The Classic Hoosier Cookbook

The Classic Hoosier

Illustrated by Jackie Lacy

Cookbook

Edited by
Elaine Lumbra

Indiana University Press

This book is a publication of

Indiana University Press
Office of Scholarly Publishing
Herman B Wells Library 350
1320 East 10th Street
Bloomington, Indiana 47405 USA

iupress.indiana.edu

Quotation on page 211 is from Rachel Peden, *Speak to the Earth*, p. 35. Copyright © 1974 by Rachel Peden. Reprinted by permission of Alfred A. Knopf, Inc.

The Library of Congress has cataloged the original edition as follows:

The Hoosier cookbook.
Includes index.
1. Cookery, American-Indiana.   I. Lumbra, Elaine.
II. Lacy, Jacqueline.
TX715.H7855   641.5'9772   75-31420
ISBN 0-253-13865-5

ISBN 978-0-253-03277-5 (hdbk.)
ISBN 978-0-253-03343-7 (pbk.)
ISBN 978-0-253-03346-8 (ebk.)

1 2 3 4 5   23 22 21 20 19 18

Contents

Foreword

To read through Indiana's bicentennial cookbook, with all of its delicious associations, is to reconstruct the state's bountiful heritage. Man has cooked here for much longer than two hundred years. In lands already under cultivation the earliest explorers found prospects of wealth almost as appealing as those promised by the fur trade. Their first attempts to mix the corn, the wild game and fish, and the alien plants in the American Indian's diet with the dishes of their homelands came from necessity. But with generous dashes of French, English, Scotch-Irish, Creole, and Swiss ingenuity, Indiana pioneers and settlers rapidly made this bounty from land and water their own. The later flavors of German, Polish, Hungarian, Slavic, and Italian cooking brought cuisines of the world to Indiana's kitchens.

Yet how could it have evolved any other way? The ingredients were here. Indiana's soils and climates promised and produced the meats, poultry, and dairy foods that are based on its famous grains. Fruits and vegetables, wild game and fish were abundant. First linked strongly to the South through its settlers, its rivers and canals, Indiana's trade expanded to the Eastern Seaboard with the coming of the railroads. Eventually, the state's central location in the nation's transportation system brought quickly to our markets foods that we could not produce here.

The sciences of food and agriculture have played a major role in this rich heritage. The late nineteenth century saw the beginning of experimental work in agriculture that has improved farm production and farm life throughout the world. Purdue University, as part of the land-grant system, has fostered research that may alter the present world-wide problems of hunger and poor nutrition.

The Cooperative Extension Service, in turn, has transformed the results of this research into practical information and applications. From its beginnings the Extension Service has provided informal education for Indiana residents. The Indiana Extension Homemakers Association, whose members have shared their recipes in this book, includes approximately 3,000 clubs with 55,000 members.

Food is one of the great joys of life. It does not take long for homemakers to transform the benefits of science into an art. Prized recipes have long been the best of the tried-and-true—mother's secret ingredients, the State Fair's awards, the fastest disappearing dishes at family reunions. Even masters of *haute cuisine* acknowledge their debt to those who have preserved these family recipes on paper instead of carrying them, tantalizing and unreliable, in the memory.

Nevertheless, the tried-and-true is changing, too. Just as the European ethnic cuisines enlivened Indiana menus earlier, now we are even more receptive to experimentation. With the recipes of our Asian, African, and Latin-American friends, we are heading in new directions. Then, too, women are discovering that many men share their enjoyment of cooking. Young people, especially, are rekindling the pride in "starting from scratch" and the interest in the cooking methods and ingredients of yesteryear. We are rediscovering the need for, and the sense of achievement from, growing and preserving our own food.

Have we come full circle then? In a way, yes. Like our ancestors, we still seek the good life. If, in the vast storehouse of experience, education, and technology that we have built over two centuries, we have found some ingredients for the good life, we should certainly preserve the recipes.

Mary E. Fuqua
Assistant Director
Cooperative Extension Service
Purdue University

Preface

Indiana means "the land of the Indians." From whence came the name Hoosier? Many believe it came from the greeting, "Who's Yere?", extended to visitors who might come to a cabin after dark. Others believe it began with an early contractor named Hoosier whose workers were called "Hoosier men." Still others believe it originates from the term "Husher," as that term was used in reference to strong and husky men, especially rivermen, who could often "hush" their opponents. Whatever the origin, few will deny that the term today stands the world around for both hospitality and friendliness.

With homemakers this friendliness often extends from one home to another with the exchange of a favorite recipe. There are many who believe that an unshared recipe is a poor thing. Thanks are due the over 8,000 extension homemakers, representing most of the counties in Indiana, who submitted recipes for sharing. It is sincerely regretted that space restrictions limited the number of recipes actually printed.

The pages of *The Hoosier Cookbook* are filled with favorite recipes which have stood the test of both time and kitchen testing and bear the endorsement of the homemaker submitting the recipe. The bits and pieces of history, Hoosier farm wisdom, and culinary folklore have been included in the hope of providing a nostalgic dimension to your recipe reading.

Bloomington, Indiana

ELAINE LUMBRA

The Classic Hoosier Cookbook

Appetizers and Beverages

Eye-catching appetizers serve to stimulate both hunger and conversation. They should have character, but not be rich and filling, because they are intended to whet, not satisfy the appetite. Remember to serve cold appetizers crisp and cold and hot appetizers really hot.

The offer alone of a cup of cheer—a cup of coffee, tea, milk, or spirits—makes guests feel welcome.

Appetizers

BISCUIT CANAPES

2 pkg. large biscuits	2 4-oz. pkg. Roquefort or
2 sticks butter	blue cheese

Cut biscuits into halves and the halves into thirds. Melt butter in pan, add crumbled blue cheese. Spread over the bottom of a large flat pan and put biscuit pieces on top. Bake 10 to 12 min. at 375 to 400°. Makes 120 bite-size canapés.

Mrs. James Garwood
Marion County

CHILI NUTS

4 T. butter or margarine	2 12-oz. cans cocktail
1 envelope Chili-O Mix	peanuts (or mixed nuts)

Melt butter in large shallow baking pan; add nuts, stirring to coat with butter. Sprinkle contents of Chili-O Mix over nuts. Heat at 250° for 30 min. Stir occasionally.

Betty Ratliff
Hendricks County

1

CHEESE PUFFS

2 c. grated sharp cheddar cheese	½ c. butter or margarine
1 c. flour	3–4 doz. small stuffed olives
½ t. paprika	

Mix first 4 ingredients well and chill. For each puff use 1 t. of the above mixture and shape in ball. Punch hole in center to make deep depression, insert olive and shape around olive to fully cover. Bake at 400° for 15 min., or until light brown. Makes 3–4 dozen.

Mrs. Dwight Amstutz
Adams County

CHESTNUT CANAPES

1 can whole water chestnuts	½ c. catsup
Bacon slices	½ c. brown sugar

Wrap water chestnuts in bacon strips and tack with toothpicks. Bake 30 min. at 350°. Make mixture of catsup and brown sugar. Mix well; dip canapés, and bake 20 min. more.

Donna Floyd
Vanderburgh County

HAM ROLL-UPS

1 3-oz. pkg. cream cheese	½ t. horseradish
2 T. sour cream	1 3-oz. pkg. thinly sliced smoked ham or dried beef
1 T. dried parsley	

Mix all the ingredients except ham. Place a small amount of cheese mixture on a piece of ham and roll starting with a corner of the meat. Secure with toothpick.

Patricia Harmon
Harrison County

HOT PRETZELS

1 envelope yeast	3¼–4 c. flour
1½ c. warm water	1 beaten egg
1 T. sugar	coarse salt or table salt
1 t. salt	

In a bowl, dissolve yeast, sugar, and salt in warm water. Stir in flour. Put on floured board and knead 10 min. Pinch off small strips of dough, roll into ropes (about 12″ long), and twist into figure 8. Place on cookie sheet. Brush with beaten egg. Sprinkle with coarse salt or plenty of table salt. Bake at 425° for 12–15 min. Makes 20 pretzels.

Mrs. Roger Thayer
Marshall County

MINI-FRANK FONDUE

3 c. peanut oil	1 lb. miniature smoked sausages or wieners
1 t. salt	
1 c. water	
1½ c. pancake mix	

Put oil and salt into fondue pot and heat at highest setting about 15 min. or until a 1″ cube of soft bread browns in 40 to 60 seconds. Mix water and pancake mix. Place in a serving bowl. Cut meat in small pieces. Spear the meat; dip into batter, letting excess drip off. Fry in oil until golden and crispy. Serves 20.

Mrs. Harold Spear
Boone County

NACHO APPETIZERS

Nacho cheese chips	Refried beans
Jalapeña pepper slices	Mild colby cheese or mild brick cheese

On each chip, spread some beans, add small slice of pepper, top with slice of cheese. Put on cookie sheet, heat at 350° for 5 min.

Lynn Pulley
Wells County

OLIVE TARTS

2 c. sharp American cheese, grated	1 c. flour
	½ t. salt
	1 t. paprika
½ c. soft butter	48 stuffed olives

Blend cheese with butter. Stir in flour, salt, and paprika and mix well. Wrap this mixture around each olive, covering it completely. Arrange on baking sheet. Freeze firm, put in plastic bag, tie, and return to freezer. To serve: Bake 15 min. or until brown at 400°.

Mrs. F. T. Miller
Putnam County

ORIENTAL HOT MUNCH

¼ c. butter	1 c. chow mein noodles
2 T. soy sauce	
1 t. salt	1 c. small pretzels
½ t. celery salt	
2 t. Worcestershire sauce	1 c. Rice Chex
	1 c. Wheat Chex
½ t. Tabasco sauce	½ c. pecans (or other nuts)
¼ t. garlic salt	½ c. cashews (or other nuts)

Blend the first 7 ingredients in a 9×2×13″ pan. Then add the cereals and the nuts. Bake in a slow oven (250°) for about 1 hr. Stir occasionally. Makes 5 cups.

Mrs. Joe Swain
Rush County

PARMESAN PATE A CHOUX

2½ T. milk	1 egg, unbeaten
½ t. butter	2 T. grated Parmesan cheese
½ t. lard	
¼ c. flour	
pinch of salt	

Scald milk with butter and lard. Add flour and salt and stir vigorously. Remove from heat; add egg, and beat the mixture until thoroughly blended and light. Add grated Parmesan cheese. Shape into tiny rounds and bake in a hot oven.

Mrs. Thelma Reedy
Jay County

PIEROGI

2 eggs	2 c. flour
½ c. water	½ t. salt

Mound flour on kneading board and make hole in center. Drop eggs into hole and cut into flour with knife. Add salt and water and knead until firm. Let rest 10 min. covered with a warm bowl. Divide dough into halves and roll thin. Cut circles with large biscuit cutter. Place a small spoonful of filling a little to one side on each round of dough. Moisten edge with water, fold over and press edge together firmly. Be sure pierogi are well sealed. Drop into salted boiling water. Cook gently for 3 to 5 min. Lift out of water carefully with perforated spoon.

Fillings:

(1) Cheese and Potato

1 c. dry cottage cheese	salt and pepper to taste
2 c. mashed potato	

Mix thoroughly.

(2) Sauerkraut

2 c. sauerkraut	¼ c. butter
1 2″ onion, chopped	

Rinse and squeeze kraut. Sauté onion in butter, add kraut, and sauté 2 min. Cool.

Mrs. Joe Pavolka
LaPorte County

ROASTED SOYBEANS

Wash 1 c. soybeans and let soak for 8–10 hr. (1 c. unsoaked soybeans will make 2½ to 3 c. soaked soybeans.) Drain. Preheat oven to 425°. Spread soybeans on cookie sheet. Stir 2 or 3 times while roasting 40–50 min. When beans get lightly brown and crunchy, take out of oven. Put in bowl. While still warm, stir in margarine (approximately 1 T.). Sprinkle with fine salt.

Mrs. Donald McNabney
Wabash County

RUMAKI

½ lb. chicken livers	1 5-oz. can water chestnuts
1 lb. sliced bacon	soy sauce
brown sugar	

Wrap ½ slice bacon around a small piece of chicken liver and a sliver of water chestnut. Secure with a tooth pick. Marinate in soy sauce overnight. Sprinkle brown sugar over tops before baking. Bake at 350° for about 15–20 min. on broiler pan. Then place under broiler for about 5 min. Drain on paper towels and serve hot.

Anna Sinnet
Putnam County

SHRIMP AND RICE ROLLS

½ c. tomato juice	1 t. chopped parsley
1 egg, well beaten	½ t. celery salt
½ c. dry bread crumbs	1 5-oz. can shrimps, mashed
1 c. cooked rice	12 bacon slices, cut in halves
dash of pepper	

Mix tomato juice and egg; add crumbs, rice, pepper, parsley, celery salt, and shrimps; mix thoroughly. Roll into finger lengths. Wrap each roll with half slice bacon and fasten with toothpicks. Place on rack in shallow pan. Bake at 425° for 10 to 15 min., or until bacon is well done. Serve hot.

Theresa Pankau
Lake County

STUFFED MUSHROOMS

12 large mushrooms	¼ c. grated Parmesan cheese
1 T. onion, minced	3 T. walnuts, chopped
¼ c. butter	
¼ t. salt	1 T. steak sauce
1 c. soft bread crumbs	1 T. water

Clean mushrooms; remove and chop stems. Sauté onions and chopped stems until onions are golden. Mix with rest of ingredients. Stuff the mushrooms with this mixture. Place stuffed mushrooms in a shallow pan with ½ c. of water. Bake at 400° for 20–25 min., or until golden brown.

Edith Ayers
Lake County

CHEESE AND MEAT BALLS

BACON LOG

1 lb. bacon, fried crisp and crumbled	½ c. pecans
	¼ t. garlic salt
	¼ t. Worcester-
1 8-oz. pkg. cream cheese	shire sauce
	1 T. chili powder

Mix together, except chili powder, and make two 1″ logs. Sprinkle with chili powder.

Galeda Anderson
Sullivan County

BLACK OLIVE CHEESE BALL

2 8-oz. pkg. cream cheese, softened	3 T. black olives, finely chopped
1 T. mayonnaise	1 t. Worcester- shire sauce
1 T. onion, finely chopped	1 pkg. dried beef, finely chopped

Mix well all ingredients except dried beef. Form ball. Roll in finely chopped dried beef. Let chill overnight.

Lynn Pulley
Wells County

BRAUNSCHWEIGER BALL

1 large pkg. braun- schweiger or liverwurst, at room tempera- ture	2 T. salad dressing
	Icing:
	1 small pkg. cream cheese
2 T. lemon juice	2 T. milk
3 T. dry onion soup	dash of garlic salt

Blend first 4 ingredients and form ball. Chill at least 2 hr. or overnight if possible.

Mix icing together. Ice ball. Chill until served. Serves 15–20.

Mrs. S. Luann Daub
Marion County

BRAUNSCHWEIGER LOG

1 lb. braun- schweiger	**Frosting:**
	1 large pkg. cream cheese
½ can tomato soup	2 heaping T. mayonnaise
2 T. onion, diced	

Mix first 3 ingredients; form a thick log shape. Mix cream cheese and mayonnaise. Frost log. Chill.

Betty VanWinkle
Wells County

CHEDDAR CHEESE-ALE BALL

6 c. (1½ lb.) shredded cheddar cheese	1 t. dry mustard
	¼ t. crushed red pepper
1 3-oz. pkg. cream cheese	½ c. walnuts, finely chopped
4 T. soft butter or margarine	½ c. parsley, chopped
¾ c. ale or beer	

With electric mixer, beat cheddar cheese, cream cheese, and butter or margarine in large bowl until smooth. Gradually beat in ale, mustard, and crushed red pepper. If mixture is very soft, refrigerate until firm. Divide mixture in half and shape into 2 balls. Combine walnuts and parsley on sheet of waxed paper. Roll cheese balls in nut mixture to cover completely. Refrigerate. Makes 2 balls about 4″ in diameter.

May be decorated by pressing 3″ round of waxed paper on top of each ball before rolling in nut mixture; remove paper. Cut pimiento in petal shapes and arrange on ball to resemble a flower; add a sprig of parsley as the stem.

Rita Carpenter
Pulaski County

CHEESE BALL (1)

1/4 c. green pepper, chopped	1 small can crushed pine-apple, drained
2 T. onion, chopped	2 c. pecans, chopped
2 8-oz. pkg. cream cheese	

Mix all ingredients together, except nuts, and chill. Form into a ball and roll in chopped nuts.

Shirley Rutherford
Orange County

CHEESE BALL (2)

1 8-oz. pkg. cream cheese	1/2 t. seasoned salt
1/2 tube soft smoked cheese	1/2 pkg. dried beef, chopped
1/4 t. garlic salt	1 t. parsley flakes
1 t. onion flakes	1/4 c. pecans, finely chopped
1 t. Worcester-shire sauce	

Mix all ingredients together, except pecans and parsley flakes, and chill until cold and stiff. Shape into a ball and roll in pecans and parsley flakes.

Mrs. Perry Miller
Ripley County

CHESTNUT MEATBALLS

2 c. soft bread crumbs (2 1/2 slices)	1/2 c. milk 1 T. soy sauce 1/2 t. garlic salt
1/4 t. onion powder	1 can (5 or 6 oz.) water chest-nuts, drained and finely chopped
1/2 lb. ground beef	
1/2 lb. bulk pork sausage	

Combine bread crumbs, milk, soy sauce, garlic salt, and onion powder. Add ground beef, pork sausage, and water chestnuts. Mix well. Form meat mixture into 1" balls. Place on 15 1/2×10 1/2×1" baking pan. Bake at 350° for 18 to 20 min. Makes about 5 dozen tiny meatballs.

Mrs. Alfred Pfister
Posey County

HOLIDAY CHEESE BALL

4 3-oz. pkg. cream cheese, softened	1 6-oz. jar bacon-cheese spread
1 6-oz. jar pimiento cheese spread	2 T. onion, grated
1 6-oz. jar olive-pimiento cheese spread	1 t. Worcester-shire sauce garlic to taste
1 6-oz. jar English cheddar cheese spread	1 c. pecans, ground 1/2 c. parsley, finely chopped paprika

In medium bowl combine cheeses, onion, Worcestershire sauce, and garlic. Beat well until blended thoroughly. Stir in 1/2 c. pecans and 1/4 c. parsley. Shape into a ball. Wrap in waxed paper, then in foil. Refrigerate overnight. About 1 hr. before serving, roll cheese ball in remaining pecans and parsley. Sprinkle with paprika. Serves 30.

Mrs. Robert D. Fawver
Scott County

HOT CHEESE BALLS

2 lb. Velveeta cheese, softened	2 t. garlic powder
	1 t. red pepper
1 large pkg. cream cheese, softened	1 c. chopped nuts

Mix cheese and cream cheese. Add garlic powder, red pepper, and 1 c. nuts. Mix together and form into balls. Top with nuts and sprinkle with chili powder.

Judy Rupp
Steuben County

LITTLE SAUSAGE BALLS

1 lb. sausage	1 pint applesauce
dash of sage	1 11-oz. pkg. red
6–8 slices bread	hots

Toast bread and make into fine crumbs. Mix sausage, bread crumbs, and sage. Form balls about size of walnut. Bake at 400° about 20 min., or until browned. Heat applesauce; add red hots. Stir and heat slowly, until red hots are dissolved. Add sausage balls to sauce. Serve hot. Makes 30 to 35 balls.

Mrs. Wilbur Whitehead
Boone County

LOUISIANA SHRIMP BALLS

1 lb. peeled, cooked shrimp	2 T. green pepper, finely diced
3 T. cream cheese	
1 T. chili sauce	1 hard-cooked egg, chopped
1 t. Worcestershire sauce	
2 t. horseradish	1 T. onion, grated
dash of black and red pepper	1 T. parsley, chopped
¼ c. celery, finely diced	¾ t. salt

Chill shrimp; mash. Add other ingredients, except parsley, and roll into small balls. Roll the balls in chopped parsley. Serves 6–10.

Mrs. Alice Ann Pearce
Floyd County

PICKLE SNOWMAN

2 c. grated Swiss cheese	1 c. sweet mixed pickles, chopped
4 8-oz. pkg. cream cheese, softened	½ c. onion, finely chopped
6 hard-cooked eggs, chopped	1 T. salt
	½ t. pepper
dill pickles	

Combine Swiss cheese and 3 pkg. cream cheese and blend thoroughly. Add eggs, sweet mixed pickles, onion, salt, and pepper. Blend well. Shape a quarter of mixture into a ball and wrap in waxed paper. Shape remaining mixture into a larger ball and wrap in waxed paper. Chill at least 3–4 hr. Remove waxed paper and place small ball on top of large ball to form head of snowman. Soften remaining package of cream cheese and beat until smooth. Spread over both balls. Garnish with dill pickles to form hat, face, and buttons. Makes about 6 cups.

Frances Barden
Sullivan County

POLYNESIAN BEEF BITES

1½ lb. ground beef	dash of Tabasco sauce
¾ c. oatmeal, uncooked	1 egg
	½ c. milk
½ t. onion salt	2 T. cornstarch
½ t. garlic salt	1 c. beef bouillon
1 T. soy sauce	

1 can pineapple
tidbits, drained
1 c. brown sugar,
packed firmly
½ c. vinegar

2 T. soy sauce
⅓ c. green
pepper,
chopped

Meatballs: Mix first eight ingredients. Form into bite-size balls. Brown meatballs at 475° in a shallow pan. Sauce: Drain pineapple, reserving liquid. Mix sugar and cornstarch in medium saucepan; add pineapple juice, bouillon, vinegar, and soy sauce. Bring to a boil, stirring constantly until thickened and clear; boil one minute. Stir in green pepper and pineapple. Add meatballs to sauce and simmer about 10 min. Serve hot. Can be simmered longer— for a couple of hours. Or let set in refrigerator overnight. Makes 4–6 dozen.

Bernardine Weatherford
Posey County

SALMON LOG

1-lb. can (2 c.)
salmon
8-oz. pkg. cream
cheese, softened
1 T. lemon juice
2 t. grated onion
1 t. prepared
horseradish

¼ t. salt
¼ t. liquid
smoke
½ c. chopped
pecans
3 T. snipped
parsley

Drain and flake salmon. Remove skin and bones. Combine salmon with next 6 ingredients and mix thoroughly. Chill several hours. Combine pecans and parsley. Shape salmon into log and sprinkle with parsley and pecans. Chill well. Serves 12–15.

Helen Hollingsworth
Monroe County

VERSATILE CHEESE BALL

2 c. (8 oz.)
shredded
cheese
1 c. (4 oz.)
crumbled
blue cheese
1 3-oz. pkg.
Philadelphia
cream cheese
1 T. milk

1 T. grated onion
½ t. dry mustard
½ t. paprika
¼ t. garlic salt
1 t. Worcester-
shire sauce
¼ t. celery salt
¼ c. toasted
sesame seeds

In large mixing bowl beat cheeses together until smooth. Blend in all other ingredients except sesame seeds. Chill for ease in handling. Shape into a ball; roll in sesame seeds. Wrap and chill.

Mrs. Walton Allbright
Martin County

DIPS

CALICO DIP

4 T. minced
radish, onions,
green pepper,
cucumber
½ c. salad
dressing

1 c. sour cream
2 T. sugar
1 t. salt
1 T. minced
garlic

Mix together and use for dip with cucumber sticks, celery, carrot sticks, and cauliflower.

Mrs. Alice Ann Pearce
Floyd County

CHEESE DIP

3 eggs, beaten
2 T. sugar
1 8-oz. pkg.
cream cheese
1 onion, size of
walnut, grated

3 T. vinegar
½ green pepper,
grated
1 c. pecans, cut
up

Cook eggs, sugar, and vinegar over hot water until thick, stirring constantly. Add cream cheese, onion, green pepper, and pecans. Beat until smooth. Age in refrigerator 6–8 hr.

Dorothy Cooper
Monroe County

DEVILED HAM DIP

1 8-oz. pkg. cream cheese	1 small can deviled ham
1 very small onion, grated fine	2 or 3 T. salad dressing
	salt and pepper to taste

Mix all together and serve.

Mary Bible
Ripley County

FRESH FRUIT DIP

1 10-oz. pkg. strawberries	4-oz. cream cheese

Combine strawberries and cheese in blender until well blended. Chill. Use as dip for pineapple, strawberries, bananas, grapes, or any of your favorite fruits.

Miss Diana Hall
Jennings County

HOT CRABMEAT DIP

1 8-oz. pkg. cream cheese	½ t. cream style horseradish
1½ c. (7 oz.) flaked crabmeat	¼ t. salt dash of pepper
2 T. finely chopped onion	⅓ c. sliced almonds,
1 T. milk	toasted

Combine softened cream cheese and remaining ingredients except almonds. Mix well. Spoon mixture into oven-proof dish.

Sprinkle with almonds. Bake at 375° for 15 to 20 min.

Mrs. Ward H. Smith
Harrison County

HOT DRIED BEEF DIP

1 8-oz. pkg. cream cheese	2 T. onion flakes
2 T. milk	½ t. garlic salt
1 pkg. dried beef, shredded	½ t. black pepper
¼ c. green pepper	½ c. chopped pecans
½ c. sour cream	

Mix all together except nuts. Sauté nuts in butter; sprinkle on top. Bake at 350° for 20 min.

Beverly Gardner
Vanderburgh County

LIVER SAUSAGE DIP

1 8-oz. pkg. cream cheese	2 t. lemon juice
1 8-oz. pkg. liver sausage	1 t. Worcestershire sauce
1 T. chopped onion	dash of salt and pepper

Combine cream cheese and liver sausage, mix until well blended; add lemon juice, onion, Worcestershire sauce. Shape in round ball and wrap in waxed paper or foil and place in refrigerator until well chilled or overnight.

Marie LeGrand
Ripley County

VEGETABLE DIP (1)

2 c. sour cream	1 medium green pepper, chopped
1 pkg. onion soup mix	

2 small tomatoes, 1 stalk celery,
  seeded and   chopped
  chopped   2 t. chili powder

Mix together.

Susan Goldman and Pat Heichelbech
Spencer County

VEGETABLE DIP (2)

⅔ c. mayonnaise   1 t. parsley flakes
⅔ c. sour cream   1 t. dill weed
  (or imitation   1 t. Accent
  cream)   1 t. green onion
1 t. garlic salt   flakes

Mix and refrigerate.

Thelma Noch
Lake County

MOLDS AND SPREADS

BLUE CHEESE MOLD

1 3-oz. pkg.   ¾ c. (4 oz.)
  lemon or lime   crumbled blue
  gelatin   cheese
1 c. boiling water 1 T. vinegar
½ c. dry white   1 T. minced
  wine   parsley
½ c. sour cream   ½ t. Worcester-
¼ t. salt   shire sauce

Dissolve gelatin in boiling water. Cool
and add the wine. Blend in sour cream,
salt, parsley, Worcestershire sauce, and
vinegar. Chill until slightly thickened. Stir
in crumbled blue cheese. Turn into an
oiled, 3-c. mold. Chill until firm.

Mrs. Richard W. Sipe
Rush County

CHEESE APPETIZER

2 c. sharp   1 c. white
  cheddar cheese,   Munster cheese,
  shredded   shredded

½ c. pickles,   1 T. horseradish
  diced   2 T. catsup
½ c. onions,   1 t. Worcester-
  finely diced   shire sauce
1 c. pimiento-   1 T. prepared
  stuffed olives,   mustard
  sliced, diced

Mix well. Keep for several days in refrigerator. Spread on thin slices of French
bread or rye bread. Put under broiler for
3 min.

Leatha Koontz
Randolph County

CHEESE SPREAD

1 lb. cheddar   Small jar of
  cheese   pimientos
4 or 5 boiled   Salad dressing,
  eggs   as needed
1 small onion

Grind together and then add enough salad
dressing to make it a spread.

Dorothy Leighty
Noble County

CHICKEN LIVER PATE

1 medium onion,   1 t. salt
  minced   ½ t. pepper
¼ c. melted   1 T. red wine
  chicken fat   2 hard-cooked
1 lb. chicken   eggs
  livers

Sauté onion and chicken livers in chicken
fat. Put sautéed onion and livers, seasonings, wine, and whites of eggs into blender,
cover and process at Blend until smooth,
using rubber spatula to aid in processing.
Garnish with chopped eggs. Makes 1½
cups.

Kay Baugh
Hendricks County

CREAM CHEESE APPETIZER

1 8-oz. pkg. cream cheese	1 T. cornstarch
1 small can crushed pineapple	½ c. brown sugar (or to taste)
	½ c. raisins
	¼ t. dry mustard

Drain juice from pineapple and thicken juice with cornstarch; add sugar and cook. Add pineapple, raisins, and mustard. Place cream cheese in center of a platter, pour hot mixture over cream cheese.

Eugenia Fisher
Posey County

PATE A LA MAISON

1 envelope unflavored gelatin	1 c. cold water
	½ c. salad dressing
1½ c. (2 oz.) liver sausage	½ c. dairy sour cream

2 T. mild onion, finely chopped   1 t. Worcestershire sauce

Soften gelatin in cold water. Then stir over low heat until dissolved. Combine liver sausage, salad dressing, sour cream, onion, and Worcestershire sauce and mix well. Stir in gelatin. Pour into a 1-qt. mold and chill until firm. Unmold and serve with toasted, thinly sliced cocktail rye bread or crackers. Serves 8.

Eleanor Croak
Daviess County

SPREAD FOR CRACKERS

1 4-oz. can deviled ham	3 T. catsup
1 8-oz. pkg. cream cheese	3 T. prepared mustard

Mix all together. Refrigerate.

Elsie Senn
Crawford County

Beverages

CHAMPAGNE FRAPPE

1 can frozen lemonade	Fifth of pink champagne, chilled
3 cans cold water	

Mix juice and water according to directions on can. Just before serving, add chilled champagne. Fill glasses ½ full of crushed ice. Pour champagne mixture over ice.

Mrs. Roy Bowser
Steuben County

ORANGE JULIUS

½ 6-oz. can (⅓ c.) frozen orange juice	½ c. milk
	½ c. water
	¼ c. sugar

½ t. vanilla   5 or 6 ice cubes

Combine all ingredients in blender container; cover and blend till smooth, about 30 seconds. Serve immediately. Makes about 3 cups.

Tonya Paddock
Union County

RASPBERRY SPARKLE

½ c. sugar	4 c. pineapple juice
1 envelope raspberry Kool-Aid	7-Up

Mix first 3 ingredients and freeze in ice cube trays. Pour 7-Up over the cubes in each glass. Garnish with fresh mint. Serve with a straw. Serves 8–10.

Patricia Harmon
Harrison County

SUMMER MINT COOLER

6 oz. jar mint   1 qt. orange
  jelly   sherbet
                1½ qt. ginger ale

With electric mixer beat jelly and sherbet together. Add ginger ale and serve. Yields 15 sherbet glasses.

Mrs. Penn Peek
Wells County

CHOCOLATE DRINKS

HOT CHOCOLATE MIX

1 8-qt. carton   1 11-oz. jar
  powdered milk   Coffee Mate
1 16-oz. box   ½ c. powdered
  Nestle's Quik   sugar

Mix ingredients and store in a covered container. Use ⅓ cup of mix per cup of hot water. Makes 1 gallon of mix. Serves 48.

Mrs. Diana Sturm
Montgomery County

INSTANT COCOA MIX

3 c. powdered   ⅓ c. cocoa
  milk   pinch of salt
1 c. sugar

Sift ingredients together several times until well blended. Store in tightly covered container. Put 3 heaping tablespoonfuls in large mug; add boiling water. Stir and top with marshmallows.

Mrs. James Brown
Montgomery County

COFFEE

Use your coffee maker to at least two-thirds to three-fourths of its capacity. Coffee should be fresh; do not buy more than you can use within one week of opening. Always use fresh, cold water, because sometimes hot water pipes will deposit minerals in the water that may give coffee an off-flavor. Occasional boiling of water with baking soda in the pot removes stains and improves the taste of your coffee.

BOILED COFFEE

For 49 cups of coffee: Mix an egg, shell and all, into 1¼ lb. of coffee. Add 1 c. cold water. Tie coffee in a cheesecloth bag. Immerse coffee in 9 qt. cold water. Bring to a boil. Remove the pot from the heat. Allow coffee to remain in water no longer than 3–4 min. Remove the coffee bag. Stir and serve.

EGGNOGS

EGGNOG (Alcoholic)

6 eggs, separated   1½ qt. milk
1 c. sugar   3 c. whipped
1½ c. brandy   cream
½ c. rum

Beat egg yolks until very thick and light. Gradually add sugar, beating constantly. While still beating, add brandy and rum gradually. Chill for an hour, stirring occasionally. Then add milk slowly. Fold in whipped cream, then the stiffly beaten egg whites. Store in covered jars in refrigerator for a day before serving. Sprinkle each serving with nutmeg. Serves 20.

Mrs. James Armstrong
Lake County

(1) EGGNOG (Nonalcoholic)

6 eggs, separated	2 qt. scalded
1½ c. sugar	milk and light
dash of salt	cream
1 t. vanilla	

Beat egg yolks and 1 c. sugar until thick and very light. Add salt; slowly add scalded milk and cream. Cook in top of double boiler over hot, but not boiling, water, until mixture coats a spoon. Stir constantly while cooking. Cool quickly. Beat egg whites until stiff and fold in remaining ½ c. sugar. Fold egg whites carefully into mixture. Flavor with vanilla, mixing thoroughly. Chill for several hours. Serve in punch cups with nutmeg or cinnamon sprinkled over each serving. Serves 12.

Mrs. James Armstrong
Lake County

(2) EGGNOG (Nonalcoholic)

½ pint	¼ t. cinnamon
whipping	¼ t. cloves
cream	1 can Eagle
1 qt. milk	Brand
juice of 1 orange	sweetened
1 T. vanilla	milk
¼ t. nutmeg	2 eggs

In a blender (or mixer) mix the eggs, spices, orange juice, and the sweetened milk. Pour this into your final container. In the blender (or mixer) whip the cream. Add whipped cream to egg mixture and add milk. Stir. Serve cold. Makes approximately ½ gallon.

Charlene Deckebach
Dearborn County

PUNCHES

PUNCH

2 c. strong tea	3 small cans
2 large cans	frozen
pineapple juice	lemonade
2 large cans	2½ lb. sugar
orange juice	6 c. warm water
4 qt. ginger ale	

Mix tea, pineapple juice, orange juice, and lemonade together. Dissolve sugar in warm water and add to tea mixture. Just before serving add ginger ale and large chunk of ice. Serves 150.

Kathleen Maxwell
Daviess County

CRANBERRY CHRISTMAS PUNCH

1 3-oz. pkg.	3 c. cold water
cherry gelatin	1 qt. cranberry
1 c. boiling	juice cocktail,
water	chilled
1 6-oz. can frozen	1 1-pt., 12 oz.
lemonade or	bottle ginger
pineapple-	ale, chilled
orange	
concentrate	

Dissolve cherry gelatin in boiling water. Stir in the frozen juice concentrate. Add the cold water and cranberry juice cocktail. Place 2 trays of ice cubes or a molded ice ring in a large punch bowl. Pour punch over ice. Slowly pour in ginger ale. Fruit-flavored sherbet may also be added. Serves 25.

Mrs. Russell Payne
Wells County

GELATIN PUNCH

1 3-oz. package lime gelatin	juice of 4 lemons or ½ can frozen lemonade
2 c. hot water	
1½ c. sugar	1 46-oz. can pineapple juice
1 qt. cold water	
2 qt. ginger ale	

Dissolve gelatin in the hot water, add sugar, cold water, and the juices and mix well. Add ginger ale just before serving. Instead of adding ice cubes to the punch, pour some of the punch into trays, adding a mint leaf or cherry to each cube. Freeze and add these to the punch bowl. Yields 30 punch cups.

Fern Johnson
Crawford County

HOLIDAY WINE PUNCH

2 1-lb. cans jellied cranberry sauce	1 c. lemon juice 1 qt. white wine 1 qt. dry ginger ale

Blend cranberries and lemon juice with beater. Add wine and pour over large piece of ice in punch bowl. Just before serving add cooled ginger ale. Yields 30 punch cups.

Ardella Reust
Whitley County

HOT CRANBERRY PUNCH

1 lb. fresh cranberries	juice of three lemons
1 c. red hots (candy)	juice of three oranges
12 whole cloves	2 c. white sugar

Cover cranberries with water and cook until tender. Drain. Add the red hots and cloves to the juice. Cook until the candy is melted. Remove the cloves. Add lemon juice, orange juice, and sugar. Add 20 c. of water. Heat to serve. The cranberries may be used in another recipe.

Ruth Enkoff
Martin County

HOT SPICED CRANBERRY PUNCH

6 pt. bottles cranberry juice	10 c. freshly brewed tea
1 10-oz. can frozen lemonade	4 sticks cinnamon 20 whole cloves

Combine cranberry juice, lemonade, and spices. Heat to a point just under a boil. Add freshly brewed tea. Serve hot. Serves 24.

Mrs. Larry Brock
Bartholomew County

PARTY PUNCH

1 pkg. Cherry Kool-Aid	1 pkg. Strawberry Kool-Aid
2 c. sugar	3 qt. water
1 6-oz. can frozen orange juice	1 6-oz. can frozen lemonade
1 qt. ginger ale	

Dissolve soft drink powders and sugar in water. Add frozen juices, stir until dissolved. Stir in ginger ale just before serving. A nice touch is an ice ring made of Kool-Aid to float in the punch bowl. Makes 1½ gallons.

Mrs. Gaylord Cole
Morgan County

PERCOLATOR PUNCH

1 qt. apple cider	1 c. orange juice
1 pt. cranberry juice	¾ c. lemon juice
	1 c. sugar

1 t. whole allspice 3 sticks
1 t. whole cloves cinnamon

Combine juices in the percolator. Place sugar and the spices in the perk basket. Allow it to go through the perk cycle. Serve hot. Makes 16½ cups.

Mary Ellison
Lawrence County

PINK PUNCH

1 c. sugar 2 48-oz. large
2 c. water cans Hawaiian
1 6-oz. can frozen punch
lemonade 2 qt. ginger ale
2 6-oz. cans 1 4-oz. bottle
frozen orange maraschino
juice cherries and
2 large cans juice
pineapple juice

Heat sugar and water. Cool. Mix the frozen lemonade and frozen orange juice as directed. Add to the first mixture together with the rest of the ingredients. Chill. Serves 60.

Mrs. Kenneth Culp
Elkhart County

RHUBARB PUNCH

3 c. rhubarb 2 c. pineapple
3 c. water juice,
1 c. sugar unsweetened
2 T. lemon juice 1½ c. ginger ale

Cook rhubarb in water until tender and strain. Add sugar and the juices. Chill. When ready to serve, add ginger ale. Makes approximately ½ gallon.

Mrs. J. Ward Leeper
Marshall County

SHARON'S PUNCH

½ gal. sherbet, 2 c. pineapple
lime, pine- juice or
apple, or lemonade,
orange chilled
12 6-oz. size
bottles 7-Up,
chilled

Place sherbet in punchbowl; stir in fruit juice. Pour in 7-Up, mixing well. Serves 36.

Pauline Dixon
Johnson County

TEMPERANCE TODDY

1 qt. apple juice 1 stick cinnamon
1 pt. grape juice 2–3 whole cloves
juice of 2 oranges ¼ t. allspice
juice of 1 lemon ¼ t. nutmeg
2 T. sugar

Combine ingredients in a saucepan and bring to a boil. Remove cinnamon and cloves. Serve piping hot in small cups. Serves 8–10.

Donna Handley
Union County

VERY BERRY PUNCH

1½ gal. vanilla 3 48-oz. cans
ice cream Very Berry
3 28-oz. bottles Hawaiian
Sprite (or punch
7-Up)

Pour punch in bowl and add ice cream. Pour Sprite in and stir slightly. Serves 75 or more.

Mrs. Judy Carter
Rush County

WEDDING RECEPTION PUNCH

1 qt. sherbet to go with 1 pkg. of Kool-Aid (any flavor) (usually pine-apple sherbet will go with any flavor of Kool-Aid)	2 qt. water 2 c. sugar 1 46-oz. can of pineapple juice 1 qt. vanilla ice cream 1 large bottle soda, ginger ale, or 7-Up

Mix first 5 ingredients and stir well. Add food coloring to go with the bride's chosen color. Chill. Just before serving, add 1 large bottle of chilled ginger ale, 7-up, or club soda. Yields 50 punch cups.

Mrs. Alma Jane Simmons
Jennings County

SLUSHES

BRANDY SLUSH

4 tea bags	1 6-oz. can frozen
2 c. water	lemonade
2 c. sugar	2 c. (¾ pt.)
7 c. boiling water	brandy, plain or flavored
1 6-oz. can frozen orange juice	

Boil 2 c. water, place tea bags in water and steep for 4 hr. Dissolve sugar in 7 c. boiling water. After sugar water has cooled to room temperature, combine with steeped tea and stir well. Add juices and brandy. Put the container in the freezer. When mixture is frozen, use ice cream dipper to put slush in a glass and cover with about 1 c. 7-Up. If drink is too sweet, decrease sugar. Makes about 2 quarts of slush.

Joyce Lake
Franklin County

FROZEN WHISKEY SLUSH

1 large can Awake	7 t. instant tea
	7 c. water
2 large cans frozen lemonade	1½ c. sugar
	2 c. whiskey

Mix and freeze. To serve, put ½ slush and ½ 7-Up in glass.

Tina Hoar Perkins
Fulton County

PUNCH SLUSH

4 c. sugar	2 small cans frozen orange juice
6 c. water	
5 bananas	
2 small cans frozen lemonade	1 46-oz. can pineapple juice
	6 qt. ginger ale

Put bananas in blender. Bring sugar and water to boil and boil for 5 min. Cool. Add to juices and bananas. Put into six 1-qt. size containers. Freeze. Before serving, take from freezer and let thaw for a short time. Add 1 qt. ginger ale to each portion and stir until slushy. Serves 50–60.

Glenna Borggren
Marshall County

TEAS

If you are making tea "from scratch," there are those who still suggest one teaspoon of tea per serving and one for the pot placed in a *warm* pottery teapot. Pour boiling water over and steep—five minutes for a small pot and seven for a large one. Store tea in an airtight container and remember it loses flavor if stored too long.

CRANBERRY TEA

4 c. cranberries	4 sticks cinnamon
3½ quarts water	12 whole cloves

2 oranges, sliced	or less,
2 lemons, sliced	according to
3 c. sugar (more	taste)

Put all ingredients except sugar in pan, cover, and bring to a boil. Cook slowly 25 min., without stirring. Put through a cheesecloth bag. While still hot, add sugar. Serve hot or cold. Serves 25.

Mrs. Grace Bechner
Rush County

ICE TEA SYRUP

4 c. water	1½ c. sugar
¾ c. loose tea	

Boil water and pour over loose tea. Steep 7 min. Strain. Add sugar and put in a covered jar. Store in refrigerator. Put 3 T. in a 9-oz. glass and fill with ice cubes and water. Yields 24 glasses.

Sandy Montcastle
Boone County

ROSE PETAL TEA

Pour 4 c. boiling water over 5 t. dried rose petals. Steep 3–5 min. Sweeten with honey.

Edith Wiseman
Crawford County

RUSSIAN TEA MIX

1 1-lb., 2-oz. jar	2 t. ground cloves
Tang	2 t. ground
1 3-oz. pkg.	cinnamon
lemonade mix	½ c. instant tea
2 c. sugar	mix

Mix thoroughly and store in Tang or tea jars. For 1 cup of hot tea, use 2 generous t. of mix in boiling water. Yield: 4–6 cups.

Mrs. Howard (Lucille) Newton
Tippecanoe County

SASSAFRAS TEA

Take red sassafras roots and wash clean.

Cover with water and let set 2–3 hr. Place on stove and let simmer (never boil). The color is a lovely light pink. Pour into a cup and add 1 t. sugar.

Mrs. Raymond Nicoll
Carroll County

WINES

DANDELION WINE

1 qt. dandelion	1 sliced lemon
blossoms	3 lb. granulated
1 gal. rainwater	sugar
1 cake com-	2 slices bread,
pressed yeast	toasted

Put dandelion blossoms in 2-gal. stone jar. Pour over them boiling rainwater. Let stand 24 hr. Drain. To water add lemon, yeast, sugar, and toasted bread slices. Let stand 3 weeks, stirring every day. Strain and bottle, but not airtight.

Mrs. Thelma Reedy
Jay County

GRAPE WINE

Use dark grapes; prepare as for jelly. Put 2 qts. pure grape juice and 2 qts. sugar in a glass gallon jug and fill with water. Bore a hole in the cork and insert a rubber tube (can be purchased at drugstore). The tube should not protrude below the bottom of the cork. Place the cork on the jug and seal so that no air can enter the inside of the jug, and place the other end of the tube in a jar of water. When it starts working, the air goes through the tube and into the water. When it stops working completely, siphon the wine into the bottles and seal. This makes a sweet, smooth wine, rich in color and flavor.

Mrs. George Conrad, Sr.
Miami County

Soups, Stews, and Chowders

Nowadays soup is seldom a meal, but a great soupmaker still holds her old-time prestige. Soups can be found for any season—chilled when the thermometer goes up and steaming hot when a chill wind is blowing.

The dictionary defines a soup as "a liquid food made by cooking meat, vegetables, fish, etc., in water, milk, etc.," while a chowder is "a dish consisting of fresh fish, clams, etc., stewed with vegetables, often in milk." Has Webster never heard of corn chowder?

Soups

GRANDPA'S BARLEY SOUP

5 lb. chuck roast or soup beef (use beef bouillon cubes with less beef)

salt and pepper

11 oz. barley (quick kind)

46 oz. can tomato juice

4 large onions, diced

6 medium potatoes, cubed

2 No. 2 cans white whole kernel corn

16 oz. elbow macaroni

Cut beef in 2 to 3" chunks; season with salt and pepper. Cook approximately 2 hr., or until done. Remove meat and keep warm. Add tomato juice, onions, potatoes, and barley to broth and cook until tender. Add macaroni and corn. When macaroni is tender, the soup is ready to serve. Fat may be removed from meat and smaller pieces returned to soup, or meat may be served separately on a platter.

Mrs. Gerald Krueger
Fayette County

18

FAMOUS BEAN SOUP

2 lb. small navy beans	1 small onion, chopped
4 qt. water	butter
1½ lb. smoked ham hocks	salt and pepper

Wash navy beans, place in colander and pour boiling water over them until skins pop open. Place beans in large pot, add water and ham hocks. Boil slowly 3½ hr. When nearly done, braise onion in a little butter and add to beans. Season with salt and pepper.

Joanna Williams
Martin County

PIONEER SOUP BEANS

1 lb. dried beans	1 t. salt
hambone	large onion

Cover beans with water and soak overnight. Next day add the hambone, salt, and onion. Bring to a boil, cover and simmer gently for several hours or until the beans are tender. Serve with slabs of corn bread and homemade butter and apple butter.

"Blue River Pioneer Cookin' "
Shelby County Historical Society

CHERRY SOUP

1 pkg. frozen sour cherries	3 sticks cinnamon
2 c. water	sugar to taste
cornstarch or flour	

Add water to thawed sour cherries and bring to a boil. Thicken lightly with cornstarch or flour. Add sugar and cinnamon. Drop in your own dumpling recipe and cook until done. Remove cinnamon sticks and serve. Serves 4.

Mrs. Hart Swanson, Jr.
LaPorte County

CHILI SOUP

1 lb. hamburger	2 cans tomatoes, or 1 each of
1 large onion, chopped	tomatoes and
2 cans kidney beans	tomato sauce
1 lb. spaghetti, cooked and drained	chili powder
	salt and pepper
	1 c. catsup

Brown hamburger and onion in a skillet, drain, and put into a large kettle. Add beans, tomatoes, spaghetti, and catsup, and stir well. Add chili powder, salt, and pepper to taste. Cook over low heat for 10 to 15 min., then let simmer for 1 hr. Serves 5.

Dorothy Fowler
Daviess County

HAM SOUP

1 lb. chunk of ham	2 c. celery, diced
1 qt. water	1 head of cauliflower,
2 c. carrots, diced	cut up
1 c. onion, diced	1 qt. green beans
1 qt. corn	1 qt. tomatoes
salt and pepper	

Cook ham in quart of water, adding more if needed. When ham is tender, cut up. Add celery, onions, beans, corn, and carrots. Cook. When these are tender, add cauliflower and tomatoes. Serves 8.

Mrs. Lee Wells
Morgan County

HUNGARIAN GOULASH SOUP
(*Gulyassuppe*)

1 lb. chuck roast	1 T. caraway
2 T. lard	seeds
1 large onion,	½ t. marjoram
diced	1 clove garlic
1 heaping T.	2 qt. water
sweet paprika	3 medium
salt and pepper	potatoes, peeled
2 T. vinegar	and diced
1 T. tomato paste	

Cut beef into ¾″ cubes. Heat lard and sauté onions. Sprinkle with paprika; sauté a few more min. Add beef; let sear and brown slightly. Add salt, pepper, vinegar, and tomato paste. Simmer 3 min., then add caraway seeds, marjoram, garlic, and water. Bring to boiling point, cover and simmer gently 45 min., or until meat is almost done. Add diced potatoes and cook slowly 15 to 20 min. Check seasoning and serve in deep bowls. Serves 6.

Ada Pfaffenberger
Scott County

GRANDMA'S POTATO SOUP

4 or 5 slices	1½ to 2 qt. water
bacon	1 c. flour
1 medium onion,	1 t. baking
chopped	powder
3 or 4 c. potatoes,	½ t. salt
finely diced	1 egg
1 t. salt	1 c. milk
dash of pepper	

Fry bacon in skillet; remove and crumble. Sauté onion in bacon fat. Add onion, bacon, drippings, 1 t. salt, pepper, and water to the potatoes. Cook until potatoes are tender. On a plate pour flour, baking powder, and ½ t. salt. In center break egg. Sift through fingers until all flour is moistened. Mixture should be size of small peas. Drop by handfuls into the potato liquid. Stir while adding. More water may be needed. Simmer 5 or 10 min. Remove from heat. Stir in milk. Serve hot.

Faye Barks
Harrison County

PUMPKIN SOUP

2½ c. canned	2 T. butter
pumpkin	1 t. chopped
1½ c. water	parsley
3 c. milk	salt and pepper
⅓ c. boiled rice	

Mix pumpkin with water. Bring almost to boiling point. Add milk. Reheat. Add remaining ingredients. Cook 15 min. in double boiler. Serves 6 to 8.

Karen Merkel
Dearborn County

MEATLESS VEGETABLE SOUP

2 c. tomato juice	1 medium onion,
2½ c. water	chopped
4 pkg. instant	1 green pepper,
beef broth or	chopped
beef bouillon	2 cans French-
1 medium head	style green
cabbage,	beans
chopped or	*No Salt*
sliced	

Mix all ingredients in pan and simmer 2 to 3 hr.

Viola Peterson
Pulaski County

SPEEDY VEGETABLE SOUP

1 lb. ground beef	2 bouillon cubes
½ c. onion,	2 c. cabbage,
chopped	shredded
2 T. fat or oil	1 c. potatoes,
2 qt. water	diced

1 No. 2 can (2½ c.) tomatoes	1 c. carrot, diced
1 c. celery, diced	1½ T. salt
	½ t. pepper

Brown ground beef and onion in oil. Add remaining ingredients and cook 30 or 40 min. until done. Even better when simmered on low all afternoon to mingle flavors. Serves 8–10.

Joy Rembe
Floyd County

VEGETABLE AND BEEF SOUP

1 lb. can tomatoes	2 medium onions, diced
1–2 lb. beef shank or stew beef	3 carrots, sliced
	3. c. water
	1 t. salt
3 stalks celery with tops, sliced	3 beef bouillon cubes
	1 can whole kernel corn
5 medium potatoes, diced	1 can green beans

Put all ingredients except corn and green beans in Crock-Pot. Cover and cook on Low for 7 to 10 hr. Add corn and green beans during last 2 hr. of cooking.

Cordilla George
Martin County

Stews

BAKED STEW

2 lb. boneless beef stew meat	¼ to ½ c. water
6 carrots in large chunks	3 onions, chopped
6 potatoes (optional)	1 T. dark brown sugar
⅛ t. pepper	1 t. salt
½ c. tomato juice	2 T. Minute Tapioca

Put in Dutch oven, cover tightly. Bake at 225° for 4 hr. or 275° for 3 hr. Potatoes may be added 1 hr. before serving. Serves 6.

Mrs. Richard Watson
Delaware County

BEEF STEW

2½ lb. stew beef	1 can celery soup
6 potatoes	1 pkg. dry onion soup
6–8 carrots	
2 cans mushroom soup	1 can water

Brown beef and season. Use 5-qt. greased pan. Peel and slice potatoes and carrots. Layer beef, potatoes, and carrots. Top with remaining ingredients. Seal with foil and lid. Bake at 325° for 5 hr.

Mrs. Dave Fox
Adams County

CABBAGE PATCH STEW

1 lb. ground beef	1 c. cooked tomatoes
2 medium onions, sliced thin	1 t. salt
2 c. cabbage, shredded	dash of pepper
	1 t. chili powder
½ c. celery, diced	2 c. hot mashed potatoes
1 1-lb. can red kidney beans	(optional)

Brown beef in hot fat over medium heat; add onions, cabbage, and celery, cook until yellow. Add water to cover (about 2 c.); simmer 15 min. Add beans, tomatoes, and seasonings. Cook 15 to 20 min. Serve in

bowls topped with spoonfuls of mashed
potatoes.

Lena Peters
Franklin County

MULLIGAN STEW

1 lb. hamburger	1 pt. tomato juice
1 medium onion, chopped	1 c. cooked elbow macaroni
salt and pepper	cheddar cheese as desired, for top
1 pt. whole kernel corn	

Brown hamburger and onion with seasonings. Add other ingredients in order. Cook
until thoroughly heated. Serves 4.

Myrna Keith
Daviess County

OYSTER STEW

¼ c. butter	1½ t. salt
1 pt. oysters	pepper
1 qt. milk	1 t. paprika

Pick over oysters, removing all bits of
shell. Melt butter; cook oysters in it for
3 min., or until edges curl. Add milk and
seasonings and bring nearly to a boil; be
careful not to scorch.

Mrs. Darrell Cropp
Martin County

SPANISH STEW (*Estofado*)

1 lb. lean beef, cut in 1″ cubes	1½ t. salt
	⅛ t. pepper
1 T. cooking oil	1 recipe Bouquet Garni
1 c. dry red wine	
1 8-oz. can (1 c.) tomatoes	½ c. fresh mushrooms, sliced
1 large onion, cut in ¼″ slices	¼ c. ripe olives, sliced
¼ c. raisins	1 T. all-purpose flour
¼ c. dried apricots, halved	1 c. cold water
	hot cooked rice
1 clove garlic, halved	

In large skillet brown meat in hot oil. Add
wine, tomatoes, onion, green pepper,
raisins, apricots, garlic, salt, and pepper.
Add Bouquet Garni to stew. Simmer covered for 1 hr. Add mushrooms and olives;
simmer 30 min. more. Discard Bouquet
Garni. Combine flour and cold water; stir
into stew. Cook, stirring constantly, until
mixture thickens and bubbles. Serve over
hot cooked rice. Serve with tossed green
salad, crusty bread, and dry red wine.
Serves 6.

Bouquet Garni: Tie 1 t. dried basil, 1 t.
dried thyme, 1 t. dried tarragon, and 1
bay leaf in cheesecloth.

Mrs. Austin Sink
Floyd County

Chowders

CORN CHOWDER (1)

1 large onion, sliced	6 slices bacon
1 1-lb. can whole kernel or cream style corn	2 T. parsley, chopped (optional)
	3 c. milk

2 c. potatoes, diced	1 t. salt

Cook bacon in heavy saucepan. Crumble
and reserve. Pour off all but 4 T. of the
fat. Add onion and cook until tender but
not brown. If whole kernel corn is used,

drain corn and add liquid to saucepan. If cream style, add ½ c. water to saucepan. Bring to boil and add potatoes Cover and cook 10 min. Add corn, milk, and bacon. Add salt. Heat to serving temperature. Sprinkle with parsley. Serves 4.

Anna Lou Arnett
Randolph County

CORN CHOWDER (2)

2 c. potatoes, diced	¼ c. margarine
½ c. carrots, sliced	¼ c. flour
	2 c. milk
½ c. celery, sliced	1 10-oz. stick sharp cheddar cheese, shredded
¼ c. onion, chopped	
1½ t. salt	2 c. (1 lb. can) cream style corn
¼ t. pepper	
2 c. boiling water	

Combine potatoes, carrots, celery, onion, salt, and pepper. Add water. Cover and simmer 10 min. Do not drain. Make a cream sauce with margarine, flour, and

milk. Add cheese; stir until melted. Add corn and undrained vegetables. Heat; do not boil. Serves 6–8.

Dorothy Stevens
Jefferson County

TUNA MANHATTAN CHOWDER

2 7-oz. cans tuna in vegetable oil	1 2-oz. envelope dry vegetable soup mix
1 small onion, sliced	½ t. dried leaf thyme
1 1-lb. can peeled tomatoes	1 12-oz. can whole kernel corn
3 c. water	

Drain 2 T. oil from tuna into a large saucepan. Add onion and cook until tender but not brown. Add tomatoes, water, soup mix, and thyme. Mix well. Bring to a boil, stirring occasionally; cover and cook over medium heat for 10 min. Stir in tuna and corn with liquid. Cook 5 min. longer, or until thoroughly heated.

Mrs. Edwin Patesel
St. Joseph County

Salads and Salad Dressings

Salads play many roles: They can begin a meal, accompany a main dish, be the main dish, or be a satisfying finale to the meal. In addition to providing valuable vitamins and minerals, salads also furnish needed variety to a meal.

A wit once said that it takes four persons to make a good sauce for a salad: a spendthrift to provide the oil, a miser to measure the vinegar, a counselor to dole out the salt and spices, and a madman to stir the ingredients.

Salads

MAIN DISH SALADS

CHICKEN SALAD (1)

2 c. chicken, chopped	¼ c. slivered almonds
¾ c. celery, chopped	½ c. olives
1 c. white grapes	1 3-oz. pkg. cream cheese
1 T. lemon juice	¾ c. mayonnaise

Cream cream cheese and mayonnaise. Mix all ingredients. Chill. Serves 6.

Mrs. Clarence Zeigler
Whitley County

CHICKEN SALAD (2)

2½ c. chicken, chopped	1½ t. onion, grated
1 c. celery, chopped	1 t. vinegar
1 box Lemon Jello	2 t. garlic salt
¾ c. boiling water	½ c. mayonnaise
	½ c. sour cream
	½ c. pecans

Dissolve Jello in boiling water. Cool and add onion, vinegar, and garlic salt. Chill until slightly thickened. Add sour cream and mayonnaise. Add Jello mixture to chicken, celery, and pecans. Stir well and chill several hours. Stir again before serving. Serve on lettuce. Serves 10–12.

Mrs. Paul D. Douglas
Shelby County

CHICKEN OR TURKEY FRUIT SALAD

1 c. turkey or chicken, diced	½ c. grapes, sliced
1 c. pineapple, chopped	½ c. walnuts, chopped
1 c. apple, chopped	½ c. mayonnaise
½ c. orange, chopped	¼ c. pineapple or orange juice
1 large banana	2 t. sugar

Combine turkey or chicken, fruit, and nuts. Chill. Mix mayonnaise, juice, and sugar; pour over turkey/chicken mixture. Serves 6.

Zello Owen
Rush County

CRUNCHY CHICKEN SALAD

1 c. raw carrots, shredded	2 T. pickle relish
1 c. celery, diced	1 c. mayonnaise, thinned with cream
¼ c. onion, minced	3 small cans potato sticks
1 cooked chicken, diced	

Mix first 6 ingredients together. Chill. Add potato sticks just before serving.

Mary Fleenor
Randolph County

HOT CHICKEN SALAD (1)

2 c. cooked chicken, diced	¼ c. French dressing
1½ c. celery, chopped	½ c. mayonnaise
	⅓ c. sour cream

¼ c. almonds, chopped	2 c. potato chips, crushed
1 c. cheese, grated	

Marinate chicken and celery in French dressing for 6 hr. Add the rest of the ingredients, except potato chips and cheese. Pour in greased 9x12″ Pyrex dish and bake at 350° for 20 min. Then sprinkle chips and cheese over the top and return to oven to broil until the cheese is bubbly.

The salad, without the cheese and potato chips, can be used for hot chicken sandwiches.

Mrs. Lester Alexander
Wells County

HOT CHICKEN SALAD (2)

1 medium cooked chicken or 2 cans boned chicken	1 can cream of chicken soup
1 c. onion, chopped	1 T. lemon juice
1 c. green pepper, chopped	½ t. Accent
butter	¾ c. mayonnaise
1 c. cooked rice	4 hard-cooked eggs, chopped
	potato chips, crushed

Brown onion and green pepper in a little butter. Mix together rice, chicken, onions, green peppers, and the rest of the ingredients except potato chips. Put into greased 9x13″ pan. Sprinkle crushed potato chips on top. Bake at 350° for 30 min. If mixed and refrigerated, bake 10 or 15 min. longer.

Hazel Douglas
Parke County

CORNED BEEF SALAD

2 beef bouillon cubes	1 pkg. Lemon Jello

1 c. hot water
1 large pkg.
  cream cheese
1 small pkg.
  cream cheese
2 c. celery,
  chopped
2 T. onion,
  chopped

1 c. mayonnaise
½ c. green
  pepper,
  chopped
1 can corned
  beef
4 hard-boiled
  eggs

Dissolve bouillon cubes in hot water; add Jello and dissolve. Chill until slightly thickened. Add cream cheese and mayonnaise. Add rest of ingredients. Mix well. Chill overnight. Serves 12–15.

Mrs. Charles Russell
Miami County

COTTAGE CHEESE SALAD

3 pt. cottage
  cheese
1 envelope
  gelatin,
  softened in ¼ c.
  cold water
1 small onion,
  grated
1 green pepper,
  chopped

4 T. mayonnaise
1 small jar olives,
  chopped
1 medium
  cucumber,
  grated
¼ c. pecans,
  chopped
1½ t. salt
½ t. paprika

Dissolve gelatin over hot water and combine with cottage cheese. Add remaining ingredients and put into mold. Turn out on lettuce and garnish with sliced tomatoes. Serves 15–18.

B. J. Grant
Switzerland County

CRAB SALAD (Sonny Liston's)

3 hard-boiled
  eggs
1 c. celery,
  chopped finely

10 oz. chilled
  crab meat,
  flaked into
  salad shreds

⅔ c. mayonnaise
1 T. lemon juice
½ t. Worcester-
  shire sauce

1 T. ketchup
¾ t. salt
¼ t. pepper
½ t. garlic salt

Mash the eggs and add to crab meat and celery in a medium-sized bowl. Mix the rest of the ingredients. Mix the mayonnaise mixture with the crab meat mixture. Serve with tomato wedges on lettuce bed. Serves 4.

B. J. Grant
Switzerland County

LIMA BEAN AND EGG SALAD

1 10-oz. pkg.
  frozen limas,
  cooked
1 T. minced
  onion
2 T. French
  dressing
½ c. mayonnaise

4 hard-cooked
  eggs, sliced
1 c. celery and
  leaves
salt and pepper
  to taste
salad greens
paprika

Mix all except greens and paprika. Place on greens and sprinkle with paprika. Serves 4–6.

Patricia Harmon
Harrison County

MOCK LOBSTER SALAD

2 lbs. fresh
  haddock
2 c. salted water
1 medium onion,
  sliced
¾ c. sour cream
½ c. chili sauce

2 T. horseradish
2 T. mayonnaise
salt to taste
1 T. fresh lemon
  juice
2 c. celery, diced

Simmer fish in salted water with sliced onion until fish are white (5 min.). Drain and cool. Flake fish in large pieces. Add celery. Combine sour cream, chili sauce, horseradish, mayonnaise, and lemon juice.

Blend well with fish. Refrigerate. Stir well before serving. Serve on lettuce with light dusting of paprika. Serves 6–8.

Lilly Jane Hall
Noble County

PATIO SALAD

1 pkg. frozen peas	½ c. dill pickles, chopped
1½ c. Minute Rice	1 t. onion, grated
½ t. salt	1 c. cooked ham, slivered
1½ c. water	1 c. Swiss cheese, slivered
¾ c. mayonnaise	

Add frozen peas and salt to water. Cover. Bring to full boil. Add Minute Rice. Stir with fork to moisten. Cover and remove from heat. Let stand 13 min. Add mayonnaise, pickle, and onion, mixing with a fork. Chill. Before serving add ham and cheese. Serve on crisp lettuce with a ring of tomato wedges. Garnish top with ham and cheese slivers. Serves 6.

Lois Torney
Daviess County

HOT SEAFOOD SALAD

3 slices white bread, toasted	1 5-oz. can shrimp or ½ lb. frozen shrimp, cooked as directed
½ c. mayonnaise	
¼ c. sweet pickle, diced	
¼ c. onion, chopped	2 T. parsley, chopped
1 6½-oz. can crab meat or 1 pkg. frozen crab meat, cooked as directed	2 hard-cooked eggs, diced
	¼ c. celery, diced
	lettuce leaves

Cut toast into ½″ cubes. Combine with mayonnaise; mix well. Add remaining in-

gredients, tossing well. Heat in top of double boiler over hot water for about 20 to 30 min., or until mixture is piping hot. Serve garnished with paprika on top of lettuce leaf. Serves 4.

Mrs. Ernest Ford
Marshall County

SHRIMP AMEN

1½ c. cooked shrimp	1 small onion, minced
¼ c. salad oil	1 T. green pepper, minced
1½ T. lemon juice	½ c. olives, sliced
1 t. salt	1 tomato, diced
pepper to taste	head lettuce, coarsely chunked
⅛ t. dry mustard	
1 t. curry powder	

Beat salad oil with lemon juice, salt, pepper, mustard, curry powder, onion, and green pepper. Toss with tomato, olives, and shrimp. Chill well. Toss with lettuce.

Mrs. La Mar Cooper
Elkhart County

SOUFFLE SALAD

1 c. boiling water	¼ t. salt
1 3-oz. pkg. fruit-flavored gelatin	dash of pepper
	1 to 2½ c. vegetables, fruit, meat, poultry, fish, cheese, hard-cooked eggs
½ c. cold water	
1 to 2 T. lemon juice	
½ c. mayonnaise	

Pour boiling water over gelatin in bowl; stir until completely dissolved. Add cold water, lemon juice, mayonnaise, salt and pepper. Blend with rotary beater. Pour into freezing tray or metal loaf pan. Chill in freezing unit until firm about 1″ from sides of pan, but still soft in the center (about

20 min.). Turn chilled gelatin mixture into bowl and beat with rotary beater until fluffy and thick. Fold in desired variation of ingredients. Pour into one quart mold or individual molds. Chill in refrigerator until firm (45–60 min.). Unmold on salad greens. Serves 4.

Note: When making vegetable and meat salads, add ½ to 1 T. finely chopped onion. When making fruit salad, omit pepper. Suggested Combinations: Ham, pineapple, and celery; tuna, cucumber, and olives; peaches, almond, and cream cheese; oranges, cottage cheese, and nuts.

Friendly Neighbors Club
LaPorte County

TUNA SALAD

2 c. unpeeled apple, diced	1 6- or 7-oz. can tuna, drained
1 11-oz. can mandarin oranges, drained	⅓ c. walnuts, coarse chopped
	½ c. mayonnaise
	2 t. soy sauce
	1 t. lemon juice

Toss all ingredients together and serve on lettuce leaf. Serves 4.

Mrs. Tom Lanphier
Marshall County

SEA ISLAND TUNA SALAD

7-oz. pkg. macaroni (2 c. dry)	17-oz. can peas, drained
½ c. mayonnaise or salad dressing	2 T. green pepper, minced
½ c. sour cream	1 T. pimiento, diced
½ t. celery seed	7-oz. can tuna, drained, or substitute ham, chicken or other meat
½ t. onion salt	
¾ c. mild cheddar cheese, diced	

Cook macaroni as directed on package. Stir in mayonnaise or salad dressing blended with sour cream and seasonings. Gently stir in peas and remaining ingredients. Chill.

Mrs. Adeline Busse
Dearborn County

VEGETABLE SALADS

ARTICHOKE-RICE SALAD

1 pkg. chicken-flavored rice mix	¼ t. curry powder
2 6-oz. jars marinated artichoke hearts, sliced	2 green onions, sliced
	½ green pepper, chopped
½ c. mayonnaise	8 stuffed olives, sliced

Cook rice as directed, but omit butter and use ¼ c. water less. Do not brown. Gently turn into salad bowl and cool. Drain artichoke hearts. For marinade use liquid from one jar artichokes combined with mayonnaise and curry powder. Layer rice, green vegetables, and artichoke hearts. Pour marinade dressing over and toss lightly. Chill. Toss again lightly and serve.

Mrs. Richard W. Sipe
Rush County

ASPARAGUS SOUP SALAD

1 can asparagus soup	⅓ green mango, chopped
1 3-oz. pkg. Lime Jello	1 t. onion, chopped
8-oz. cream cheese	½ c. mayonnaise
1 c. celery, chopped	½ c. water
	⅓ c. nuts, chopped

Heat the asparagus soup and water to boiling point. Dissolve the Jello into hot mixture, and while still warm add the cream cheese and stir until melted. Cool and add the rest of the ingredients. Put all into a round mold and chill until firm. Unmold and garnish with parsley. Serves 8.

Mrs. George Cook
Bartholomew County

BEAN SALAD

1 No. 2½ can kidney beans	1 T. sugar dash of salt
4 medium pickles, sliced	2 T. salad dressing
1 medium onion, sliced	2 hard-boiled eggs, sliced

Mix pickles, onions, and eggs. Add to kidney beans. Stir in sugar and salt, and salad dressing. Serves 6.

Sandra Barber
Daviess County

GREEN BEAN SALAD

2 cans cut green beans, drained	1 small jar pimiento, drained
1 can peas, drained	1½ c. sugar
4 stalks celery, diced	1 c. white vinegar ½ c. cooking oil
2 medium onions, sliced	1 t. salt 1 T. water

Mix the last 5 ingredients; then mix all the ingredients together. Let set for 24 hr. before serving. Serves 15.

Mrs. Tom Bonnell
Bartholomew County

HOT BEAN SALAD

1 20-oz. can red kidney beans	1 c. celery, thinly sliced

½ c. Swiss cheese, diced	¼ c. home-style salad dressing with mini croutons and flavor bits
1 T. onion, chopped	
½ t. salt	
½ c. mayonnaise	

Combine all ingredients except salad dressing. Place in 4 10-oz. baking dishes. Sprinkle with salad topping and bake at 450° for 10 min.

Barbara Davis
Sullivan County

THREE BEAN SALAD

1 can green beans, drained	1 small can pimiento, chopped
1 can yellow wax beans, drained	1 medium onion, chopped
1 can red beans, drained	¾ c. sugar
½ c. celery, chopped	¾ c. vinegar
½ green pepper, chopped	¼ c. vegetable oil

Mix and let stand for 24 hr. before serving.

Helen Hevron
Spencer County

FIVE BEAN SALAD

1 can French cut beans, drained	1 can garbanzos or peas, drained
1 can kidney beans, drained	½ c. onion, cut in rings
1 can wax beans, drained	½ c. green mango, cut in rings
1 can green limas, drained	
1 small pimiento (or small can), chopped	1 c. vinegar
	2 T. salad oil
	1 c. sugar

Mix and let stand for 24 hr. before serving.

Mrs. Neil Moody
Delaware County

BEET SALAD (1)

1 lb. can sliced beets, drained	¼ c. salad oil
1 small onion, cut into rings	¼ c. cider vinegar
¼ c. sugar	¼ t. seasoned salt
	dash of pepper

Add drained beets to onion rings. Make a salad dressing by mixing together the sugar, oil, vinegar, and seasonings. Combine all ingredients and marinate for at least 1 hr. Serves 4.

Mrs. Charles McIntyre
Fayette County

BEET SALAD (2)

1½ c. cooked diced beets, drained	⅓ c. vinegar
2 pkg. Lemon Jello	1 t. onions, grated
3 c. beet juice	2½ T. horseradish
	1 c. celery, diced

Dissolve Jello in boiling beet juice. Add vinegar, onions, horseradish, and chill mixture slightly. Add beets and celery. Refrigerate.

Leatha Koontz
Randolph County

RED BEET SALAD

1 pkg. Strawberry Jello	¾ c. pineapple juice
1 pkg. Raspberry Jello	¾ c. beet juice
1 pkg. Cherry Jello	½ c. sweet pickle juice
4 c. boiling water	⅛ t. salt
	1 T. vinegar

1 No. 303 can sliced beets, drained	1 c. mayonnaise
	1 c. celery
	1 c. green pepper
1 No. 303 can crushed pineapple, drained	¼ c. onion
	1 avocado

Mix Jellos with boiling water, dissolve, and cool. Mix juices with salt and vinegar, then add beets and pineapple. Mix with the Jello and let set. In blender mix last 5 ingredients and use as dressing for the salad.

Sharon Fifer
Posey County

BROCCOLI SALAD

2 10-oz. pkg. frozen broccoli spears (do not use chopped)	1 small sweet onion (optional)
1½ c. stuffed olives, sliced	6 hard-cooked eggs, chopped
	mayonnaise

Cook broccoli in salt water for 3 min. Chop into bite-size pieces. Add onion and eggs, olives, and generous amount of mayonnaise (enough to coat well). Serves 6.

Mrs. Evelyn Mousa
Jennings County

CABBAGE-PEANUT SALAD

1 small head cabbage, finely chopped	2 t. salt
	2 t. pepper
	1 T. butter
1 lb. salted peanuts, finely chopped	2 T. flour
	2 egg yolks
	1 t. dry mustard
3 large red delicious apples, finely chopped	¾ c. vinegar
	¾ c. sugar

Mix chopped cabbage, peanuts, and apples. Add salt and pepper. Cream together butter, flour, sugar, mustard, stir in vinegar, and cook in double boiler until stiff. Add egg yolks. Pour over cabbage mixture. Serves 6–8.

Eloise White
Porter County

FROZEN SLAW

1 head cabbage, shredded	2 carrots, shredded
1 T. salt	1 c. cider vinegar
3 stalks celery, shredded	2 c. sugar
	½ c. water
1 mango, shredded	1 t. celery seed
	1 t. mustard seed

Add salt to cabbage. Let stand for 1 hr., then squeeze out juice. Add celery, mango, and carrots. (The number of carrots and mangoes can be more or less, as preferred.) Mix the last 5 ingredients and bring to a boil. Cool and pour over cabbage. Slaw may be served immediately or it can be boxed and frozen. It does not have to be completely thawed to be served, and it will keep after thawing for quite a long time in refrigerator.

Mrs. Kathryn Carr
Bartholomew County

PINEAPPLE COLESLAW

4 c. cabbage, shredded	1 c. miniature marshmallows
1 c. unpeeled red apples, diced	½ c. celery, chopped
1 c. pineapple chunks	salad dressing
	lettuce

Combine cabbage, apples, pineapple, marshmallows, celery, and enough salad dressing to moisten; toss lightly. Serve in lettuce-lined salad bowl.

Mary Ann Boger
Pike County

SKILLET SALAD

¼ c. onion, chopped	2 c. cabbage, shredded
½ c. green pepper, chopped	½ t. sugar
	1 t. salt
½ c. celery, diced	dash of pepper
	2 T. butter or margarine
1 c. fresh tomatoes, diced	

Melt margarine in a skillet. Add remaining ingredients and cover. Simmer for 12 to 15 min. until the vegetables are tender.

Patty Held
Fulton County

STAY-CRISP GARDEN SLAW

2 qt. (8 c.) finely shredded cabbage	1 green pepper, cut in strips
	½ c. onion, sliced thin or chopped
2 shredded carrots	½ c. ice water

Use very sharp, thin, long-bladed knife—not a shredder—for cutting cabbage into thin shreds. Peel carrots with vegetable peeler or scrape with a knife; shred on medium shredder. Cut green pepper in thin strips, then across in about 1″ lengths. Put cabbage in large bowl. Add carrots, pepper strips, and sliced or chopped onion. Sprinkle ice water over all. Cover bowl and refrigerate to chill thoroughly. Drain chilled mixture; pour dressing over top; mix lightly with salad fork to coat vegetables with dressing. Serve immediately or store in refrigerator in covered container. Stir just before serving to separate pieces.

Dressing:

1 envelope unflavored gelatin	¼ c. cold water
	⅔ c. cider vinegar

⅔ c. sugar	¼ t. black
2 t. celery seed	pepper
1½ t. salt	⅔ c. salad oil

In small saucepan measure cold water and sprinkle gelatin in it. Let stand to soften (about 5 min.), then add sugar, vinegar, celery seed, salt, and pepper. Place on low heat and stir until mixture is hot and gelatin is dissolved. Cool until slightly sirupy. Gradually beat in salad oil.

Rosella Elliott
Ripley County

WINTER VEGETABLE SALAD

1 3-oz. box	½ c. celery, diced
lemon gelatin	½ c. pimiento,
1 c. hot water	chopped
1 c. cold water	1½ c. cabbage,
1 t. salt	shredded
1 t. vinegar	

Dissolve gelatin in hot water; add vinegar, salt, and cold water. Chill until slightly thickened. Fold in remaining ingredients and chill until firm. Serve with mayonnaise if desired. Serves 8.

Mrs. Harold Coffman
Union County

CARROT-PINEAPPLE MOLD

1 1-lb., 12-oz. can	1 c. carrots,
crushed pine-	grated
apple (3½ c.)	¾ c. nuts,
1 c. water	chopped
1 3-oz. pkg.	2 c. cottage
lemon gelatin	cheese
1 3-oz. pkg.	1 c. whipping
orange gelatin	cream, whipped
1 c. celery, finely	½ c. mayonnaise
diced	

Heat pineapple and water to boiling. Add

gelatins and stir until dissolved. Chill until partially thickened. Fold in remaining ingredients. Turn into 16 individual molds or two 1-quart molds. Chill until firm. Serves 16.

Mrs. Richard Soliday
Greene County

CARROT-RAISIN SALAD

6 carrots	½ t. salt
½ c. seedless	¼ c. mayonnaise
raisins	2 t. Tang

Peel or scrape carrots; grate or put through food chopper. Combine with raisins, salt, mayonnaise, and Tang. Chill. Serve on letture or watercress. Serves 6.

Mrs. James T. Wheeler
Knox County

CAULIFLOWER SUPREME SALAD

1 medium head	1-lb. bacon, fried
of cauliflower,	and crumbled
broken into	2 c. mayonnaise
small flowerets	⅓ c. sugar
1 medium head	(optional)
of lettuce, torn	⅓ c. grated
as for tossed	Parmesan
salad	cheese
1 medium onion,	½ t. salt
finely chopped	dash of pepper

In a large bowl, layer ingredients as follows: cauliflower, lettuce, onion, and bacon. In another bowl mix the last 5 ingredients. Pour dressing mixture over top of layered mixture. Cover and refrigerate for at least 6 hr. or overnight. Toss before serving. Serves 12.

Mrs. Kay McIntire
Boone County

CUCUMBER SALAD MOLD

1 3-oz. pkg. Lemon Jello	1 cucumber, finely chopped
½ c. boiling water	1 small onion, finely chopped
1 small pkg. small curd cottage cheese	1 c. mayonnaise small amount of stuffed olives,
½ c. nuts, finely chopped	chopped (optional)

Dissolve Jello in boiling water. Set aside to cool. Prepare the rest of ingredients and mix together. Mix with cooled Jello and put into mold for several hr.

Anna Vibbert
Vanderburgh County

DANDELION SALAD

4 c. dandelion greens, shredded	1 small onion, cut fine
	¼ c. vinegar
4 medium boiled potatoes, diced	salt
	4 slices bacon
4 hard-boiled eggs, chopped	

Combine greens, potatoes, and eggs in bowl with onion. Fry bacon and crumble over greens. Put vinegar into bacon grease and heat. Pour over entire mixture. Salt to taste. Serves 6.

Suggestion: When dandelions are not in season, use endive.

Mrs. Charles Warner
Whitley County

GUACAMOLE SALAD

3 ripe avocados	3 t. onion, grated
2 small ripe tomatoes	
	3 t. lemon juice
3 T. mayonnaise	1 t. salt

Peel ripe avocados and put through a sieve. Peel tomatoes. Take out all seeds and cut tomatoes into small pieces with scissors. Mix all ingredients. Serve on a bed of lettuce. Serves 6–8.

Lillian Ehlbert
Vanderburgh County

WILTED LEAF LETTUCE

8 c. leaf lettuce, torn into small pieces	¼ c. water
	½ c. green onions, sliced
6 slices bacon	4 t. sugar
¼ c. vinegar	

Fry bacon until crisp. Drain and crumble. Add onions to drippings and cook until tender. Add vinegar, water, sugar, salt, and bacon to onions. Pour hot dressing over lettuce. Toss to coat. Garnish with radishes and hard-cooked eggs if you wish.

Marilyn Jackson
Sullivan County

MIXED VEGETABLE SALAD

1 large pkg. frozen mixed vegetables	½ green pepper, chopped
	3 stalks celery, chopped
1 can kidney beans, drained	¾ c. sugar
1 large onion, chopped fine	½ c. vinegar
	1 t. mustard

Cook vegetables. Cool and drain well. Cook sugar, vinegar, and mustard until slightly thick. Cool sauce and pour over vegetables. Chill thoroughly.

Minnie Crawe
Pike County

HOT VEGETABLE SALAD

2 cans French-cut green beans	1 large mango, sliced in thin strips
1 can shoe string carrots	1 c. celery, chopped
1 large can tomatoes or ⅔ qt. home canned	2 T. sugar
	2 T. cornstarch
	buttered bread crumbs
1 large onion, sliced thin	

Butter 8½×11″ baking dish and layer vegetables in it as follows: 1 can green beans, carrots, mango, celery, onion, and 1 can green beans. Combine tomatoes, sugar, and cornstarch and cook until mixture starts to thicken. Pour over vegetables in baking dish. Top with bread crumbs. Bake at 350° for about 2 hr.

Mrs. Max Tribbett
Montgomery County

WONDER SALAD

1 can green peas, drained	3 medium onions, sliced thin
1 can green beans, drained	2 c. celery, sliced thin
1 large can Chinese vegetables, drained	1 c. white sugar
	¾ c. vinegar
1 small can watercress, drained	

Make alternate layers of first 6 ingredients in large bowl. Mix vinegar and sugar and pour over vegetables. Do not stir. Cover and leave in refrigerator overnight. Will keep for several days.

Betty Ratliff
Hendricks County

PEA SALAD

½ head of lettuce, shredded	small bunch of parsley, chopped
2 pkg. of frozen peas	½ c. celery, chopped
1 small sweet red onion, sliced thin	1 c. sour cream
	⅔ c. mayonnaise
1 small carrot, grated	½ lb. bacon, cooked and crumbled

Cook frozen peas slightly. Drain and cool peas. In large mixing bowl add lettuce, peas, onion, carrot, parsley and celery. In a smaller bowl blend sour cream and mayonnaise, add to lettuce mixture and blend well. Sprinkle bacon on top. Refrigerate overnight. Serves 12.

Mrs. Linda Kerber
Tippecanoe County

BAKED POTATO SALAD

8 medium cooked potatoes, diced	1 c. mayonnaise
	salt and pepper to taste
1 lb. soft American cheese, diced	½ c. uncooked bacon, chopped
¼ c. onions, chopped	½ c. olives, sliced

Combine potatoes, cheese, onions, mayonnaise, salt, and pepper and turn into baking dish. Top with uncooked bacon and olives. Bake 1 hr. at 350°. Serves 8.

Nell Lester
Switzerland County

DANISH POTATO SALAD

¼ c. vinegar	¼ c. sugar
¼ c. water	¼ t. salt

1 t. prepared
  mustard
2 eggs,
  well-beaten
1 c. salad dressing
2 hard-cooked
  eggs, chopped
4 c. cookd pota-
  toes, cubed
  (about 2 lbs.)

dash of pepper
½ c. cucumber,
  chopped
  (optional)
1 T. onion,
  minced
1 T. green
  pepper,
  chopped
  (optional)

Combine first six ingredients. Bring to a boil. Reduce heat; gradually beat in well-beaten eggs. Cook, stirring constantly, until slightly thickened (about 5 min.). Beat in salad dressing. Toss remaining ingredients together. Pour dressing over potato mixture, toss gently. Adjust seasoning, if it's necessary. Serves 6.

Rita Carpenter
Pulaski County

GERMAN POTATO SALAD

6 to 8 medium
  potatoes,
  unpeeled
1 medium onion,
  chopped very
  fine

½ lb. bacon, cut
  in small pieces
3 eggs
1 c. sugar
½ c. vinegar

Boil potatoes with skins until done. Pare and slice when cool. Pour about a quart of boiling water over the sliced potatoes; drain. Mix onion with potatoes. Fry bacon pieces. Pour fat and bacon over potatoes and mix well. Beat eggs and blend in sugar and vinegar. Cook over low heat until very thick. Pour over potatoes and mix well. Allow the salad to stand to blend flavors before serving. Serves 6–8.

Erma Stearley
Clay County

SPECIAL POTATO SALAD

12 to 14 large
  cooked pota-
  toes, cubed
  (about 3½ qt.)
6 hard-boiled
  eggs
1½ c. sweet
  pickles,
  chopped
1 small mango,
  chopped fine

1½ c. red
  radishes, sliced
2½ c. mayonnaise
2 t. salt
½ t. pepper
1 small jar
  pimiento, cut
1 c. green onions
  with tops,
  chopped

Combine potatoes with remaining ingredients in a large bowl and mix lightly. Liberally coat 10″ angel food cake pan with mayonnaise. Press salad firmly into pan. Chill at least two hours or overnight in refrigerator. To serve, run knife around sides of pan to loosen salad. Turn out on large platter or serving dish. Serve cold cuts around edge of salad with tomato wedges and parsley. Serves 12–14.

Hazel Henley
Brown County

SAUERKRAUT SALAD

1 large can
  sauerkraut,
  drained (chop,
  if shredded)
1 c. green or red
  pepper,
  chopped
1 c. celery,
  chopped

1 medium red or
  white onion,
  chopped
1 c. granulated
  sugar (or
  ¾ c., if
  preferred)
¼ c. vinegar
½ c. salad oil

Mix all ingredients well. If possible, let stand in refrigerator 48 hr. before serving.

Mabel Collins
Washington County

SPINACH SALAD

1 1-lb. pkg. fresh spinach, chopped	3 or 4 hard-boiled eggs, chopped
1 can bean sprouts, drained, washed under cold water	6 slices bacon, fried and broken in pieces

Combine and serve with dressing.

Dressing:

½ c. sugar	¼ c. vinegar
1 c. salad oil	1 medium onion, chopped
pinch of salt	
½ c. ketchup	

Mix together and chill. Pour over spinach mixture.

Trudy Gentry
Perry County

EASY PERFECTION SALAD

2 3-oz. pkg. lemon gelatin	6 small green onions, chopped
2 c. boiling water	ripe olives
1 T. vinegar	carrot curls
12 to 15 ice cubes	1 t. horseradish
1 1-lb. can sauerkraut	1 c. mayonnaise or salad dressing
1 pimiento, chopped	

Place gelatin in 8½×4½×2½" loaf dish. Add boiling water and stir until gelatin is dissolved. Add vinegar and ice cubes. Stir until gelatin begins to thicken (about 3 min.). Remove any ice cubes remaining. With scissors, cut through sauerkraut. Add sauerkraut, onions, and pimiento to gelatin. Stir gently to dis-

tribute vegetables. Chill until set (about 4 hr.). Unmold onto crisp greens on serving plate. Garnish with ripe olives and crisp carrot curls. Stir horseradish into mayonnaise or salad dressing. Serve with salad. Serves 8–10.

Eva Eherenman
Kosciusko County

CALORIE CONSCIOUS SALAD

2 envelopes unflavored gelatin	1 t. Worcestershire sauce
3¼ c. tomato juice	¼ t. Tabasco sauce
½ t. salt	¼ c. lemon or lime juice

Sprinkle gelatin over 1 c. tomato juice in a medium saucepan. Place over moderate heat. Stir in remaining 2¼ c. tomato juice and other ingredients. Pour into 1-quart ring mold. Chill until firm. Unmold and fill center with coleslaw. Serves 6.

Mrs. Odelia Lohman
Ripley County

TOMATO SPICE FOR GARLIC LOVERS

1½ c. tomato juice	1 3-oz. pkg. Lemon Jello
1 bay leaf	½ t. salt or celery salt
6 whole cloves	
¼ t. instant minced garlic	

Heat tomato juice with one bay leaf, 6 whole cloves, and instant minced garlic. Add Lemon Jello and salt. Cool until ready to set. Add ground celery and onion. Put in 1-quart mold. Chill until firm. Serves 6.

Clara F. Burroughs
Switzerland County

FRUIT AND DESSERT SALADS

AMBROSIA SALAD

1 small pkg. orange gelatin	2 peeled oranges, cut in small pieces
1 c. boiling water	
⅓ c. sugar	½ c. flaked coconut
1 9-oz. can crushed pineapple, drain and save juice	½ c. sour cream
	½ t. vanilla

Dissolve gelatin and sugar in hot water. Stir in pineapple juice. Chill until syrup stage. Add sour cream and vanilla. Whip until fluffy. Fold in pineapple, oranges, and coconut. Pour in 9×9″ pan and chill.

Mary Loper
Franklin County

APPLESAUCE-RASPBERRY SALAD

1 3-oz. pkg. raspberry gelatin	1 10-oz. pkg. frozen raspberries
1 c. boiling water	
1 c. applesauce	1 c. small marshmallows
1 c. sour cream	

Dissolve gelatin in boiling water; add frozen raspberries; stir until thawed. Stir in applesauce. Pour into 10×6×1¾″ baking dish. Chill until set. Combine sour cream and marshmallows. Spread on top of gelatin. Cover and chill 2 hr. more. Cut in squares; serve on lettuce leaf. Serves 6.

Minnie Hofherr
Delaware County

CINNAMON-APPLESAUCE MOLD

2 pkg. Lemon Jello	1 8-oz. pkg. cream cheese
2 c. hot water	2 c. applesauce
½ c. red hots	2 T. mayonnaise

Dissolve Jello and red hots in water. Cool and add applesauce. Mix cream cheese and mayonnaise. Combine with gelatin mixture. Pour in mold and refrigerate until firm. Serves 8–10.

Helen Wilson
Washington County

APRICOT SALAD

1 29-oz. can of apricots, drained and mashed	2 pkg. Orange Jello
	2 c. boiling water
	1 c. fruit juice
1 29-oz. can crushed pineapple, drained	¾ c. miniature marshmallows

Drain fruit and save juice. Dissolve Jello in boiling water. Add fruit juice. Chill until thickened. Fold in fruit and marshmallows. Chill until firm. Serves 15.

Topping:

½ c. sugar	¾ c. cheddar cheese, grated
1 egg, beaten	
1 c. fruit juice	3 T. flour
1 c. whipped cream	1 T. butter

Mix flour and sugar. Blend in egg and gradually add fruit juice. Cook over low heat until thick, stirring constantly. Remove from heat. Add butter. Cool. Fold in whipped cream and spread over Jello. Sprinkle grated cheese on top.

Jean Burns
Parke County

APRICOT JELLO SALAD

2 pkg. Apricot Jello	2 c. cool water
2 c. boiling water	1 c. small marshmallows

2 c. bananas
1 No. 2 can
   crushed pine-
apple, drain
and reserve
juice

Mix and let set.

Topping:

½ c. sugar
½ c. pineapple
   juice
1 egg, slightly
   beaten
2 T. flour
2 T. butter
1 8-oz. pkg.
   cream cheese
1 envelope
   Dream Whip

Cook together the first 5 ingredients; remove from fire, and add cream cheese. Let cool. Whip Dream Whip and fold into mixture. Spread on Jello.

Mrs. Louis Houston
Marshall County

BANANA SALAD

6 large bananas
1 small pkg.
   peanuts,
   ground
4 eggs
1 c. sugar
1. T vinegar
1 c. butter

Cook last 4 ingredients until thick. Set to cool. Slice and quarter bananas. Spread layer of bananas, layer of dressing, layer of bananas, layer of dressing, etc., until bananas are all used. Sprinkle ground peanuts over top. Serves 12.

June Harbison
Putnam County

CAMPAIGN SALAD

1 8-oz. pkg.
   cream cheese
¾ c. sugar
1 12-oz. pkg.
   frozen
   strawberries,
   thawed
2 bananas, cut up
1 large can
   crushed pine-
   apple, drained
1 c. nuts,
   chopped
1 10-oz. carton
   Cool Whip

Blend well cream cheese and sugar. Add rest of ingredients. Mix well and freeze. Remove from freezer ½ hr. before serving. Serves 20.

Shirley Copple
Marion County

CHERRY SALAD SUPREME

1 3-oz. pkg. rasp-
   berry gelatin
2 c. boiling water
1 21-oz. can
   cherry pie
   filling
1 3-oz. pkg.
   lemon gelatin
⅓ c. mayonnaise
   or salad
   dressing
1 3-oz. pkg.
   cream cheese
1 8¾-oz. can
   (1 c.) crushed
   pineapple
½ c. whipping
   cream
1 c. miniature
   marshmallows
2 T. nuts,
   chopped

Dissolve raspberry gelatin in 1 c. boiling water; stir in pie filling. Turn into 9×9× 2″ baking dish; chill until partially set. Dissolve lemon gelatin in 1 c. boiling water. Beat together cream cheese and mayonnaise. Gradually add lemon gelatin. Stir in undrained pineapple. Whip whipping cream, fold into lemon mixture with marshmallows. Spread on top of cherry layer; top with chopped nuts. Chill until set. Serves 12.

Carol Sargent
Pulaski County

SOUR CHERRY SALAD

1 1-lb. can sour
   cherries,
   drained
1 1-lb., 4-oz. can
   crushed pine-
   apple, drained
1 3-oz. pkg.
   lemon gelatin
1 3-oz. pkg.
   cherry gelatin
1 c. water
¾ c. sugar

1 California orange, grated rind and juice
1 lemon, grated rind and juice
few drops of red food coloring (optional)
nut meats, chopped (optional)

Add water to drained juice from cherries and pineapple. Add sugar to dry gelatins. Heat ½ of liquid to boiling and use to dissolve both packages of gelatin and sugar. Add grated rinds and remaining juices. Add drained cherries and pineapple. Chill until mixture begins to thicken. Stir well and pour into 9" square pan or molds. Top with dressing.

Dressing:

1 3-oz. pkg. cream cheese
½ c. mayonnaise
¼ c. nuts, chopped

Mix well and spread on gelatin.

Dianna Crouse
Union County

CRANBERRY SALAD (1)

2 3-oz. pkg. raspberry gelatin
2 c. hot water
1 c. sour cream
1 can jellied cranberries
1 c. pecans, chopped

Mix jellied cranberries and 1 c. hot water in blender or mixer until smooth. Dissolve both packages of gelatin in 1 c. hot water. Add cranberry mixture and pecans to gelatin. Put ½ of mixture in 8" square pan and chill in freezer until firm (35–40 min). Spread sour cream over top of chilled mixture. Add second half of gelatin over sour cream. Refrigerate until firm. Serves 8–12.

Mrs. Judy Gaffney
Jefferson County

CRANBERRY SALAD (2)

2 c. raw cranberries, ground
2 c. unpeeled apples, ground
2 c. sugar
1 large pkg. Lemon Jello
2 c. hot water
2 c. pineapple juice
1 c. Tokay grapes, halved and seeded
½ c. pecans, ground

Combine cranberries, apples, and sugar. Dissolve Jello in hot water; add pineapple juice. Chill until partially set. Add cranberry-apple mixture, grape halves, and nut meats. Pour into 9×13×2" pan and keep in refrigerator. Keeps well for several days. Use salad oil if put into mold. Serves 12.

Mrs. Charles Ayers
Delaware County

CRANBERRY-APPLE-7 UP MOLD

2 3-oz. or 1 6 oz. pkg. cranberry or red raspberry gelatin
2 c. applesauce, hot
2⅔ c. chilled 7-Up
1 c. celery, chopped
½ c. nuts, chopped

Dissolve gelatin in hot applesauce. Add 7-Up, blending gently. Chill until slightly thickened. Add celery and nuts. Put in 1½-qt. mold or 12 individual molds. Chill until firm.

Jay County

FROZEN CRANBERRY SALAD

2 envelopes Dream Whip
12-oz. cream cheese
4 T. mayonnaise
4 T. sugar
2 15-oz. cans cranberry sauce
2 c. crushed pineapple, drained
2 c. nuts, chopped

Prepare Dream Whip; refrigerate. Cream cream cheese, mayonnaise, and sugar. Add cranberry sauce, pineapple, and nuts. Fold in Dream Whip. Pour into 10×13″ Pyrex dish. Freeze. Serve on lettuce. Serves 18–24.

Mrs. John Clark
LaPorte County

RAW CRANBERRY SALAD

1 large pkg. raspberry gelatin	2 c. fresh or frozen cranberries
1 small can crushed pineapple, drained	1 whole apple with peel
1 whole orange with peel	1 c. sugar
	½ c. nuts, chopped

Grind cranberries, orange, and apple. Add sugar and pineapple to ground mixture. Prepare gelatin, using some of pineapple liquid for some of water. Fold cooled gelatin into cranberry mixture. Refrigerate. Cut into squares to serve. Serves 15.

Mrs. George Conrad, Sr.
Miami County

FROZEN DATE AND CHEESE SALAD

2 3-oz. pkg. cream cheese	1 c. cream, whipped
¼ c. maple syrup	½ c. dates, chopped
1½ c. pineapple or bananas, diced	1½ c. nuts, chopped

Cream cream cheese until very soft; add maple syrup. Fold in whipped cream. Then add chopped dates and pineapple or bananas. Add nuts, fold into mold and freeze. Serves 10–12.

Norma Headley
Monroe County

DRY GELATIN SALAD

1 pkg. dry gelatin, any flavor desired	1 14-oz. can crushed pineapple, drained
1 14-oz. pkg. small curd cottage cheese	1 pkg. whipped topping (small Cool Whip or 1 pkg. Dream Whip)
1 can mandarin oranges, drained	

Put cottage cheese in bowl and fold in dry gelatin. Fold in the other ingredients and blend well. Cover and chill in refrigerator over night. Serve as a dessert or on lettuce leaf as a salad.

Mabel Ehrhardt
Porter County

FIVE-CUP SALAD

1 c. miniature marshmallows	1 c. cottage cheese
1 c. hot water	1 c. (8¼-oz. can) crushed pineapple
1 pkg. Orange or Lime Jello	
1 c. Cool Whip	

Mix Jello and marshmallows with hot water. Congeal in refrigerator. Mix (at low speed) cottage cheese, pineapple, and Cool Whip into Jello mixture. Pour into a square baking dish. Refrigerate until firm enough to cut into small servings.

Maxine Froman
Crawford County

FROZEN SALAD

1 8-oz. pkg. cream cheese	2 t. vanilla
1 c. sugar	1 can crushed pineapple, drained
2 envelopes Dream Whip	1 c. miniature marshmallows
1 c. milk	

1 3-oz. pkg.	½ c. coconut
black walnuts	

Cream together cream cheese and sugar. Add Dream Whip, milk, and vanilla. Beat until thick. Fold in pineapple, black walnuts, marshmallows, and coconut. Freeze until serving time.

Lee Hadley
Franklin County

FROZEN GELATIN SALAD

1 3-oz. pkg. lime	1 8-oz. pkg.
gelatin	colored butter
2 13½-oz. cans	mints, chopped
crushed pine-	fine
apple, drained	2 c. whipping
1 pkg. miniature	cream, whipped
marshmallows	

Sprinkle gelatin over hot pineapple juice; stir to dissolve. Add marshmallows. Store in refrigerator 4 to 5 hr., stirring occasionally. Fold mints into whipped cream. Fold in pineapple. Turn into a 13×9×2″ pan. Cover with clear plastic. Freeze until firm. Serve partially frozen.

Mrs. Russell Payne
Wells County

GINGER ALE SALAD

1 pkg. Lemon	1½ c. ginger ale
Jello	¼ c. celery,
½ c. boiling	finely diced
water	1 c. fruit
¼ c. nuts,	cocktail,
chopped	drained

Pour boiling water over Lemon Jello. Dissolve over hot water, stirring constantly. Cool and add ginger ale. Refrigerate until it begins to thicken. Stir in celery, nuts, and fruit cocktail. Refrigerate. Serve with mayonnaise, if desired.

Carrie Bonnell
Bartholomew County

GOLDEN GLOW SALAD

2 3-oz. pkg.	1 16-oz. can
Orange Jello	yellow peaches,
2 c. boiling	drained and
water	cut up
1½ c. cold water	1 c. seedless
1 11-oz. can man-	white grapes
darin orange	2 large bananas,
slices, drained	sliced

Dissolve Jello in boiling water. Add cold water and cool until rather thick. Reserve 1 c. of drained fruit juices for topping. Fold fruits into the Jello and pour into baking dish. Place in refrigerator overnight. Serves 10–12.

Fluffy Topping:

6 T. sugar	1 pkg. Dream
2 T. corn starch	Whip or
1 egg, well	whipped cream
beaten	1 c. reserved
2 T. butter or	fruit juice
margarine	¼ c. cheese,
1 T. lemon juice	grated

Combine sugar and corn starch in heavy saucepan. Blend in fruit juice and egg, stirring constantly until it thickens. Remove from heat and stir in butter and lemon juice. Fold in beaten Dream Whip and spread topping over Jello. Sprinkle grated cheese on top.

Myrtle Wilkie
Greene County

GOOSEBERRY SALAD

1 can goose-	1 c. miniature
berries, drained	marshmallows
1 3-oz. pkg. any	⅔ c. sugar
flavor gelatin	1 c. celery,
juice of goose-	chopped fine
berries plus	1 orange, grated
water to make	and chopped
2 c.	

Dissolve gelatin and marshmallows in heated juice and water mixture. Chill until thickened. Combine gooseberries and sugar. Grate rind of orange and chop the pulp. Add fruits, celery, and rind to gelatin. Chill until firm.

Mrs. Kay Rouse
Jennings County

GRAPE SUPREME SALAD

1 c. pineapple tidbits	1 pkg. Dream Whip
1 c. white grapes	1 3-oz. pkg.
2 c. miniature marshmallows	cream cheese, softened
3 bananas, sliced	½ c. walnuts,
1 can mandarin oranges	chopped

Combine fruit and marshmallows. Whip Dream Whip. Blend in softened cream cheese. Mix cream cheese mixture with the combined fruit. Top with walnuts. (Black walnuts are especially good in this recipe.) Serves 10–12.

Mrs. Max Tribbett
Montgomery County

SPICED GRAPE SALAD

1 family-size pkg. Lime Jello	1 small can chunk pineapple or
1 average-size can spiced grapes, drained	crushed pineapple, drained
1 c. celery, cut in small pieces	½ c. stuffed olives, cut crosswise

Mix Jello according to directions, using drained juice from grapes to make up liquid required. Add spiced grapes and chunk pineapple to Jello; add celery and olives. Put in large baking dish and refrigerate. Serve on lettuce leaf with dash of mayonnaise on tip. For dessert: omit celery and olives and add nuts as desired.

Mrs. Garrel Ritchie
Delaware County

LEMON-LIME COTTAGE SALAD

1 3-oz. pkg. Lemon Jello	1 c. ground celery
1 3-oz. pkg. Lime Jello	1 c. ground nuts
2 c. boiling water	1 c. cottage cheese
1 c. crushed pineapple, drained	1 c. mayonnaise
	1 large can Milnot, whipped

Dissolve Jello in boiling water. Cool. Add pineapple, celery, nuts, cottage cheese, and mayonnaise. Fold Milnot into this mixture. Pour into 1½-quart serving dish. Chill until firm. Serves 15.

Opal Jean Sedam
Marion County

LIME JELLO SALAD

2 pkg. Lime Jello	½ c. pecans, chopped
16-oz. bottle 7-Up	2 c. hot water
1 large can crushed pineapple, drained	1 8-oz. pkg. cream cheese
2 t. vanilla	2 T. sugar

Soften cream cheese to room temperature. Dissolve Jello in hot water and add cream cheese; use mixer to blend. Add 7-Up, sugar, and vanilla and set slightly. Add drained pineapple and nuts. Pour into 9× 13″ pan. Chill in refrigerator and serve with crackers. Serves 15.

Marsha Guthrie
Martin County

MACADAMIA NUT CREAM

2 3-oz. pkg. lemon gelatin	3 c. miniature marshmallows
2 c. boiling water	2 c. whipping cream, whipped
1 20-oz. can crushed pineapple, undrained	½ c. dates, choppd
	1 c. Macadamia nuts, chopped

Dissolve gelatin in boiling water. Cool. Add pineapple. Chill until partly set. Fold in remaining ingredients. Turn into individual molds or one large mold. Chill until firm. Serves 12.

Mrs. Albert Pfaffenberger
Jackson County

FROZEN MINT SALAD

1 c. mint jelly	½ c. green minted cherries
1 c. mayonnaise	
1 c. canned pears, diced	1 c. miniature colored marshmallows
1½ c. pineapple tidbits	
½ c. nutmeats	1 c. cream, whipped until stiff
½ c. maraschino cherries	

Melt jelly over hot water until liquefied; cool well. To the jelly add mayonnaise very slowly, stirring with a fork. Add all the other ingredients and fold in the whipped cream. Pour into a 2½-qt. mold or a flat glass or aluminum pan. Freeze for at least 8 hr. Unmold and garnish with whipped cream or salad dressing and cherries. Can be cut in squares and topped with a cherry and a bit of salad dressing. Serves 12.

Mrs. Archie B. Roberts
LaPorte County

ORANGE-PINEAPPLE SALAD MOLD

1 3-oz. box Orange Jello	⅓ bag miniature marshmallows
1 c. hot water	½ c. chopped walnuts
2 cans mandarin segments and pineapple tidbits, drained	¼ c. chopped cherries
	1 or 2 bananas, sliced
1 pt. vanilla ice cream, softened	

Dissolve Jello in hot water and add ice cream until dissolved. While this mixture thickens, drain mandarin-pineapple. Add with other ingredients to Jello-ice cream mixture. Pour into mold and refrigerate. Serves 6–8.

Virga Shoemaker
Boone County

FROZEN ORANGE SLUSH SALAD

½ c. sugar	1 16-oz. can crushed pine-apple, drained
2 c. hot water	
juice of 2 lemons	
1 6-oz. can frozen orange juice, undiluted	1 small jar maraschino cherries, quartered
2 bananas, chopped	

Dissolve sugar in hot water. Add lemon juice, frozen orange juice, bananas, pineapple, and cherries. Freeze in 9×13″ cake pan, stirring often while freezing. Serves 8–10.

Marilyn Hostetter
Greene County

SPICY ORANGE MOLD

1 1-lb., 13-oz. can peaches	12 whole cloves
¼ c. vinegar	3 cinnamon sticks
½ c. sugar	boiling water

4 3-oz. pkg.	¼ c. nuts,
Orange Jello	chopped
2 c. cold water	

Drain peaches, reserving juice. Cut peaches into chunks; set aside. Combine reserved juice, vinegar, sugar, cloves, and cinnamon sticks in saucepan; bring to boil. Reduce heat and simmer 10 min. Strain syrup and add enough boiling water to make 3½ c. Dissolve gelatin in hot syrup. Stir in cold water. Chill until thick and syrupy. Fold in peaches and nuts. Turn into 6-cup mold. Chill until set. Serves 10–12.

Phyllis McConnell
Gibson County

PINEAPPLE SALAD

1 can chunk	2 T. cornstarch
pineapple,	8 oz. miniature
drain and	marshmallows
reserve juice	1 T. butter
2 c. pineapple	1 1-lb. pkg.
juice and water	English walnuts
2 eggs	1 t. vanilla
1 c. sugar	(optional)

Beat eggs, sugar, and cornstarch. Add to hot (not boiling) juice and water; boil until thick. Add vanilla (if used). When cold, add in layers: filling-pineapple, nuts, and marshmallows.

Marge Grostefon
Porter County

PINK SALAD

2 c. chunk	1 medium
pineapple,	jar maraschino
drained	cherries, cut
20 large marsh-	and drained
mallows, cut	4 t. cherry juice

2 3-oz. pkg.	4 t. pineapple
cream cheese	juice
3 T. salad	½ pint whipping
dressing	cream, whipped

Cream cream cheese with beater. Add salad dressing and juices. Add to whipped cream. Mix pineapple, cherries, and marshmallows lightly into the cream mixture.

Linda Harris
Posey County

PISTACHIO SALAD

1 small carton	pistachio instant
cottage cheese	pudding (use
1 No. 2 can	dry)
crushed pine-	1 small container
apple, drained	Cool Whip
1 small can	⅔ c. miniature
mandarin	marshmallows
oranges,	
drained	

Mix together and refrigerate until ready to serve. Serves 12.

Opal Moffett
Fountain County

RASPBERRY SALAD

2 3-oz. pkg.	4 10-oz. pkg.
Orange Jello	frozen red
2 3-oz. pkg.	raspberries
Raspberry Jello	2 No. 303 cans
3 c. boiling	applesauce
water	4½ c. miniature
1 pt. sour cream	marshmallows

Dissolve Jello in boiling water. Add frozen raspberries—using juice, too. Break up blocks of raspberries to hasten thawing. This mixture will thicken quickly. Add the applesauce. Pour mixture into a 9×13″ glass dish. Refrigerate. Beat the marshmallows and sour cream in a mixer until the marshmallows completely dissolve. This will take some time. A blender may also be used for this. Pour this mixture over the Jello and allow the salad to stand overnight. This must be served from the container in which it is made. Serves 12.

Mrs. Carter Meharry
Tippecanoe County

RASPBERRY-RICE SALAD

1 small pkg. raspberry gelatin	1 c. whipping cream
1 c. boiling water	1 c. cooked rice, drained and sweetened
1 small can crushed pineapple, drained	1 c. miniature marshmallows

Dissolve gelatin in boiling water. Add rice. Chill 2–3 hr. so rice will take up flavor of gelatin. Blend pineapple, marshmallows, and whipped cream into gelatin mixture. Serve on crisp lettuce after it sets firm. Serves 8.

Eleanor Purdue
Daviess County

RECEPTION SALAD

1 pkg. Lemon Jello	1 8-oz. pkg. cream cheese
drained pineapple juice with water added to make 1 c.	1 small can pineapple, drained
1 medium can pimientos, chopped	½ c. celery, finely chopped
⅛ t. salt	1 small carton Cool Whip

Dissolve the Jello in the heated pineapple juice-water. Put into refrigerator to con-

geal. Add rest of ingredients in order and allow mixture to set before serving. Serves 12.

Mrs. Ralph E. Partridge
Spencer County

RHUBARB SALAD

2¼ c. rhubarb	1 small can crushed pineapple, drained
½ c. water	
¾ to 1 c. sugar	½ c. nuts
1 3-oz. pkg. Strawberry Jello	

Cook rhubarb with water and sugar until tender. While hot, add Strawberry Jello, pineapple, and nuts. Place in mold and chill.

Donna Bolinger
Noble County

RIBBON SALAD

2 3-oz. pkg. lime gelatin	1 1-lb., 4-oz. can crushed pineapple, drained
5 c. hot water	
4 c. cold water	1 c. drained pineapple juice
1 3-oz. pkg. lemon gelatin	1 c. heavy cream, whipped
½ c. miniature marshmallows, cut in pieces	1 c. mayonnaise
1 8-oz. pkg. cream cheese	2 3-oz. pkg. cherry gelatin

Dissolve lime gelatin in 2 c. hot water. Add 2 c. cold water. Pour into 14×10×2″ pan. Chill until partly set. Dissolve lemon gelatin in 1 c. hot water in top of double boiler. Add marshmallows and stir to melt. Remove from heat. Add drained pineapple juice and cream cheese. Beat until well blended and stir in pineapple. Cool slightly. Fold in whipped cream and mayonnaise. Chill until thickened. Pour in layer over lime gelatin. Chill until almost set. Dissolve cherry gelatin in 2 c. hot water. Add 2 c. cold water. Chill until syrupy. Pour over pineapple layer. Chill until firm. Serves 24.

The colors of gelatin may be changed according to the seasons, such as green and yellow or orange for Easter.

Mrs. Jennings Draut
Ripley County

STRAWBERRY SALAD

2 small boxes frozen strawberries	3 medium size bananas, mashed
1 large can crushed pineapple, undrained	1 large carton sour cream
1 can pecans, chopped	1 large pkg. Strawberry Jello
	1 c. hot water

Mix strawberries, pineapple, bananas, and pecans. Dissolve Jello in hot water and pour into strawberry mixture. Pour half of mixture in container and jell until firm (one hr.). Spread sour cream over jelled half and pour remainder of mixture over sour cream. Then jell.

Menage Lore
Vanderburgh County

TWENTY-FOUR HOUR SALAD

2 eggs, beaten	4 T. vinegar
4 T. sugar	2 T. butter
2 c. white cherries	2 c. pineapple chunks, drained
2 c. marshmallows, quartered	1 c. whipping cream, whipped

Put eggs in double boiler; add vinegar

and sugar. Beat until thick and smooth, stirring constantly. Remove from heat; add butter and let cool. Combine fruits and marshmallows. Fold whipped cream and fruit mixture into egg mixture. Turn into ring mold and cool. Serves 12–14.

Marguerite Stanley
Pulaski County

WALDORF SALAD

3 or 4 red apples, cut in cubes	1 c. miniature marshmallows
1 No. 2 can pineapple cubes, drain and reserve juice	⅓ c. American or sharp cheddar cheese, cubed
white grapes, same amount as apples	1 c. pineapple juice
	2 T. flour
	⅓ c. sugar
	1 egg

Cook pineapple juice, flour, sugar, and egg until thick. Cool and fold in fruits, cheese, and marshmallows. Serves 8–10.

Naomi Hawes
Bartholomew County

FROZEN WALDORF SALAD

1 9-oz. can crushed pineapple, drain and reserve juice	2 medium apples, unpeeled and diced
2 eggs, slightly beaten	½ c. nutmeats
	½ c. miniature marshmallows
½ c. sugar	½ c. whipped cream
¼ c. lemon juice	1 c. celery, diced
¼ t. salt	
¼ c. mayonnaise	

Mix together egg, sugar, lemon juice, salt, and the reserved pineapple juice. Cook over low heat, stirring constantly until slightly thickened (about 20 min.). Remove from heat and cool; fold in mayonnaise. Combine well-drained pineapple, diced apples, celery, nuts, and marshmallows. Mix well. Beat whipping cream and fold into cooled egg mixture. Pour over fruit mixture and toss. Fill a 6-cup mold and freeze until firm. Serves 9.

Mrs. Carroll Groves
Johnson County

YUM YUM SALAD

2 c. crushed pineapple, undrained	½ pint whipping cream, whipped stiff
juice of 1 lemon	2 T. celery, finely chopped
¾ c. sugar	
2 T. gelatin	2 T. green pepper, finely chopped
½ c. cold water	
¾ c. American cheese, grated	½ c. mayonnaise

Heat pineapple. Add lemon juice and sugar; stir until sugar is dissolved. Soak gelatin in cold water for 10 min. Add to hot mixture. When cool and beginning to set, add grated cheese and whipped cream. Mix thoroughly, place in 2-quart Pyrex rectangular pan, and chill until firm. To serve: Cut in squares and top with mayonnaise in which celery and peppers have been mixed. (Homemade mayonnaise mixed with additional whipped cream may be substituted.) Serves 12.

Martha W. Bain
Monroe County

WHITE SALAD

1 lb. marshmallows	1 No. 2 (20-oz.) can crushed pineapple, drained
½ c. milk	
1 8-oz. cream cheese	1 pkg. Dream Whip
1 pint cottage cheese	

Melt marshmallows in milk over low heat. Watch and stir often. Beat cream cheese with cottage cheese. Add to marshmallow mixture. Add pineapple. Prepare Dream Whip and fold in. Place in 9×13″ pan. Chill. Serve on lettuce and garnish with red or green cherry half.

Martha Jo McGaughey
Putnam County

Salad Dressings

SALAD DRESSING (Catsup)

1 c. Wesson Oil	1 T. onion, minced (onion salt may be used)
½ c. sugar	
⅓ c. catsup	
⅓ c. vinegar	
pinch of salt	1 T. paprika
½ T. celery seed	

Mix all together in blender or mixer. Let set for a day or two. Makes approximately 1¼ cups.

Mrs. Evelyn Armstrong
Madison County

SALAD DRESSING (Tomato Soup)

1 can tomato soup	1 T. Worcestershire sauce
1 c. salad oil	
1 c. sugar (½ c. for less sweet dressing)	1 T. onion juice
	¾ c. vinegar
	1 T. dry mustard
1 t. salt	(mix with sugar)
½ t. paprika	

Mix all ingredients together in a mixer, or shake well until blended. Will keep for weeks in the refrigerator.

Janet G. Meyer
Pulaski County

BOILED SALAD DRESSING

1 c. vinegar	2 eggs
1 c. sugar	½ c. cream
1 small lump	1 T. flour
butter	1 t. dry mustard

Heat vinegar, sugar, and butter in double boiler. Beat eggs and add cream, flour, and mustard. Pour heated vinegar mixture over egg mixture and mix. Return to double boiler and cook until it thickens, stirring frequently. Dressing keeps well in refrigerator. It is good for fruit or vegetable salad. When heated, it makes a delicious sauce for broccoli.

Mary McKinney
Wayne County

SPECIAL SALAD DRESSING (No Oil)

3 T. flour	½ c. evaporated
3 T. sugar	milk
1 t. salt	½ c. water
¼ t. dry mustard	1 egg, well-
½ t. paprika	beaten
⅛ t. black pepper	⅔ c. cider
½ t. celery seed	vinegar

Mix all dry ingredients in a saucepan. Add evaporated milk and water and bring to boil, boil 3 min., stirring constantly. Remove from fire and stir hot mixture into well-beaten egg which has been combined with vinegar. Chill. Makes about 1½ cups. Store in refrigerator. This dressing is good for potato or macaroni salad, or whereever an oil dressing is not desired.

Daisy Lowe
Vigo County

CELERY SEED DRESSING

⅔ c. sugar	1 small onion,
1 t. dry mustard	grated
1 t. salt	1 c. salad oil
⅓ c. vinegar	1 T. celery seed

Combine sugar, mustard, salt, onion juice, and ½ of vinegar. Beat at second speed with electric mixer. Add oil gradually and then add remaining vinegar. Then add celery seed. Makes 1 pint.

Dorothy J. Taylor
Kosciusko County

FRENCH-CHEESE SALAD DRESSING

1 t. pepper	1 c. catsup
1 t. salt	⅓ c. sugar
1 t. dry mustard	½ c. sharp
1 T. grated onion	cheese, grated
½ c. vinegar	½ c. salad oil

Combine ingredients. Let stand a few hours. Makes 1 pint.

Mrs. Perry Strasser
Vanderburgh County

FRUIT SALAD DRESSING

4 T. sugar	½ pt. whip-
4 T. vinegar	ping cream,
2 T. butter	whipped, or
2 eggs, beaten	1 pkg. Dream
	Whip, whipped

Heat sugar, vinegar, and butter to boiling. Add beaten eggs and stir all the time until it thickens. Cool. Then add whipped cream. Fold into fruit. Makes 3 cups.

Mrs. E. W. Knee
Kosciusko County

GOOD FRUIT SALAD DRESSING

½ c. sugar	1 c. pineapple
1 T. flour	juice
1 egg, unbeaten	

Mix sugar and flour. Add unbeaten egg; stir until well mixed. Add pineapple juice. Cook over low heat until mixture coats spoon.

Minnie Beeson
Monroe County

UNCOOKED FRUIT SALAD DRESSING

juice of 2 lemons	1 large can evap-
1 c. sugar	orated milk

Mix lemon juice and sugar. Gradually add evaporated milk, stirring while adding. Will become as thick as mayonnaise.

This amount of dressing is for a large salad bowl.

Laurette Green
Jefferson County

BLENDER MAYONNAISE

1 egg	1 c. salad oil
2 T. vinegar or	½ t. salt
lemon juice	½ t. sugar
½ t. dry mustard	

Blend egg, vinegar, sugar, salt, and mustard for 70 seconds, adding oil in a steady stream through opening in lid while motor is running. Makes approximately 1 cup.

Mrs. Margaret Johnson
Jennings County

ROQUEFORT DRESSING

1 qt. mayonnaise	3 oz. blue cheese
1 T. instant	3 oz. Roquefort
minced onion	cheese
¼ t. garlic salt	1 8-oz. container
¼ c. lemon juice	sour cream

Mix ingredients together. Yields 1½ quarts.

Lucy Smith
Greene County

THOUSAND ISLAND DRESSING

3 c. mayonnaise	1 hard-boiled
1 c. catsup	egg, grated
⅔ c. onions,	1 t. salt
chopped	1 t. pepper
⅔ c. dill pickle,	1 t. dry mustard
chopped	1 T. lemon juice
⅓ c. ripe olives,	2 T. sugar
chopped	(optional)

Combine ingredients. Makes 3 pints.

Virginia Watson
Harrison County

ZERO SALAD DRESSING
(For low cholesterol diets)

½ c. tomato	1 T. onion, finely
juice	chopped
2 T. lemon juice	salt and pepper
or vinegar	

Combine ingredients in a jar with a tightly fitted top. Shake well before using. Chopped parsley or green pepper, horseradish, or mustard, etc., may be added if desired.

Thelma M. Hardwick
Rush County

Vegetables

We are fortunate to have such a large variety of vegetables available the year round—fresh, frozen, or in a can. Vegetables add valuable minerals, vitamins, and bulk to the daily diet. Avoid overcooking and don't throw precious cooking liquid down the drain.

A "mess" of vegetables is the amount a homemaker goes out and gathers in her apron to carry into the house. The exact quantity of a mess varies with the size of the family.

Corn was usually the first crop on new ground. Early settlers ate the corn, fed it to their cattle, and used it as fodder for the hogs. With the husks they filled their ticks or mattresses and braided rugs for their thresholds. Out of the cobs they fashioned pipes for the men and toys for the children. The dried cobs were used as fuel for their fires.

Pumpkin or "punkin" was another vegetable favored by pioneers. It was often stewed, spread on clapboards, and dried before the fire for winter use.

Tomatoes were called "love apples," and were used as ornamental shrubs in gardens. Not until the early 1830s did anyone dare eat the tomato, because most people thought it was poisonous.

ASPARAGUS SOUFFLE

1 can cream of asparagus soup
4 egg whites, beaten stiff
¾ c. sharp American cheese, shredded
4 egg yolks

Heat and stir soup over low heat. Add cheese; stir until melted. Remove from heat. Beat egg yolks until thick and lemon-colored. Slowly add cheese mixture to beaten egg yolks, stirring constantly. Pour mixture slowly onto beaten egg whites, folding thoroughly but gently. Pour into ungreased 2-qt. soufflé dish or casserole. Bake in slow oven (300°) 1 hr. and 15 min., or until mixture doesn't adhere to knife. Serves 4.

Tonya Paddock
Union County

CHEESY ASPARAGUS

2 No. 2 cans asparagus, cut and drained	1 2½-oz. jar mushroom pieces or 1 2½-oz. jar pimientos
3 eggs, hard boiled	
½ lb. processed cheese	White Sauce:
cracker crumbs	2 T. butter
paprika	2 T. flour
	1 c. milk

Place asparagus in bottom of buttered glass pan. Slice eggs both ways to make small chunks. Sprinkle eggs over asparagus. Make white sauce of butter, flour, and milk. Add cheese and stir until melted. Pour over asparagus mixture. Pour cracker crumbs over top. Sprinkle paprika over top. Bake 45 min. at 325°. Serves 8.

Mrs. Mary Smith
Jennings County

SAUCE FOR ASPARAGUS AND BROCCOLI

4 T. vinegar	salt and pepper to taste
2 egg yolks	
¼ lb. butter	

Beat egg yolks. Add vinegar and butter. Cook over low heat until butter is melted. Season with salt and pepper. Serve over cooked asparagus or broccoli.

Mrs. Berneice Mauntel
Dubois County

BEANS

Use pinto, pink, brown, navy, chili or kidney beans. Inspect, wash, then soak overnight in water 2½ times the amount of beans. In the morning pour off water and place beans between two terry towels, keeping them damp for two days or until tiny end of the sprout breaks through or is just barely visible. Then place beans in bean pot and cover with boiling water. Cook very slowly—never boiling. Beans may be placed in electric fry pan, turn controls to 200° or less and just forget about them. (Beans may be cooked in Corning ware or stainless steel, but not aluminum.) Beans take about 3–6 hr. to cook; do not overcook. When done, salt to taste with sea salt or sea water.

Lovina VanEmon
Adams County

BAKED BEANS

4 No. 303 cans Great Northern beans	1 medium onion, chopped
	2 T. butter
½ bottle catsup	½ mango, chopped
½ lb. brown sugar	bacon slices
½ c. white syrup	

Combine first four ingredients. Sauté onion and mango in butter and add to bean mixture. Top with bacon and bake in bean pot for 3 hr. at 350°.

Mrs. George W. McCammon
Lawrence County

SWEET-SOUR BAKED BEANS

8 slices bacon, fried crisp, drained, and crumbled	1 T. dry or prepared mustard
	1 1-lb. can lima beans, drained

1 1-lb. can red beans, drained
1 1-lb., 11-oz. can pork and beans or New England style baked beans
4 onions, sliced in rings
¾ c. brown sugar
1 t. salt
½ t. garlic powder
½ c. vinegar

Cook all ingredients, except beans and bacon, covered for 20 min. Lay the beans in a large shallow baking dish. Add the cooked mixture to the beans and top with bacon. Bake at 350° for 1 hr.

Mrs. Wilbur Nussbaum
Adams County

GREEN BEAN CASSEROLE (1)

2 medium cans mushrooms
1 medium onion, chopped
½ c. margarine
¼ c. flour
½ c. cream
½ c. milk
¾ lb. Velveeta cheese
½ t. Tabasco sauce
2 t. soy sauce
½ t. salt
¼ t. pepper
1 quart green beans
1 c. water chestnuts, sliced thin
almonds, chopped

Sauté mushrooms and onion in margarine. Add flour and brown. Add cream, milk, cheese, sauces, salt, and pepper. Simmer until cheese melts. Add green beans and water chestnuts. Put in casserole and sprinkle with almonds. Bake at 350° for 40–45 min.

Mrs. Fred Cole
Steuben County

GREEN BEAN CASSEROLE (2)

1 box Triscuits, crushed
1 can green beans, well drained
1 lb. browned beef or chicken chunks
½ c. mayonnaise

2 cans cream of mushroom soup or cream of chicken soup
with chicken chunks
1 small jar water chestnuts

Layer Triscuits (reserve some for topping), green beans, beef or chicken, and water chestnuts in 13×9×2" baking dish. Heat the soup and mayonnaise thoroughly and pour over green bean mixture in casserole. Sprinkle remaining Triscuits over top. Bake at 350° for 1 hr. Serves 12.

Mrs. Roland Bentrup
Allen County

GREEN BEAN, POTATO, AND BACON CASSEROLE

¼ lb. bacon, diced
3 c. raw potatoes, sliced
1 can cream of celery soup
1 medium onion, diced
1 pkg. frozen green beans
1 t. salt

Brown bacon until medium dark in dutch oven. Remove half of drippings. Add potatoes, soup, onion, green beans, and salt. Cover and simmer over low heat for two hr. May be baked at 350° for 1 hr. Serves 8.

Mrs. Leona Ness and Mrs. R. D. Smith
Whitley County

BARBECUED GREEN BEANS

4 slices bacon, finely cut
¼ c. onion, chopped
½ c. catsup
¼ c. brown sugar
1 T. Worcestershire sauce
2 cans French-style green beans, drained

Brown bacon and onions. Add catsup, brown sugar, and Worcestershire sauce. Simmer 2 min. Place beans in casserole;

pour bacon mixture over beans but do not stir. Bake at 350° for 20 min. Serves 6–8.

Mrs. Donna Kraft
Marion County

SPECIAL GREEN BEANS

2 T. butter	1 c. sour cream
¼ c. onion,	2 pkg. frozen
minced	green beans,
2 T. flour	cooked and
1 t. salt	drained
¼ t. pepper	grated cheddar
¼ t. dry mustard	or Parmesan
¾ t. Worcester-	cheese
shire sauce	

Sauté onion in butter. Add flour, salt, pepper, dry mustard, and Worcestershire sauce. Cook until thickened, stirring constantly. Add sour cream and mix with green beans. Put all in casserole. Top with grated cheese. Bake at 350° for 20 min.

Marylin Staley
Parke County

KIDNEY BEAN HOT POT

2 c. dried kidney	small piece bacon
beans	1 large onion,
1 green pepper,	chopped
chopped	1 c. carrots, sliced
2 c. tomatoes	2 c. cooked
salt and pepper	macaroni

Soak the beans overnight; add bacon, and cook until almost tender. Add carrots, green pepper, onions, and tomatoes. Continue cooking until all of the vegetables are tender. Add macaroni which has been cooked separately. Season to taste.

Potatoes or rice may be used in place of macaroni.

Mrs. Harry Brink
Martin County

LIMA BEAN CASSEROLE (1)

1 c. dried lima	2 T. green pep-
beans	per, chopped
1 t. salt	2 T. green chives,
½ c. onions,	chopped
chopped	2 c. stewed
½ c. celery,	tomatoes
diced	½ t. chili powder

Cover beans with water and soak overnight. Drain, cover with water, and simmer until tender. Add remaining ingredients, pour into casserole, and bake at 350° for 40 min.

Mary Overpeck
Parke County

LIMA BEAN CASSEROLE (2)

1 pkg. frozen	4 oz. Velveeta
lima beans	cheese,
1 pkg. frozen	shredded
baby lima beans	1 small can water
1 can cream of	chestnuts, sliced
mushroom	small amount of
soup, undiluted	diced onions
1 small can mush-	
rooms, cut up	

Prepare frozen lima beans as directed, cook. Mix remaining ingredients and add to lima beans. Put in flat baking dish. Bake at 350° until casserole bubbles up and cheese is melted.

Mrs. Jennie Wright
Sullivan County

CRANBERRY BEETS

1 1-lb. can diced	2 T. orange juice
beets, drained	1 t. grated orange
1 1-lb. can whole	rind
or jellied cran-	dash of salt
berry sauce	

Combine all ingredients in saucepan. Heat thoroughly, stirring occasionally. Serves 4.

Mrs. Russell Payne
Wells County

BROCCOLI CASSEROLE

1 20-oz. bag frozen chopped broccoli, partially cooked	1 can cream of mushroom soup
1 3½-oz. can water chestnuts, drained and sliced	6 oz. Velveeta or American cheese, cubed bread crumbs or crushed potato chips

Mix well all ingredients and pour into casserole. Top with bread crumbs or potato chips. Heat at 350° for approximately ½ hr., or until top is brown and bubbling.

Dawnelle Gregory
Greene County

BROCCOLI-CHEESE CASSEROLE
(*Prysnac Serbia*)

6 unbeaten eggs	1 pkg. frozen broccoli, thawed and chopped
2 lb. small-curd cottage cheese	
6 T. flour	
½ lb. processed cheese, diced	2 green onions, chopped
¼ lb. soft butter	

Layer ingredients in large mixing bowl. Beat until well blended. Pour into greased 9×12″ baking dish. Bake at 350° for 1 hr. Should be golden brown and bubbly. Let set at least 10 min. before serving. Serves 10–12.

Margaret Schubert
Putnam County

ITALIAN BROCCOLI CASSEROLE

2 10-oz. pkg. frozen cut broccoli	2 eggs, beaten
	1 8-oz. can stewed tomatoes, cut up
1 can cheddar cheese soup	1 4-oz. pkg. pizza cheese (blended cheeses)
½ t. dried, crushed oregano	

Cook frozen broccoli in unsalted water 5 to 7 min., or until tender. Combine eggs, cheddar cheese soup, and crushed oregano. Stir in stewed tomatoes and cooked broccoli. Turn the vegetable-cheese mixture into a 10×6×2″ baking dish. Sprinkle with the pizza cheese. Bake the casserole, uncovered, at 350° for about 30 min.

Mrs. August W. Smith
Marion County

BROCCOLI AND LIMA BEAN CASSEROLE

1 pkg. frozen chopped broccoli	1 can cream of mushroom soup
1 pkg. Fordhook frozen lima beans	1 pkg. dried onion soup mix
	1 stick margarine
1 can water chestnuts, drained and sliced	3 c. bread crumbs or Rice Krispies, crushed after measuring
1 c. sour cream	

Cook broccoli and lima beans in small amount of water until tender-crisp. Add water chestnuts. Mix soups with sour cream and layer with vegetables in 2-qt. casserole. Brown crumbs in margarine and sprinkle over top. Bake 30 minutes at 350°. Serves 8.

Mrs. William Taylor
St. Joseph County

BROCCOLI PUFFS

1 10-oz. pkg. frozen or fresh broccoli	¼ c. milk
	½ c. salad dressing
1 10½-oz. can cream of mushroom soup	1 egg, beaten
	¼ c. fine, dry bread crumbs
½ c. sharp American cheese, shredded	1 T. butter or margarine

Cook frozen broccoli according to directions, omitting salt; drain. Place in 10× 6×1½" baking dish. Mix soup with cheese. Add milk, salad dressing, and beaten egg to soup mixture. Pour over broccoli. Combine bread crumbs with butter. Sprinkle evenly over mixture. Bake at 350° for 45 min. Serves 4–6.

Pauline Wood
Whitley County

BROCCOLI AND RICE CASSEROLE
(Irish Rice)

1 c. boiling water	½ stick margarine
1 c. instant rice	2 oz. Cheese Whiz
½ c. frozen broccoli	1 can cream of mushroom soup, undiluted
¼ c. onion, chopped	
¼ c. celery, chopped	½ t. salt
	¼ t. pepper

Add instant rice to boiling water, cover, and let stand 5 min. Cook broccoli and drain. Sauté onion and celery in margarine. Add Cheese Whiz and soup to hot rice. Add vegetables, salt, and pepper. Put into greased casserole. Bake at 350° for 30 to 40 min. Serves 6.

Mrs. O. W. Ruffner
Marshall County

BROCCOLI AND CAULIFLOWER CALIFORNIA CASSEROLE

1 pkg. broccoli, cooked	1 jar of Cheese Whiz with pimiento
1 pkg. cauliflower, cooked	1 pkg. frozen or canned French-fried onions
1 can cream of chicken soup	
1 can cream of celery soup	

Place cooked vegetables in casserole. Heat soups and Cheese Whiz until blended and pour over vegetables. Cover with French-fried onions and bake at 350° for 20 to 25 min. Serves 8–10.

Mrs. Reba Reeves
Parke County

CABBAGE DISH

1 head cabbage, shredded	1 egg, beaten
	2 T. sugar
½ c. butter	2 T. lemon juice
1 c. sour cream	

Cook cabbage in butter until crisp-tender. Combine rest of ingredients and pour over cabbage. Heat until warm and serve.

Connie Clauss
Allen County

SCALLOPED CABBAGE

1 medium head cabbage, chopped	2 T. pimientos, chopped
	6 slices bacon
1½ c. cream sauce	½ c. bread crumbs
2 T. peppers, chopped	1 c. (or less) cheese, grated
2 T. fat	

Boil cabbage for 7 to 8 min. Drain well. Prepare cream sauce. Sauté and mince bacon slices. Toss bread crumbs lightly in melted fat. Place layers of drained cabbage in greased baking dish. Sprinkle layers with minced bacon, peppers, pimientos, and grated cheese. Cover with cream sauce. Top with the sautéed bread crumbs. Bake cabbage in moderate oven (375°) for 10 min. Serves 8.

Mary Hickey
Marion County

SWEET-SOUR RED CABBAGE

1 medium head red cabbage, chopped ¼″ thick	1 T. bacon fat or butter
½ white onion, sliced	1 tart apple, chopped and cored
¾ c. white vinegar	½ t. salt
½ c. brown sugar	¼ t. (or less) pepper
	1½ c. water

Bring all ingredients to a boil; then turn down heat and simmer 45 min. Serves 6.

Mrs. Patricia McLaughlin
St. Joseph County

HARVARD CARROTS

½ c. sugar	4 c. cooked sliced carrots
1½ T. cornstarch	
¼ c. vinegar	¼ c. butter
¼ c. water	

Combine sugar and cornstarch. Add vinegar and water. Mix well and cook until thick, stirring constantly. Add cooked carrots. Let stand over low heat 5 to 10 min. Add butter and serve. Serves 8.

Mrs. Keith Hines
Boone County

MARINATED CARROTS
(Copper Pennies)

4 c. sliced carrots, cooked until fork tender	1 can tomato soup
	1 c. sugar
	½ c. salad oil
1 medium sweet onion, sliced thin	¾ c. vinegar
	1 t. prepared mustard
1 green pepper, sliced thin	1 t. salt
	1 t. pepper

Mix the carrots, onion, and green pepper lightly. Mix the rest of the ingredients and combine with carrot mixture. Put in qt. cans and refrigerate at least 12 hr. Carrots will keep 6 weeks in refrigerator.

Mrs. Fred L. McCain
Carroll County

SCALLOPED CARROTS AND CHEESE

12 medium carrots, sliced	2 c. milk
	⅛ t. pepper
1 small onion, minced	¼ t. celery salt
	½ lb. sliced American or sharp cheese (10 slices)
¼ c. butter or margarine	
¼ c. flour	
1 t. salt	3 c. buttered, soft bread crumbs
¼ t. dry mustard	

Make the day before and refrigerate. Cook carrots covered in 1″ boiling salted water until barely tender, about 10 min. Drain. In saucepan gently cook onion in butter 2 or 3 min. Stir in flour, salt, and mustard; then milk, cooking and stirring until smooth. Add pepper and celery salt. In 2-qt. casserole arrange a layer of carrots, then layer of cheese. Repeat, ending with carrots. Pour sauce over carrots. Top with crumbs. Refrigerate. Bake at 350° for 35 to 40 min. Serves 8.

Bonnie Norris
Delaware County

SUNSHINE ORANGE CARROTS

5 medium carrots	¼ cup orange
1 T. sugar	juice (thawed
1 t. cornstarch	frozen juice
¼ t. salt	may be used)
¼ t. ground	2 T. butter
ginger	

Cut carrots crosswise on the bias in 1" chunks. Cook covered in boiling salted water until just tender, about 20 min.; drain. Meanwhile, combine next 4 ingredients in small saucepan. Add orange juice; cook, stirring constantly until mixture thickens and bubbles. Boil 1 min. Stir in butter. Pour over hot carrots, tossing to coat evenly. Serves 4.

Mrs. Clinton J. Florey
Fountain County

CAULIFLOWER CASSEROLE

3 10-oz. pkg. fro-	¼ c. green
zen cauliflower	peppers, diced
⅓ c. butter	1 recipe white
1 small can mush-	sauce
rooms, sliced	grated cheese

Cook cauliflower in salted water and drain. Brown mushrooms and green pepper in butter; mix into white sauce. Alternate layers of cauliflower, grated cheese, and white sauce mixture in 1½-qt. casserole. Bake at 350° for 15 min. Serves 6.

Linda Abrams
Rush County

CORN BALLS

½ c. onion,	1¼ t. pepper
chopped	1 c. water
1 c. celery,	1 8-oz. pkg.
chopped	bread stuffing
1 13-oz. can	3 beaten egg
creamed corn	yolks

½ c. butter,	1 t. salt
melted	

Mix all ingredients except stuffing, egg yolks, and butter. Add corn mixture to stuffing; fold in egg yolks. Shape into 18 balls and place in baking dish or pan. Pour melted butter over balls and bake 15 min. at 375°. Serves 8.

Thelma Conner
Delaware County

CORN CASSEROLE

2 T. butter	1 c. sour cream
½ c. onion, diced	3–4 bacon slices,
¼ c. green pep-	cooked,
per, chopped	drained, and
2 cans whole ker-	crumbled
nel corn,	
drained	

Sauté onion and green pepper in butter in large skillet. Add sour cream and drained corn. Heat through and serve. Top serving dish with bacon. Serves 8–10.

Mrs. Stanley Griffin
Delaware County

CRUNCHY CORN CASSEROLE

½ c. green pep-	1 egg, slightly
pers, chopped	beaten
1 t. margarine	½ can French-
1 1-lb. can cream	fried onions,
style corn	crushed
2 t. pimientos,	
chopped	

Sauté green peppers in margarine until soft. Add remaining ingredients. Pour into 1½-qt. casserole. Bake at 350° for 25 min. Sprinkle remaining onions in can on top of casserole and bake for 5 min. Serves 6.

Emma Lou Kramer
Spencer County

CORN FRITTERS

1 can cream style corn	1 t. baking powder
2 eggs, beaten very light	½ t. salt
1¼ c. flour	¼ t. pepper

Combine corn and eggs. Sift together rest of ingredients. Add to corn and eggs. Fry in deep fat at 350°.

Mrs. Vance Ratcliff
Randolph County

CORN PUDDING

6 strips bacon	½ c. soft bread crumbs, buttered
2 T. green pepper, minced	
2 T. onion, minced	2 eggs, beaten
	1⅔ c. milk
1 No. 303 can whole kernel corn	1 3-oz. can mushrooms, sliced
	1 t. salt

Fry bacon until crisp, remove from fat, drain. Cook peppers and onion in 2 T. of the fat over moderate heat until tender. Mix in corn, crumbs, eggs, milk, mushrooms, and salt. Add bacon pieces, pour into buttered casserole or baking dish, top with buttered crumbs. Bake at 350° about 45 min. or until set.

Eva Dwyer
Martin County

CORN PUFFS

⅓ c. milk	1 egg, separated
1 T. butter, melted	1 c. sifted flour
½ c. cream-style corn	1½ t. baking powder
	1 t. salt

Beat egg yolk. Add milk, butter, corn, and dry ingredients. Fold in stiffly beaten egg white. Drop by tablespoonfuls into deep, hot fat and fry till brown, about 3 min., turning once. Makes 12 puffs.

Nancy Hewitt
Wells County

CORN SHORTCAKE

1 large sweet onion, peeled and diced	⅓ c. milk
	1 c. sour cream
¼ c. butter or margarine	1 can cream style corn
1½ c. corn muffin mix	¼ t. salt
	1 c. cheddar cheese, grated
1 egg, beaten	

Slowly sauté onion in butter. Combine muffin mix, egg, and corn. Pour into buttered baking dish. Mix onion, sour cream, salt, and half of cheese. Pour on top of other mixture. Sprinkle rest of cheese on top. Bake at 425° for 25 to 30 min.

Mrs. Helen Bricker
Wayne County

CORN-TOMATO SKILLET

1 green pepper, chopped	4 tomatoes, peeled and sliced
2 T. butter	
1 T. sugar	1 t. salt
½ c. onion, chopped	⅛ t. pepper
	2 c. corn

Cook green pepper and onion in butter until soft. Add remaining ingredients and cook until tomatoes and corn are tender. Serves 6.

Mayme Benjamin
Pike County

FRIED CORN WITH CHEESY TASTE

4 slices bacon
1 c. green pepper strips
1 can cheddar cheese soup
3 c. cooked whole kernel corn
½ can chopped tomatoes

Cook bacon until crisp. Remove from heat and crumble into bite-size pieces. Pour off all but 2 T. fat. Cook green peppers in fat until tender. Add soup, corn, and tomatoes. Heat until corn is tender, stirring occasionally. Serves 12.

Mrs. Janice Lowe
Jennings County

SAUTEED CORN

8 ears fresh corn or two 12-oz. cans corn, drained
¼ c. butter or margarine
1 c. thin onion rings
½ c. green pepper strips
1½ t. salt
¼ t. monosodium glutamate
¼ t. dried oregano
½ c. light cream
2 medium tomatoes, sliced and halved

Melt butter in a 10″ heavy skillet (or chafing dish or electric skillet), using medium heat. Add the corn, onion rings, green pepper strips, salt, monosodium glutamate, and oregano. Cover the skillet and cook mixture 6–7 min., or until corn is just tender. While cooking, shake skillet gently or stir once or twice with wooden spoon. Add cream and tomato slices. Let it simmer uncovered 1–2 min., or until tomatoes are hot but still firm. Serves 6–8.

Variation: Omit green peppers, tomatoes, and 1 t. salt, and add ½ c. sliced stuffed olives.

Mrs. Dale Kaufman
Marshall County

FRIED CUCUMBERS

Peel cucumbers. Slice lengthwise and put in salt water for 1 hr. Roll in flour and fry until done.

Mrs. Joseph Bertke
Perry County

FRIED DANDELION BLOOMS

Pick dandelion blooms close to bloom. Wash; soak in salt water for 10–15 min. Drain. Make a batter of egg, flour, and milk. Dip blooms in batter, then roll in flour. Fry in corn oil or other shortening.

Opal Osborn
Putnam County

EGGPLANT AND CHEESE CASSEROLE

1 large eggplant
3 T. vegetable oil
1 c. chopped onion
1½ c. soft white bread crumbs
1½ t. salt
1 t. oregano
¼ t. pepper
1 lb. cottage cheese
2 eggs
¼ c. chopped parsley
2 medium tomatoes
1 8-oz. pkg. mozzarella cheese

Slice, pare, and dice eggplant; sauté in oil until soft. Sauté onion, and stir in bread crumbs. Add 1 t. salt, oregano, and pepper. Remove from heat. Combine cottage cheese, eggs, parsley, and ½ t. salt in bowl. Spoon half of eggplant mixture into 8×8×2″ baking dish. Spread cottage cheese mixture over eggplant mixture. Top with remaining eggplant mixture. Overlap slices of mozzarella cheese. Bake at 350° for 45 min. Remove and let set for 10 min. before serving. Serves 8.

Bette Underwood
Monroe County

EGGPLANT PATTIES

1 eggplant	1 egg
3 medium ripe tomatoes	cracker crumbs or cracker meal

Peel and dice eggplant and tomatoes in 1" squares. Salt and cook like potatoes until soft. Drain in colander. Put in mixing bowl and mash with spoon or fork. Add 1 egg, stir. Add cracker crumbs or cracker meal until batter drops from spoon. Fry until done.

Mrs. Joseph Bertke
Perry County

EGGPLANT SOUFFLE

1 medium eggplant	½ c. grated cheese
1 c. water	1½ T. onion, grated
2 T. margarine	
2 T. flour	1½ t. salt
1 c. milk	1 c. fresh or frozen corn
¾ c. bread crumbs	2 eggs, separated

Peel eggplant and dice. Cook in water about 10 min. Drain. Melt margarine in double boiler or heavy saucepan. Blend in flour, then milk. Cook, stirring frequently, until thick, about 10 min. Add cooked eggplant, corn, crumbs, onion, and salt. Beat egg yolks lightly and stir into eggplant mixture. Beat egg whites until stiff and fold into eggplant mixture. Pour into greased 1-quart casserole and bake uncovered at 350° for about 45 min. or until firm. Serves 6.

Mrs. Earl H. Green
Dearborn County

ITALIAN DELIGHT

1 small eggplant, quartered and sliced ½" thick	6 medium zucchini, cut in ½" slices
1 green pepper, cut in ½" strips or slices	2 8-oz. cans tomato sauce
½ lb. fresh mushrooms, sliced	1 t. salt
	½ t. oregano
¼ c. olive oil	¼ t. pepper
1 medium onion, thinly sliced	1 1-lb. can green beans, well drained
1 T. sugar	

Sauté eggplant, zucchini, green pepper, onion, and mushrooms in oil. Add tomato sauce, sugar, oregano, salt, and pepper. Cover and simmer for 20 min. Add green beans and heat through. Serves 8.

Mrs. Richard L. Wigent
St. Joseph County

FAMILY MEAL IN A CASSEROLE

¼ c. margarine	1 10-oz. pkg. frozen mixed vegetables
¼ c. flour	
1 envelope mushroom gravy	1 small onion, chopped
1 t. celery salt	
1 t. salt	2 T. dry parsley
⅛ t. black pepper	¼ lb. cheddar cheese
3½ c. milk	
1 pkg. frozen French fries	paprika (after baking)

Cook mixed vegetables. Melt margarine. Mix flour, mushroom gravy, celery salt, salt, and pepper. Add to melted margarine with milk. Cook until smooth. Add cheese, onion, frozen French fries (no pre-cooking). Drain cooked vegetables and add parsley. Pour into 9×9" 2-qt. casserole. Add cheese sauce. Bake at 400° for 30 min. until bubbly around the edge. Sprinkle with paprika and allow to stand a few minutes before serving. Serves 6.

Mrs. Henry Sanderson
Fayette County

MIXED VEGETABLES

1 pkg. frozen peas	Sauce:
	1½ c. mayonnaise
1 pkg. frozen green beans	3 hard-boiled eggs, chopped
1 pkg. frozen baby limas	1 small onion, grated
1 pkg. frozen carrots	1 t. Worcestershire sauce
(Or 1 large pkg. frozen mixed vegetables instead of the 4 pkg.)	1 t. table mustard juice of 1 lemon or 2 T. bottled lemon juice

Mix all sauce ingredients together. Keep at room temperature 2 hr. before using. Cook vegetables according to directions on pkg.; drain. Add sauce at once and serve. Serves 18–20.

Mrs. Roy Weist
Whitley County

MIXED VEGETABLES SUPREME

2 pkg. frozen mixed vegetables	2 c. liquid (use reserve stock, plus ½ c. cream, plus enough milk to make 2 cups)
1 c. water	
½ c. butter, melted	
¼ c. flour	
1½ t. salt	2 c. fresh bread crumbs (without crust), the size of thumbnail
¼ t. nutmeg	
¼ t. garlic salt	
¼ c. grated Parmesan cheese	
2 T. sherry or white port wine	¼ c. butter, melted

Cook frozen mixed vegetables in water just until thawed. Drain and reserve liquid. Combine in saucepan all ingredients except bread crumbs and butter. Cook until

thick. Put vegetables in well-buttered baking dish. Pour sauce over vegetables. Sprinkle bread crumbs over top. Pour melted butter over crumbs. Bake at 350° for 30 min. Serves 8.

Mrs. James Bryan
Montgomery County

MOCK MUSHROOMS

1 can cream of mushroom soup	1 or 2 eggs, beaten
30 soda crackers, crumbled	

Mix together. Drop by spoonfuls into hot fat and fry until brown. Drain on brown paper.

Mrs. Donna Mundy
Martin County

BAKED ONIONS

8 medium onions (1¼ lb.)	½ t. salt
	¾ c. catsup
1 T. butter, melted	1 c. water
	parsley sprigs
1 T. brown sugar	

Peel onions, cut in half crosswise, and place in a greased 1-qt. casserole. Combine butter, brown sugar, salt, catsup, and water. Pour over onions. Bake covered at 350° for 1 hr., or until onions are tender. Serve garnished with parsley.

Lois Bowers
Delaware County

FRENCH-FRIED ONION RINGS

4 large Spanish onions	¼ t. salt
	1 egg, well-beaten
1 c. sifted flour	1 c. milk
1 t. baking powder	1 t. salad oil

Cut onions into ¼″ slices and separate into rings. Sift flour, baking powder, and salt. Add milk and salad oil to egg. Stir into sifted ingredients. Beat only until smooth. Preheat shortening (about 1″ deep in electric skillet or other fryer). With a long-handled two-tined fork dip onion rings in batter so that each is completely coated. Let drain a second. Drop a few rings at a time into the heated oil. Brown, turn only once, using a second fork. Do not crowd rings. Drain on paper towels and serve piping hot. May be kept hot briefly in 325° oven. Serves 5.

Ruby Welch
Switzerland County

PARTY ONIONS

2 lbs. small or medium white onions	1 t. salt
5 T. butter or margarine	1 t. Worcestershire sauce
3 T. flour	dash of pepper
1 c. water	¼ t. paprika
1 T. brown sugar	2 T. slivered almonds

Peel and quarter onions. Cook covered in boiling water 25–30 min. Drain well and place in 2-qt. casserole. Make a white sauce of the margarine, flour, water, brown sugar, salt, Worcestershire sauce, and pepper. Pour white sauce over the onions. Sprinkle with paprika. Cover and bake at 375° for about 20 min. At serving time garnish with the slivered almonds. Serves 8–10.

LaVonne Boyer
Rush County

DELMONICO POTATOES

9 medium red potatoes	½ lb. Old English cheese
½ pt. whipping cream, not whipped	1 t. dry mustard
1 c. milk or 1 pt. half and half	1½ t. salt
	dash of pepper
	dash of nutmeg

Boil unpeeled potatoes until just soft. Cool, peel, and slice into a baking dish. Make a sauce of cheese, whipping cream, milk, mustard, salt, pepper, and nutmeg. Heat until cheese is melted and pour over potatoes. Refrigerate 24 hr. Bake 1 hr. at 325°. Serves 6–8.

Ferne Moore
Randolph County

GERMAN POTATO PANCAKES

5 c. grated potatoes	½ t. baking powder
2 large or 3 small eggs, beaten	3 or 4 t. salt (to taste)
⅓ c. milk	

Combine ingredients as listed. Bake in several skillets with plenty of oil for about 5 min. or until brown and crispy around the edges.

Mrs. Fay Hooton
St. Joseph County

GOURMET POTATOES

6 medium potatoes	⅓ c. green onion, finely chopped
2 c. cheddar cheese, shredded	1 t. salt
¼ c. butter	¼ t. pepper
1½ c. sour cream	2 T. butter
	paprika

Cook potatoes in skins; cool. Peel and shred coarsely. In saucepan over low heat, combine cheese and ¼ c. butter. Stir occasionally until almost melted. Remove from heat and blend in sour cream, onion, and seasonings. Fold in potatoes and turn into greased 2-qt. casserole. Dot with 2 T. butter and sprinkle with paprika. Bake uncovered at 350° for 30 mins. Serves 8.

Bonnie Whitehair
Delaware County

POTATO BAKE

8 large potatoes, cooked and cubed (about 8 c.)	1 c. mayonnaise
	½ c. onion, diced
	½ c. olives
	½ c. fried bacon, crumbled
12 oz. American cheese, cubed	

Mix potatoes, mayonnaise, cheese, and onion together; put in large Pyrex baking dish. Top with olives and bacon. Cover dish and bake at 350° for 45 min. Uncover and bake 15 min. longer. Serves 12.

Mrs. George W. McCammon
Lawrence County

POTATO AND CHEESE CASSEROLE

2 lb. pkg. frozen hash brown potatoes, partly thawed	1 13-oz. can evaporated milk, undiluted
2 10-oz. cans cheddar cheese soup	1 can French-fried onion rings
salt and pepper to taste	

Combine potatoes, soup, milk, and half the onion rings. Pour into greased 3½-qt. Crock-Pot. Add salt and pepper. Cover and cook on Low 8–9 hr. (High 4 hr.). Sprinkle remaining onion rings over top before serving.

Carol Ruby
Perry County

POTATO PUDDING

2 c. potatoes, finely diced	⅓ c. onion, minced
1 c. boiling water	1½ t. salt
	⅛ t. pepper
1½ c. milk	½ T. parsley, chopped
3 or 4 eggs, slightly beaten	

Cook potatoes in boiling water until tender; drain. Heat milk and stir slowly into eggs. Add potatoes, minced onion, salt, pepper, and parsley. Mix well. Pour into greased 1½-qt. casserole. Bake at 350° for 40 min., or until set. Serve with (or without) sour cream. Serves 6.

Marie Keiser
Whitley County

POTATOES ROMANOFF

5. c. potatoes (8 medium), cooked and diced	1 c. sour cream
	1 c. green onion, finely chopped (other onions may be used)
2 t. salt	
2 c. small-curd cottage cheese	1 c. sharp cheese, shredded

Combine first 5 ingredients. Sprinkle grated cheese on top. Bake at 350° for 45 min. Serves 12.

Mrs. Max Tribbett
Montgomery County

QUICK BAKED POTATO

When baking potatoes, wrap in foil and boil until almost done. Then bake. Much faster than baking the whole time.

Kathleen Ingle
Crawford County

SCALLOPED POTATOES

8 medium pota- toes (2 qt.), pared and sliced	1 can cream of mushroom soup 1 c. milk
¼ c. green pep- per, chopped	2 t. salt dash of pepper
¼ c. onion, minced	

Alternate layers of potatoes, green pepper, and onion in greased 2-qt. baking dish. Combine remaining ingredients; pour over potatoes. Cover and bake in moderate oven (350°) 1½ hr., or until potatoes are done. Serves 8.

Irene Jones
Scott County

SPECIAL POTATOES

1 2-lb pkg. frozen hash browns	1½ c. grated cheddar cheese
1 2½-oz. can sliced mush- rooms	1 8-oz. carton sour cream 1 can cream of celery soup
2 T. onions, chopped	1 can cream of chicken soup
1 green pepper, chopped	½ t. seasoned salt pepper to taste

Mix together. Reserve part of cheese to sprinkle on top. Put in greased casserole and bake 40 min. at 350°.

Ruth M. Hamm
Allen County

STUFFED WHITE POTATOES

For each baked potato:

½ t. salt	2 T. shortening
dash of pepper	dash of paprika
1 egg	¼ c. grated
2–3 T. milk, heated	cheese

Cut baked potato in half lengthwise; scoop out pulp and mash. Add salt, pepper, shortening, and milk to pulp. Beat egg until foamy; add to pulp mixture; beat until fluffy. Pile pulp mixture lightly into skins, sprinkle with paprika and cheese. Bake at 350° for 5–7 min.

Mrs. Allan Rogers
Dearborn County

SWEDISH GREEN POTATOES

6 large potatoes	2 T. chives or
¾ c. milk or light cream	green onion, chopped
1 t. sugar	½ t. dried dill
¼ lb. butter	1 pkg. frozen
2 t. salt	chopped
¼ t. pepper	spinach

Boil potatoes until tender. Cook spinach and drain well. Mash potatoes with milk, sugar, butter, salt and pepper. Beat until fluffy. Add chives, dill, and spinach. Beat until blended. Bake in greased casserole at 350° for 30 min. Serves 6–8.

Mrs. Henry A. Pictor
Ohio County

SAUERKRAUT AND APPLES

2 c. sauerkraut	½ t. salt
¼ c. fat	1 T. sugar
¼ c. water	½ t. caraway
3 apples, cored and quartered	seed 2 potatoes, grated
1 small onion, sliced	

Combine sauerkraut, fat, water, apples, and onion. Cook slowly until apples are tender. Add salt, sugar, caraway seed, and grated potatoes. Continue cooking for 5 minutes, or until potatoes are done. Serve with broiled or steamed wieners, or your favorite sausage. Serves 6.

Mrs. Fredric W. Banta
Kosciusko County

HERB SPINACH BAKE

1 10-oz. pkg. chopped spin-ach, cooked and drained	2 T. soft butter or margarine
1 c. cooked rice	1½ T. dried minced onion
1 c. sharp cheddar cheese, shredded	½ t. Worcester-shire sauce
2 eggs, slightly beaten	1 t. salt
⅓ c. milk	¼ t. rosemary, crushed

Combine spinach and rice with other ingredients. Pour into a greased 10×6×1½" baking dish. Bake at 350° for 25 min. Cut into squares to serve. Serves 8.

Bertha Fifer
Posey County

SPINACH CASSEROLE

1 10-oz. pkg. frozen chopped spinach	6 oz. cream cheese, cubed
2 hard-boiled eggs, sliced	about 3 slices bread, cubed
1 c. thick cream sauce	margarine, melted

Arrange half of first 4 ingredients in thin layers in 1½-qt. casserole dish in order named. Repeat layering with the other half. Dip bread cubes in melted margarine. Sprinkle over top of casserole. Bake 30 min. at 350°. Serves 6.

Thick Cream Sauce:

3 t. margarine	dash of pepper
4 T. flour	1 c. milk
¼ t. salt	

Melt margarine. Stir in flour, salt, and pepper. Add milk. Stir until thick and bubbly.

Cris Freeman
Monroe County

SPINACH SOUFFLE

2 10-oz. bags fresh spinach (do not use frozen)	6 eggs, beaten
	1 stick margarine, cut in chunks
1 large carton small-curd cottage cheese	½ lb. Velveeta cheese, cut in chunks
	6 T. flour

Chop fresh spinach. Put in large bowl. Add cottage cheese, eggs, margarine, cheese, and flour. Mix all together and put in greased 9×13" casserole. Bake at 350° for 1 hr. Serves 12.

Mrs. Norval Maguire
Monroe County

SWISS CHEESE-SPINACH CASSEROLE

1 lb. frozen chopped spinach	3 T. onion, chopped
2 t. salt	1¼ c. milk
3 T. butter or margarine	2 c. natural Swiss cheese, shredded
2 T. flour	2 eggs, beaten

Grease a 10×6" baking dish. In medium saucepan over high heat and in 1" boiling water, heat spinach and ½ t. salt to boiling; cover and cook 10 minutes; drain; set aside. In medium saucepan over medium heat, melt butter or margarine; stir in flour and 1½ t. salt until smooth. Add onion and cook 1 min. Slowly stir in milk; cook, stirring constantly, until mixture thickens and begins to boil; remove from heat. Stir Swiss cheese and spinach into mixture until cheese melts slightly; stir in beaten eggs. Pour into greased 10×6″ baking dish and bake at 325° for 30 min., or until center is firm to the touch. Serves 8.

Mrs. Erna Lloyd
Spencer County

SQUASH MEDLEY

4 medium un-peeled summer squash or 4 c. frozen summer squash	6 slices bacon, fried and chopped
½ green pepper, chopped	⅓ c. onion, chopped
2 ripe tomatoes, peeled and chopped	½ t. salt
	½ c. fine bread crumbs
	2 T. butter

Parboil squash (zucchini for 3 min.; yellow crookneck or small white pattypans, 5 min.). If you use frozen squash do not parboil. Combine remaining ingredients except butter and crumbs. Mix well. Slice squash thinly. Place in baking dish, alternating squash and green pepper-tomato mixture. Top with bread crumbs and dot with butter. Bake in moderate oven (375°) for 35 min. Serves 8–10.

Frances Long
Scott County

SUMMER SQUASH

1 lb. yellow squash	¼ t. dill
2 T. butter	¼ t. salt
1 T. parsley	onion powder

Slice squash crosswise ¼″ thick. Melt butter in skillet. Add squash, parsley, dill, salt, and onion powder. Cover and cook on low heat 8–10 min., stirring occasionally.

Marianna Roth
Spencer County

ZUCCHINI CASSEROLE (1)

3 c. zucchini squash, sliced in ¼″ pieces	½ t. salt
	1 4-oz. jar pimiento, diced
1½ c. cracker crumbs	1 c. milk
3 eggs, beaten	2 c. (2 pkg.) shredded cheddar cheese
½ c. margarine, melted	

Combine all ingredients. Pour into greased 2-qt. baking dish. Bake uncovered at 300° for 30–40 min.

Helen Heinley
Whitley County

ZUCCHINI CASSEROLE (2)

4 medium zucchini, diced	6. T. margarine
¾ c. carrots, shredded	2¼ c. herb stuffing mix
½ c. onions, chopped	1 can cream of chicken soup
	1 c. sour cream

Cook zucchini in small amount of salted water; drain. Cook carrots and onions until tender. Stir in 1½ c. stuffing mix, soup, and sour cream. Gently fold in zucchini and 3 T. margarine. Pour into a greased casserole. Melt remaining margarine with remaining stuffing mix and sprinkle over top of casserole. Bake at 350° for 30 min. Serves 6–8.

Mrs. Everett Hoesel
Marshall County

ZUCCHINI, CORN, AND TOMATOES

2 lb. zucchini	dash of pepper
4 T. butter	¼ t. dried oregano leaves or dried basil leaves
¼ c. onions, thinly sliced	
1¾ t. salt	

3 medium toma-
toes, peeled and
cut into eighths

1 12-oz. can
whole kernel
corn, drained

Scrub zucchini well; do not pare. Cut into
1/4" diagonal slices. Sauté onion in hot
butter in large skillet until onion is tender,
about 5 min. Add zucchini and seasonings.
When mixture boils, reduce heat and simmer covered for 15 min., or until zucchini
is tender. Stir several times while cooking.
Add tomatoes. Cook uncovered for 5 min.
longer. Add corn and cook for a few min.
until corn is heated through. Serves 6–8.

Anne Reiff
Allen County

BUTTERNUT SQUASH
(Mock Sweet Potatoes)

2 lb. fresh butter-
nut squash
1 c. orange juice
1 packet artificial
sweetener

1/8 t. nutmeg
1/8 t. cinnamon
orange slices for
garnish

Boil squash in orange juice. Mash squash
and add sweetener, nutmeg, and cinnamon. Bake at 350° for 30 min. Serves 4.

Mrs. Minnie Mikesell
Monroe County

BUTTERNUT SQUASH CASSEROLE

3 c. hot mashed
butternut or
buttercup
squash
1/4 c. butter or
margarine
1 t. salt
1/8 t. pepper

1 t. onion,
minced
1/4 c. milk
3 eggs, well
beaten
1/4 c. buttered
bread crumbs

Add butter to hot squash; beat until butter
melts. Stir in salt, pepper, and onion. Blend
milk into eggs; add to squash mixture.

Pour into greased 1½-qt. casserole; top
with buttered bread crumbs. Set in pan of
warm water and bake in moderate oven
(350°) until knife inserted in center
comes out clean (about 45 min.). Serves
6.

Mrs. Albert Lichtenbarger
St. Joseph County

FRIED SQUASH BLOSSOMS

Gather a pan of pumpkin and/or squash
blossoms when fully opened. Remove sta-
mens. Wash and drain. Make a batter,
using 1 egg, about ½ c. of flour and milk.
Dip the blossoms in batter and drop into
deep, hot fat. Serve as a vegetable.

Kay Kinder
Monroe County

MASHED SWEET POTATOES

3 c. sweet pota-
toes, mashed
½ c. butter,
melted
1 t. vanilla
1 c. sugar
½ c. milk
2 eggs

Topping:
1/3 c. butter
1 c. brown sugar
1/3 c. flour
1 c. pecans,
chopped

Mix first 6 ingredients together and put in
buttered baking dish. Mix topping ingredients until coarse like meal or pie
dough and sprinkle over top of sweet potatoes. Bake at 350° for 30–40 min. Serves
6.

Mrs. Barney Thomas
Daviess County

MARSHMALLOW-DATE SWEET
POTATOES

4 medium sweet
potatoes

1/4 c. butter
1 egg

1 9-oz. can crushed pineapple	18 dates, cut up
	2 t. brown sugar
	2 t. butter
2 t. salt	8 marshmallows,
1 t. nutmeg	quartered

Boil and mash sweet potatoes. Combine potatoes, pineapple, butter, egg, salt, nutmeg, and dates. Beat until creamy. Spoon into 8″ round baking dish. Sprinkle with brown sugar and dot with butter. Top with marshmallows and bake uncovered at 350° for 30 min., or until marshmallows are brown. Serves 6–8.

Mary Allbright
Martin County

ORANGE-GLAZED SWEET POTATOES

2-lb. or 1 1-lb., 13-oz. can sweet potatoes	½ c. butter or margarine
	½ c. orange juice
½ c. dark corn syrup	½ t. salt

Cook sweet potatoes (unpared, if using fresh potatoes) in boiling salted water until tender. Drain (and peel, if fresh). Cut potatoes in halves. Mix corn syrup, margarine, orange juice, and salt in large skillet. Cook until mixture comes to boil. Boil 3 min. Add sweet potatoes. Cook slowly, turning occasionally (about 12 to 15 min.) until sweet potatoes are well glazed. Serves 8.

Mrs. Charles McIntyre
Fayette County

SWEET POTATO-APPLE CASSEROLE

1 lb. sweet potatoes, cooked	¼ t. cinnamon
	¼ t. salt
⅓ c. light brown sugar, firmly packed	2 c. apples, peeled, thinly sliced

⅓ c. raisins (optional)	⅓ c. slivered almonds or chopped pecans
¼ c. butter or margarine	

Peel sweet potatoes and slice 1″ thick. Mix brown sugar, cinnamon, and salt. Arrange layer of sweet potatoes in 2-qt. baking dish. Layer brown sugar mixture, apples, then raisins and nuts and dot with butter. Repeat layers. Bake at 375° for 35 min. Serves 4–6.

Eileen Weinzapfel
Posey County

SWEET POTATO BAKE

3 lb. sweet potatoes	1 c. apricot nectar
	½ c. hot water
1 c. brown sugar	2 t. grated orange peel
1½ T. cornstarch	
¼ t. salt	2 T. butter
⅛ t. cinnamon	½ c. pecans

Cook sweet potatoes in salt water until just tender. Combine all of the ingredients, except the sweet potatoes, in medium saucepan and bring to a full boil, stirring constantly. Remove from heat. Add butter and pecans to mixture. Place sweet potatoes in an 8×12″ casserole and pour sauce over them. Bake, covered, in a moderate oven (375°) for about 25 min. Serves 6–8.

Mrs. Joe Swain
Rush County

SWEET POTATO PATTIES

2 c. sweet potatoes, mashed	1 egg, well beaten
2 T. butter	½ t. salt
2 T. brown sugar	¼ t. nutmeg
2 T. cream	

To the sweet potatoes add egg, butter, sugar, nutmeg, salt, and cream. Mix well and beat until fluffy. Pile lightly on well-greased cookie sheet by large spoonfuls. Bake at 350° until tops are brown. Serves 4.

Mrs. Margaret Hastings
Ohio County

BREADED TOMATOES

2 T. butter, melted	1 pt. tomatoes
2 T. flour	2 T. sugar
dash of salt	2 or 3 slices
1 c. milk	bread, broken in large pieces

Blend half the butter, flour, and salt; slowly add milk. Simmer until thickened, stirring constantly. Heat tomatoes, remaining butter, and sugar; add to hot sauce (in this order to prevent curdling). Stir in bread; remove from heat. Serves 4.

Mrs. Robert Belcher
Crawford County

DILLED TOMATO SLICES

4 sliced tomatoes	1 t. basil
½ t. sugar	1 t. dill seed or
salt and pepper	some fresh dill
sweet onion slices	heads

Layer tomatoes and onions. Add seasonings. Let set 3 hr. before serving.

Nisa Waltz
Ripley County

FRIED GREEN TOMATOES

Slice 4 green tomatoes; soak in salt water 2 hr. Drain, season with pepper, and turn in flour or cornflake crumbs. Fry in vegetable oil until brown on one side; turn. When nearly brown on top side, sprinkle with brown sugar. Serves 4.

Large cucumbers can be fried the same way, if peeled first. Eggplant can also be fried this way.

Mrs. Hale Thompson
Lawrence County

MYRTLE'S STUFFED TOMATOES

6 smooth, uniform tomatoes	¼ c. onion, chopped
1 c. cold left-over cooked meat, finely chopped (crisp bacon may be used)	1 c. soft bread crumbs
	¼ c. (or less) sugar
	1 t. salt
¼ c. green and red peppers, chopped	pepper to taste
	3 T. butter

Cut a slice from stem end of each tomato and scoop out the pulp. Place pulp in mixing bowl and add the rest of the ingredients except butter. Mix thoroughly and fill each tomato shell. Arrange stuffed tomatoes in baking dish. Add ½ T. of butter to each tomato. Add ¼ c. of hot water to baking dish and bake in moderate oven (350°) for 25 min. Serve at once. Serves 6.

Mary Hardman
Orange County

TURNIP SOUFFLE

2 lb. turnips	¾ t. salt
3 t. butter	½ t. pepper
3 eggs, well-beaten	1 onion, sliced cracker crumbs
1 can cream of mushroom soup	Parmesan cheese (optional)

Cook turnips and onion until tender. Drain and mash. Mix with remaining ingredients. Place in greased casserole, and top with cracker crumbs. Parmesan cheese may be used also. Bake at 350° for 30 min. or until firm. Serves 6–8.

Ruth Cox
St. Joseph County

Beef and Pork

The round purple stamp on meat shows it has passed federal inspection. This stamp guarantees all of us that the meat is from healthy animals, and has been processed under sanitary conditions. The marking fluid, used for this stamp, is a vegetable color and is harmless. It need not be trimmed from the meat.

In determining the quantity of meat required per serving, several factors must be considered, including the appetite of the person eating. A person who thinks he has just "licked his weight in wildcats" will probably feel he needs more than one who has spent the day wrestling with a computer. The meat itself makes a difference; a person happy with a quarter pound of hamburger may demand a pound of steak to be satisfied. U.S. Department of Agriculture charts allow one-quarter pound of boneless meat per serving up to one pound per serving when there is much bone. These allowances should be used as a guide only.

U.S.D.A. research shows that searing meat at a high temperature for a short time, followed by a low cooking temperature, causes excessive meat shrinkage. Constant low oven temperatures (275°–325°) for as short a time as possible are recommended. A meat thermometer provides the most accurate measurement of doneness.

Veal is baby beef and needs gentle cooking. When roasted it needs constant basting to keep it juicy and tender. Veal steaks, chops, and cutlets should be braised, not broiled.

One of the most flavorful of all meats, pork needs sufficient cooking time, since it must always be served well done. Many cooks recommend a little more spice, salt, and other seasonings be used with pork than with other meats.

Properly prepared and cooked, lamb has a delicate flavor. The outside skin called a "fell" should be removed, along with as much fat as possible, before cooking lamb.

Hamburger without a bun or Salisbury steak was promoted at the turn of the century by a physician and food faddist, J. H. Salisbury. He recommended eating ground steak three times a day for the relief of colitis, pernicious anemia, asthma, bronchitis, rheumatism, tuberculosis, gout, and hardening of the arteries.

Originally called "red hots," the name was changed to hot dogs after Tad Dorgan, a cartoonist, pictured the "red hot" as an elongated bun containing a dachshund.

Beef

ROAST BEEF

4½ lb. beef roast	¼ t. black pepper
1 T. vinegar	½ t. dry mustard
1 T. brown sugar	1 t. paprika
¼ t. allspice	2 t. salt

Mix together all ingredients except meat. Rub the mixture well into meat. Place meat in roasting pan with no cover. Do *not* add water. Bake at 200° for 6½ hr.

Mrs. Ralph Beckman
Franklin County

ROAST BEEF HASH

2 c. leftover roast beef, chopped	2–6 T. onion, minced
2–3 c. cooked potatoes, chopped	⅓ c. milk
salt and pepper	2 T. fat

Chop meat and potatoes separately; pieces should be a little smaller than ¼" cubes. Add onion, seasoning, milk; toss together lightly. Melt fat in heavy fry pan or in both sides of omelet pan. Put hash into pan; spread evenly. Cook uncovered over low heat, without stirring until underside is lightly browned, about 30–35 min. Check browning by lifting edge with spatula; if browning too rapidly, reduce heat. Run spatula around sides of pan to loosen hash.

If using omelet pan, close to put the 2 halves together, then turn on to heated platter. If using fry pan, take handle in left hand; make a cut through center of hash at right angle to handle. Tip handle up and, with aid of spatula, fold upper half over lower half. Hold edge of pan close to far edge of platter; slowly tip the two together until hash rolls onto platter. Serves 4.

Mrs. Diane Hunteman
Ripley County

APPLE POT ROAST

4 lb. chuck blade roast	¼ t. black pepper
	1 c. apple juice
2 T. solid vegetable shortening or oil	4 medium golden delicious apples, cored, pared, and quartered
1½ t. salt	
¾ t. ground ginger	1 onion, sliced
5 whole cloves	2 T. flour
1 bay leaf	¼ c. water

Brown roast on both sides in hot shortening; add salt, ginger, cloves, bay leaf, pepper, apple juice to meat. Bring to boiling and reduce heat; cover and simmer for 2 hr. Add apples and onion; return to simmer for ½ hr. longer, or until tender. Remove meat to platter and surround with apples and onions. Stir flour with water smoothly, whisk into sauce; bring to boiling, stirring. Spoon a little gravy over the meat. Serve the rest in a sauce boat.

Mrs. Jack Butler
Martin County

BEEF POT PIE

3 lb. chuck roast	¼ c. snipped
3 c. water	parsley or 3 T.
3 c. beef broth	dried parsley
3 beef bouillon	pieces
cubes	1 c. potato cubes
6 T. margarine	1 pkg. frozen
½ c. onion,	peas
chopped	1 carrot, chopped
½ c. flour	1 can plain
1 t. salt	biscuits

Pressure cook chuck roast until tender in water. Cut meat up in small pieces and set aside. Cook until tender potato cubes, peas, and carrot. In a large saucepan, sauté onion in margarine. Blend in flour and salt. Stir until thick. Add broth and bouillon cubes. Add meat and vegetables. Put in a large deep casserole. Put biscuits on top. Bake at 450° for 20 min., or until biscuits are brown.

Ann Apple
Orange County

BEEF LUNCHEON CASSEROLE

2 lb. beef or veal,	1 small can sliced
diced	mushrooms,
1 lb. broad	drained
noodles, cooked	1 small can
1 can whole	pimientos,
kernel corn,	drained and
drained	diced

salt and pepper	2 c. milk
to taste	1 to 1½ lb.
Sauce:	cheese, grated,
¼ lb. butter	diced, or
3 T. flour	shredded

Cook meat in a small amount of water. *Do not brown* the meat. When meat is tender; put in large casserole. Add cooked noodles, corn, mushrooms, and pimientos. Add salt and pepper to taste. Melt butter; add flour and mix thoroughly. Gradually add milk and cook until thickened, stirring constantly. Add cheese and stir until melted. Pour cheese sauce over first mixture and bake slowly at 350° for 45 min. Serves 15.

Mrs. Mary Germann
St. Joseph County

CUBED STEAKS IN MUSHROOM SAUCE

6 cubed steaks	½ c. sour cream
salt, pepper, flour	1 can cream of
⅓ c. shortening	mushroom soup
2 T. water	

In skillet, brown the lightly floured and seasoned meat in hot shortening. Transfer meat to 13×9×2″ baking pan. Pour water into pan; cover pan with foil. Bake at 350° for 30 min. Uncover and pour in the soup and sour cream. Recover and bake for 15 minutes or more. Serves 6.

Sharon Edwards
Putnam County

FRESH CRANBERRY SAUERBRATEN

4–5 lb. beef pot	2 medium onions,
roast, chuck	thinly sliced
or round	2 c. fresh
2 t. salt	cranberries
⅛ t. black pepper	½ c. granulated
2 T. salad oil	sugar

2½ T. vinegar dash of garlic
1½ c. water powder
⅛ t. cloves 2 T. water
1½ T. cornstarch

Season meat with salt and pepper. Heat oil in heavy kettle or Dutch oven. Brown meat on both sides in oil. Add onions, cranberries, sugar, vinegar, 1½ c. water, cloves, and garlic powder. Simmer covered 2 to 2½ hr., or until tender. Remove meat to platter; keep warm. Mix cornstarch to smooth paste with 2 T. water. Stir into cranberry mixture. Cook, stirring constantly, until gravy thickens and clears. Serves 6.

Mrs. Ernest Ford
Marshall County

GERMAN SAUERBRATEN

2 c. vinegar ¼ t. mustard seed
2 c. water 1 4–5 lb. beef
4 onions, sliced rump roast
1 stalk celery, 1 t. salt
  chopped ¼ t. pepper
1 carrot, chopped ¼ c. salad oil
2 bay leaves 4 T. flour
8 peppercorns, ½ c. seedless
  crushed raisins
8 whole cloves ½ c. sour cream

Combine vinegar, water, onions, celery, carrot, bay leaves, peppercorns, cloves, and mustard seeds in sauce pan. Bring to boil; cool. Place meat in large bowl. Pour marinade over meat. Place in refrigerator; marinate 2–3 days, turning several times. Remove meat from marinade; dry well. Sprinkle meat with salt and pepper. Heat oil in Dutch oven. Brown meat on all sides. Add 2 cups of marinade; cover; simmer 2–3 hr., or until meat is tender. Remove meat; keep warm. Strain sauce; skim off fat; measure liquid. Add water or mar-

inade to make 2 cups. Stir in flour. Return to pan. Cook over low heat, stirring and scraping browned bits, until thickened. Stir in raisins and sour cream; blend well. Serve with meat. Serves 6 to 8.

Ann Picht
Allen County

HUNGARIAN GOULASH

2 lb. lean, bone- paprika to taste
  less chuck, cut dried marjoram
  into cubes caraway seeds,
onion, sliced (for crushed
  each lb. of meat 1 16-oz. can
  add 1 onion) tomato puree
bacon fat or olive beef bouillon,
  oil if needed
garlic clove, red wine
  crushed

Sauté onion in hot bacon fat or olive oil until tender, then add beef cubes, paprika, garlic clove, marjoram, and a fair portion of caraway seeds. Add tomato puree; cover and simmer 1½ hr. If liquid is too thick, add beef bouillon. About 15 min. before serving add a generous amount of red wine. Serve over noodles.

Barbara Cooper
St. Joseph County

ITALIAN BEEF

3 lb. chuck roast 1 carrot
salt and pepper 2 green peppers,
1 large onion sliced
8 whole cloves butter
2 stalks of celery

Brown meat on all sides, then poke holes in it. Salt and pepper meat. Put in roaster. Put whole cloves in large onion. Lay beside meat along with celery and carrot. Cover and bake. Slice meat when done. Put back into juice. Sauté green peppers in butter.

Place over meat. May be served on French bread as sandwiches. Serves 6–8.

Mrs. Alice Bauer
Pulaski County

SAVORY BLADE POT ROAST

3 lb. blade bone pot roast	2 T. Worcester- shire sauce
¼ c. wine vinegar	1 t. dried rose- mary, crushed
¼ c. cooking oil	½ t. garlic powder
¼ c. catsup	½ t. dry mustard
2 T. soy sauce	

In skillet, brown meat slowly in a small amount of hot oil. Sprinkle meat with a little salt. Combine vinegar, oil, catsup, soy sauce, Worcestershire sauce, rosemary, garlic powder, and mustard; pour over meat. Cover tightly and simmer 2 hr., or until tender. Remove meat to heated platter. Skim excess fat from sauce; spoon sauce over meat. Serves 6–8.

Mrs. Donna Peter
Perry County

SIZZLING SHORT RIBS

4 lb. beef short ribs or 2 lb. chuck roast, cut in pieces	½ t. horseradish
	1 t. Worcester- shire sauce
½ c. catsup	½ t. mustard
1 t. garlic salt	1 t. salt
4 t. vinegar	½ t. monosodium glutamate
½ t. lemon juice or Real-Lemon	2 T. sugar
	pepper

Brown short ribs or roast in roasting pan. Pour off fat. Make a sauce of remaining ingredients; pour over meat. Cover and bake at 325° for 2 hr., or until fork-tender. Serves 4–6.

Mrs. Loys Rees
Rush County

CORNED BEEF

CORNED BEEF CASSEROLE

1 8-oz. pkg. me- dium noodles	1 12-oz. can corned beef, broken into pieces
3 T. butter	
½ c. green pep- per, chopped	1 c. condensed cream of chicken soup
½ c. onion, chopped	
2 c. (8 oz.) ched- dar cheese, cubed	1 c. milk
	¼ c. fine dry bread crumbs
1 T. butter, melted	green pepper rings

Cook noodles according to directions; drain. In a small skillet melt 3 T. butter; add onions and green pepper; sauté for 5 min. In buttered 2½-qt. casserole layer half the noodles, half the onion and green pepper mixture, half the cheese, and all the corned beef. Repeat layers of noodles, vegetables, and cheese. Stir soup and milk together, pour over casserole. Combine crumbs and 1 T. melted butter and sprinkle over the top. Bake at 350° for 40 min. Garnish with green pepper rings.

Progressive Homemakers
Lake County

REUBEN CASSEROLE

1 lb., 11 oz. can sauerkraut, drained	2 4-oz. pkg. sliced corned beef, shredded
2 medium toma- toes, sliced	2 cups (8 oz. pkg.) shredded Swiss cheese
2 T. thousand island dressing	1 can biscuits
2 T. butter	¼ t. caraway seed
2 rye crackers, crushed	

Spread sauerkraut in bottom of 12×8″ baking dish. Top with tomato slices; dot with dressing and butter. Cover with corned beef; sprinkle with cheese. Bake at 425° for 15 min. Remove casserole from oven. Separate each biscuit into three layers; slightly overlap biscuit layers on casserole to form three rows. Sprinkle with crackers and caraway seed. Bake at 425° for 15 to 20 min. until biscuit topping is golden brown. Serves 6–8.

Jan Hriso
Vanderburgh County

DRIED BEEF

DRIED BEEF CASSEROLE

1 can condensed cream of mushroom soup
1 c. (¼ lb.) processed cheddar cheese, cut fine
3 T. onion, finely chopped
1½ c. milk
1 c. uncooked elbow macaroni
¼ lb. dried beef, cut in bite size pieces
2 eggs, hard-cooked

Mix soup, milk, cheese, onion, macaroni, and dried beef. Fold in eggs. Turn into buttered ½-qt. baking dish. Store covered in refrigerator at least 3 hr. or overnight. Bake 1 hr. at 350°.

Thelma Richards
Sullivan County

SKILLET DRIED BEEF AND CORN

2½ oz. dried beef
2 T. butter
1 T. flour
1 No. 303 can cream-style corn
2 T. onion
½ c. shredded cheddar cheese
¾ c. milk
2 T. green pepper, diced

Lightly fry beef and onion in melted butter until beef begins to curl. Stir in flour. Add milk; cook, stirring until thickened. Add corn; heat until hot. Add cheese and green pepper, stir over low heat until cheese melts. Serve at once on buttered toast or in toast cups. Serves 6–8.

Hallie Tyson
Greene County

FLANK STEAK

FLANK STEAK BROIL

¼ c. soy sauce
¼ c. Worcestershire sauce
⅓ c. cooking oil
1 flank steak

Combine sauces and oil. Poke holes into steak. Marinate meat at least 2 hr., turning and making holes whenever you think of it. Broil each side 5–6 min. (Check for doneness by inserting knife). Makes 2 large servings or 3–4 smaller servings.

Betty VanWinkle
Wells County

FLANK STEAK MARINADE

3 cloves garlic, chopped
1 T. ground pepper
⅔ c. soy sauce
½ T. Tabasco sauce
⅓ c. sherry or dry vermouth
flank steak

In glass dish, combine ingredients. Place steak in dish; turn every hour, and at least 1 hr. for each side. Keep at room temperature. Grill steak over hot charcoal fire until done. Slice thinly against the grain.

Mrs. James Sammer
Hamilton County

FLANK STEAK MIGNONETTE

1 lb. flank steak	1 c. mushroom
seasoned instant	caps
meat tenderizer	¼ c. margarine
¼ t. pepper	fresh parsley
6 bacon strips	

One hour before broiling: Sprinkle steak with tenderizer. Cut flank diagonally in strips the width of the bacon. Season with pepper. Wrap bacon around each strip of flank and fasten with toothpick. Broil about 8 min. per side. Sauté mushrooms in margarine. Arrange mignonettes on platter, removing toothpicks. Top with mushrooms and garnish with parsley.

Violet Ferguson
Sullivan County

ROUND STEAK

ALMOND BEEF

2 lb. round steak,	1 4-oz. can mush-
cut in 1″ cubes	rooms & stems
2 T. vegetable oil	1 10-oz. can
1 t. salt	mushroom soup
1½ c. celery,	½ c. water
chopped	1 8-oz. pkg. nar-
½ c. green pep-	row noodles,
per, chopped	cooked and
½ c. onion,	drained
chopped	1 c. almonds,
¼ c. canned	sliced
pimiento,	1 c. sour cream
chopped	

Brown beef cubes in oil; pour off fat. Add salt, mushrooms and liquid, mushroom soup, and water. Simmer about 45 min., until meat is tender. Cook noodles, drain. Combine noodles, sour cream, beef mixture, celery, green pepper, onion, and pimiento and pour into greased casserole.

Top with sliced almonds. Bake at 325°–350° for about 30 min. Serves 4–6.

Helen Hickman
Noble County

BARBEQUE STEAK

1 or 2″ round	1 T. dry mustard
steak	chopped onion to
1 c. catsup	taste
¼ c. water	3 T. brown sugar
⅓ c. vinegar	pepper

Heat all except the steak to a boil. Boil for 1 min. Put steak in 9 × 13″ pan; pour mixture over steak. Bake at 350° for 2 hr. Serves 4–6.

Lola Hay
Jefferson County

BEEF BIRDS

1 round steak, cut	1 4-oz. can mush-
½″ thick	room stems &
3 T. flour	pieces, drained
1 t. salt	3 T. lard or
⅛ t. pepper	drippings
½ c. onion,	1 beef bouillon
chopped	cube
½ t. poultry	1 c. boiling water
seasoning	

Combine flour, salt, and pepper and pound into round steak. Cut into 5 or 6 serving pieces. Combine onion, mushrooms, and poultry seasoning. Place about ¼ c. mixture on each piece of meat. Roll as a jelly roll and fasten with wooden picks. Brown meat in lard or drippings. Dissolve bouillon cube in boiling water. Add to meat. Cover tightly and cook slowly 1½–1¾ hr., or until meat is tender. Remove meat to a heated platter. Thicken cooking liquid with flour to make the best gravy. Serves 4.

Sandra Cripe
Noble County

BEEF STEAK PIE WITH POTATO CRUST

1 lb. round steak, cut in 1″ cubes	¼ t. pepper
3 T. fat	dash thyme
3 small onions, sliced	dash garlic salt
	2 c. water
3 T. flour	3 medium pota-
1½ t. salt	toes, thinly
	sliced

Dredge meat in flour. Place in skillet with fat. Brown meat until very brown and crusty about 15 minutes per side. Add onions and cook until golden brown; about 10 minutes. Put in 2-qt. baking dish. Sprinkle with flour and seasonings; pour water over top. Bake at 350° for 45 min. to 1 hr., or until meat is tender. Remove from oven, increase temperature to 450°. Place potatoes on top and sprinkle with salt and paprika. Return to oven and bake for about 30 min., or until potatoes are browned and tender. Serves 4–6.

Emmalou Turpin
Martin County

BEEF STROGANOFF (1)

1 lb. round steak	¼ c. shortening
1 clove garlic	1 can condensed
3 T. flour	consommé
1¾ t. salt	½ c. water
1 t. paprika	1 small can
¼ t. pepper	mushrooms
½ c. onion, chopped	½ c. sour cream

Rub both sides of meat with garlic; then cut into 1½×1″ strips. Mix flour, salt, pepper, and paprika. Add meat strips and toss lightly until strips are well coated with flour. Reserve remaining flour mixture. Heat shortening in heavy skillet. Add meat and brown well. Add onions and continue cooking until onions are transparent. Add remaining flour mixture, consommé, water, and mushrooms. Cover and cook slowly until meat is tender (about 1½ hr.), stirring occasionally. Remove cover and continue cooking until mixture is slightly thickened. Add sour cream and blend. Serve with broad noodles. Serves 4–5.

Arlene McDill
Boone County

BEEF STROGANOFF (2)

round steak, cubed	½ can water
	1 pkg. dry onion
1 small can mushrooms	soup
	1 small onion
1 can cream of mushroom soup	butter
	¼ c. sour cream

Sauté onion in butter. Add steak and mushrooms. Combine mushroom and onion soups in bowl. Add water. Pour over steak. Bake at 325° for 2 hr. Ten minutes before serving stir in sour cream. Serve over rice.

Liqueta Eubank
Vanderburgh County

DAD'S ROUND STEAK

2 round steaks, ½″ thick	8 oz. fresh mushrooms, sliced
1 12-oz. can pitted black olives, drained and chopped	1½ c. red wine
	salt, pepper, flour
	butcher twine
	(6 ft.)
1 8-oz. can green olives, drained and chopped	2 T. cornstarch
	1 c. water
1 large sweet onion, chopped	

Debone the steak; overlap the boned ends. Sprinkle with flour, salt, and pepper. Pound both sides of steak with the side of a plate. Spread olives, onions, and mushrooms (reserve ½ c.). Roll up from end (jelly-roll fashion). Tie with twine. Cook in covered heavy pan 2 hr. at 325°. After 1 hr. pour ½ the wine over the rolled steak. Half an hour later put the rest of the mushrooms alongside the roast. Pour remaining wine over meat. Leave the lid off to brown. Take out the roast. Mix cornstarch in water. Add to drippings in pan. Stir over low heat until thickened. Slice roast cross-wise. Serve gravy alongside. Serves 6–8.

Mrs. Jon C. Trusty
Shelby County

FAVORITE ROUND STEAK
Sprinkle round steak with garlic salt on one side, with celery salt on the other. Layer in casserole. Pour 1 can tomato soup over all. Bake covered for 40–45 min. at 350°.

Phyllis Kirts
Brown County

FILLED AND ROLLED STEAK

1 thin slice round steak, pounded	1 small can mushrooms
¾ lb. ground beef	¼ c. milk
1 clove garlic	¼ t. oregano
2 T. butter	2 c. water
½ c. bread crumbs	½ c. white wine
	1 small onion, chopped

Sprinkle round steak with salt and pepper. Sauté onion and garlic in butter; cool. Add bread crumbs, mushrooms, milk, and oregano. Pour over ground beef and mix well; spread mixture on steak and roll; fasten with skewers or tie with string. Dredge with flour. Place in roasting pan; brown

quickly at 500°; add water and cover. Reduce heat to 350° and cook for 1½ hr. Pour wine over steak before last 15 min. of cooking. Slice and serve with gravy.

Mrs. Wilbert Seehausen
Lake County

GREEN PEPPER STEAK AND RICE

1½ lb. boneless round steak	¼ c. water
1 T. paprika	1 c. onion, chopped
2 T. margarine	2 c. green pepper strips
½ c. red wine	2 large, fresh tomatoes, diced
2 T. soy sauce	
2 t. garlic powder	3 c. hot, cooked rice
2 t. garlic salt	
¼ t. pepper	
1 T. cornstarch	

Partially freeze meat to make slicing easier. Cut in strips ⅛″ thick. Sprinkle steak with paprika. Using high heat, brown meat rapidly in margarine on all sides. Reduce heat. Add wine, soy sauce, and seasonings. Cover and simmer 25 min. Blend cornstarch and water. Stir into meat. Arrange onions, green peppers, and tomatoes over steak. Replace cover; simmer 10–15 min. longer. Serve over rice. Serves 6.

Mrs. Steve Plew
Whitley County

PEPPER STEAK

1½ lb. boneless round steak	salt and pepper to taste
2 T. shortening	2 medium green peppers
1 pkg. onion soup mix	1½ T. cornstarch
2½ c. water	

Cut meat into thin 2″ strips. In large skillet, heat shortening; brown meat. Stir in 2 c. water and onion soup mix. Simmer

30 min. Add green peppers. Cover. Simmer 10 min., or until tender. Blend cornstarch with ½ c. water. Stir into steak mixture. Serve over rice on noodles.

Mrs. Floyd Baker
Adams County

ROLL 'EM UPS

1 large onion, chopped	round steak, cut into 4″ strips
bacon slices, cut in small pieces	salt and pepper

Put onion and bacon pieces on round steak strips; roll and tie. Season with salt and pepper. Brown meat on all sides in skillet. Remove to Dutch oven. Scrape all drippings from skillet; add to meat. Add water to cover. Cook covered and on low heat for 1½ hr., or until meat is tender. Use broth for gravy.

Mrs. Jerry Krueger
Fayette County

ROUND STEAK IN BEER

1–1½ lb. round steak	2 carrots, chopped
2 T. vinegar	1 t. sugar
1 c. beer	¼ c. tomato
2 c. onion soup (make according to pkg. directions)	sauce celery tops and parsley pinch of thyme

Salt and pepper steak to taste. Brown in hot oil, then remove steak from pan. Add remaining ingredients to pan drippings. Bring to boil. Place meat in a roasting pan and pour broth over. Bake 2½–3 hrs. at 300°. Serves 4–6.

Mrs. John Stephenson
Monroe County

SIRLOIN TIPS IN OVEN

2–3 lb. sirloin tips or round steak, cut in strips	1 can cream of chicken soup
	½ pkg. dry onion soup
1 can cream of mushroom soup	½ c. port wine

Mix all ingredients together and place in 3-qt. covered casserole. Cook for 6 hr. at 250°. Stir once or twice during cooking. Serve over hot cooked rice or chow mein noodles.

Mrs. Fred L. McCain
Carroll County

SKILLET BEEF AND GREEN BEANS

1½ lb. lean, *tender* beef	1 T. cornstarch
2 T. Wesson oil	1 T. soy sauce
1 onion, chopped	¾ c. liquid (using liquid
2 c. French-cut green beans (fresh or frozen)	from mushrooms and water)
1 c. celery, sliced	1 can mushrooms, drained

Cut beef in strips (about 2″ long, ⅛″ to ¼″ thick). In skillet, brown beef in oil. Add onions, green beans, and celery. Cook 4–6 min. Combine cornstarch and soy sauce with liquid. Add to skillet with mushrooms. Stir and cook until liquid is shiny. Cover and cook until beans are tender. Serve with rice.

Mrs. Maynard Bosserman
Allen County

STRIPS OF BEEF CASSEROLE

1 lb. round steak, cut in ½″ strips	1½ c. onion, chopped
¼ c. shortening	2 T. flour

1 c. canned	½ t. Worcester-
tomatoes	shire sauce
1 c. water	¾ to 1½ c. fresh
1 c. (6 oz.)	or canned
tomato paste	mushrooms, cut
1 T. sugar	in pieces
1½ t. salt	¾ c. sour cream
¼ t. pepper	

Brown steak in shortening in large skillet, stirring occasionally. Stir in onion and flour. Cook until onions are tender, stirring occasionally. Add remaining ingredients except mushrooms and sour cream. Cover and simmer for 1½ hours or until meat is tender, stirring occasionally. Add mushrooms and sour cream. Continue cooking 5 minutes. Place mixture in 2-qt. casserole. Top with sour cream puffs. Brush with cream and sprinkle with sesame seed. Bake uncovered at 425° for 20 to 25 min. until golden brown.

Sour Cream Puffs:

1¼ c. flour, sifted	½ t. salt
2 T. baking	¼ c. shortening
powder	¾ c. sour cream

Sift together sifted flour, baking powder, and salt into mixing bowl. Cut in shortening until particles are fine. Add sour cream, stirring with fork until dough clings together in a ball. Pat out on well-floured surface to ½" thickness. Cut six to eight 2½" biscuits and top each with a 1" biscuit.

Mrs. William Oliger
Shelby County

STRIPS OF BEEF ORIENTAL

1 lb. round steak	1 garlic clove,
2–3 T. cooking	minced
oil	2 c. mushrooms
1 c. water	(2 cans or ½ lb.
2 T. soy sauce	fresh)

1 c. carrot slices	½ c. Parmesan
1 c. celery slices	cheese
¾ c. cold water	hot, cooked rice
2 T. cornstarch	

Cut meat into strips ¼" wide and 3" to 4" long. Brown meat in oil; drain. Add water, soy sauce, and garlic. Cover; simmer 45 min. Add vegetables; cover and cook 15 to 20 min. Combine cornstarch and water, stirring until blended. Gradually add to hot meat mixture, stirring constantly until thickened. Remove from heat and stir in Parmesan cheese. Serve over rice. Serves 4.

Mrs. Michael Jones
St. Joseph County

SUKIYAKI

1½ lb. steak, cut	1 c. celery, cut in
in thin strips	1" strips
2 T. salad oil	1 can bamboo
¼ c. sugar	shoots, sliced
¾ c. soy sauce	thin
¼ c. mushroom	1 can mushrooms,
stock or water	sliced thin
2 medium onions,	1 bunch green
sliced	onions, cut in
1 green pepper,	1" slices, using
sliced in thin	green tops
strips	

Heat oil in skillet or wok; add meat and brown slightly. Mix sugar, soy sauce, and mushroom stock. Cook half of mixture with meat. Push meat to one side of skillet and add sliced onions, green pepper, and celery. Cook a few min.; add remaining soy sauce mixture, bamboo shoots, and mushrooms. Cook 3–5 min. Add green onions. Cook 2 min. more. Stir well and serve over rice or chow mein noodles.

Mrs. Fred L. McCain
Carroll County

SWISS BLISS

2 lb. chuck or Swiss steak	½ green pepper, sliced
½ T. butter	1 lb. can tomatoes, drain and use
1 envelope onion soup mix	½ c. juice also
½ lb. mushrooms, sliced	½ t. salt
1 T. cornstarch	1 T. steak sauce

Lay steak on heavy foil. Mix together rest of ingredients. Pour over steak; fold foil in double folds and seal tightly. Bake at 350° for 2 hr.

Ann Apple
Orange County

SWISS STEAK

2 lb. round steak, cut in strips	1 4-oz. can mushrooms
1 onion, sliced	1 can cream of celery soup
1 green pepper, cut in strips	1 c. mayonnaise
½ c. water	

Brown steak, onion, and green pepper in skillet. Simmer ½ hr. in a little water. Mix mushrooms, celery soup, mayonnaise, and water together. Pour over steak. Mix well and heat. Pour over cooked noodles. Serves 4–6.

Marilyn Ralston
Marshall County

LIVER

BAKED LIVER

Coat liver with flour. Brown on both sides; put in casserole. Add cut-up onions, salt, and pepper. Make a thin gravy; pour over liver. Top with bacon strips and cracker crumbs. Bake at 350° for 25 min.

Mrs. Gladys Smith
Ripley County

LIVER AND ONIONS

1 lb. liver, cut in bite-sized pieces	1½–2 c. water
1 pkg. onion soup mix	2 T. margarine
	3 T. flour
	2 T. chili sauce

Brown liver in margarine. Add soup mix and flour. Stir in water and chili sauce. Cook for 10–20 min. over low heat. Serve over rice. Serves 4–6.

Lavonne Boyer
Rush County

HAMBURGER

BACON-WRAPPED BEEF PATTIES

2 lb. ground beef	2 T. Parmesan cheese
1 c. shredded cheddar cheese	2 T. Worcestershire sauce
⅔ c. onion, chopped	1 t. salt
¼ c. ketchup	¼ t. pepper
2 eggs	12 strips bacon

Combine ground beef, cheddar cheese, onion, ketchup, Parmesan cheese, Worcestershire sauce, salt, pepper, and eggs. Mix well. Divide mixture in half. Shape each half into an 11″ roll. Place 6 strips bacon on waxed paper. Place beef roll on one end of bacon strips. Roll up, using waxed paper as an aid, so that roll is wrapped with bacon. Cut into 6 patties. Secure bacon ends with toothpicks. Place on broiler rack. Repeat with other roll. Broil 7″ from source of heat for 6 min. Turn patties over and broil 3 min.

Note: Whole beef roll can be baked, if you wish. Bake at 375° for 40 min. Serves 6.

Mrs. Lewis W. Lafuse
Rush County

BARBECUED HAMBURGERS

1 c. bread crumbs	pepper
½ c. milk	4 T. Worcester-
1 lb. ground beef	shire sauce
1 medium onion,	2 T. vinegar
minced	¼ c. sugar
¼ c. fat or salad	1 c. catsup or
oil	chili sauce
½ t. salt	

Combine crumbs, meat, and onion. Form into cakes and brown in fat or salad oil. Combine remaining ingredients; pour over meat cakes. Cover; simmer ten min.

Mrs. Cleora Morgan
Brown County

BEEF PINWHEELS

Pinwheels:

1 lb. ground beef	½ t. oregano,
¼ c. chili sauce	crushed
1 t. chili powder	2 T. milk
1 t. prepared	1 egg
mustard	1 t. Worcester-
1 medium onion,	shire sauce
minced	1 t. salt
⅓ c. fine dried	dash of garlic
bread crumbs	powder

Mix together all ingredients.

Mashed Potato Filling:

1½ c. mashed	1 8½-oz. can
potato flakes	peas & carrots,
1 egg	drained

Cook potatoes according to directions on package, reducing liquid by ¼. Remove from heat and beat in egg. Fold in peas and carrots. Cool.

To assemble:

With rolling pin roll pinwheel mixture between two sheets of waxed paper into a rectangle (½″×6″). Spread potato mixture evenly on meat. Roll up like a jelly roll. Wrap in waxed paper and chill several hours or overnight. Cut into 1″ slices and place on cookie sheet. Broil about 4″ from heat for 10 min.; turn; broil 12 min. longer, or until brown. Serve warm with your favorite tomato or spaghetti sauce.

Anna Pine
Vigo County

DILLY BURGERS

1½ lb. ground	salt and pepper
beef	1 can tomato
6 onion slices	soup
⅔ c. dill pickle	2 t. Worcester-
slices	shire sauce

Make 12 thin patties of ground beef. Sprinkle each patty with salt and pepper. Place onion slice on top of each of 6 patties, then evenly distribute dill pickle slices on top of onion slices. Top each with remaining 6 patties; press edges together to seal. Place in baking dish. Combine undiluted tomato soup with Worcestershire sauce and spoon over meat patties. Bake at 375° for 40–45 min. Serves 6.

Brenda Summers
Putnam County

JAPANESE FRIED PIES (*Giyoza*)

1 pkg. Giyozo	5–6 green onions,
shells or Won	finely chopped;
Ton skins	top half, too
1 lb. hamburger	1 t. garlic powder
or ground pork	¼ t. salt
1 medium onion,	¼ t. pepper
finely chopped	Aji-no-moto,
¼–½ c. cabbage,	sprinkle to taste
finely chopped	

Brown meat; drain to taste. Add remaining ingredients to meat and simmer to cook onions and cabbage. Place teaspoon of meat mixture into shell or skin, folding over and sealing shell with water along the edges. Fry Giyoza in 1½″ shortening, browning both sides. Drain on paper towel. Serve hot with hot sauce or soy sauce.

Alda Kemp
Crawford County

Brown ground beef, half of chopped onion, salt, pepper, and garlic. Drain off excess grease. Add beef taco filling, taco sauce, and refried beans (if used). Cook until hot and bubbling. Heat tortillas in a greaseless frying pan or oven at 200°. Put filling in tortillas and fold. Lettuce, cheese, remaining onion, and tomato may be added to tacos as desired. Serves 12.

Mrs. Randall Blair
LaPorte County

SALISBURY STEAK

1 lb. ground meat	1 can mushroom
1 egg	soup
½ t. onion	1 can mushroom
½ t. salt	steak sauce
2 T. catsup	(optional)
1 T. Worcester-	2 T. water
shire sauce	

Combine meat, egg, onion, salt, catsup and Worcestershire sauce. Mix well. Shape into six patties. Roll in flour and brown in hot fat. Place in loaf pan. Add soup, sauce, and water. Bake 45 min. at 300°. Serves 3–6.

Mrs. John Schipper
Whitley County

TACOS

1 dozen flour or	½ t. garlic salt
corn tortillas	½ head lettuce,
1½ lbs. ground	shredded
beef	8 oz. sharp
1 large onion,	cheddar cheese,
chopped	shredded
1 can beef taco	1 can refried
filling	beans
1 can taco sauce	(optional)
½ t. salt	1 tomato,
½ t. pepper	chopped

UPPER MICHIGAN PASTIES

Crust:	3 c. potatoes,
3 c. flour	diced
pinch of salt	½ c. carrot or
⅓ c. shortening	rutabaga, finely
or lard	grated
⅓ c. water	½ c. onion,
Filling:	chopped
1 lb. ground	½ t. salt
chuck or beef	dash of pepper
½ lb. ground	1 T. butter
pork	

Mix together flour and salt; cut in shortening. Gradually mix in water. Pat mixture together to form a ball. Divide into 5 or 6 portions. Roll each dough ball out to the size of a salad plate (about 8″ in diameter). Set aside while making filling. Mix together meat, potatoes, carrots, and onion. Add salt and pepper. Place about 1 c. of mixture on half of each rolled crust. Top with pat of butter. Fold crust over and seal edges with tines of a fork. Bake at 475° for 20 min.; reduce heat to 375° for 30 min. more. Pasties may be served as a main meal or packed for lunch boxes.

Patricia Marshall
Morgan County

HAMBURGER CASSEROLES

BEEF AND CABBAGE CASSEROLE

1 medium onion, chopped	⅛ t. pepper
3 T. butter	6 c. cabbage, coarsely
¾ lb. ground chuck	shredded
¾ t. salt	10½ oz. can tomato soup

Sauté onion in butter; add ground chuck, salt, and pepper. Heat through; do not brown. In 2-qt. baking dish, spread 3 c. of cabbage. Cover with meat mixture, top with 3 more c. of cabbage. Pour soup over top. Bake at 350° for 1 hr. Serves 4–5.

Mrs. Ann Neel
Floyd County

CALORIE CONSCIOUS CASSEROLE

1 lb. ground beef	1 can French-
1 small onion, finely chopped	style green beans
1 green pepper, finely chopped	1 can bean sprouts
1 c. celery, finely chopped	soy sauce to taste

Brown hamburger, onion, pepper, and celery. Add green beans and bean sprouts. Add soy sauce to taste. Stir together. Bake in casserole at 350° for 1 hr.

Esther Swift
Steuben County

CHINESE HAMBURGER CASSEROLE
(With Mixed Vegetables)

½ lb. ground beef	1 can mixed vegetables, drain and reserve liquid
1 onion, chopped	
salt and pepper	
1 can cream of mushroom soup	½ c. liquid from vegetables

celery, if desired | ¼ c. Chinese
1 T. soy sauce | noodles

Brown hamburger and onion; salt and pepper; cook and pour off fat. Mix rest of ingredients and add to hamburger. Bake 25 min. at 350°. Top with additional noodles; bake 5 min. more.

Louise Richey
Scott County

CROWN CASSEROLE

1 lb. ground beef	1 pkg. brown
1 pkg. frozen mixed vegetables	gravy mix
	dash of salt
	dash of garlic
⅓ c. green pepper, chopped	powder
	1 can biscuits
1¼ c. hot water	⅓ c. mayonnaise

Brown beef in skillet over medium heat, stirring frequently; drain fat. Add next 6 ingredients; bring to a boil. Remove from heat; stir in 1½-qt. casserole. Flatten biscuits slightly, arrange overlapping around edge of casserole. Brush biscuits with additional mayonnaise; bake at 425° for 15 min., or until heated and the biscuits are browned. Serves 4–6.

Nyla Willis
Pike County

DINNER IN A DISH

3 ears fresh corn, cut from cobs	1 lb. hamburger
	onion salt
6 large tomatoes, peeled and sliced	salt
	pepper

Brown hamburger in skillet and pour off grease. Place hamburger in 1½-qt. casserole and cover with corn and tomatoes. Season to taste. Bake at 350° for 30–40 min. Serves 6–8.

Note: Frozen corn or drained canned corn and canned tomatoes with liquid may be used.

Mrs. W. H. Frick
Marion County

ENCHILADA SQUARES

1 lb. ground beef	1 envelope enchi-
¼ c. onion,	lada sauce mix
chopped	⅓ c. pitted ripe
4 eggs	olives, sliced
1 5½-oz. can	2 c. corn chips
evaporated	1 c. shredded
milk	natural cheddar
1 8-oz. can	cheese
tomato sauce	

Cook ground beef and onion in skillet until beef is browned and onion is tender. Drain off excess fat. Spread beef in bottom of 10×6×1½″ baking dish. Beat together eggs, milk, tomato sauce, and enchilada sauce mix. Pour over meat layer. Sprinkle with olives and top with corn chips. Bake uncovered at 350° for 20–25 min. or until firm in center. Sprinkle with cheese and return to oven for 3–5 min.

Wanda Mason
Putnam County

GREEN BEAN, HAMBURGER, AND CHEESE CASSEROLE

1 16-oz. can cut	2 eggs, slightly
green beans,	beaten
drained	1½ c. cream-style
1½ lbs. ground	cottage cheese
beef	with chives
1 8-oz. can (1 c.)	¼ c. grated Par-
tomato sauce	mesan cheese
½ t. garlic salt	2 T. pitted ripe
⅛ t. cinnamon	olives, sliced

Place green beans in 1½-qt. casserole. In medium skillet, brown ground beef; drain off excess fat. Stir in tomato sauce, garlic salt, and cinnamon. Spread over green beans. Combine eggs and cottage cheese. Spread over meat mixture. Sprinkle with Parmesan cheese. Bake at 350° for 30 min. Garnish with olive slices. Serves 6.

Mrs. Carl Smith
Allen County

HAMBURGER CASSEROLE
(With Tomatoes)

2 lb. ground beef	1 t. chili powder
½ c. onion,	2 t. salt
chopped	½ lb. pasteurized
2 8-oz. cans	cheese
tomatoes	1 green pep-
2 6-oz. cans	per, chopped
tomato paste	

Brown meat; drain off excess fat. Add onion; cook until tender. Blend in tomatoes, tomato paste, chili powder, green pepper, and salt. Layer meat mixture and half of cheese in 2-qt. casserole. Bake at 350° 15–20 min. Top with remaining cheese. Return to oven until melted. Serves 8.

Nancy Schuman
Wabash County

HAMBURGER CORN-PONE PIE

1 lb. ground beef	1 c. canned
½ c. onion,	tomatoes
chopped	1 c. canned kid-
1 T. shortening	ney beans,
2 t. chili powder	drained
¾ t. salt	1 c. corn bread
1 t. Worcester-	batter
shire sauce	

Brown meat and chopped onion in melted shortening in electric skillet. Add seasonings and tomatoes. Cover and simmer over low heat for 15 min.; then add kidney beans. Top with corn bread batter, spreading with wet knife. Cook for about 20 min., or until corn bread is done. Serves 6.

Possible substitutions: tomato paste and water for tomatoes; chili beans for kidney beans and chili powder.

Mrs. Robert S. Perkins
Putnam County

HAMBURGER-LIMA BEAN BAKE

1 c. dry lima beans	¼ c. flour
5 c. water	1 T. salt
1 c. onions, sliced	¼ t. pepper
1 lb. hamburger	1 c. celery leaves, chopped
3 T. fat	

Soak beans overnight in water. *Do not drain.* Brown onions and meat in fat. Add flour, salt, and pepper. Mix thoroughly. Add beans and soaking water and celery. Cover and simmer, adding water when needed, for 1 hr., or until beans are tender. Top with cornbread. Bake at 425° for 35 min., or until done.

Cornbread:

½ c. sifted flour	1 t. salt
¾ c. corn meal	2 T. shortening
½ t. soda	1 egg, beaten
½ t. baking powder	1 c. buttermilk

Sift dry ingredients. Cut in shortening. Add egg and buttermilk. Stir only until mixed. Pour over beans before baking.

Mrs. Stella Burge
Jennings County

HAMBURGER QUICHE

1 unbaked 9″ pastry shell	½ lb. ground beef
½ c. mayonnaise	1½ c. (½ lb.) cheddar or Swiss cheese, chopped
½ c. milk	
2 eggs	
1 T. cornstarch	
⅓ c. green onion, sliced	dash of pepper

Brown meat in skillet over medium heat. Drain fat and set aside. Blend next 4 ingredients until smooth. Stir in meat, cheese, onion, and pepper. Turn into pastry shell. Bake at 350° for 35 to 40 min., or until golden brown on top and knife inserted in center comes out clean. Serves 6–8.

Mrs. Norma G. Naegele
Floyd County

HOT TAMALES

1½ lb. ground beef	2 T. chili powder
3 medium onions, chopped	½ t. red pepper
	1 c. mangoes or olives, chopped
1 c. oil	1 can whole kernel corn
1 No. 2 can tomatoes	1 c. sweet milk
1 T. salt	2 c. cornmeal

Cook hamburger and onions in oil until meat is done. Add tomatoes, salt, chili powder, red pepper, and mangoes or olives. Cook about 5 min. Add corn, milk, and cornmeal. Mix well and put in 9×13″ pan. Bake for 45 min. in a slow oven. Serves 12–16.

Glenda Chestnut
Monroe County

PICADILLO

2 T. bacon drippings or cooking oil	1½ c. onions, chopped
1½ t. salt	2 cloves garlic, minced

2 lb. lean ground beef
½ t. pepper
¼ t. chili powder
⅓ c. Chablis or any dry white wine
½ c. raisins
1 c. tomato sauce
½ c. pimiento-stuffed olives
½ c. blanched, slivered almonds
¼ c. capers
fluffy cooked rice

Heat oil or bacon drippings in large skillet and sauté onions and garlic until golden brown. Add meat and crumble. Cook until browned. Add salt, pepper, tomato sauce, wine, raisins, and chili sauce. Cover; simmer over low heat, stirring frequently for 15 min. Uncover, simmer 10 min. more, stirring occasionally. Add olives and almonds; simmer 5 min. longer. Add capers just before serving with or over rice.

Mrs. Mahalia Nunez
Jennings County

QUICK AND EASY BEEF STROGANOFF

1 lb. ground beef
½ c. onion, finely chopped
2 T. butter
2 T. flour
1 t. salt
⅛ t. pepper
2 T. parsley, minced
1⅓ c. canned mushroom pieces, drained
1 10½-oz. can cream of chicken soup
1 c. sour cream
8 oz. pkg. chow mein noodles

Sauté ground beef and onion in butter in skillet until brown and tender. Add flour, seasonings, and mushrooms. Cook 5 min. Add soup; simmer uncovered 10 min. Stir in sour cream. Serve over warm chow mein noodles. Garnish with parsley. Serves 4–6.

Mrs. Charles Zila
LaPorte County

HAMBURGER CASSEROLES WITH PASTA

CALIFORNIA CASSEROLE

¾ c. onion, chopped
¾ c. green pepper, chopped
2 lb. lean ground beef
1 can cream style corn
1 8-oz. can tomato sauce
1 can tomato soup
1 4-oz. can pitted ripe olives, sliced
1 4-oz. can pimiento, diced
1½ t. salt
½ t. chili powder
⅛ t. pepper
⅛ t. dry mustard
1 8-oz. pkg. medium noodles, cooked as directed on pkg.
1 c. cheddar cheese, grated

Sauté onion, green pepper, and ground beef. Add corn, tomato sauce, tomato soup, ripe olives, and pimiento. Season with salt, chili powder, pepper, and dry mustard. Layer cooked noodles and meat sauce in 9×13″ casserole or 2-qt. (or larger) round casserole. Sprinkle with grated cheese. Bake at 350° for 45 min. Serves 8–10.

Kay Wegener
Marion County

CRAZY CASSEROLE

1 lb. ground beef
1 onion, chopped
1 5-oz. bottle soy sauce
1 medium head cabbage, chopped small
1 4-oz. can of mushrooms
1 small can bean sprouts
1 7-oz. package spaghetti

Brown meat and onions in skillet. Turn heat low and add ⅓ of soy sauce. Add cabbage and simmer for 5 min. Add mushrooms, bean sprouts, and ⅓ of soy sauce. Simmer 5 min. more; add rest of soy sauce. Add cooked spaghetti; cover and simmer a few more min. Serves 6.

Esther Tibbetts
Clay County

DAD'S SPECIAL CASSEROLE

1 lb. ground beef	¼ t. pepper
½ c. onion, chopped	¼ t. thyme
	4 oz. (2 c.)
1 can cream of mushroom soup	noodles, cooked
	2 c. (8 oz.)
½ c. milk	shredded sharp
½ t. salt	cheddar cheese

Brown meat. Add onion; cook until tender. Stir in soup, milk, and seasonings. Layer half of noodles, meat sauce, and cheese in 1½-qt. casserole. Repeat layers of noodles and meat sauce. Bake at 350° for 20 min. Sprinkle with remaining cheese; return to oven until cheese melts.

Mrs. DeWayne Heagy
Miami County

"FOR THE CROWD" CASSEROLE

1½ lb. ground beef	1 can cream of mushroom soup, not diluted
1 c. onion, chopped	
¼ c. pimiento, chopped	1 c. sour cream
	½ t. Accent
1 12-oz. can whole kernel corn, drained	¾ t. salt
	¼ t. pepper
	3 c. medium noodles, cooked
1 can cream of chicken soup, not diluted	1 c. buttered soft bread crumbs

Brown meat; add onion and cook until tender but not brown. Add next 8 ingredi-

ents; mix well. Stir in noodles. Pour into 2-qt. casserole dish. Sprinkle crumbs over top. Bake in moderate oven (350°) for 30 minutes. Serves 8–10.

Jeannie Johnson
Monroe County

GROUND BEEF CASSEROLE

1½ lb. ground beef	1 can tomato soup
	1 can mixed vegetables
1 t. salt	
½ c. onion, diced	1 can vegetable soup
1 c. celery, diced	
1 pkg. noodles	1 T. soy sauce

Brown ground beef, onion, and salt in skillet. Cook celery and noodles together and drain. Combine all ingredients together in casserole. Bake at 350° for 30 min. Serves 8–10.

Marily Seib
Posey County

GROUND BEEF NOODLE SCALLOP

8 oz. fine noodles	1½ t. salt
2 lb. hamburger	pepper as desired
2 c. onions, chopped	¼ c. soy sauce
	1 t. Worcestershire sauce
1 4-oz. can mushrooms, drained	8 oz. shredded cheese
1 10¾-oz. can cream of chicken soup	1 8-oz. can chow mein noodles
1¼ c. milk	slivered almonds

Cook, wash, and drain noodles and put in a large, flat greased baking pan. Fry hamburger and onions together. Drain off excess fat and place on noodles. Mix drained mushrooms, chicken soup, milk, salt, pepper, soy sauce, and Worcestershire sauce. Stir and pour over hamburger-noodle layer. Sprinkle shredded cheese over this. Put chow mein noodles over the cheese. Top with slivered almonds. Bake 20–30 min. at 350°. Serves 8–10.

Pearl Baugher
Kosciusko County

GROUND BEEF IN SOUR CREAM

1 c. chopped onion	⅔ c. broiled sliced mush-
1 lb. ground beef	rooms
3 c. tomato juice	2 T. fat
1½ t. celery salt	3 c. medium
2 t. Worcester-	noodles
shire sauce	1 c. dairy sour
1 t. salt	cream
dash of pepper	

Cook onion in hot fat until tender but not brown. Add beef; brown lightly. Place noodles in layer over meat. Combine tomato juice and seasonings; pour over noodles. Bring to boiling; cover and simmer over low heat 30 min. Stir in sour cream and mushrooms; heat just through. Season to taste. Serves 6.

Deborah Peterson
Randolph County

(1) HAMBURGER CASSEROLE
(With Noodles)

1 lb. ground beef	½ t. onion salt
½ lb. Longhorn Colby cheese	2 c. dry noodles
1 c. celery, chopped	1 No. 2 can tomatoes
	¼ can water

Brown beef; salt and pepper to taste. Layer cheese over beef. Layer other ingredients in order. Cook on high until steaming. Cover; reduce heat to low for 30 min. Serves 6.

Sarah Jane Collett
Brown County

(2) HAMBURGER CASSEROLE
(With Noodles)

1½ lb. hamburger	1 c. sour cream
1 c. onion, chopped	½ c. pimiento or mango, chopped
1 can corn, drained	¾ t. salt
1 can cream of chicken soup	½ t. pepper
	6 oz. noodles
	½ stick butter
1 can cream of mushroom soup	1½ c. bread crumbs

Cook noodles and drain. Brown hamburger and onion. Add corn, soups, sour cream, pimiento or mango, salt, and pepper and mix well. Add noodles to hamburger mixture. Put in 2½-qt. casserole. Melt butter and mix well with bread crumbs. Put on top of casserole. Bake at 350° for 45 min. Serves 6–8.

Mrs. Ruth Brouwer
Tippecanoe County

MAKE-AHEAD CASSEROLE

1 lb. ground beef	1 c. sour cream
1 T. margarine	¼ c. fresh parsley, chopped
¼ c. onion, minced	1 c. sliced, cooked carrots
2 8-oz. cans tomato sauce	8-oz. medium noodles, cooked and drained
1 t. salt	
¼ t. pepper	
1 c. cream-style cottage cheese	1 c. shredded cheddar cheese

Brown beef in melted margarine in skillet. When meat begins to turn color, add onion. Sauté until meat is well browned. Stir in tomato sauce, salt, and pepper. Simmer uncovered for 5 min. Combine sour cream, cottage cheese, parsley, and carrots. Add to cooked noodles; mix well. Alternate layers of the meat mixture and cottage cheese mixture in greased 3-qt. casserole, beginning and ending with noodles. Top with cheddar cheese. Bake at 350° for 30 min., or until hot. If frozen, heat covered at 400° for 1 hr., or until bubbly. Serves 6–8.

Mrs. Lewis W. Lafuse
Rush County

MEXICALI MACARONI

½ lb. ground beef	½ c. green pepper, chopped
1½ c. shredded American cheese	¼–½ c. onion, chopped
1 8-oz. can stewed tomatoes, broken in small pieces	1 t. Worcestershire sauce
2 small hot finger peppers, seeded and chopped	½ c. mayonnaise
	½ lb. macaroni, cooked and drained
	½ c. tortilla chips, crumbled

In a large skillet, brown ground beef; stir in next 6 ingredients. Heat over medium heat, stirring occasionally, 10 min., or until cheese melts. Stir in mayonnaise; toss with macaroni. Turn into greased 1½-qt. casserole; top with tortilla chips. Bake at 350° for 10 min., or until warm. Serves 6.

Mary Crisler
Monroe County

PIZZA CASSEROLE

1 lb. hamburger	1 t. oregano
1½ c. macaroni	2 cloves garlic
1 8-oz. tomato sauce	mozzarella cheese
½ c. onion, chopped	pepperoni
	mushrooms
	peppers

Brown hamburger; cook macaroni. Combine hamburger, macaroni, and sauce. Put in 13×9″ baking dish. Top with cheese and other ingredients. Bake at 350° until cheese is melted. Serves 6.

Mrs. Dave Fox
Adams County

ROMAN HOLIDAY BAKE

1 lb. ground beef	1 can tomato soup
½ lb. hot Italian sausage, cut in ½″ slices	1 c. water
	4 c. wide noodles, cooked
2 t. oregano	4 slices cheddar cheese, cut in half diagonally
1 can cheddar cheese soup	

In skillet, brown beef and cook sausage and onion with oregano until done; stir to separate meat. Pour fat off. Add soups and water. Chill overnight. In a separate container, chill cooked noodles overnight. Combine meat mixture and noodles; pour into 2½-qt. shallow baking dish. Cover; place in cold oven. Bake at 400° for 40 min., or until hot; stir. Top with cheese; bake until cheese melts. Serves 6.

Cyndie McKee
Dearborn County

SKILLET MARZETTI

1 lb. hamburger	2 t. salt
1 qt. tomato juice	1 4-oz. can mushrooms
¼ t. pepper	¼ lb. Velveeta cheese or ¼ lb. cheddar cheese, diced
8 oz. broad noodles	
1 medium onion, chopped	

Cook and brown hamburger and onion together, draining off excess fat. Add tomato juice, salt, and pepper and cook for 30 min. Add mushrooms and noodles. Cover and cook for 20 min. Just before serving add the cheese and keep warm until it melts. Serves 6.

Mrs. Jack Haisley
Delaware County

SPAGHETTI CASSEROLE

1 lb. spaghetti, cooked	1 large can mushrooms or frozen mush- rooms
1 lb. ground beef	
½ lb. sausage	
1 onion, chopped	1 can cream-style corn
1 bell pepper, chopped	
1 large can tomatoes	2 cans pitted ripe olives
1 pkg. frozen peas	garlic salt
	grated cheese

Brown meat, onion, and bell pepper. Add cooked spaghetti and rest of vegetables and mix. Season with garlic salt. Simmer for 15 min. Bake at 350° for 45 min. with grated cheese on top.

Catherine Anderson
Whitley County

HAMBURGER CASSEROLES WITH POTATOES

CINDER LANE'S CASSEROLE

1 lb. ground chuck	Tater Tots
1 can peas, drained	1 small onion, chopped
	salt to taste
1 can cream of mushroom soup	pepper to taste
	garlic salt to taste

Put onion, salt, pepper, and garlic salt in ground chuck. Line casserole with meat, going up the sides a little. Put peas in the center and pour the mushroom soup over the top. Cover with Tater Tots. Bake *uncovered* for 1 hr. at 350°. Serves 4–6.

Mrs. Howard White
LaPorte County

HAMBURGER CASSEROLE— GERMAN STYLE

4 medium potatoes	1–1½ c. tomatoes
	oregano
1 medium onion	salt and pepper
1 lb. hamburger	

Slice potatoes and place in bottom of medium casserole. Slice onion thin and put on top of potatoes. Shape hamburger into patties and place on top. Salt and pepper to taste. Pour tomatoes over hamburger and add a dash of oregano. Bake at 350° for 2 hr. Serves 6.

Clara Rogers
Switzerland County

HAMBURGER PIE

1 medium onion, chopped	1 can tomato soup
1 lb. ground beef	potato fluff topping
¾ t. salt	
dash of pepper	5 medium pota- toes, cooked
2 c. green beans or mixed vege- tables, cooked	½ c. warm milk
	1 egg

Cook onion in small amount of fat. Add meat and seasonings. Brown lightly. Add vegetables and soup. Put in casserole. Whip potatoes with milk and eggs. Drop potatoes in mounds over meat mixture. Bake at 350° for 25–30 min.

Mrs. Clifford Baker
Wabash County

LAZY LAYER OVEN MEAL

2 c. raw potatoes, diced	1 c. green pepper, finely chopped
2 c. celery, chopped	1 c. raw onions, sliced
2 c. hamburger, uncooked	2 c. canned tomatoes

salt and pepper   12 soda crackers,
1 T. Worcester-   crumbed
   shire sauce

Place ingredients in 2½-qt. baking dish in order given. Sprinkle each layer with salt and pepper. Sprinkle top with cracker crumbs. Bake at 375° for 1½ hr. Serves 6.

Mrs. Sandra Shelton
Jefferson County

ONE DISH MEAL
1 lb. ground beef   ½ c. rice,
2 c. potatoes,   uncooked
   diced   2 c. canned
¾ c. onion, diced   tomatoes
1 c. celery, diced   salt and pepper
1 No. 303 can
   kidney beans

Arrange half of first 5 ingredients in layers in greased 3-qt. casserole. Add rice and rest of first five ingredients. Pour tomatoes on top. Cover and bake at 350° for 2 hr.

Norma Wasson
Randolph County

POTATO AND MEAT SCALLOP
¾ lb. ground   1 T. butter or
   beef   margarine
1 t. onion,   1½ c. milk
   chopped   2 c. raw potatoes,
1½ t. salt   thinly sliced
1 T. flour

Brown the beef and onion; add salt. Melt the fat; blend in flour. Add the milk; cook until thick. Stir constantly. Place alternate layers of sliced potatoes, beef, and sauce in a greased baking pan. Cover and bake at 350° for 50–60 min. If desired remove cover and brown in broiler about 5 min. Serves 4.

Variation: Use 2 c. sliced raw ham in place of the beef. Reduce salt to ½ t. It is not necessary to brown the ham.

Uva Lesley
Whitley County

HAMBURGER CASSEROLES WITH RICE

BEEF-RICE CASSEROLE
1 lb. ground beef   1 10½-oz. can
¼ c. celery, diced   chicken-rice
¼ c. mushrooms,   soup
   sliced   1 10½-oz. can
1 c. onion, diced   cream of celery
1 T. vegetable oil   soup
½ t. salt   2 c. water
¼ t. pepper   fresh parsley for
½ c. uncooked   garnish
   rice

Brown beef and sauté celery, mushrooms, and onion in oil in a large skillet. Pour off excess fat. Season with salt and pepper. Stir rice and soups into mixture and blend in water. Pour into 11½×7½×1½" baking dish and bake 1 hr. and 15 min., or until rice is thoroughly cooked. Stir occasionally during baking. Garnish with parsley. Serves 6.

Dorothy Langenbahn
Pulaski County

BUSY-DAY CASSEROLE
1 lb. hamburger   1 c. celery, diced
1 small onion,   2 cans water
   diced   3 t. soy sauce
2 cans cream of   1 c. uncooked
   chicken, celery,   rice
   or mushroom   1 t. Worcester-
   soup   shire sauce

Brown together hamburger, celery, and onion. Mix browned mixture with soup and water. Add soy sauce, rice, and Worcestershire sauce. Stir well. Bake at 350° in two 1-qt. casseroles for 1 hr. Crumb topping may be added if desired. Serves 12.

Mrs. Merrill Kirkpatrick
Kosciusko County

CABBAGE ROLLS

1 c. cooked rice	2½ t. salt
1 lb. ground beef	1½ t. chili
½ lb. ground	powder
pork	1 t. sugar
¾ c. onion,	2 T. catsup
chopped	1 8-oz. can
2 garlic cloves,	tomato sauce
chopped, or ¼	1 head cabbage
t. garlic powder	1 c. cabbage
½ t. pepper	liquid

Prepare cabbage leaves by removing heart of leaves. Preboil leaves only until pliable. Set aside. Mix rice with half of tomato sauce and all other ingredients except cabbage, rest of tomato sauce, and liquid. Mix well. Spoon about 1 T. of mixture into center of a cabbage leaf. Fold base of leaf over mixture. Fold sides. Place in greased casserole dish. Pour rest of tomato sauce over rolls, then liquid. Cover and bake at 350° for one hr.; uncover and bake ½ hr. longer. Serves 6.

Marsha Paris
Shelby County

CHINESE HAMBURGER CASSEROLE
(With Rice)

1 lb. ground beef	½ c. celery,
2 small onions,	chopped
chopped	1 can cream of
4 T. soy sauce	chicken soup

½ c. uncooked	1 can chow mein
rice	noodles
1 c. water	

Brown ground beef, onions, and celery; drain off fat. Combine soup, rice, and water; mix well with browned beef mixture. Bake 45 min. at 350°. Remove from oven; add chow mein noodles to top of casserole. Bake 15 min. longer.

Mrs. Lilburn W. McEuen
Vanderburgh County

HAMBURGER AND RICE CASSEROLE

1 lb. hamburger	1½ c. boiling
½ c. onion,	water
chopped	1 pint tomato
½ c. celery,	juice
sliced	1 T. sugar
½ t. salt	½ t. salt
1 c. rice	dash of pepper

Fry hamburger, onion, celery, and salt until meat loses red color; drain off fat. Simmer rice in boiling water 10 to 12 min.; rice will not be tender. Combine tomato juice, sugar, salt, and pepper and heat to near boiling. Grease baking dish with 1 T. oleomargarine. Add ½ c. rice; add meat mixture; add balance of rice. Pour tomato juice over all. Bake at 350° about 45 min. Serves 6.

Edna Winters
Pulaski County

HAMBURGER-ZUCCHINI
CASSEROLE

1 zucchini, sliced	2 c. cooked rice
1 large onion,	1 or 2 lb.
sliced	hamburger
1 large tomato,	1 or 2 t. salt
sliced, or 1 can	1 can cream of
tomato sauce	mushroom soup

Salt hamburger (1 t. to 1 lb.). Scramble and drain. Place layer of zucchini in bottom of skillet. Place half of onion slices, half of tomato slices, 1 c. cooked rice, and half of hamburger over zucchini. Pour half can of soup over top. Make layers again, starting with zucchini. Cook on top of stove about 1 hr. Stir through now and then so it will not stick. Serves 6.

Lola Mae Taylor
Greene County

TEXAS HASH

1 lb. ground beef	2 c. (1 can)
3 large onions,	tomatoes
sliced	1 t. chili powder
1 large green	1 t. salt
pepper, minced	⅛ t. pepper
1 c. uncooked rice	

Fry ground beef, onions, green pepper until mixture falls apart. Stir in rest of ingredients. Pour into 2-qt. casserole. Cover and bake at 350° for 1 hr. Remove cover last 15 min. Serves 6–8.

Alma Woody
Parke County

MEATBALLS

ITALIAN MEATBALLS IN TANGY SAUCE

1 lb. ground beef	1 egg
1 envelope onion	½ c. croutons
soup mix	

Mix together well. Form into small balls and brown.

Sauce:

1 bottle tangy	1 jar apple jelly
catsup	

Mix sauce in pan, add browned meatballs and simmer 20 min. Serves 4.

Mrs. Tom Lanphier
Marshall County

MEATBALL CASSEROLE

1 lb. ground beef	½ c. mango,
½ c. fresh bread	chopped
crumbs	¼ c. onion,
1 egg	chopped
1 t. salt	½ lb. cheese,
all-purpose oil	cubed
2 c. water	1 c. uncooked
2 large carrots,	rice
quartered	

Combine meat, bread crumbs, egg and salt; mix lightly. Shape into 18 meatballs; brown in small amount of oil on all sides in large skillet. Drain; add water, rice, carrots, mango, and onion. Cover and simmer 25 min. Add cheese; heat until cheese melts. Serves 4–6.

Mrs. Jack Butler
Martin County

MEATBALLS WITH PEACHES

¾ c. quick oats	¼ c. onion,
1½ lb. ham-	chopped
burger	¼ c. catsup
1 c. Milnot or	1 1-lb. can peach
milk	halves, drained
1½ t. salt	brown sugar
¼ t. pepper	vinegar

Mix first 7 ingredients and form into 6 balls. Put in 13×9″ loaf pan and bake at 350° for 45 min. Arrange peach halves around meatballs. On each peach put 1 T. brown sugar and ½ t. vinegar. Place back in oven and bake 15 min. longer. Serves 6.

Nancy Beghtel
St. Joseph County

NORWEGIAN MEATBALLS

1 lb. pork	½ c. onion,
1½ lb. round	finely cut
steak	1 egg

1 T. cornstarch   ¼ t. pepper
1 t. salt   3⅓ c. cream
¼ t. nutmeg   2 T. flour

Have butcher grind meats together. Mix in egg, onion, cornstarch, and seasonings. Mix in ⅓ c. cream and shape into small balls, about the size of a blue plum. Brown these carefully in a skillet in chicken fat or butter. Remove balls from skillet and stir flour into drippings. Stir rapidly to avoid burning or lumping. Add 3 c. of thin cream. Pour this over meatballs in a casserole and bake covered for 1½ hr. at 350°. Serves 12.

Dorothy Kelley
Hendricks County

ONE DISH MEAL

1 lb. ground   4 large tomatoes,
  chuck   chopped
1 egg   2 large sweet
salt and pepper   onions, cut in
4 large green pep-   rings
  pers, cut in ½″ ¼ scant c. olive
  strips   oil

Add egg and seasoning to ground chuck and make small meatballs the size of a teaspoon. Sauté in butter and simmer until done. Cook peppers, onions, and tomatoes until peppers are glassy looking. Add meatballs to this mixture. Add olive oil. Let simmer until flavors blend. May be served over rice or plain spaghetti. Serves 4–6.

Mrs. Virgie LeRoy
LaPorte County

PORCUPINE MEATBALLS

1 lb. hamburger   1 egg, beaten
½ c. raw rice   few dashes of
1 t. salt   Worcestershire
½ t. pepper   sauce
1 onion, chopped

Sauce:
1 small can   2 cans water
  tomato sauce   ¼ c. vinegar
  or paste   3 T. sugar

Mix together first 7 ingredients and make into small balls. Put in baking dish. Mix sauce. Pour over meatballs. Bake in moderate oven (375°) for 30–40 min. Serves 4–6.

Mrs. Homer Allbright
Orange County

SOUR CREAM PORCUPINES

1½ lb. ground   ⅓ c. precooked
  beef   or instant (un-
1 t. paprika   cooked) rice
1 t. salt   ¼ c. onion, diced
2 T. hot   ½ c. water
  shortening   1 beef bouillon
1 can mushroom   cube
  soup   1 t. Worcester-
Chinese noodles   shire sauce

Combine beef with rice, paprika, salt, and onion. Shape into 16–20 balls. Brown balls in hot shortening. Arrange in 1½-qt. casserole or 8″ baking dish. Drain fat. Combine in skillet water, bouillon cube, Worcestershire sauce, and soup. Stir until well blended and hot. Stir in the sour cream and pour mixture over meatballs. Cover and refrigerate or bake, uncovered, in moderate oven (350°) for 45 min. Pour Chinese noodles over top for last 10 min. of baking. Serves 6.

Alberta L. Dickerson
Fountain County

SAUERKRAUT AND MEATBALLS (1)

1 c. sauerkraut   1 onion, sliced
1 T. brown sugar   1 c. quick rice
½ t. caraway seed salt and pepper
1-lb. ground   1 c. tomato juice
  round

Place sauerkraut, sugar, and caraway seed in buttered casserole or skillet. Place onion slices over kraut. Mix meat, rice, and seasoning. Makes about 16 meatballs. Place on top of onion slices. Pour tomato juice over all, cover, and bake at 350° for 1 hr. Remove cover and bake ½ hr. after turning meatballs. Check after 15 min. Serves 6.

Harriet Teboe
Hamilton County

SAUERKRAUT AND MEATBALLS (2)

1 medium can sauerkraut, drained	½ t. pepper
	Sauce:
1 egg	¼ c. brown sugar
1 lb. hamburger	1 c. catsup
¼ c. bread crumbs	1 c. water
½ t. salt	1 c. gingersnap cookies, rolled

Mix hamburger, egg, bread crumbs, salt, and pepper and form meatballs. Brown; remove from pan. Make sauce and bring to boil slowly. Add sauerkraut. Drop in meatballs and cook for 45 min. over low heat, stirring occasionally.

Mrs. H. Dale Mace
Marion County

SWEDISH MEATBALLS

1½ lb. ground beef	½ c. evaporated milk
1½ t. salt	Sauce:
¾ c. bread crumbs	½ c. catsup
½ t. pepper	3 T. Worcestershire sauce
1 or 2 eggs	1 t. garlic salt
1½ T. Worcestershire sauce	½ t. chili powder
⅓ c. onions, chopped	¼ c. water

Mix all ingredients except sauce. Form into balls, using one teaspoon for each. Place on a cookie sheet and brown in the oven 12–15 min. at 400°. Mix sauce; heat and pour over meatballs.

Joyce Burr
Noble County

SWEET-SOUR MEATBALLS

5 slices dry bread, cut in cubes	Sweet-Sour Sauce:
2 lb. ground beef	1 1-lb., 12-oz. can tomatoes (about 3½ c.)
½ c. onion, grated	1 c. brown sugar
½ t. garlic salt	¼ c. vinegar
¼ t. pepper	½ t. salt
1 t. salt	1 T. onion, grated
2 eggs, slightly beaten	10 gingersnaps, crushed

Soak bread cubes in a little cold water until soft. Squeeze out water. Combine with remaining ingredients except Sweet-Sour Sauce. Shape in balls the size of walnuts (1½"). Place on 15½×10½×1" jelly roll pan and bake in very h oven (450°) for 15 to 18 min. (or brown balls in skillet containing a little hot fat). Combine all ingredients for Sweet-Sour Sauce. Cook to boiling. Add baked meatballs and simmer 10 min. Makes 36 meatballs. Serves 8–9.

Rita Carpenter
Pulaski County

MEAT LOAF

MEAT LOAF (1)

3 eggs	1 t. nutmeg
1½ t. salt	pinch of cloves
¼ t. pepper	¼ c. milk
¼ t. dried thyme leaves	1 c. soft white bread crumbs

¼ c. sour cream
1½ lb. ground
  beef
¼ lb. ground
  pork
¼ lb. ground
  veal
2 T. onion, finely
  chopped

2 T. parsley,
  chopped
2 T. celery leaves,
  chopped
1 t. chives,
  chopped
¼ t. garlic, finely
  chopped
6 slices bacon

In a large bowl, beat eggs with salt, pepper, thyme, nutmeg, and cloves until well mixed. Stir in milk, sour cream, and bread crumbs. Let stand 5 min. Add beef, pork, veal, onion, parsley, celery leaves, chives, and garlic; mix lightly until well blended. Shape; place in a loaf pan and put bacon strips over top. Bake 45 min. at 350°. Add chili sauce. Serves 6.

Chili Sauce:

1 bottle chili
  sauce
dry mustard, start
  with 1 t.

brown sugar, start
  with 2 T.

Combine chili sauce, brown sugar, and dry mustard and mix well. Taste to see if enough brown sugar and mustard have been added. Use on top and sides of meat loaf. Bake 30 min. longer brushing several times with sauce.

Mrs. Diane Hunteman
Ripley County

MEAT LOAF (2)

2 lb. ground
  round steak
2 eggs
1½ c. bread
  crumbs
¾ c. ketchup
1 t. Accent

½ c. warm water
1 pkg. onion
  soup mix
3 bacon strips
1 8-oz. can
  tomato sauce

Mix thoroughly first 7 ingredients. Put in loaf pan. Cover with bacon strips. Pour tomato sauce over all. Bake for 1 hr. at 350°. Serves 6.

Kathryn Bucher
Greene County

MEAT LOAF (3)

1 lb. ground beef
1½ t. salt
⅔ c. tomato juice
½ c. oats
¼ c. onion,
  chopped
¼ t. pepper

Topping:
3 T. brown sugar
¼ c. catsup
¼ t. nutmeg
1 t. dry or pre-
  pared mustard

Combine meat loaf ingredients thoroughly and pack firmly in loaf pan. Mix topping ingredients well and pour on top of meat loaf. Bake at 350° for 1 hr.

Bernice Begle
Dubois County

ITALIAN MEAT LOAF

½ c. medium
  cracker crumbs
  (about 11
  crackers)
1½ lb. ground
  beef
1 6-oz. can (⅔ c.)
  tomato paste
2 eggs
½ c. onion, finely
  chopped
¼ c. green pep-
  per, finely
  chopped
¾ t. salt

dash of pepper
Filling:
½ c. medium
  cracker crumbs
1 12-oz. carton
  (1½ c.) small
  curd cottage
  cheese
1 3-oz. can (½ c.)
  chopped mush-
  rooms, drained
1 T. parsley,
  snipped
¼ t. dried ore-
  gano, crushed

In large bowl combine first 8 ingredients. Mix well. Pat half the mixture into bottom of 8×8×2″ baking pan. Combine filling ingredients. Spread mixture evenly over meat in pan. Top with remaining meat mixture. Bake in moderate oven (350°) for 1 hr. Let meat loaf stand 10 min. before serving. Serves 8.

Fran Gehring
Noble County

POTATO MEAT LOAF

3 eggs, beaten	2 lbs. lean ground
2½ t. salt	beef
2½ c. raw pota-	¼ t. pepper
toes, ground	4 slices bacon,
1 small onion,	ground
ground	

Combine eggs with ground beef. Mix well and season with salt and pepper. Combine potatoes, onions, and bacon, then add to beef mixture. Bake at 350° for 1 hr. and 15 min. May be covered with brown gravy before serving.

Pauline Brummett
Morgan County

SICILIAN MEAT ROLL

2 eggs, beaten	2 lb. ground beef
¾ c. soft bread	8 slices boiled
crumbs	ham
½ c. tomato sauce	6 oz. (½ c.)
2 T. parsley	shredded moz-
½ T. oregano	zarella cheese
¼ t. salt	3 slices American
¼ t. pepper	cheese, halved

Mix eggs, bread, tomato sauce, and seasonings. Stir in meat and mix well. Pat meat into a rectangle on waxed paper. Arrange ham on top of meat. Sprinkle Mozzarella cheese on meat; roll. Place roll in a 13× 9×2″ pan. Bake at 350° for 1 hr. and 15 min. Add American cheese halves and bake 5 min. longer.

Ruth Hygema
Kosciusko County

Pork

GINGER-GLAZED PORK ROAST

1 4- or 5-lb.	½ c. apricot jam
smoked pork	¼ c. orange juice
roast	1 T. ginger

Blend together jam, juice, and ginger. Pour over roast. Bake at 350°. After baking 1 hr., brush every 15 min. until done.

Peggy Szeman
Steuben County

ERNIE'S FAVORITE CASSEROLE

2 lb. lean pork,	1 small pkg.
cubed	medium-fine
1 lump of butter	noodles
3 stalks celery,	1 can cream of
chopped fine	chicken soup
1 green pepper,	1 small can
chopped fine	mushrooms
1 can whole	potato chips,
kernel corn	crushed

Cook noodles and drain. Put butter in a pan; add meat, celery, pepper, and mushrooms. Simmer 15–20 min. Place a layer of noodles; then a layer of meat mixture; then a layer of corn in a casserole. Pour chicken soup over all. Sprinkle potato chips on top. Bake 1 hr. in moderate oven.

Jean Martin
Monroe County

KRAUT-PORK PINWHEEL

1 lb. ground pork	1 1-lb. can (2 c.)
½ c. fine dry	sauerkraut,
bread crumbs	drained and
1 egg, slightly	snipped
beaten	¼ c. onion,
1 t. salt	chopped
dash of pepper	5 bacon slices
½ t. Worcester-	
shire sauce	

Combine ground pork, bread crumbs, egg, salt, pepper, and sauce and mix thoroughly. On waxed paper, pat meat mixture to 10×7″ rectangle. Combine sauerkraut and onion and spread evenly over meat. Starting with narrow side, roll up meat jelly-roll fashion. Place in shallow baking dish. Arrange bacon slices across top. Bake at 350° for 40–45 min. Serves 5–6.

Karen Emrich
Allen County

PORK MANDARIN

1½ lb. pork, cut	1 can mandarin
in 1″ cubes	orange sections,
oil for frying	drain and
1 c. chicken broth	reserve liquid
or 1 bouillon	2 T. vinegar
cube dissolved	2 T. corn starch
in 1 c. hot water	1 t. grated ginger
¼ c. corn syrup	root
2 T. soy sauce	onion rings

Brown pork cubes in oil. Add chicken broth or bouillon. Simmer about 1 hour or until tender. Add mandarin orange liquid and remaining ingredients (except onion rings). Cook until mixture thickens. Add orange slices and onion rings just before serving. Serve over cooked rice. Serves 6–8.

Edna B. Hysell
Switzerland County

SCRAPPLE

2 lb. bony fresh	⅔ c. corn meal
pork	1 onion,
2 t. salt	chopped
1 quart boiling	salt and pepper
water	

In deep pan, put pork, salt, and boiling water. Cover and cook until meat drops from bone. Strain broth. Chop meat and add to broth. Stir in corn meal. Add onion. Season with salt and pepper. Simmer 1 hr. Cool. Pack in small loaf pan. Chill. To fry, cut in ¼″ slices, coat with flour, and pan fry until golden brown.

Mrs. Gladys Smith
Ripley County

SUB GUM CHOP SUEY

¼ c. margarine	1 can mixed
or butter	Chinese
2 c. celery, cut	vegetables, well
in 1″ pieces	drained
1 t. salt	
¼ t. pepper	Thickening:
1½ c. hot water	2 T. cold water
1 lb. lean pork,	2 t. soy sauce
cut in bite	1 T. brown gravy
size pieces	sauce
½ c. onion,	1 t. sugar
chopped	2 T. flour or
1 small can sliced	cornstarch
mushrooms,	
drained	

Melt butter in hot skillet. Add meat, stir and sear quickly, without browning. Add onions; fry 5 min. Add celery, salt, pepper, and hot water. Cover and cook 5 min. Add Chinese vegetables and mushrooms; mix thoroughly. Heat to boiling point. Combine thickening ingredients. Add thickening; stir lightly. Cook 1 min. Serve hot on cooked Minute Rice or, if you prefer, on chow mein noodles. Flavor individual servings with soy sauce.

Mrs. Hallas Mullen
Delaware County

SWEET-SOUR PORK (*Subuta*)

1½ lb. pork, cut in cubes
1 T. soy sauce
2 T. corn starch
3 carrots, cubed and boiled until not quite tender
2 large onions, sliced
2 green peppers, cut in ½″ slices
1 pkg. fresh mushrooms
3 stalks celery, sliced

1 15¼-oz. can chunk pineapple, drained
oil for frying, about 3 T.

Sauce:
1 c. pineapple juice
4 T. ketchup
3 T. sugar
2 T. corn starch
½ t. monosodium glutamate
dash of salt

Mix soy sauce with cubed pork and marinate for 10 min. Add 2 T. corn starch and coat thoroughly. Deep fry until crisp and brown. Drain. In large cooking pan, fry vegetables quickly in hot oil until barely cooked. Mix sauce. Add to vegetables. Cook for 5 min. Add pork. Cook until it starts to bubble. Serves 6.

Mrs. David Takamori
Adams County

HAM

BAKED HAM

5 lb. ham
1 small can evaporated milk

¾ c. brown sugar
whole cloves

Place ham in roaster and stick a few cloves in it. Mix milk and sugar together. Pour over ham. Cover roaster and bake at 300° for about 1½ hr. Add more milk for gravy. Serves 20.

Marcia Powders
Greene County

CHARCOAL-GRILLED SUGARED HAM

2 fully cooked center cut smoked ham slices (1″ thick, about 3½ lb.)
1 c. brown sugar, packed
¼ c. lemon juice
⅓ c. horseradish

Score each side of ham ¼″ deep in diamond pattern. Combine brown sugar, lemon juice, and horseradish in small saucepan. Heat to boiling, stirring constantly. Place ham slices on grill 3″ from medium coals. Cook 15 min. on each side, basting frequently with brown sugar mixture. Serves 6–8.

Pauline Dixon
Johnson County

GLAZED HAM AND APPLESAUCE BAKE

5 lb. canned ham
¼ c. honey
1 T. prepared mustard
2 t. lemon juice
1 can cream of celery soup
½ c. applesauce

Score ham; place in roasting pan. Bake at 325° for 1 hr.; pour off fat. Combine honey, mustard, and lemon juice; spread over top of ham. Bake 15 min. more (15 min. per pound or 130° on meat thermometer). Remove to platter. On top of range, in roasting pan, add remaining ingredients to drippings. Heat, stirring now and then. Serve with ham. Serves 8–10.

Mary C. Green
Floyd County

HOLIDAY BAKED HAM

1 fully cooked smoked ham (12–15 lb.)	1 20-oz. can pineapple slices, drained
½ c. honey	Maraschino
1 c. orange marmalade	cherries, drained
½ t. cloves	

Wrap ham completely in long length of aluminum wrap. Line shallow roasting pan with aluminum wrap. Place ham into it and roast at 350° for 3 hr. Remove from oven, turn back foil. In a bowl, mix glaze of honey, marmalade, and cloves. Cover ham with pineapple slices and fasten with toothpicks. Fill center of slices with maraschino cherries. Spoon some glaze over ham. Replace in oven and roast another 20 min. Baste with remaining glaze and roast 20 min. more. Serve on platter garnished with small bunches of frosted, green, red and blue grapes, and holly leaves. Serves 12–14.

Lilly Phillips
Martin County

HAM AND BROCCOLI ROYALE

1 c. uncooked rice	2 onions, chopped fine
2 10-oz. pkg. frozen broccoli spears	1 t. salt
	¼ t. pepper
	3 c. milk
6 T. butter or margarine	1½ lb. (about 4 c.) ham, cubed
2 c. fresh bread crumbs	1 8-oz. pkg. sliced American cheese
3 T. flour	

Cook rice, following directions. Spoon into greased 9×13″ pan. Cook broccoli, drain, and place in a layer over rice. Melt butter in a pan. Measure out 2 T. and sprinkle over crumbs. Set crumbs aside. Stir onions into butter in pan. Sauté until soft. Stir in flour, salt, and pepper. Stir in milk. Continue cooking until thick. Stir in ham. Pour over layers in pan. Place cheese slices over sauce. Sprinkle buttered crumbs over all. Bake 45 min. at 350°.

Barbara Sondgerath
Tippecanoe County

HAM CASSEROLE SUPREME

½ c. milk	¼ t. pepper
1 can condensed cream of mushroom soup	4 oz. wide noodles, cooked and drained
2 t. prepared mustard	2 c. cooked ham, diced
1 t. dehydrated minced green onion	1 c. sour cream
	¼ c. potato chips, crushed

Combine all ingredients except potato chips. Pour into a buttered 2-quart casserole. Top with potato chips. Bake at 350° for 20–25 min. Serves 6.

Mrs. Howard Hensler
St. Joseph County

HAM LOAF

2 lb. ham	Sauce:
1 lb. pork	½ c. chili sauce
2 eggs	1 T. vinegar
2 T. milk	3 T. brown sugar
1 c. rolled oats	1 T. flour
	1 scant t. mustard

Have ham and pork ground together. Stir eggs, milk, and oats into meat mixture. Mix into a loaf and bake at 350° for 1¼ hr. Mix ingredients for sauce. Pour sauce on loaf and bake an additional ½ hr. Serves 12.

Cyndie McKee
Dearborn County

HAM WITH PEACHES

1 or 2" thick ham slice	4–6 peach halves, drained and re-
1 T. dry mustard	serve liquid
4 T. brown sugar	2 sticks cinnamon
⅓ c. wine vinegar	2 whole cloves
	¼ t. ginger

Cut gashes in fat of ham slice every inch or so. Brown on both sides in heavy skillet. Place in shallow baking dish. Make a paste of dry mustard and spread over top of ham. Sprinkle brown sugar on top of mustard. Lay peach halves flat side down. Mix drained liquid from canned peaches, wine vinegar, cinnamon, cloves, and ginger. Simmer 10 minutes; strain. Pour over ham. Bake in slow oven (320°) for 1½ hr.

Charlene Walton
Martin County

HAM AND SWEET POTATO ROLL

¾ lb. ground ham	½ c. cracker crumbs
½ lb. ground pork	¾ c. milk
1 egg	2 c. mashed sweet potatoes

Combine all ingredients except sweet potatoes. Spread on waxed paper to ½" thickness, making a rectangle about 6× 10". Spread with sweet potatoes and roll like a jelly roll. Place in pan and bake about 1 hr. in a moderate oven (350°). Serves 6.

Mrs. Aleda Green
Dearborn County

SMOKED PORK SHOULDER CASSEROLE (*Choucroute al Alsocienne*)

2 1-lb., 11-oz. cans sauerkraut, drained	3 bay leaves
	¼ t. whole peppercorns
1 1-lb. can white potatoes, drained, or fresh potatoes	1 carrot, sliced
	8 juniper berries (or gin)
2 lb. smoked boneless pork shoulder, cut in ¾" crosswise slices	2 T. onion, minced
	1 10½-oz. can condensed consommé
	1 can water
¼ lb. bacon in 1 piece or ½ lb. sliced bacon	1 c. white wine
	4 knockwurst or franks

Drain and rinse sauerkraut; repeat if salty. Place half in 4-qt. casserole. Top with half of potatoes, then half of carrot slices. Arrange half of pork slices on top of carrots. Cover with rest of sauerkraut. Arrange rest of pork, potatoes, and carrots on top of sauerkraut. Place bacon on top. Tuck bay leaves in sauerkraut. Sprinkle onions, peppercorns, and juniper berries over top. Pour undiluted consommé, water, and wine over sauerkraut. Cover casserole tightly with close-fitting lid or foil. Bake 2 hr. at 400°. Remove paper-thin layer of skin of knockwurst or franks (or use franks as is); arrange on top of casserole. Recover and bake ½ hr. longer. Serves 8.

Mrs. Larry Kovaleski
Dubois County

GROUND HAM MEATBALLS

2 lb. ham	Sauce:
2½ lb. lean fresh pork	¾ c. brown sugar, packed
1½ c. fine bread crumbs	⅛ c. vinegar
1 t. salt	1 T. dry mustard
4 eggs, slightly beaten	2 c. crushed pineapple
pepper	2–3 c. apple juice

Grind ham and pork together. Mix with bread crumbs, eggs, salt, and pepper. Shape into balls. Combine ingredients for sauce. Pour over meatballs in shallow baking dish. Bake 1 hr. at 350° for small balls. Bake extra 15 min., if balls are larger.

Peggy Price
Monroe County

HAM BALLS (1)

⅔ c. milk	1 egg
¾ c. dry bread	1⅓ c. cooked
crumbs	ham, ground
½ t. dry mustard	⅓ c. fresh ham,
dash of Worces-	ground
tershire sauce	

Moisten bread crumbs and mustard in milk. Add egg, Worcestershire sauce, and cooked and fresh ham. Mix well and make into small balls (about 2 dozen). Place on cookie sheet and bake at 325° for 25 min. Put on platter or serving dish. Pour hot sauce over balls.

Sauce:

2 T. flour	1 c. sour cream
2 T. drippings	1 t. dill seed
from balls	¼ t. salt

Stir flour into drippings. Add sour cream, dill seed, and salt. Heat, but do not boil. Pour over balls and serve.

Mrs. Olive Sumner
Parke County

HAM BALLS (2)

1 lb. pork	Sauce:
sausage	½ c. water
1 lb. ham	¼ c. vinegar
2 c. soft bread	¼ c. orange juice
crumbs	1½ c. brown
2 eggs	sugar
1 c. milk	1 T. dry mustard
½ t. salt	15 whole cloves

Grind sausage and ham together. Mix with bread crumbs, eggs, milk, and salt. Shape into 24 balls and place in shallow pan. Use a pan large enough to have only one layer of ham balls. Mix ingredients for sauce. Bring to boil and pour sauce over ham balls. Bake at 325° for 1½ hr. Turn and baste after 1 hr. Serves 8–10.

Estelee Clark
Hamilton County

PORK CHOPS

CREOLE PORK CHOPS

6 to 8 pork chops,	1 t. Worcester-
cut 1″ thick	shire sauce
2 T. shortening	1 t. salt
½ c. catsup	¼ t. pepper
½ c. water	1 pkg. medium
1 t. Tabasco sauce	noodles
2 T. brown sugar	

Heat shortening in a skillet large enough for chops and sauce. Add chops and sauté until brown on both sides. Mix other ingredients except noodles and pour over chops. Cover and simmer for 1–1½ hr. Chops should be spoon tender. Cook noodles in salted water, drain; rinse in hot water and drain again. Season with margarine. To serve: Place noodles on large platter and arrange chops in center. Pour sauce over chops and noodles. Serves 4.

Evelyn Vonderschmidt
Monroe County

PORK APPLE BAKE

8 thick pork	Sauce:
chops	½ c. brown
salt and pepper	sugar, packed
8 apple rings	½ c. soy sauce

½ c. apple sauce	3 T. catsup
or juice	½ t. ginger
2 T. cornstarch	

Place chops flat in large pan or cookie sheet with edges. Bake 1 hr. at 350°, turning once. If there is much fat, drain. Combine ingredients of sauce and cook until thickened. Place apple ring slices on each chop and pour sauce over all. Bake for 30 more min. Serves 8.

Mrs. Rex Parker
Putnam County

PORK CHOP CASSEROLE

6 pork chops or	1 large or 2 small
3 pork shoulder	onions, sliced
steaks cut ¾"	1½ c. tomato
thick	juice
flour and salt	¾ t. crushed
2 T. cooking oil	rosemary
6 large potatoes,	¾ t. salt
pared and sliced	¼ t. pepper
3 T. cornstarch	½ c. Parmesan
¾ c. cooking	cheese
sherry	

Season chops and dust with flour. Brown chops in oil on both sides. Place potato slices in 4-quart casserole and top with onion slices. Place chops on top. Combine cornstarch, sherry, tomato juice, rosemary, salt, and pepper; stir until smooth. Pour over mixture in casserole. Cover tightly and bake 45 min. at 400°. Remove from oven and sprinkle with cheese. Bake uncovered 30 min. at 350°. Serves 6.

LaVonne Peterson
Pulaski County

PORK CHOP SKILLET MEAL

| 4 1" thick pork | 4 ¼" thick slices |
| chops | Bermuda onion |

4 T. fat	4 T. uncooked
1 c. diced celery	Minute Rice
4 rings green	3 c. stewed
pepper	tomatoes

Brown chops in fat until well browned on both sides. Place 1 slice of onion and 1 pepper ring on each pork chop. Place 1 T. rice in each ring. Pour tomatoes around meat, add celery. Place cover on skillet. When steam appears, turn to low heat and allow to cook for one hour. Serves 4.

Sara Cantwell
Knox County

PORK CHOPS WITH CRANBERRY SAUCE

8 pork chops	3 T. sugar
1 t. cinnamon	½ c. port wine
¼ t. ground	1 1-lb. can whole
cloves	or jellied cran-
¼ t. nutmeg	berry sauce

Brown pork chops very well on both sides in skillet. Remove to large shallow baking dish. Combine remaining ingredients, except cranberry sauce, and heat until sugar dissolves. Add sauce and heat. Pour over chops and cover baking dish with foil. Bake in moderate oven (350°) about 45 min.

Judy Roemke
Steuben County

PORK CHOPS AND RICE

6 pork chops	1 4-oz. can mush-
2 T. drippings	rooms, drain
1 c. uncooked rice	and reserve
1 pkg. onion	liquid
soup mix	hot water
2 T. pimientos,	
diced	

Brown pork chops in drippings. Spread uncooked rice on bottom of 13×9" pan. Reserve 1 T. of onion soup mix; spread remaining onion soup mix over rice. Spread mushrooms and diced pimientos over rice. Add enough hot water to mushroom liquid to make 3 c. liquid, and pour over rice. Arrange browned pork chops over rice and sprinkle the 1 T. onion soup mix over chops. Cover tightly with foil and bake at 350° for 45 min. to 1 hr. Remove foil and bake about 10 min. more, or until liquid evaporates.

Mrs. Donald C. Rader
Monroe County

STUFFED PORK CHOPS

6 double thick pork loin chops with pockets cut	¼ c. mushrooms, finely sliced
3 T. margarine	½ c. (about 3 oz.) blue cheese, crumbled
1 t. minced onion	¾ c. fine dry
dash of salt	bread crumbs

Melt butter in skillet. Add onions and mushrooms. Cook 5 min. Remove from heat and stir in blue cheese, crumbs, and salt. Stuff pockets in each chop with dressing. Secure with picks. Bake at 325° for 1 hr., or until meat is nicely browned and cooked through.

Mrs. Alice Baker
Jay County

PORK STEAKS

BAKED PORK AND VEGETABLES

4 pork steaks, cut about ¾" thick	½ c. milk
2 T. salad oil	1 10½-oz. can cream of asparagus soup
1 c. green onion, chopped	4 potatoes, sliced

1½ t. seasoned salt	¼ medium head cabbage, shredded
½ t. seasoned pepper	

About 1 hr. and 45 min. before serving: Preheat oven to 350°. In large skillet over medium heat, in hot salad oil, brown pork steaks well on both sides. Meanwhile, in greased 13×9" baking dish, toss well remaining ingredients. Arrange pork steaks on top. Cover dish with foil and bake 1 hr. and 15 min. or until pork steaks are fork tender. Serves 4.

Frances Barden
Greene County

GREEN BEANS AND PORK OVER RICE

4 or 5 pork steaks, diced	1 c. bean sprouts, well drained
salt and pepper	1½ c. celery, ¼" slices
cooking oil	
2 cans green beans, drained; reserve ½ liquid	1½ c. green pepper, diced in ¼" squares
3 T. soy sauce	1 small onion, diced

Season diced pork and brown in oil. Add green beans and ½ liquid, bean sprouts, and soy sauce. Simmer about 15–20 min. Add celery, green pepper, and onion. Cook 30–35 min. until celery and green pepper are transparent. Serve over hot rice. Top with chow mein noodles if desired.

Mrs. Jerry Krueger
Fayette County

PORK CABBAGE ROLLS IN KRAUT

1 16-oz. can kraut, drain and reserve liquid	1 medium head of cabbage (10 to 12 leaves)
2 T. bacon fat	1 c. rice

2 boneless pork steaks, cut in ½" cubes
¼ c. onion, chopped
2 c. water
¼ c. green pepper, chopped
salt and pepper
1 slice bacon
½ c. water

Cook rice in 2 c. water for 5 min. Cover and remove from heat and let water absorb before using. Remove cabbage leaves and soften in hot water. Brown pork cubes slightly in bacon fat. Add green pepper and onion. Stir in partially cooked rice and salt and pepper to taste. Mix all thoroughly. Place 1 to 2 T. of mixture on each cabbage leaf and roll up. Put ½ of kraut on bottom of pressure cooker, place cabbage rolls on kraut, then place remainder of kraut on top. Add slice of bacon for seasoning. Add ½ c. water and reserved kraut juice. Cook in pressure cooker 10 to 15 min. If cooker is not available, simmer about 1 hr. on low heat.

Mrs. Leona Salitros
Marion County

PORK STEAK ITALIANO

4 ¾" thick pork steaks
3 T. drippings
½ t. salt
¼ t. pepper
¼ t. Italian seasoning
¼ t. basil
¼ c. water
1 8-oz. can tomato sauce
4 green pepper rings, diced
4 slices or 1 pkg. grated mozzarella cheese

Brown steaks in drippings and pour off liquid. Mix salt, pepper, Italian seasoning, basil, water, and tomato sauce together; pour over steaks. Cover tightly and simmer 30 min., then add green pepper and cheese. Cover and simmer 30 min. more.

Rosalie Williams
Sullivan County

SAUSAGE

BAR-B-QUE SMOKED SAUSAGE

½ c. brown sugar
4 t. Worcestershire sauce
1 c. water
2 T. vinegar
1 small onion, chopped
few drops to ½ t. Tabasco sauce
¾ c. spicy catsup
1 lb. smoked sausage, cut in 1½" chunks

Put sausage chunks and water in skillet and simmer for 10 min.; add all the ingredients and simmer for 30 min. Cool. Marinate for 4 hr. or more. Simmer for 2 hr. Serves 6.

Mrs. James Paschall
Delaware County

ITALIAN SAUSAGE AND ZUCCHINI

1 lb. Italian sweet sausages, sliced
½ c. onion, chopped
2 c. tomatoes, peeled and chopped
4 c. unpared zucchini, shredded
1 t. lemon juice
¼ t. salt
¼ t. Tabasco sauce
¼ t. dried leaf oregano
¼ c. grated Parmesan cheese

Brown sausage in skillet, stirring occasionally. Add onion and cook 5 min. Add remaining ingredients except Parmesan cheese. Cook uncovered for 5 min., stirring occasionally. Sprinkle with Parmesan cheese before serving. Serves 4.

Mrs. Richard L. Wigent
St. Joseph County

SAUSAGE AND ALMOND CASSEROLE

2 lb. bulk sausage
1 large onion, chopped
1½ c. rice
1 small jar pimientos, chopped
2 c. water

1 green pepper, chopped	1 can cream of chicken soup
2 c. celery, chopped	½ lb. slivered almonds
salt and pepper to taste	butter

Brown sausage and drain off grease. Add onion, green pepper, pimientos, and celery and brown. Salt and pepper to taste. Stir in rice, soup, and water. Refrigerate overnight or at least for eight hr. Pour into casserole and bake for 1 hr. and 15 min. at 325°. Stir several times while baking. Brown almonds in butter and add to casserole. Bake 15 min. longer. Serves 6–8.

Georgia Cater
Allen County

SAUSAGE BALLS AND SAUERKRAUT

1 lb. pork sausage	1 egg
1 c. quick oats, uncooked	1 large can sauerkraut
½ c. dark seedless raisins	½ c. brown sugar

Place sausage, oats, eggs, and raisins in bowl; mix thoroughly. Shape to form small balls. Place in ovenproof pan and bake at 350° for 30–35 min. Combine sauerkraut and brown sugar in saucepan. Cover and simmer 30 minutes, stirring occasionally. To serve, make a ring of sauerkraut on platter or in serving dish. Place sausage balls in center of ring. Serves 4–5.

Hilda Evrard
Spencer County

SAUSAGE AND EGG SOUFFLE

6 eggs	1 t. dry mustard
2 c. milk	1 lb. mild sausage
6 slices white bread	1 c. grated cheddar cheese, slightly packed
1 t. salt	

Crumble and slightly brown sausage. Drain off grease. In mixing bowl, beat eggs; add milk, salt, and mustard. Add cubed bread and stir well. Add cheese and sausage. Place in 8×12″ glass baking dish and place in the refrigerator overnight. Bake at 350° for 45 min., or until done. Let set for a few min. before cutting and serving. Serves 10.

Ethel Mount
Hamilton County

SAUSAGE WITH MUSH

1 c. cornmeal	1 lb. sausage
1 t. salt	drained sausage grease
1 c. cold water	
3 c. boiling water	

Mix cornmeal and salt in cold water. Stir mixture into boiling water. Cook 5 min. Fry sausage until nearly done. Drain grease. Put sausage into mush and continue cooking very slowly on low heat for 15 min. Pour sausage-mush into loaf pan. When cold, slice and fry in drained sausage grease. Serves 4.

Mildred West
Scott County

SAUSAGE SUPREME

1 lb. pork sausage, crumbled	1 c. shredded cheese
1 onion, chopped	1 small pkg. (8 oz.) fine noodles
1 can cream of mushroom soup	
½ c. milk	

Fry crumbled sausage with onion long enough to fry out fat, but not until crisp. Drain thoroughly. Cook noodles and drain. Mix all ingredients together in a casserole and bake at 325° for 25–35 min. Serves 8.

Mrs. Russell McCann
Dearborn County

SOUR CREAM SKILLET SUPPER

1 lb. sausage	2 c. tomatoes
1 large onion, chopped	3 T. brown sugar
	1 T. chili powder
1 large green pepper, diced	1 t. salt
	2 c. (1 pt.) sour cream
1 c. cooked elbow macaroni	

Cook sausage, onion, and green pepper until done, but *not* brown. Pour off part of fat. Add tomatoes, cooked macaroni, brown sugar, chili powder, and salt. Cook for a few min. Add sour cream and cook to thickness you desire.

Anna Mae Troxler
Delaware County

SPARERIBS

BARBECUED SPARERIBS

1 envelope onion soup mix	1 clove garlic, minced
1½ c. water	1 t. ginger
⅓ c. honey	4 lb. spareribs, cracked and cut into 1 rib portions
¼ c. soy sauce	
2 T. sherry	
1 T. sugar	

In large mixing bowl, combine onion soup mix, water, honey, soy sauce, sherry, sugar, garlic, and ginger; add ribs and marinate 2 hours turning frequently. Place ribs on rack in shallow roasting pan. Roast at 350° 1¼ hr., or until tender and crisp; turning and basting occasionally with marinade. Serves 6.

Marcia Powers
Greene County

SPARERIBS WITH BARBECUE SAUCE

spareribs	½ c. catsup
1 onion, diced	1 t. sugar
1 t. vinegar	½ c. Worcestershire sauce
½ t. chili powder	
½ c. celery, chopped	salt and pepper

Cut ribs into convenient sizes; salt and pepper. Cover with sauce. If not enough liquid to cook meat, add water, as sauce cooks down. Cover. Bake at 325° until done (2–2½ hr.).

Karen Roberts
Wells County

SPARERIBS AND CARAWAY KRAUT

3 lb. spareribs	1 1-lb., 11-oz. can (3½ c.) sauerkraut
2 t. salt	
¼ t. pepper	
1 unpared tart apple, chopped	2 T. brown sugar
	2 or 3 t. caraway seed
1½ c. tomato juice	

Season ribs with salt and pepper; place in Dutch oven, and brown well. Combine remaining ingredients. Spoon over ribs. Simmer, covered, for 1½ hr., basting with juices several times. Skim off fat; add Stuffing Balls; cook 15 min. more. Serves 6.

Stuffing Balls:

1½ c. water	seasoned stuffing mix (3½ c.)
½ c. butter or margarine	
	2 eggs, slightly beaten
1 8-oz. pkg. herb-	

Heat together water and butter or margarine. Add stuffing mix and toss lightly until stuffing is moistened. Stir in eggs. Shape into 6 balls. Place on kraut; cook, covered 15 min., as directed above.

Ann Vacek
Pulaski County

SWEET-AND-SOUR SPARERIBS

3½ lb. spareribs (chops)	2 large onions, sliced
½ c. vinegar	⅓ c. brown sugar
⅔ c. pineapple juice	1 T. soy sauce
	1 c. pineapple chunks
⅓ c. water	
½ t. salt	⅛ t. pepper
1 T. cornstarch	1 T. cold water

Fry pork until brown. Place onions in Dutch oven or kettle with 2 T. pork fat from fryings. Sauté 2 min., add brown sugar, vinegar, soy sauce, pineapple juice and chunks, ⅓ c. water, salt, pepper, and pork. Cover and simmer 2 hr. (or 1 hr., if less pork used). Remove meat. Thicken sauce in pan with cornstarch dissolved in 1 T. cold water. Replace meat in sauce. Serve at once over or with rice.

Deanna Bredwell
Delaware County

TENDERLOIN

TENDERLOIN DELUXE

1 lb. pork tenderloin, sliced ¼″ thick	1 mango, sliced thin
1 lb. soda crackers, rolled into fine crumbs	1 onion, sliced thin
½ c. milk	½ pint catsup
4 eggs	2 c. boiling water
salt and pepper	¼ pt. piccalilli or chili sauce

Lay each slice of tenderloin separately on a mound of crumbs and cover with crumbs. (Reserve some crumbs for a second coating.) Roll to 3 times its original size. Cut into serving pieces as desired. Beat eggs and milk together. Dip meat pieces into egg and milk mixture. Recoat with re-served cracker crumbs. Fry just until golden brown in hot fat. Remove from fat to large roaster and cover each piece of meat with a slice of onion, then top with a mango ring, and inside the ring put piccalilli or chili sauce, then top with catsup. After arranging meat on bottom of pan, stagger remaining meat pieces so as not to disturb topping. Pour boiling water carefully around meat. Cover with tight lid and bake 1 hr. at 350°. Serves 20.

Thelma D. Appleby
Parke County

TENDERLOIN AND NOODLE CASSEROLE

1 lb. pork tenderloin, diced	1 small can mushrooms, drained
2 small onions, cut fine	1 can cream of mushroom soup
1 green pepper, cut fine	1 c. milk
salt and pepper	½ 4-oz. pkg. Velveeta cheese
1 pkg. noodles, cooked	

Dice pork and brown well. Add onions, green pepper, salt and pepper and cook slowly 15 min. Add mushrooms, soup, and milk to cooked noodles. Mix pork and noodle mixtures together in casserole and top with cheese. Bake in moderate oven (350°) for 30 min.

Mrs. Cleo Scott
Marion County

FRANKFURTERS OR HOT DOGS

CORN DOGS

1 c. flour, sifted	1½ t. baking powder
2 T. sugar	

1 t. salt   2 T. shortening
⅔ c. yellow corn   ¾ c. milk
  meal   1 lb. (8 to 10)
1 egg, slightly   franks
  beaten

Sift together flour, sugar, baking powder, and salt. Stir in corn meal. Cut in shortening until mixture resembles fine crumbs. Combine egg and milk; add to corn meal mixture, stirring until well blended. Insert wooden skewer into end of each frank. Spread franks evenly with batter. Fry in deep, hot fat (375°) until brown (4–5 min.). Serve with chili sauce or mustard. Serves 4–5.

Janet Kluemper
Dubois County

COWBOY DINNER

¾ c. uncooked   1½ c. onions,
  rice (makes   sliced (2
  about 2 c.)   onions)
3 T. cooking fat   1 No. 2 can
  or oil   tomatoes
1½ t. salt   4 T. green pep-
1 bay leaf   per, chopped
3 whole cloves   (½ whole
9 frankfurters,   pepper)
  cut up   1 T. sugar

Cook rice until tender. Drain. Meanwhile cook onions in fat until tender. Add remaining ingredients. Simmer for 15 min.; remove bay leaf and cloves. Add rice. Arrange ⅓ of mixture in greased 1½-qt. casserole. Cover with 3 cut-up franks. Repeat layers until all ingredients are used. Bake at 325° for 1 hr. Uncover and bake another 15 min. Serves 6.

Rhea Dawn Thomas
Lawrence County

HOT DOG-POTATO SUPPER

6–8 large pota-   1 pkg. hot dogs
  toes, sliced 1 large mango,
2 large onions,   sliced
  sliced

Fry potatoes and onions in enough shortening to brown in a large skillet. After second turning, add hot dogs and mango. Simmer until potatoes are done and hotdogs are well heated. Serves 6.

Mrs. Joan Bentz
Jennings County

MUSTARD CABBAGE AND FRANKS

8 c. cabbage,   1 t. salt
  finely shredded 1 lb. (8 to 10)
½ c. water   frankfurters

Place cabbage, water, and salt in saucepan; top with frankfurters; cover. Bring to a boil; cook over medium heat 12 to 15 min., or until cabbage is tender; drain. Meanwhile make Mustard Sauce. Pour sauce over cabbage topped with frankfurters. Serves 6–8.

Mustard Sauce:

2 T. butter or   ¼ c. sweet pickle,
  margarine   chopped
1 T. flour   2 T. mayonnaise
1 T. mustard   or salad
2 t. sugar   dressing
½ t. salt   4 dashes of
½ c. water   Tabasco sauce
¼ c. vinegar

Melt butter or margarine; blend in flour, prepared mustard, sugar, and salt. Combine water and vinegar and gradually stir into mustard mixture. Cook and stir until thick. Add sweet pickle, mayonnaise or salad dressing, and Tabasco sauce; mix well.

Joan Jones
Lawrence County

Poultry, Fish, and Wild Game

Don't wait for company to plan a chicken dinner. Poultry is an excellent source of high-quality protein. Both chicken and turkey supply calcium, thiamine, riboflavin, and niacin. Serving for serving, both are also lower in calories than most meats. Raw poultry keeps two days and cooked about five. Freeze chicken livers separately and save up enough to make a paté. Always remove stuffiing from the bird and store separately.

Fish is high in protein, high in mineral content, low in fats—and the fats are polyunsaturated. Fat fish, like salmon and mackerel, are excellent sources of vitamins A and D. Naturally tender, fish cooks in a hurry, so avoid overcooking. It is best to thaw frozen fish before cooking, because there is a danger of overcooking on the outside before the center is sufficiently cooked. Allow one-third pound per serving for fish steaks and fillets.

Do not overcook venison; the meat toughens quickly. When roasting, broiling, or pan frying, lay strips of bacon or beef suet across the meat.

Poultry

CHICKEN

BARBECUE CHICKEN

½ c. corn oil	¼ c. water	2 broiler-fryer chickens (1½ to 2½ lb. each), cut up	1 T. sugar
½ c. vinegar	2 t. salt		1 t. paprika
		¼ t. pepper	1 T. onion, minced

Mix corn oil, vinegar, water, salt, pepper, sugar, paprika, and onion together. Let stand 15 min. Brush each chicken piece with barbecue sauce and place on grill. Baste chicken while cooking. Turn after 15 to 20 min. Baste frequently and continue cooking until chicken is tender. Chicken pieces and sauce may be put in medium size roaster and baked at 350° for 1½ hr. Serves 4–6.

Mrs. Diane Hunteman
Ripley County

THE BEST FRIED CHICKEN

1 2½- to 3-lb.	1 t. paprika
fryer, cut up	¼ t. pepper
1½ c. flour	oil or shortening
1½ t. salt	water
½ t. sage	

Mix dry ingredients. Place cut-up chicken in bowl of very cold water. Roll each piece of chicken in flour mixture to coat well. Fry at 325° in electric skillet with about 1½″ oil or shortening. Cover with lid for first 10 minutes. Turn and finish frying uncovered (about 30–40 min.). Turn often to brown evenly. Moisten remaining flour with water and drip from fork into hot shortening to make extra "crusties."

Phyllis Stevens
Posey County

CUBAN CHICKEN WITH FRUIT

2 2½-lb.	1½ c. water
chickens, cut in	2 T. lime juice
quarters	1 t. salt
¼ c. margarine	1 t. Accent
or butter	¼ t. allspice or
1 medium onion,	black pepper
cut in slices	¼ t. nutmeg
1 small can sliced	¼ c. unsulphured
mushrooms	molasses

2 t. cornstarch	4 bananas (not
4 slices of pine-	too ripe), cut
apple, cut in	in half
half	

In a big frying pan, brown chickens, in the margarine. Add onions and cook slightly. Add mushrooms, with liquid. Add 1¼ c. water, lime juice, salt, and spices. Cook for 30 min. over low heat. Dissolve cornstarch in ¼ c. water; add to pan, and cook until it is transparent and thick. Add fruits and let cook another 30 min.

Mrs. Mahalia Nunez
Jennings County

CHICKEN BAKED IN FOIL

¾ c. uncooked	2 medium zuc-
regular rice	chini, sliced, or
1 fryer chicken,	1 can zucchini
cut up	1 medium onion,
1½ t. salt	sliced
1 6- or 8-oz. can	1 15-oz. can
mushrooms,	tomato sauce
drain and re-	½ t. oregano
serve liquid	½ t. basil
1 green pepper,	grated Parmesan
cut in strips	cheese

Place 3 T. rice in center of each of four 12″ squares of aluminum foil. Sprinkle chicken with ½ t. salt and place on rice. Divide mushrooms, zucchini, green pepper, and onion into four portions and place over chicken. Mix together tomato sauce, mushroom liquid, 1 t. salt, oregano, and basil and spoon over vegetables and chicken. Fold foil over food. Place in shallow baking pan and bake 1 hr. at 375°. Sprinkle with Parmesan cheese before serving. Serves 4.

This recipe can be made in a regular casserole instead of dividing into four portions. You may wish to fry the onion and green pepper before adding them to the vegetables.

Eileen K. Brown
Greene County

CHICKEN FRICASSEE
WITH DUMPLINGS

1 4½- to 5-lb. stewing chicken, cut up	paprika, if desired shortening
1 c. plus 3 T. flour	1 c. water
2 t. salt	lemon juice
¼ t. pepper	celery salt

Dumplings:

1½ c. flour	¾ t. salt
2 t. baking powder	3 T. shortening
	¾ c. milk

Coat chicken in 1 c. flour, salt, pepper, and paprika. Brown chicken in shortening in skillet or Dutch oven to make gravy. Drain off excess. Add water, lemon juice, and celery salt to season. Cover tightly. Cook chicken slowly 2½-3 hours, until tender, adding water if necessary. Remove chicken from liquid. Make enough gravy in skillet using 3 T. flour to equal 3 c. Boil about 1 min. Return chicken to gravy. Make dough for dumplings: Mix flour, baking powder, and salt in bowl. Cut in shortening. Stir in milk. Drop spoonfuls into hot chicken. Cook uncovered for 10 min.; cover and cook 20 min. longer. Serves 6–8.

To fricassée a broiler fryer: use a 3–4 lb. chicken and follow as above except cook about 1 hr., or until tender.

Joyce Day
Allen County

CHICKEN AND HERB RICE

6 pieces of chicken	1 t. thyme (optional)
1 c. long-grain rice	1 pkg. onion soup
1 t. powdered sage (optional)	1 can cream mushroom soup
	1 can water
	paprika

Put rice in 9×13″ dish, mix herbs with onion soup and sprinkle over rice. Add mushroom soup and water. Arrange chicken on top, skin side up. Dust with paprika. Cover with foil and bake 1½ hr. at 350°. Uncover last 10 min.

Pearl Lybarger
Adams County

CHICKEN LOAF

4 lb. chicken (approximately 3 c.)	1 c. rice, uncooked (approximately 3 c. when cooked)
2 c. bread crumbs	1 c. milk
¾ c. broth	4 eggs, well beaten
¼ c. chicken fat	
½ c. celery, chopped	

Cook rice and rinse. Pour warm broth over bread crumbs and cooked rice. Add chicken and eggs and milk. Press into greased shallow pan and spread fat over top. Bake 1 hr. at 350°.

Pimiento and/or mushrooms may be added if desired. Gravy or mushroom sauce may be served over each serving.

Anna Jeanne Moorlag
Porter County

CURRIED CHICKEN

Skin and cut up chicken fryers. Shake in flour mixture in paper bag. Brown golden in peanut or safflower oil. Place in baking pan and bake at 370° for 40 min. Make a sauce with butter and oil and flour. Add 1 t. curry powder per cup and make a gravy with chicken drippings. Pour over chicken and bake another 20 min., or until tender.

Lovina VanEmon
Adams County

HAWAIIAN CHICKEN

1 chicken, cut up	1 can pineapple
¾ c. soy sauce	chunks and
1 T. onion	liquid
1½ t. ginger	2 T. lemon juice
½ stick mar-	flour
garine	

Place cut-up chicken in large bowl. Combine soy sauce, onion, and ginger in measuring cup. Pour over chicken. Let chicken soak in this mixture for 30 min. or longer; turn chicken pieces occasionally so sauce will be on each piece. Remove chicken from sauce; drain. Put margarine in shallow baking dish and place in hot oven (425°) until melted. Coat chicken pieces with flour; place skin side down in buttered dish. Bake for 30 min., or until brown on bottom. Remove from oven and turn pieces. Mix pineapple chunks and liquid, lemon juice, and soy sauce mixture. Pour over chicken; return to oven; bake 15 to 20 min. more.

Brenda Cash
Posey County

HERB BROILED CHICKEN

2 1½-lb. chick-	¼ t. thyme
ens, halved	½ t. salt
juice of 2 lemons	¼ t. pepper
¼ t. basil	½ stick butter
¼ t. tarragon	

Heat the last 7 ingredients to make sauce and keep hot. Place chicken halves on broiler racks. Broil 4–6″ from heat until done; basting and turning frequently.

Patricia Harmon
Harrison County

JAPANESE STYLE SWEET-SOUR CHICKEN

10 or 12 chicken	½ c. chicken
wings, tipped	broth
and cut in two	4 T. ketchup
1 egg, beaten	2 T. Kikkoman
cornstarch,	soy sauce
enough to coat	½ t. monosodium
chicken	glutamate
½ c. sugar	dash of salt
½ c. vinegar	

Dip chicken pieces in egg, then roll in cornstarch. Fry in hot oil until brown. Mix last seven ingredients to make sauce. Line chicken in ovenware. Pour sauce over chicken, cover with foil. Bake at 375° for 45 min. Turn chicken after 25 min. of baking.

Mrs. David Takamori
Adams County

OVEN BAKED CHICKEN

Chicken pieces—	⅓ c. evaporated
thighs, legs, and	milk
breasts	garlic salt
Rice Krispies,	paprika
crushed	2 T. butter
4 or 5 eggs	

Roll generous amount of Rice Krispies and place in bowl. Beat eggs and add milk, garlic salt, and paprika. Dip chicken pieces in egg and milk. Roll in Rice Krispie crumbs generously. Place in 13×9″ shallow pan with skin side up. If any egg and milk are left, pour over chicken. Add extra crumbs, if you wish. Dot with butter and a little extra salt to suit taste. Bake at 375° for about 1½ hr., depending on size of chicken pieces. Do not turn chicken.

Mrs. Harry E. Rohrer
Marshall County

OVEN BARBECUED CHICKEN

1 frying chicken (2½- to 3-lb.), cut into serving pieces	½ c. chili sauce or catsup
	3 T. Worcestershire sauce
¼ c. water	1½ t. salt
¼ c. vinegar	½ t. pepper
1 T. dry mustard	

Combine all ingredients except chicken in saucepan, place over heat, and simmer for 5–10 min. Place chicken, skin side up, in large baking pan. Pour half of the barbecue sauce over the chicken and bake, uncovered, at 350° for about 45–60 min. Baste with remaining barbecue sauce every 15 min. during cooking. Serves 4.

Mrs. Lynn Rieckers
Jackson County

OVEN FRIED CHICKEN

2 c. potato chips, crushed	¼ c. water
½ t. pepper	1 2½- to 3-lb. chicken, cut up
½ t. curry powder	salt
2 eggs, beaten	¼ c. butter or margarine, melted
½ c. frozen orange juice	

Blend together potato chips, pepper, and curry powder (use blender for easiest way). Mix together eggs, orange juice, and water. Lightly salt chicken. Dip chicken in egg mixture, and then in seasoned potato chips. Place chicken pieces side by side in a greased pan. Drizzle with melted butter and bake until tender 40 to 45 min. Serves 4.

Anita Thompson
Parke County

QUICK BARBECUED CHICKEN

1 frying chicken, cut up	1 c. tomato catsup
1 c. barbecue sauce	1 small (6½ oz.) Coca-Cola
1 t. salt	

Combine all ingredients in pressure cooker and cook for 15 min. Remove chicken from cooker and place in hot oven for 10 to 15 min. Serves 4.

Peggy Crutchfield
Martin County

CHICKEN BREASTS

ALMOND CHICKEN
(*hsing-jen chi ting*)

1 lb. chicken breasts, boneless	1 hot red pepper, remove seeds and cut into pieces (optional)
1 small green pepper, chopped	
1 spring onion (green onion), chopped	1 T. dry sherry
2 slices fresh ginger	2 T. light soy sauce
½ c. cooked almonds, remove the brown skins	1 T. corn starch
	5 T. peanut oil or cooking oil
	1 T. salt

To remove the brown skins from almonds: Soak them in boiling water with lid on for 10 min. Then peel the skins with fingers.

Remove bones from the chicken meat. Cut all the meat into ¾″ square pieces. Add dry sherry, 1 T. light soy sauce, and corn starch to the chicken meat and mix well. Mix hot pepper, spring onion, ginger, salt, and 1 T. light soy sauce in a small bowl for later use. Pour oil in the wok over high heat. Give the chicken mixture a quick stir to recombine it. Put the mixture in the wok when the oil becomes warm, but has not yet begun to smoke. Stir-fry the chicken meat for 2 min., and then take the pieces out with a slotted spoon. Leave remaining oil in wok. Put green pepper in wok and stir-fry for 1 min. Add hot pepper mixture in wok, stir-frying them well. Then put the chicken back in wok and stir-fry with vegetables until the meat turns white completely. Drop in almonds and stir with other ingredients in wok. Serve hot with rice. Serves 4–6.

Mrs. Raymond Bauer
Vanderburgh County

CHICKEN BREASTS WITH BACON

6 whole chicken breasts, halved, skinned, and boned	2 bunches green onions, chopped (include lots of the green)
12 slices of bacon	
8-oz. cream cheese	

Cream cheese with onions and form into 12 balls, about the size of a walnut. Wrap ½ chicken breast around each cheese ball. Wrap each ½ chicken breast with 1–2 slices of bacon. Cover chicken as much as possible. Secure with toothpicks. Broil on rack, with drip pan below. Have broiling rack 6–8″ below heat. Broil approximately 30 min., or until bacon is well done. Turn

chicken occasionally to brown evenly. Serves 6–12.

Mrs. Richard W. Sipe
Rush County

PARTY CHICKEN

8 chicken breasts, deboned	1 can mushroom soup
1 3-oz. pkg. chipped beef	2 T. white cooking wine
½ pint sour cream	sliced bacon

Line baking dish with chipped beef cut fine with scissors. Season chicken with salt and pepper. Wrap each breast with bacon; secure with pick. Add soup, cream, and wine. Bake covered at 350° approximately one hour. Remove cover, continue baking until bacon is browned. Serves 8.

Mrs. Walter Zinkan
Knox County

TANGY BAKED CHICKEN

6–8 chicken breasts or 1 chicken, cut up	1 10-oz. glass apricot preserves
1 8-oz. bottle Russian salad dressing (red)	1 pkg. (envelope) dry onion soup

Place chicken in glass baking dish. Mix together the other ingredients. Spread this over chicken pieces, add no other salt or seasoning, and bake uncovered in 275° or 300° oven until tender, about 1½ hr. As soon as chicken starts to boil, turn oven down until it is just bubbling. Before serving, pour off liquid that has formed, save and use later on pork chops or in meat loaf.

Thelma Ransdell
Tippecanoe County

CHICKEN CASSEROLES

ALICE'S SCALLOPED CHICKEN

1 5- to 6-lb. stew-	4 c. day-old bread,
ing hen	toasted and
salted water	cubed
¾ c. chicken fat	¼ c. onion,
1⅛ c. flour	chopped
1 T. salt	1 c. celery,
¼ t. white	chopped
pepper	1 t. salt
4½ c. chicken	½ t. sage
broth	⅓ c. butter or
2 c. rich milk	margarine

Simmer chicken in salted water to cover, or pressure cook until tender. Remove meat from bones. Melt fat in heavy skillet; blend in flour, salt, and pepper. Cook on low heat until bubbly, stirring constantly. Slowly stir in liquids; boil 3 min., stirring constantly. Lightly toss together bread cubes, onion, celery, salt, sage, and butter. Arrange in two 2-qt. baking dishes. Top with chicken; cover with white sauce. Mix with fork to moisten dressing. Bake in moderate oven (350°) for 1 hr. Serves 16.

Nora Warren
Pulaski County

CHICKEN ASPARAGUS CASSEROLE

4 c. bread cubes	1 c. grated sharp
or herb-	cheddar cheese
seasoned	1–2 pkg. frozen,
croutons	cut asparagus,
8 T. butter,	cooked
melted	2 c. chicken,
⅓ c. flour	cooked and
1 t. salt	diced
pepper to taste	4 oz. mushrooms,
2 c. milk	drained

Toss together bread cubes and 4 T. melted

butter. Make sauce of 4 T. melted butter, flour, salt, pepper, milk, and cheese. Cook until thick. Line buttered 1½-qt. casserole with half of bread crumbs. Add asparagus, chicken, and mushrooms. Pour sauce over all and top with remaining bread cubes. Bake at 350° for 30 min. Serves 6.

Mrs. Carl Raffel
LaPorte County

CHICKEN CREOLE

1 2-lb. or larger	1 T. Worcester-
stewing hen,	shire sauce
cooked and cut	3½ oz. can
in fairly large	pimientos, cut
pieces	into small strips
1 green pepper,	8 oz. (2 4 oz. cans)
chopped	mushrooms, cut
1 medium-sized	up
onion, chopped	¾ lb. mild ched-
butter	dar cheese or
9 oz. box elbow	American
spaghetti	cheese, cut up
salt to taste	1 qt. broth

Heat broth until it is boiling; add spaghetti. Cook until it is tender, about 5–7 min. Put spaghetti in a casserole. Cook green pepper and onion slightly in butter. Add chicken, Worcestershire sauce, salt, pimientos, mushrooms, green pepper, onion, and cheese to spaghetti. Allow casserole to age in refrigerator at least 24 hr. For serving, bake at 350° for 30–45 min. Serves 14.

Mrs. Carter Meharry
Tippecanoe County

CHICKEN DIVAN

2 10-oz. pkg.	2 c. sliced or
frozen broccoli	cut-up cooked
spears	chicken

2 10¾-oz. cans cream of chicken soup	½ c. shredded cheese (such as cheddar)
1 c. mayonnaise or salad dressing	1 c. soft bread crumbs
1 t. lemon juice	1 t. poultry seasoning
1 t. paprika	1 T. melted butter or margarine
½ t. curry powder	
1 t. dry mustard	

Cook broccoli according to package directions. Drain and arrange in 12×12″ shallow casserole. Place chicken on top. Combine soup, mayonnaise, lemon juice, curry powder, paprika, and mustard. Pour over chicken. Sprinkle with cheese. Combine bread crumbs, butter, and poultry seasoning. Sprinkle over casserole. Bake at 375° for 30 to 35 min., or until bubbly and browned. Serves 8.

Each step may be done separately, stored in refrigerator, then entire casserole combined when ready to bake, thus saving last minute work and giving the cook time for the foods that cannot be prepared ahead. As another time saver, I sometimes use dressing mix for topping in place of bread crumbs, poultry seasoning, and butter.

Mrs. Dale Maines
Marion County

CHICKEN AND DRESSING CASEROLE

1 stewing chicken	½ t. celery seed
2 qt. water	½ t. sage
1 T. salt	2 T. onion, chopped
1 loaf day-old bread, cubed or broken up	2 qt. chicken broth
	⅓ c. butter

¾ c. flour bread crumbs	6 eggs, well-beaten

Cook chicken in water and salt until tender, bone, and cut up. Mix with bread cubes, celery seed, onion, sage, and 1 qt. chicken broth. Put in greased 10×13″ pan. Make gravy of butter, flour, and 1 qt. chicken broth; add eggs slowly. Cook until bubbly and pour over chicken and dressing. Sprinkle top with bread crumbs. Bake at 350° for 1 hr.

Mrs. Dale George
Kosciusko County

CHICKEN AND GREEN BEAN CASSEROLE (1)

2 cans French-cut green beans, drained	1 can cream of mushroom soup
4 large chicken breasts, cooked and diced	2 cans cream of chicken soup
	2 cans Chinese vegetables
1 can button mushrooms, drained	1 can French-fried onions

Add ingredients as listed in 13×9″ pan: green beans, chicken breasts, 1 can chicken soup, Chinese vegetables, mushroom soup, 1 can chicken soup, mushrooms. Bake at 350° for 45 min. to 1 hr. Ten min. before done, sprinkle French-fried onions on top. Serves 8.

Doris Siferd
Delaware County

CHICKEN AND GREEN BEAN CASSEROLE (2)

5 chicken breasts, cooked, boned, skinned, and cut up in bite-size pieces	1 can water chestnuts
	1 can whole green beans
	1 t. curry

2 cans cream of	2 t. lemon juice
chicken soup	½ c. grated ched-
¾ c. milk or	dar cheese
mayonnaise	(optional)

Spread water chestnuts on bottom of casserole. Lay chicken on top of chestnuts. Then cover with green beans. Mix cream of chicken soup with either milk or mayonnaise. Add curry and lemon juice to the cream of chicken soup; mix together and spread over the beans. Bake 30 min. at 350°. Sprinkle grated cheddar cheese over the top during the last 18 min. of baking, if you wish.

Mrs. Edward W. Smith
LaPorte County

CHICKEN NOODLE CASSEROLE

2 c. cooked	1 can cream of
chicken	mushroom soup
4 c. cooked	¼ c. canned pi-
noodles	miento, diced
½ lb. American	bread crumbs
or pimiento	butter
cheese, diced	

Fold diced cheese into boiling hot noodles. Stir until almost completely melted. Fold in cream of mushroom soup, chicken, and pimiento. Place in casserole, top with generous layer of bread crumbs, and dot with butter. Bake at 350° for about 1 hr., or until brown. Serves 6.

Edna Krammes
Rush County

CHICKEN PIE

1 frying chicken	1 oz. butter
water	¼ c. flour
1 bay leaf	5 oz. chicken
parsley	stock
thyme	4 oz. cream

2 oz. wine	1 small onion,
juice of 1 lemon	chopped
1 can mushrooms,	6 oz. ham, thinly
or fresh	chopped
dash of salt	2 eggs, boiled
pastry	egg white
celery, chopped	

Cover chicken with water. Add bay leaf, parsley, and thyme and simmer until chicken is done. Cool and debone. Set aside. Melt butter with flour. Stir until it looks like a sandy mixture. Pour into it chicken stock and cream. Stir well and add wine. Cook 1 minute. Set aside. Sauté mushrooms; add lemon juice, and salt (no pepper). Set aside. Line deep baking dish with pastry. Add onion, celery, cut-up chicken, ham, and boiled eggs. Add wine sauce and mushrooms. Cover with pastry crust. Brush with egg white and bake at 350° until well browned. Serves 6.

Lorene Bedwell
Vigo County

CHICKEN AND RICE SUPREME

1 whole stewing	1 can water chest-
chicken or 1	nuts, sliced
canned chicken	1 small jar
1 pkg. chicken-	pimiento
flavored rice,	1 can French-style
prepared	green beans
according to	½ c. mayonnaise
package	salt and pepper
directions	to taste
1 can cream of	2 cans French-
mushroom or	fried onion
cream of celery	rings
soup	

Cook stewing chicken until done, remove from bones, and cut up. Combine with next seven ingredients in casserole dish or 9×13½″ baking pan. Top with onion rings and bake at 350° for 35 min. Serves 12.

Carole Harding
Allen County

CHICKEN TOMATO CASSEROLE

1 small hen or 1	2 T. fat
large frying	1 qt. canned
chicken	tomatoes
⅔ c. uncooked	2 t. salt
rice	1 T. chili powder
1 c. onion,	pepper to taste
chopped	

Cut chicken in serving pieces. Arrange in greased 3-qt. casserole. Mix together rice, onion, fat, tomatoes, and seasonings. Pour over chicken. Cover. Bake at 325° until tender. Serves 6–8.

Mrs. Venice Morrison
Putnam County

CHICKEN VEGETABLE CASSEROLE

1 fryer, cut up	4 carrots, peeled
salt and pepper	and quartered
butter	4 onions, peeled
4 potatoes,	and quartered
peeled and	2 cans cream of
quartered	mushroom soup

Place cut-up fryer in broiler pan. Salt and pepper and dot with butter. Place under broiler until lightly brown; turn and brown other side. Place potatoes, carrots, and onions alongside the chicken. Pour undiluted mushroom soup over all and cover tightly with foil. Bake 1½ hr. at 350°. Serves 4.

Marion Walker
Hamilton County

CHICKEN AND WALNUTS

3 T. oil	1½ c. chicken
2 c. uncooked	broth, heated
chicken cubes	¼ t. salt
2 T. soy sauce	¼ t. MSG
⅓ c. bamboo	⅓ c. dried black
shoots	mushrooms
½ c. walnuts	½ c. snow peas
2 T. cornstarch	2 T. water
2 T. corn syrup	

Blanch and deep-fry walnuts; set aside. Soften dried mushrooms for 15 min. in lukewarm water and cut in half. Cook salted chicken over high heat in oil 1 min., tossing and turning to sear evenly. Stir in soy sauce, MSG, bamboo shoots, and dried mushrooms. Stir-fry for 1 min. Stir in heated broth and snow peas. Cook briskly, covered, 2–3 min. Uncover, stir in walnuts and syrup, heat through. Gradually stir in cornstarch dissolved in water. Cook, stirring for 2 min., until thickened. Serve with rice and other Chinese dishes. Serves 2–4.

Mrs. George Weaver
Putnam County

CHINESE CHICKEN

½ c. onion, finely	1 4-oz. can mush-
chopped	rooms, pieces
1 c. celery, diced	and stems
2 c. chicken,	2 cans water
diced (tuna	chestnuts, sliced
may be used)	1 can bamboo
1 can mushroom	shoots
soup	½ lb. cashew
1 No. 2½ can	nuts (split
chow mein	pieces)
noodles	potato chips,
1 jar pimientos	crushed

Combine all of these ingredients. Do not dilute soup, but do use the juice from the mushrooms and chestnuts. Put entire mixture into greased 2-qt. casserole. Cover the top with crushed potato chips. Bake at 325° for 45 to 60 min. Serves 8.

Mrs. Walter Lechlitner
Elkhart County

EASY CHICKEN CASSEROLE

1 c. rice	1 c. water or
chicken pieces	milk
1 can cream of	1 pkg. dry onion
mushroom soup	soup

Grease 9×13″ pan. Sprinkle rice on bottom. Cover with layer of chicken pieces. Dilute mushroom soup with water or milk. Sprinkle dry onion soup over all. Cover pan with aluminum foil. Bake 1½ hr. or longer at 325°.

Donna Bruce
Pulaski County

ITALIAN CHICKEN

1 stick butter or	1 can tomato soup
margarine	1 medium green
1 small bottle of	pepper,
green olives	chopped
(about ½ c.),	2 c. chopped
chopped	chicken
1 T. chili powder	1 lb. American
1 large onion,	cheese, diced
diced	1 lb. box spa-
½-oz. garlic buds	ghetti, cooked
1 can cream of	2 t. salt
chicken soup	

Melt butter in pan. Add onion and green pepper. Cook in butter until tender. Add chili powder, olives, garlic, and salt and stir well. Simmer 5 min. Add soups, stir-

ring constantly until lumps are gone. Add chicken and mix well. Mix in cooked spaghetti. Fold in chopped cheese. Bake 45 min. at 325°. Serves about 20.

Helen Nash
Daviess County

NIGHT BEFORE CASSEROLE

1¾ c. uncooked	½ lb. soft Ameri-
macaroni	can cheese, cut
2 c. cut-up	up
chicken	3 hard-boiled
2 cans mushroom	eggs, chopped
soup (or 1 can	1 pimiento
chicken and 1	1 green pepper
can mushroom)	2 c. milk

Combine all ingredients, let stand overnight in refrigerator. Pour into buttered casserole and bake at 350° for 1 hr. and 15 min. Serves 10.

Doris Gillum
Pike County

TANGY CHICKEN BAKE

⅔ c. corn flake	2 3-oz. cans
crumbs	mushrooms,
2 T. margarine or	chopped, drain
butter, melted	and reserve
2 c. uncooked	liquid
noodles	½ c. sour cream
½ c. flour	2 c. cooked
1 c. milk	chicken
3 chicken	¼ c. fresh parsley
bouillon cubes	(optional)

Mix corn flake crumbs with butter or margarine. Reserve for topping. Cook noodles; drain well. Add enough water to reserved mushroom liquid to measure 2 c. Set aside. Make sauce: measure flour and milk into saucepan; place over low heat stirring until smooth. Add bouillon cubes. Gradually add the 2 c. liquid, stirring constantly. Increase heat to medium and cook until bubbly and thickened, stirring occasionally. Remove from heat. Stir in sour cream. Layer noodles, mushrooms, chicken, sauce, and parsley in ungreased 2-qt. baking dish. Sprinkle buttered crumbs evenly over top. Bake in moderately hot oven (400°) for about 20 min. Serves 6.

Mary Richardson
Noble County

CORNISH GAME HENS

CORNISH GAME HENS AND RICE

1 c. long grain rice	1 can cream of chicken soup
1 pkg. Italian salad dressing mix	2 Cornish game hens, cut in half lengthwise
2 c. boiling water	

Spread rice in 9×13″ baking dish and bake for 15 min. at 375°, stirring occasionally until golden brown. Combine salad dressing mix and boiling water; add chicken soup; then stir into rice. Place game hens on top of rice. Bake at 350° for 1 hr. If hens begin to brown too quickly, cover loosely with foil. Serves 4.

Mrs. H. K. Ulreich
Hamilton County

TURKEY

COACH'S TURKEY CRUNCH

3 c. cooked turkey, diced	1 2-oz. jar chopped pimientos, drained
¼ c. celery, chopped	
¼ c. onion, chopped	2 cans cream of mushroom soup
1 4-oz. can sliced mushrooms, drained	1 3-oz. can Chinese noodles
1 c. milk	½ c. cashews (optional)

Combine turkey, mushrooms, celery, onion, and pimientos in greased 2-qt. baking dish. Blend soup and milk together; pour over turkey mixture. Sprinkle noodles around edge. Bake at 325° for about 1½ hr., or until bubbly. Serves 6–8.

Evelyn Rice
Boone County

TURKEY STRATA

8 slices day-old white bread	½ c. mayonnaise
2 c. turkey or chicken, diced	¾ teaspoon salt
½ c. onion, chopped	2 eggs, slightly beaten
½ c. green pepper, chopped	1½ c. milk
½ c. celery, chopped fine	1 can cream of mushroom soup
	½ c. shredded sharp American cheese

Butter 2 slices bread; cut into ½″ cubes. Cut rest of bread into 1″ cubes. Place half of 1″ cubes in bottom of 8×8″ dish. Combine turkey, vegetables, mayonnaise, and seasonings. Spoon over bread cubes. Sprinkle rest of 1″ bread cubes on top. Combine eggs and milk. Pour over all. Cover and chill an hour or overnight. Spoon soup on top. Sprinkle with buttered cubes. Bake 50 min. at 325°. Sprinkle cheese on top for last 5 min. of baking.

Mrs. Robert L. Vore
Wayne County

Fish

BAKED FISH

Pickerel, bass, or well-cleaned carp are best for baking. Clean well; dry with a towel. Rub salt inside and out. Dot with butter. Place in a dripping pan or large baking dish. Add ¼ c. water and bake in a hot oven (400°) at 10 min. per pound. Baste with hot water and butter occasionally. Serve on a large platter, with lemon wedges surrounding the fish. Serve with tartar sauce, if desired. One large fish will serve 8–10.

Ethel Alice Vinnedge
Lake County

FISH STEAKS BAKED IN MUSTARD SAUCE

4 individual fish steaks	¾ c. milk
1 T. melted fat or oil	salt and pepper to taste
1 T. flour	¼ c. crumbs mixed with butter or margarine
½ t. powdered dry mustard	

Place steaks in greased shallow pan. Blend fat, flour, and mustard. Stir in milk. Cook, stirring until thickened. Add salt and pepper. Pour this sauce over fish and sprinkle with crumbs. Bake at 350° for 30–35 min. Serves 4.

Sherry Myers
Sullivan County

ORIENTAL ORANGE FISH

2 T. vinegar, lemon or orange juice	2 T. soy sauce (or teriyaki sauce)
3 T. vegetable oil	pepper or freshly ground pepper
dash of lemon	
4 fillets of flounder	1 T. grated orange rind

Combine vinegar, oil, soy sauce, and pepper. Place fish in a refrigerator dish; pour marinade over. Let stand at least 1 hr. Brush broiler lightly with oil. Place fish in broiler pan and broil 6 min. on one side. Turn and sprinkle top with grated rind. Broil other side 1 to 2 min., or until fish flakes when tested with a fork. Each serving has 185 calories. Serves 4.

Mrs. Arthur Jones
Ripley County

STUFFED BAKED FISH

1 6-lb. whole fish	1 4-oz. pkg. (1 c.) shredded cheddar cheese
1 T. lime juice	
¾ c. butter or margarine	½ c. milk
1 medium onion, minced	¼ c. parsley, chopped
½ c. celery, minced	1 t. salt
1¼ c. herb-seasoned stuffing	½ t. nutmeg
	½ c. dry white wine

About 3 hr. ahead: Brush inside of fish with lime juice; refrigerate 1 hour. Meanwhile, prepare stuffing. In 1-qt. saucepan over medium heat, melt ¼ c. butter or margarine; add onion and celery and cook until tender, about 5 min. In a large bowl, toss onion mixture, stuffing, cheese, milk, parsley, salt, and nutmeg. Line a large roasting pan with foil; grease foil. Fill inside of fish with stuffing; fasten opening with toothpicks. Place fish in pan. In same small saucepan, melt ½ c. butter or margarine; add wine. Bake fish at 350° for about 1 hr. and 20 min., basting about every 15 min. with butter-wine mixture.

Lift foil with fish to warm, large platter; remove foil, then remove toothpicks. Pour pan liquid into gravy boat for sauce. Serves 10.

Ann Cull
Jay County

SALMON

CELERY SALMON BAKE

1 1-lb. can salmon	½ onion, chopped
1 can condensed cream of celery soup	1 T. lemon juice
	1 c. medium white sauce
1 c. dry bread crumbs	1 hard-cooked egg to garnish
2 eggs, beaten	

Remove skin and bones from salmon and flake. Combine with remaining ingredients except the white sauce and hard-cooked egg. Place in greased casserole or loaf pan. Bake at 375° for 1 hr. Spoon white sauce across top of baked casserole and decorate with hard-cooked egg slices. Serves 6.

Mrs. Charles McIntyre
Fayette County

COHO SALMON STEAKS TERIYAKI

4 Coho (or other salmon) steaks (about 1½ lb.)	2 T. soy sauce
	½ t. dry mustard
	½ t. ginger
¼ c. oil	⅛ t. garlic powder
2 T. lemon juice	

Make a marinade of last six ingredients. Let steaks marinate several hours. Broil 12″ from heat for several min., until fish flakes.

Nina Gail Shroufe
Pulaski County

SALMON NEWBURG

3 c. canned salmon	3 egg yolks
	1 t. Worcestershire sauce
1 c. mushrooms, chopped	1 t. salt
6 T. shortening	1 t. lemon juice
2½ T. flour	¼ c. sherry
2½ c. milk	(optional)

Drain and flake salmon. Fry mushrooms in 3 T. shortening for about 10 min., or until lightly browned. Melt remaining shortening in sauce pan and stir in flour. Stir in milk and cook over medium heat until thickened. Beat egg yolks with a little of the sauce. Add to sauce mixture. Blend in Worcestershire sauce, salt, lemon juice, salmon, and mushrooms. Cook over low heat, stirring constantly, for 2 min. Serve on toast or biscuits, or in baked shells of pie crust. Garnish with boiled egg slices. Serves 4–6.

Mrs. Carl Weilhamer
Owen County

SCALLOPED SALMON

1 can salmon	dash of pepper
⅓ c. butter or margarine, melted	1 small onion, chopped
	1 egg
12 to 15 crackers, crushed	1 c. milk

Mix crackers, salmon, onions, egg, and half of milk. Place in baking dish. Add pepper, melted margarine, and milk over all. Bake 30 min. at 350°. Serves 4.

Donola Hysong
Fountain County

TUNA

TUNA CHOPSTICK CASSEROLE

1 7-oz. can tuna	1 can mushroom
1 c. celery,	soup
chopped	½ c. onion,
½ small can chop	chopped
suey noodles	½ c. salted
¼ c. water or	cashew nuts
milk	dash of pepper

Combine soup and water or milk; add 1 c. noodles, tuna, celery, cashews, onion, and pepper. Toss lightly just to mix. Sprinkle rest of noodles across top. Bake at 375° for 15 min. in greased casserole.

Mary Nenstiel
Delaware County

TUNARONI CASSEROLE

2 T. unsifted	2 c. skim milk
flour	2 c. cooked
¼ t. salt	macaroni
⅛ t. pepper	1 1-lb. can toma-
⅛ t. curry	toes, drained
powder	2 7-oz. cans
2 T. vegetable oil	tuna, drained
¼ c. onion,	2 T. margarine,
chopped	melted
2 T. parsley,	¼ c. fine bread
finely chopped	crumbs

Combine flour, salt, pepper, and curry powder. Add oil; stir until smooth. Add onion and parsley. Cook, stirring occasionally, until onion is tender. Gradually stir in skim milk. Cook, stirring constantly, until mixture comes to a boil. Mix sauce with macaroni, tomatoes, and tuna. Place in a 1½-qt. baking dish. Combine margarine and bread crumbs. Sprinkle on top. Bake at 375° for about 35 min. Serves 4.

Mrs. Leo Mosier
Kosciusko County

FROG LEGS

FROG LEGS

Sever the legs of several large green marsh frogs. Pare off the feet and turn them by inserting the stump along the skin of the other leg. Put them in salt, pepper, lemon juice, and water to steep for 1 hr. Remove legs and drain. Roll in flour; then in beaten egg and fine bread crumbs. Fry to a light brown in hot fat. Ten legs will serve 5.

Ethel Alice Vinnedge
Lake County

SEAFOOD

CRAB A LA MARTIN

3 T. butter	1 t. salt
3 T. flour	pepper to taste
1½ c. tomato	1½ c. cooked
juice	rice
1 T. onion, grated	⅔ c. mayonnaise
¼ c. green pep-	buttered bread
per, chopped	crumbs
1 can crab meat	

Melt butter, add flour, and gradually add tomato juice. Cook until thickened, stirring constantly. Remove from heat. Add onion, green pepper, and cooked rice. Fold in mayonnaise. Place in casserole or individual shells. Sprinkle with buttered bread crumbs. Bake 30 min. at 400°. Serves 6-8.

Edith Giltner
Clark County

LOBSTER NEWBURG

2 c. cooked	3 egg yolks,
lobster	slightly beaten
4 T. butter	salt and pepper
1/4 c. sherry	paprika
1 c. cream	

Preheat electric skillet to 225°. Melt butter and add lobster and seasoning. Add 1/2 of sherry and cook 1 min., stirring constantly. Lower control dial to 200°. Add cream and heat. Combine egg yolks and rest of sherry and stir into mixture. Serve as soon as slightly thickened. Serves 6.

Kay Baugh
Hendricks County

SCALLOPED OYSTER CASSEROLE

Have ready 1 qt. shucked oysters in their liquor (you can cheat a little on the oysters to economize) and a buttered deep casserole. Place in the bottom 1/2" layer of coarsely crushed soda crackers. Put in a layer of oysters, season with salt and pepper and bits of butter. Pour over this two c. cream. Sprinkle with another layer of crushed crackers (Ritz crackers may be used to add richness). Bake at 350° for 45 to 50 min. Serves 6.

Mrs. Robert Rigsby
Floyd County

SCALLOPED OYSTER AND CORN CASSEROLE

1 pt. oysters	1 stick (1/2 c.)
1 pt. whole	margarine,
kernel corn	melted
1 c. cracker	1 t. salt
crumbs	1/2 t. black pepper
1 to 1 1/2 c. half &	
half cream	

In greased 1-qt. baking dish, layer corn, oysters; sprinkle cracker crumbs, pour melted margarine over layer. Do two layers with a top layer of cracker crumbs. Sprinkle each layer with salt and pepper. Pour cream over all. Bake at 350° for approximately 1 hr. Serves 8.

Laveda Phrelkeld
Boone County

EASY CURRIED SHRIMP

1 medium onion,	1 lb. frozen
chopped	shrimp, rinsed
2 T. butter	1/2 t. curry
1 can cream of	powder
shrimp soup	few drops of red
1 c. sour cream	food coloring

Sauté onion in butter; add soup and heat well. Stir in shrimp, curry powder, and coloring. Bring to boiling point. Fold in sour cream and remove from heat. Serve over rice. Serves 4.

Mrs. William Gibbs
LaPorte County

QUICK SHRIMP GUMBO

3/4 c. celery,	1 15-oz. can
chopped	stewed
1 medium onion,	tomatoes
chopped	1 c. tomato juice
2-oz. can sliced	or 1/4 c. catsup
mushrooms	and 3/4 c. water
(optional)	3/4 c. peas (frozen
1 T. flour	are best)
salt and pepper	2/3 c. cooked rice
to taste	1 10-oz. bag
1 small hot	frozen baby
pepper or 1 t.	shrimp
chili powder	

Brown celery, onion, and mushrooms in small amount of butter or shortening. Then add flour, spices, tomatoes, tomato juice, and peas. Cook at medium heat for 20 min. Add rice and shrimp. Cook another 15 min., stirring occasionally. Serves 4.

Dearborn County

SHRIMP CASSEROLE HARPIN

2½ lb. large raw shrimp, shelled and deveined	1 t. salt
	⅛ t. pepper
	⅛ t. mace
1 t. lemon juice	1 10½-oz. can
3 T. salad oil	tomato soup
¾ c. raw rice	1 c. heavy cream
2 T. butter	½ c. sherry
¼ c. green pepper, minced	¾ c. slivered blanched almonds
¼ c. onion, minced	

Early in the day: Cook shrimp in boiling salted water for 5 min. Drain. Place in 2-qt. casserole and sprinkle with lemon juice and salad oil. Meanwhile, cook rice as label directs. Drain. Refrigerate all. Set aside 8 shrimp for garnish. In butter, sauté green pepper and onion for 5 min. Add with rice, salt, pepper, mace, soup, sherry, ½ c. almonds to shrimp in casserole. Toss well. Bake uncovered at 350° for 35 min. Top with 8 shrimp and ¼ c. almonds. Bake 20 min. longer, or until mixture is bubbly and shrimp are slightly browned. Serves 6–8.

Gertrude Crain
Steuben County

SHRIMP CREOLE

¾ c. onion, diced	½ c. celery, chopped
1 clove garlic	
1 medium green pepper, chopped	2 T. butter or margarine
	½ c. water

8 oz. can tomato sauce	⅛ t. pepper
	7 oz. pkg. frozen shrimp, thawed
1 t. parsley	
½ t. salt	

Sauté onion, garlic, green pepper, and celery in butter until tender. Remove from heat. Stir in tomato sauce, water, parsley, salt, and pepper. Simmer 10 min. Add more water if needed. Add thawed shrimp. Bring to a boil and cook for 5 min. Serve over rice. Serves 2 generously.

Mrs. Thomas Szumski
St. Joseph County

SHRIMP JAMBALAYA

2 garlic cloves or ½ t. garlic powder	1 stick butter or margarine
½ t. salt	2 medium onions, chopped
¼ t. leaf thyme	1 bunch green onions, chopped
pinch of pepper	
2 lb. cut-up shrimp or salad shrimp	1 large green pepper, chopped
2 16-oz. cans tomatoes	½ c. celery, chopped
	2 bay leaves
1 6-oz. can tomato paste	1 lb. smoked sausage, cooked and drained (optional)
½ lemon, quartered, or 1 t. lemon juice	

Cook onions, green pepper, and celery in butter until tender. Add all other ingredients except shrimp. Blend well and simmer 5–10 min. Add shrimp and cook until shrimp is done. Serve over hot rice. Serves 6.

Mrs. Harvey Hinks
Elkhart County

TED'S SHRIMP CASSEROLE

1½ lb. boiled shrimp	1 T. Worcestershire sauce
2 cans mushroom soup	½ c. mayonnaise salt and pepper to taste
2 small jars pimientos, chopped	3 hard-boiled eggs, chopped
1 medium onion, chopped	½ c. slivered almonds

6 slices bread, buttered, toasted and	crumbled (or croutons may be used)

Combine all ingredients except 2 slices of bread. Place in buttered casserole. Sprinkle with bread crumbs (2 slices). Bake for about 30 min. at 350°. Serves 6–8.

Mrs. John Hensel
Hamilton County

Wild Game

BLACKBIRD OR PIGEON PIE
(1840 recipe of Esther Ann Scritchfield)

Clean only the breasts from 25 or 30 blackbirds (which used to be very numerous in this area), or use pigeons. Boil in enough water to cover the meat for about 20 min., or until almost done. Place in a large baking pan or dish pan, add a teaspoon of salt, a little pepper, and two heaping tablespoons of butter. Add a few slices of salt pork or bacon, if desired. Add another cup or two of water. Then place a ½ or ¾″ biscuit crust over the top. Pierce a few holes in the top of the crust with a case knife or paring knife. Put the pie in the oven at 425° and bake 20 to 25 min., or until done. When crust is baked, a little flour mixed with a cup of sweet cream may be poured through the holes in the crust. Serve while hot. Serves 8–10. (This recipe may be used for rabbit, squirrel, or any wild fowl.)

Ethel Alice Vinnedge
Lake County

HASENPFEFFER (1)

1 2½ to 3 lb. rabbit, cleaned	1 t. salt
	¼ t. pepper
2 T. butter	1 T. mustard seed
2 T. chopped bacon	1 chopped onion
	¼ c. canned
2 chopped carrots	mushrooms
	1 c. cream
1 bay leaf	1 c. water or
8 cloves	vinegar
1 clove of garlic	

Cut meat from bones. Melt butter in saucepan. Add bacon, carrots, bay leaf, cloves, garlic, salt, pepper, mustard seed, onion, mushrooms and rabbit. Brown well. Add water or vinegar. Cover and simmer until tender, about 1 hr. Add cream. Mix well and serve hot. Serves 6.

Karen Merkel
Dearborn County

HASENPFEFFER (2)

3 c. water	1 t. pickling
½ c. sugar	spices
1 c. vinegar	¼ t. pepper

1 med. sliced onion	2 t. salt
	1 dressed rabbit

Mix together the first seven ingredients. Add cut up rabbit to mixture and place in a crock. Refrigerate 2 days. Remove meat and dry. Reserve 1 c. marinade. Coat rabbit with flour and brown meat in hot oil. Add reserve marinade. Cover and simmer 1 hr. or until tender. Add water if necessary. Remove meat. Thicken liquid for gravy. Strain the mixture before making gravy if you don't want spices in it. Serves 2–3.

Mrs. Diane Hunteman
Ripley County

FRICASSEED SQUIRREL

2 squirrels	1 T. sliced onion
½ t. salt	1½ t. lemon juice
⅛ t. pepper	⅓ c. broth
3 slices bacon	

Rub pieces with salt and pepper, roll in flour. Pan fry with chopped bacon for approximately 30 min. Add onion, lemon juice, and broth, and cover tightly. Cook slowly for 3 hr.

Mrs. Pat Flinn
Wabash County

POLLY'S SQUIRREL ROAST

After skinning and cleaning the fattest squirrel you can hit, pound it as flat as you can, then rub on butter or lard. Spit the pieces on cut green sticks, and broil over a clear, brisk fire. When sufficiently cooked, season with salt and pepper, and plenty of butter. It's best to eat while still hot enough to burn your hands!

"Blue River Pioneer Cookin' "
Shelby County Historical Society

BREADED VENISON

Trim edges of deer chops or small steaks and dip in beaten egg. Firmly press finely rolled bread or cracker crumbs into each piece until no more will adhere. To brown use plenty of fat in an iron skillet, adding extra shortening if needed when meat is turned. Season with salt and pepper and bake 1 hr. in moderate oven. Skillet should be covered with loose fitting lid. Do not add water.

Mrs. Pat Flinn
Wabash County

Cheese, Eggs, and Meat Accompaniments

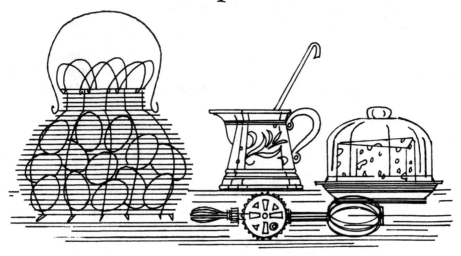

Cheese supplies protein equal to that in meat, fish, poultry, and eggs. Cheese also provides valuable amounts of calcium and riboflavin.

Overcooking makes cheese stringy and leathery. To aid in quick melting grate, shred, or dice cheese before adding to sauces or casseroles. Cheese grates easier if chilled first.

Eggs are powerhouses of nutrition—good at any meal. All government grades are wholesome. Grade AA is more expensive and grade B the least. Use A or AA for such uses as poaching, since it is a fresh egg with a well-centered yolk and a thick white. Store eggs in the refrigerator with the large ends up; this helps keep the yolks centered. The only difference between brown and white eggs is in the color of the shell.

Egg whites will not beat up to full volume if there is any trace of yolk or fat in them. An easy way to remove traces of yolk or shell is with an eggshell. Leftover egg whites may be stored in the refrigerator in a tightly covered container for ten days. Yolks may be stored two to three days in the refrigerator if covered with cold water in a covered jar.

Cheese

CHEESE AND EGG CASSEROLE

9 slices of bread, buttered and cubed	2 c. chopped ham; or 6 roasties, cut in small pieces; or 3–4 weiners, cut in pieces
½ lb. grated cheese (such as Casino brick)	
6 eggs	3 c. milk
¾ t. salt	¾ t. dry mustard
½ t. pepper	

Put bread cubes in 8×12×12″ casserole. Add grated cheese and chopped meat. Beat eggs; add milk and seasonings. Pour over bread cubes, cheese, and meat. Put in refrigerator overnight. Bake at 350° for 45 min. Serves 6.

Mrs. Doyle Lehman
Adams County

CHEESE FONDUE CASSEROLE

8 slices of bread, cubed	2 c. milk
4 eggs	½ t. salt
½ lb. grated sharp cheese	bacon, fried crisp and crumbled

Put bread cubes in greased 13×9″ baking dish. Beat together eggs, cheese, milk, and salt. Pour over bread cubes. Refrigerate 4–5 hr. Bake at 350° for 1 hr. After 45 min. sprinkle top with bacon. Serves 6.

Pauline Hyde
Switzerland County

CHEESE GRITS

4 oz. sharp cheese	1 t. pepper
4 oz. garlic cheese	2 eggs, well beaten
2 c. soaked grits	
2 T. margarine	½ c. corn flakes, crushed
1 t. salt	

Cook grits according to instructions on box. Add cheese, margarine, salt, pepper, and eggs. Stir all until cheese melts. Pour into greased 2-qt. casserole. Sprinkle corn flakes on top and bake at 300° for 10 min., or until delicately brown. Serves 8–10.

Ginger Anderson
Washington County

CHEESE, CRACKER, AND MUSHROOM CASSEROLE·

1 onion, chopped	1 can mushrooms, including liquid
25 soda crackers	
2 eggs, slightly beaten	4 oz. American cheese
¼ t. pepper	
½ c. milk	

Sauté onion until tender. Break soda crackers into bowl. Mix all ingredients. Place in greased 1½-qt. casserole. Bake covered ½ hr. and uncovered ½ hr. at 350°.

Mrs. Raymond McCarty
Starke County

CHEESE SOUFFLE

1½ c. milk	½ lb. shredded mild cheddar cheese
½ t. salt	
¼ c. Cream of Rice	
	3 eggs, separated
2 T. butter or margarine	grated Parmesan cheese

Combine milk and salt; scald. Sprinkle in Cream of Rice and cook, stirring constantly, for 1 min. Remove from heat, cover, and let stand 4 min. Add butter and cheese; stir until melted. Beat egg whites until stiff but not dry. Beat egg yolks until lemon colored. Gradually blend warm rice mixture into egg yolks. Fold in about ⅓ of beaten egg whites, then remainder. Pour into unbuttered 1½-qt. soufflé or baking dish. Sprinkle top lightly with Parmesan. Bake at 325° until puffed and golden brown (about 40 min.). Serve immediately. Serves 4.

Mrs. Charles McIntyre
Fayette County

COOKED CHEESE

½ stick butter or substitute	salt to taste
2 cartons dry cottage cheese, drained	½ t. soda
	2 eggs, slightly beaten

Stir all ingredients, except eggs, over heat until all curds are melted. Add eggs. When mixture begins to boil, remove and pour into dish. The dryer the cheese, the milder the flavor.

Tina Hoar Perkins
Fulton County

COTTAGE CHEESE BALLS

½ c. thick white sauce	bread crumbs
2 T. flour	½ c. milk
salt and pepper	1 T. fat
2 c. mashed potatoes	2 c. cottage cheese
	1 egg, beaten

Make white sauce. Gradually beat cottage cheese into it. Add mashed potatoes; season. Make into soft balls; roll in bread crumbs. Fry in kettle of deep fat until a golden brown. Delicious served with tomato sauce.

Zela Bonnell
Pulaski County

COTTAGE CHEESE ROAST

2 lb. carton cottage cheese	2 t. Accent salt to taste
5 c. Special K	¾ c. ground pecans
1 large onion, chopped	½ can of evaporated milk
1 stick margarine	
5 eggs	

Mix. Bake for 1 hr. at 350°. Serves 6.

Harriet Teboe
Hamilton County

DOUBLE GOOD MACARONI
   ## AND CHEESE

1 8-oz. pkg. macaroni	2 c. (8-oz.) shredded cheddar cheese
1-lb. carton creamed style small curd cottage cheese	1 egg, slightly beaten
¾ c. dairy sour cream	2 t. onion, grated
	1 t. salt
	pepper

Cook macaroni according to directions on package. Drain. Combine all other ingredients in large bowl and mix until blended. Fold in macaroni. Spoon in well-greased 10-c. baking dish. Bake at 350° for 45 min., or until it bubbles. Serves 8.

Wiletta Washmuth
Switzerland County

FETA CHEESE

Heat 4 gal. milk to temperature of 85° to 90° but not over 93°. Crush ½ rennet tablet into ½ glass water. (Rennet made especially for cheese.) Pour into milk; stir 1 or 2 min. real good. Cover with a blanket and do not disturb or move container for 1 or 2 hr. After 2 hr. of setting milk should be thick and whey will start to be on top.

You may take a long knife and slash 4 cuts so that whey will separate from cheese. Put all this in a cheese bag and strain to make cheese ball. It will help if you scrape the inside of cheese bag, so that the cheese will strain easier. After the cheese has formed the ball, tie with a string and let it hang for at least 12 hr. or overnight. The next day slice cheese and put it in a tray. As you slice the cheese, sprinkle canning salt on each slice. Salt will draw more whey out of the cheese and in turn make the cheese firm. Let this stay overnight and the third day put into a crock covered with salted whey and put a plate on top to weight it down. Keep cheese submerged in whey at all times. Do not disturb cheese for at least 2 weeks, but every 2 or 3 days remove scum that forms on top. You may need to add more whey when removing scum. When you remove scum, do not disturb cheese. The cheese will turn soft, but do not be alarmed. After 2 or 3 weeks it will begin to harden. Put in refrigerator after it is hard. This makes about 5 lb. cheese.

To Make Cottage Cheese:

After the third day, add 2 c. salt to whey and cook for 30 seconds. Strain as you did for cheese. Put whey aside to cool. This may be too much whey but you can put some in a jar for future use. The cottage cheese will be too salty, so pour cold water into cheese bag to remove the salt. Stir with a spoon or spatula. Let this hang overnight. Next day put into a container for table use. This makes a good cheese dip.

Eleanor Giannakeff
Allen County

GNOCCHI A LA ROMAIN

1 qt. milk	⅛ t. pepper
½ and ⅓ c. butter	1 c. Gruyère cheese, grated
1 c. grits	⅓ c. Parmesan cheese
1 t. salt	

Bring milk to a boil. Add ½ c. butter. Gradually stir in grits. Cook until thick. Remove from heat. Add salt and pepper. Beat hard until creamy, about 5 min. Pour into 9×13" pan. Chill until set. Cut into rectangles. Place over each other in buttered pan. Sprinkle with grated cheeses. Pour ⅓ c. melted butter over layered grits mixture and cheeses. Heat in hot oven (400°) about 30 to 35 min. until golden brown. Recipe can be cut in half. Serves 6 to 8.

Jane Pfaffenberger
Monroe County

QUICHE LORRAINE

½ T. butter, softened	2 c. light cream (half & half)
8 slices bacon, fried	¾ t. salt
	dash of nutmeg
¼ lb. natural Swiss cheese, grated	dash of cayenne pepper
	dash of sugar
4 eggs	

Sprinkle bacon and cheese evenly on bottom of unbaked pie crust. Beat remaining ingredients together and pour over cheese and bacon. Bake 15 min. at 425°, then 40 min. at 300° (or until knife comes out clean). Let stand 15 min. before cutting.

Pat Whittaker
Daviess County

WELSH RAREBIT

¾ c. medium	½ t. dry mustard
white sauce	toast or crackers
½ t. salt	tomato slices
⅛ t. paprika	3 bacon slices,
1 c. grated cheese	fried

Combine white sauce, cheese, and seasonings. Heat to serving temperature. Place toast or crackers on plate. Place tomato slices and bacon slices on top. Pour sauce over all.

Mrs. Allan Rogers
Dearborn County

Eggs

CORN OMELET

3 eggs, separated	2 c. corn (canned,
½ c. milk	fresh, or
1½ t. salt	frozen)
¼ t. pepper	¼ c. flour
1 T. shortening	

Beat egg yolks until light then add milk, salt, pepper, corn, and flour. Fold in whites, which have been beaten until stiff and dry. Cover bottom of frying pan with melted shortening, and turn in omelet mixture. Cook slowly until brown underneath, then put in oven at 325° for at least 20 min. Serve on a hot platter at once. Garnish with bacon. Serves 2.

Martha Minton
Lawrence County

DANDELION OMELET

2 c. dandelion	4 T. cracker
blossoms	crumbs, finely
1 egg, beaten	rolled
4 T. shortening	pinch of salt
or butter	

Bug, wash, and dry blossoms. Beat egg; add salt. Blend in blossoms lightly. Add crumbs; mix lightly. Pour in hot fat in iron skillet. Turn when brown. Reduce heat, cover and cook 12–15 min. Serve with syrup, honey, or butter. Serves 2.

Mrs. Elmo M. Beesley
Franklin County

EGGS A LA KING

4 T. margarine	Topping:
4 T. flour	2 T. margarine
2 c. milk	1 c. Rice Krispies,
1 t. salt	crushed lightly
¼ t. pepper	¼ t. salt
1 c. celery, diced	1 T. Worcester-
1 pkg. frozen peas	shire sauce
5 hard-cooked	
eggs	

Mix margarine, flour, milk, salt, and pepper and cook for about 3 min. Cook celery and frozen peas separately and drain well. Quarter hard-cooked eggs and put in sauce with peas and celery. Pour in buttered casserole. Mix topping and put on top of casserole. Bake for 20 min. at 350°.

Grace Fuson
Vigo County

EGGS PONCE DE LEON

6 eggs, hard	1 T. butter
cooked	½ onion, diced
2 c. tomato juice	½ t. Worcester-
½ c. celery,	shire sauce
chopped	½ c. white sauce
½ c. mushrooms	salt and pepper
¼ c. green pep-	to taste
pers, chopped	cracker crumbs
1 T. flour	butter

Chop whites of the eggs and mash yolks. Brown onion in butter; add flour and blend well. Put in tomato juice and peppers and cook slowly until done. Add mushrooms, seasoning, and Worcestershire sauce. When this is all done, add white sauce, egg yolks, and chopped egg whites. Place in buttered casserole. Sprinkle with cracker crumbs, dot with butter, and brown in the oven. Serves 8.

Doris W. Marple
Dearborn County

EGGS WITH TOMATO SAUCE

2 T. bacon fat	1 c. water
2 small onions, chopped	½ t. salt
1 c. tomatoes	4 eggs
2 T. flour	toast

Put fat into frying pan. When melted, add onions; cook until brown. Add tomatoes. Mix flour and water; add to mixture. Season with salt. Cook 3 min. Break eggs into the sauce. Cook until set. Serve on toast with the sauce.

Catherine Dorsey
Pike County

WOODCHUCK

1 can tomato soup	4 hard-boiled eggs
1 can mushroom soup	½ stick butter
½ can pimientos	2 T. flour
⅓–½ green pepper, chopped	1 c. milk
	4 oz. cream cheese

Melt cheese; add flour and milk. Add tomato and mushroom soup; heat until thickens. Add other ingredients except eggs. Add eggs when serving. Serve over Holland rusk or toast.

Linda Blocher
Putnam County

Soybeans

SOYBEAN SOUP OR BAKED SOYBEANS

Soybean Soup:

2 c. soybeans, washed	ham bone with meat on it (optional)
1 small onion, chopped	¼ c. tarragon leaves, crushed (optional)
1½ c. ham, cut in large cubes	

Cover soybeans with water and let soak overnight. Drain. Put in pressure cooker with water to more than cover. If using ham juice to cook, do not add salt. Add onion and cubed ham. You may use ham bone or any substitute for flavor. Cook under medium pressure for 45 min. Let pressure go down by itself. Taste and flavor as you would for navy bean soup.

If you do not care for bean soup, pour off some of juice after removing from pressure cooker. Proceed as you would for baked beans. Makes 2 casseroles of baked beans for freezer or large (10×13″) baking dish for dinner. Serves 16.

Baked Soybeans:

soybeans, left over from soup	1 c. barbecue sauce (or catsup or tomato paste)
¼ c. onion, chopped	
¼ c. molasses or brown sugar	pepper to taste
1 T. dry mustard	bacon strips

Pour off juice from beans if too juicy, and add other ingredients except bacon. Put in baking dish. Place bacon strips on top. Bake at 350° for 1½ hr.

Mrs. Carl Nelson, Sr.
Lake County

SOYBURGERS

1 c. soybeans,	2 eggs, beaten
cleaned and	2 T. milk
washed	½ onion,
1 t. black pepper	chopped fine
1 t. paprika	cheese (optional)
1½ t. salt	

Soak the soybeans overnight and cook the next morning in the same water with the pepper, paprika, and salt until tender, about 2½ to 3 hr. Drain any remaining liquid. Grind the soybeans (medium). Mix in the beaten eggs, milk, and onion. Drop by spoonfuls into a hot frying pan with a small amount of grease to make 5 patties. Flatten out. When cooked on one side, turn once. Fry until browned and done. If desired, make cheeseburgers by adding cheese and covering the skillet until the cheese melts. Serve as a pattie or on a bun. Serves 5.

Mrs. Ralph E. Partridge
Spencer County

Meat Accompaniments

BASTING BALM

2 t. MSG	2 t. black pepper
¼ t. celery salt	2 t. chili powder
2 t. onion salt	2 t. paprika
1 t. red pepper	¼ t. nutmeg
1 t. cayenne	¼ t. lemon peel
pepper	

Mix ingredients together and store. To use: Mix 2 T. mix, 4 T. lemon juice, and ¼ lb. melted butter or margarine together. Sprinkle fowl with paprika and onion salt. Bake fowl at 350° for about 1½ hr., basting with the lemon juice mixture about every 15 min.

Gingham Gals
Vanderburgh County

BATTER FOR FRYING

1 scant c. flour	1 egg
½ t. salt	2 T. salad oil
¾ c. cold water	

Put in bowl in order given and beat thoroughly. Batter will stick to what is being fried. For fish, onion rings, shrimp.

Marietta C. Swain
Lawrence County

DRESSING FOR POULTRY

1 large loaf of	1 T. ground sage
bread, broken	1 t. salt
up	1 t. pepper
1 onion, chopped	3 eggs, beaten
3 stalks of celery,	slightly
cut fine	hot broth

Mix above ingredients except broth. When ready to bake, add enough hot broth to mix to medium consistency. Bake in large pan until slightly browned. Do not overbake dressing, or it will be dry. Dry ingredients can be mixed ahead and frozen, adding eggs and broth when ready to bake.

Goldie Jones
Pike County

GOOD OLE DRESSING

24 slices bread, broken	6 boiled eggs, chopped
48 saltine crackers, broken	1 small onion, chopped
1 c. chopped chicken or turkey	½ c. chopped parsley
	hot broth, enough to moisten

Mix above ingredients. Put in 13×9″ pan. Bake at 425° until done.

Mrs. Sharon Coffey
Rush County

OYSTER DRESSING

2–3 pt. (32–48 oz.) oysters, fresh, frozen or canned	1 c. milk
	4 t. salt
	1 t. sage
3 1¼-lb. loaves white bread	1 t. pepper
1½ c. onion, chopped	2 c. celery, chopped
1⅓ sticks (⅔ c.) margarine	5 c. liquid (½ drippings with milk, butter, and water)
2 eggs, beaten	

Cube bread slices and toast in large pan in 375° oven; stir several times to brown lightly and evenly. Cover; store overnight in cool place. Cook onion gently for a few minutes in margarine until amber colored. Add beaten eggs to milk, salt, sage, pepper, celery, onions, oysters, with all liquid covering them, plus about 5 c. liquid, made up of 2½ c. of drippings from turkey and blend of milk, butter, and water, according to richness desired. Add all at once to toast; mix well. Bake at 350° for 1 hr. May be stirred once. Serves 25.

Mrs. Gertrude Moeller
Ripley County

SAUSAGE STUFFING

1 loaf white bread	1 T. poultry seasoning
¾ lb. pork sausage	2 eggs
2 c. celery, chopped	bouillon, stock or butter, if needed
2 c. onion, chopped	giblets, cooked and chopped (optional)
3 T. butter	
1 T. salt	
¼ t. pepper	

Toast bread until golden brown and dried. Fry sausage until fat is out. Pour off fat. Cook celery and onion in butter, covered, for 15 min. Soak a few slices of the toast at a time in cold water until it is spongy. Squeeze out water. Mix salt, pepper, and seasoning with vegetables, sausage, and bread; add 2 eggs and mix. If more moisture is needed, use bouillon, stock, or butter. Giblets may be added. Bake at 350° for at least 1 hr. Serves a crowd.

Mrs. Walter Vieting
Starke County

CREAM GRAVY

3 T. thick cream, sweet or sour	water, about 2 c.
2 T. flour	salt and pepper

Put thick cream in an iron skillet. Fry until the fat comes to the top of it. Add flour and brown. Add enough water to make it the correct thickness, about 2 c. Add salt and pepper to taste. This tastes like steak gravy. Serves 6–8.

This recipe was used in the 1880s when no meat or shortening was available. The gravy was served with potatoes or hot breads.

Ozetta Sullivan
Harrison County

BARBEQUE SAUCE

2 c. onion, chopped	2 T. Worcestershire sauce
1 c. celery, finely diced	1 T. dry mustard
4 T. fat	½ t. garlic, minced
3 small cans tomato sauce	1 green pepper, chopped
¾ c. molasses	salt and pepper
1 c. brown sugar	dash of nutmeg
½ c. vinegar	dash of cinnamon
¾ c. catsup	½ t. soda

Cook slowly onions and celery in fat. Do not brown. Add rest of ingredients. Simmer for 1 hr. and stir often. Makes 6 c. Good for hamburgers, oven barbequed chicken, baked pork chops or spareribs, and barbequed beef sandwiches.

Martha Daniel
Monroe County

EASY BAR-B-QUE SAUCE

½ c. soy sauce	1 t. ginger
¼ c. salad oil	1 t. Accent
1 t. powdered mustard	1 T. sugar

Put the above ingredients in a shaker and shake. Ready to use. Very good for marinating steaks and chops to be grilled.

Mrs. Noble C. Fry
Putnam County

ORANGE SAUCE

½ c. sugar	juice of 1 orange or ½ c. frozen orange juice
1 T. cornstarch	
¾ c. boiling water	
1 t. grated orange peel, fresh or dried	1 T. butter or margarine
	dash of nutmeg

In saucepan combine sugar and cornstarch. Gradually stir in boiling water until smooth. Bring to boil; reduce heat and cook and stir about 5 min. Remove from heat and stir in peel, juice, butter, and nutmeg. Makes 1¼ cups. Very tasty over roast chicken or Cornish hen.

Mrs. Ernest Ford
Marshall County

MEAT SAUCE

2 c. cooked meat, chopped	1 t. chili powder
1 t. mustard	½ t. Worcestershire sauce
½ c. catsup	¼ c. sugar
½ c. water	

Mix sauce ingredients and cook 10 min. Add meat and simmer until ready to serve.

Mary Pankop
Noble County

SEASONED SALT (1)

To ¼ c. of salt (or salt substitute), add ½ t. each of garlic powder, onion powder, thyme, and paprika plus freshly ground black pepper.

Mrs. Louise Alford
St. Joseph County

SEASONED SALT (2)

1 c. fine plain popcorn salt	½ t. poultry seasoning
1 t. black pepper	⅓ t. red pepper
1 t. paprika	3 t. garlic salt or
½ t. ginger	2 t. garlic
½ t. dry mustard	powder

Mix all together good. Pack in shaker jars. Use on fish, chicken, lamb, pork, or any meat, fried or baked.

Mrs. George Conrad, Sr.
Miami County

Cereals and Pasta

Pasta is a general term for spaghetti, macaroni, and noodles. Those who know pasta best usually want it cooked *al dente,* still slightly firm with a little bite left to it. It is not true to say that all pasta meals are budget conscious. When one considers the addition of costly cheeses, sausages, and mushrooms, the purpose of a pasta meal is more often great eating than budget control.

Rice provides the main ingredient for many casserole dishes. Short and medium grain rice particles cling together after cooking, so choose these varieties when rice is to be molded, as in a ring. Brown rice rates high in food value, because the germ and fat have not been removed. Because of the fat content, however, it may become rancid with long storage (over six months), so check before using. Cooked rice will keep in the refrigerator about five days.

GRANOLA CEREAL

7 c. old-fashioned oatmeal	sunflower seeds
	sesame seeds
1 c. wheat germ	almonds
1 c. powdered milk	chopped dates
	raisins
1 c. whole wheat flour	coconut
	¾ c. honey
1 c. brown sugar	¾ c. oil

Mix the first five ingredients well and add any amount of any or all of the following six ingredients. Mix well. In blender mix the honey and oil. Pour over mixture and stir well. Spread on shallow pans (cookie sheets) and bake at 250° for 30 min., or until slightly brown. Store in covered container. Yield: approximately 1 gal.

Betty Schuetz
Monroe County

139

NEVER FAIL DUMPLINGS

2 c. flour	1½ t. baking
¼ t. salt	powder
¾ c. milk	

Sift flour, salt, and baking powder together. Add milk and stir until blended. Drop by teaspoonfuls into boiling broth. Cover; cook 10 min. without removing the cover. Serve at once.

For variations, add to dry ingredients: 3 T. minced parsley; 3 T. chopped chives; ½ t. sage, thyme, celery salt, or your favorite herb; ½ c. grated sharp cheese.

Mrs. Arthur Jones
Ripley County

SCHMARGEL

2 c. flour	2 eggs
1 t. baking	enough milk for
powder	batter
1 t. salt	

Heat heavy skillet and add grease to coat bottom of skillet. Pour in batter. Pierce bottom occasionally with fork. Turn. When done (looks dry), cut into bite sizes and serve with syrup.

Helen Muntzinger
Allen County

HOMEMADE NOODLES

1 c. flour	water to fill half
2 eggs	eggshell

Break eggs in flour and stir. Add water. Mix well and form ball in hands. Pour on floured surface and roll thin. Cut in four strips and lay on top of each other. Roll lengthwise (like jelly roll). Slice thin. Spread out on waxed paper to separate. Place in boiling chicken or beef broth and boil 6 to 10 min. May be boiled in salted

water also. May be dried and then bagged or frozen for future use. Serves 6.

Mrs. Evelyn Heinzman
Lake County

NEVER FAIL NOODLES

6 egg yolks,	¼ c. cream
beaten	¼ c. melted
flour to make stiff	butter or
dough	margarine

Mix ingredients except flour together. Add enough flour to make a rather stiff dough; mix thoroughly. Roll thin on a floured board. Dry and cut. When ready to use, cook in broth about 20–30 minutes. These noodles dry fast because the recipe does not use salt.

Edna Hood
Rush County

CHEESE STUFFED SHELLS

¼ lb. mozzarella	¼ c. parsley
cheese, grated	flakes
1 lb. ricotta	Manicotti noodles
cheese	or rolled
1 egg	lasagna noodles
½ c. grated Par-	(such as Prince
mesan cheese	No. 67 "Shells
¼ t. salt	for Filling"),
⅛ t. pepper	cooked

Combine ingredients and stuff into noodles. These may then be frozen. To cook, place a layer of spaghetti sauce on bottom of baking dish, add filled noodles, and cover with sauce. Bake at 350° for 30 min., or if frozen, until hot. Serves 8–10.

Mrs. Victor Lechtenberg
Tippecanoe County

LASAGNA

2 small onions, chopped	1 8-oz. can tomato sauce
½ t. garlic powder	1 6-oz. can tomato paste
2 T. olive oil	¾ c. water
1 lb. ground beef	1 lb. ricotta or
1 large can (1 lb., 12 oz.) tomatoes	cream-style cottage cheese
2 t. sugar	½ c. grated Parmesan cheese
1 t. salt	½ lb. lasagna
2 t. basil leaves, crumbled	noodles
¼ t. oregano powder	½ lb. mozzarella cheese
¼ t. pepper	parsley for garnish (optional)

Sauté onions and garlic powder in oil in a large heavy kettle until soft. Add meat and cook over low heat until meat is cooked through. Break up tomatoes with fork and add along with sugar, salt, basil, oregano, and pepper. Cover and simmer one hour, stirring occasionally. Add tomato sauces and water and continue cooking covered for 30 min. longer. Meanwhile cook lasagna noodles according to package directions. Drain. In a greased 9×13″ baking pan or casserole, put ⅓ of the sauce, a layer of lasagna, ½ of the ricotta cheese and ½ of the Parmesan cheese. Repeat this procedure with ⅓ of the sauce, lasagna, remaining ricotta, and the last of the sauce. Top with mozzarella cheese. Bake at 350° for about 30 min., or until sauce is bubbling hot. Remove from oven and let stand for 15 min. before cutting into squares. Sprinkle with parsley flaked and serve hot with additional Parmesan cheese. Serves 6–8.

Alice Pohlar
Union County

NOODLE PUDDING

1 lb. broad noodles	1 lb. cottage cheese
¼ lb. butter	1 pint sour cream
salt and pepper to taste	sugar to taste (from 1–3 T.)

Cook noodles and drain. Add the remaining ingredients. Put in a casserole and bake 1–1½ hr. at 325°. Sprinkle a dash of cinnamon on top before baking, if you wish. For a moist dish, keep covered. Otherwise, remove cover the last 20 min.

Berniece Weber
Porter County

ITALIAN TOMATO SAUCE

1 small can tomato paste	¼ c. parsley leaves
1 can (3½ c.) tomatoes	¼ c. grated cheese (Parmesan or
2 T. olive oil	Roman)
¼ c. chopped onion	1 roll pepperoni or sausage
1 small clove garlic, chopped	½ lb. sausage and ½ lb.
¼ c. celery, finely chopped	ground beef fresh mushrooms
1½ t. salt	(optional)
½ t. sugar	½ t. soda
¼ t. nutmeg	(optional)
½ t. oregano	
⅛ t. pepper	

Fry onions, garlic, and celery in the olive oil until tender. Then add meat; fry until lightly browned. Drain the grease off. Add all the ingredients except soda and mushrooms and simmer in a covered saucepan for 1½ hr. or more. Mushrooms that have been sliced and sautéed for 15 min. may be added the last 15 min. Soda should be added the last 10 min. The longer sauce simmers the better taste it will have. Serve over spaghetti.

Mrs. DeWayne Heagy
Miami County

MEAT SAUCE FOR SPAGHETTI

2 lb. ground beef	1 c. tomato
1½ c. onions,	paste *or* 2 c.
minced	tomato puree
2 t. salt	1 med. bell pep-
½ t. black pepper	per, chopped
½ t. ground	fine
pickling spice	4–6 cloves of
6 bay leaves	garlic, minced
1 T. paprika	1 pt. of water
1 med. carrot,	½ pt. if puree
chopped fine	used)

Brown ground beef in small amount of fat. Add onions and cook until they are transparent. Add spices and other ingredients and bring to a boil. Lower heat and simmer from 3 to 4 hr., stirring occasionally to prevent sticking and burning. Water may be added for consistency desired, but sauce should not be watery when done.

This is a good base for chili; just add red kidney beans.

Sophia Emrich
Lake County

MEATLESS SPAGHETTI SAUCE

¾ c. onion,	1 T. sugar
chopped	1½ t. salt
2 cloves garlic,	½ t. pepper
minced	1½ t. oregano
3 T. olive oil	1½ t. sweet basil
2 lb. can whole	1 bay leaf
tomatoes	(remove after
2 6-oz. cans	1 hr. of
tomato paste	cooking)
1 c. water	

Sauté onion and garlic until tender in olive oil. Add the rest of the ingredients. Simmer for at least 2 hr., or until desired thickness.

Mrs. Victor Lechtenberg
Tippecanoe County

BAKED RICE

½ c. raw rice	¼ t. Accent
1 T. margarine	dash of each:
1 t. chicken	white pepper,
bouillon	onion salt, curry
½ t. salt	powder,
1 bay leaf	paprika
1 t. parsley	1¼ c. boiling
1 t. onion soup	water
mix	

Brown rice in margarine until golden and transparent, stirring constantly. Place in 1½-qt. casserole and swish around to grease casserole. Add remaining ingredients, stir, cover, and bake for 15 min. Uncover, remove bay leaf, recover, and bake for 30 min. Uncover, stir, and continue baking for 15 min. Serves 4–6.

Mrs. Louis Friedman
St. Joseph County

FILIPINO FRIED RICE

2 c. uncooked rice	1 fresh tomato,
½ lb. cubed pork	chopped
or bacon	1 egg
1 medium onion,	¼ c. soy sauce
chopped	salt, pepper, and
1 medium green	Accent (season
pepper, diced	to taste)

Cook rice according to package directions. Set rice aside and fry meat until done. Add cooked rice to meat in skillet and stir until well blended. Stir in egg, soy sauce, salt, pepper, and Accent. Add chopped vegetables, and mix well. Continue cooking, being cautious not to overcook vegetables.

Barbara Hibschman
Elkhart County

MOCK WILD RICE

1 cup raw rice	1 4-oz. can mush-
¼ stick of butter	rooms, drained
1 can onion soup	

Brown rice in butter with mushrooms. Reserve mushroom liquid. Mix mushroom liquid with 1 can water and onion soup. Add to rice and simmer over low heat for 1 hr. Stir often. Add more water if necessary to prevent sticking. Serves 6–8.

Mrs. Stella Burge
Jennings County

PIZZA RICE

1½ c. mozzarella cheese	¾ c. mango pepper, chopped
1½ lb. ground sausage	1 large can mushroom pieces
¼ c. onion, chopped	1 can pizza sauce
1¾ c. water	1 c. rice, uncooked

Brown sausage in a 3-qt. saucepan. Drain. Add remaining ingredients. Cover and simmer 15 min. Put in 9×13″ loaf pan. Top with mozzarella cheese. Bake 20 min. at 325°. Serves 6.

Mrs. Nelson Dyson
Wabash County

RICE CASSEROLE

1 can consommé	½ c. butter or
1 can onion soup	margarine
1 small can mushrooms	2 c. Minute Rice

Combine all ingredients in a small casserole. Cover and bake at 325° for 1 hr. or longer. Serves 6–8.

Lela Redifer
Clay County

VEGETABLE PILAF

1½ c. long-grain rice	¾ c. parsley, finely chopped
½ c. butter or margarine	¾ c. carrots, finely chopped
3 c. boiling chicken broth	¾ c. onions, finely chopped
½ t. Accent	¾ c. celery, finely chopped
¾ c. almonds, finely chopped	salt and pepper

Heat butter in a skillet. Add rice and heat for 5 min. Shake skillet occasionally so rice will brown evenly. Put into a hot buttered casserole. Add boiling broth and Accent. Cook covered at 350° for 45 min. Add vegetables and nuts. Mix well. Salt and pepper to taste. Return to oven and heat 15 min. more. If mixture looks as if it lacks moisture, add more broth the last 15 min. Serves 12.

Mrs. L. L. Richeson
Tippecanoe County

WILD RICE CASSEROLE

1½ sticks butter	½ c. diced celery
1 c. wild rice or wild brown rice mix	1 T. onion, diced
	3 c. chicken broth
1 large can mushrooms	(or 3 chicken bouillon cubes
½ c. blanched almonds	and 3 c. boiling water)

Combine above ingredients except chicken broth in skillet and brown until rice looks yellow in color. Add chicken broth. Pour into casserole. Cover and bake for 1½ hr. at 350°. May be made ahead and reheated. Serves 4.

Ruth Ann Hite
Noble County

Breads, Rolls, and Sandwiches

Nothing quite equals the tantalizing aroma of bread in the process of baking. Breadmaking itself is an emotional experience—one that can appeal to all five senses. There is particular satisfaction in the act of kneading. It's a good time to think through puzzling problems and work off one's frustrations.

For on-the-double bread baking today, use one cake or package of yeast to each cup of liquid in a recipe, or one cake or package of yeast to each three cups of flour. Active dry yeast should be dissolved in warm water (105–115°). Dissolve compressed yeast by crumbling it into lukewarm water (95°).

For a tender, soft crust, brush the loaf with shortening after you remove it from the oven, and cover with a towel. For a crisp crust, allow the loaf to cool without the towel and omit the shortening. For a highly glazed crust, before baking brush on a mixture of egg yolk beaten with a tablespoon of water.

Early cooks were advised that bread rose more quickly in the daytime when the kitchen fires were kept going than at night when only embers smoldered on the hearth. Four hours in the daytime were equal to twelve hours of rising at night.

Quick breads are leavened by baking powder or soda instead of yeast. They are "quick" because no rising period is required. In general, prepare only enough for one meal and serve them piping hot.

The texture of biscuits will be better and the biscuits will rise to greater heights if the dough is kneaded. Eighteen light strokes, or ½ minute of kneading, are sufficient. To avoid sogginess after baking, break biscuits rather than cut them.

The single most important item to remember with muffins is to stir—never beat—the batter. The ingredients should be moistened, but still lumpy. The muffin tins should be filled no more than ⅔ full, to allow for expansion.

Whatever you call them—flapjacks, pancakes, or griddle cakes—make sure the batter is not so thin that it will overspread on the griddle, or so thick that it heaps up in a lump. Test-fry a tiny pancake, and stir in more flour if too thin, or more liquid if too thick. Covered griddle cake batter may be kept in the refrigerator for several days. Cold pancakes may be frozen and reheated in a single layer on a jelly roll pan at 500°.

The knowledge of how to make sourdough probably dates as far back as 4,000 years. Sourdough is a self-perpetuating yeast mixture made by combining flour, sugar, and water. The Alaskan Sourdoughs were responsible for the identification of sourdough with America.

Quick Breads

BISCUITS AND BUNS

BUTTERMILK BISCUITS

3 t. baking powder	½ t. salt
	¼ t. soda
2 c. sifted flour	5 T. shortening
1 c. buttermilk	

Sift flour, baking powder, salt, and soda. Cut in shortening until mixture resembles crumbs. Add buttermilk all at once and stir until dough follows fork around bowl. Knead ½ min. Roll ½″ thick. Brush with melted fat. Fold over and cut double biscuits. Bake on ungreased cookie sheet at 450° for 12–15 min. Makes 2 dozen.

Mrs. Evelyn Kittle
Dearborn County

CLOUD BISCUITS

2 c. flour	½ t. salt
1 T. sugar	½ c. shortening
4 t. baking powder	1 egg
	⅔ c. milk

Sift together dry ingredients; cut in shortening until mixture resembles coarse crumbs. Combine egg and milk; add to flour mixture. Stir until dough follows fork around bowl. Turn out on lightly floured surface; knead gently with heel of hand about 20 times. Roll out and cut with biscuit cutter. Place on ungreased baking sheet. Bake at 450° for 15 min.

Phyllis McConnell
Gibson County

MOTHER'S CHEESE BISCUITS

2 c. flour	¾ c. milk
3 t. baking powder	½ c. cheddar cheese, shredded
½ t. salt	
4 T. shortening	

Sift flour with baking powder and salt. Cut in shortening and shredded cheese until mixture resembles coarse crumbs. Mixes better with the fingers than with a fork. Add milk, stir until dampened. Drop onto greased cooky sheet by heaping teaspoon-fuls. Bake at 450° for 12–15 min. Makes about 16 biscuits.

Brenda Bex
Martin County

SAVORY RAISIN STRIPS

⅔ c. raisins, coarsely chopped	2 c. biscuit mix
	1 t. dry mustard
	⅔ c. milk
½ c. cooked ham, finely chopped	½ c. butter, melted
½ c. cheddar cheese, grated	

Combine raisins with cooked ham and cheddar cheese. Stir biscuit mix with dry mustard. Add milk and raisin mixture; beat until blended. Roll out on floured board to 10×6″ rectangle. Cut in half lengthwise, then in strips 3×¾″. Pour ¼ c. melted butter into bottom of 13×9″ baking pan. Arrange raisin strips in pan. Pour ¼ c. melted butter over top. Bake in hot oven (450°) about 15 min. Serve hot. Makes 24.

Mrs. Louise Alford
St. Joseph County

STICKY CINNAMON BUNS

Filling: Dough:

½ c. brown sugar	3¼ c. flour
½ c. nuts, chopped	2 T. baking powder
1½ t. cinnamon	1½ t. salt
Topping:	¼ c. shortening
	1½ c. milk
½ c. butter or margarine	2 T. butter or margarine, melted
½ c. brown sugar	
½ c. nuts, chopped	

Prepare filling by combining 3 ingredients in small bowl; set aside. Prepare topping by melting butter or margarine in 13×9″ pan. Sprinkle brown sugar and nuts evenly over melted butter or margarine. Prepare dough: In medium bowl, mix flour, baking powder, and salt with fork. With pastry blender, cut in shortening until mixture resembles coarse crumbs; add milk. With fork, quickly mix just until mixture leaves side of bowl (dough will be sticky). Turn dough onto well-floured surface; knead 6–8 strokes to mix thoroughly. With floured rolling pin, lightly roll dough into 20×14″ rectangle. Brush dough with melted butter or margarine. Sprinkle filling evenly over dough. Starting with 20″ side, roll jelly-roll fashion. With sharp knife, cut roll into 16 slices; place over topping, cut side down. Bake at 400° for 20 min., or until lightly browned. Invert rolls immediately onto warm platter. Makes 16.

Kay Baugh
Hendricks County

CAKE BREADS

APPLE BREAD

1 c. salad oil	2 c. sugar
2 c. cooking apples, chopped	1 t. salt
	2 t. vanilla
1 c. nuts, chopped	1 t. soda
3 eggs, well beaten	3 c. flour

Mix and beat by hand all ingredients except soda and flour. Sift together soda and flour and add to mixture. Bake in angel food or bundt cake pan for 70–90 min. at 350°. Serves 12.

Mrs. Pat Kelsey
Boone County

APPLE-WHEAT BREAD AND MUFFINS

½ c. butter or margarine, melted	1½ c. whole-wheat flour
1½ c. brown sugar, firmly packed	½ c. nonfat dry milk
2 eggs	½ c. rolled oats
2 c. flour	½ c. wheat germ
2 T. baking powder	1 c. nuts, chopped
1 t. salt	1 c. dates or raisins, chopped
1¾ c. milk	1½ c. unpeeled apple, chopped

Grease an 8½×4½×2½″ loaf pan and a muffin pan (or 2 loaf pans or 2 muffin pans). Mix melted butter and sugar in a large bowl; beat in eggs. Sift flour, baking powder, and salt into another bowl; stir in whole-wheat flour, dry milk, oats, and wheat germ and then nuts, dates, and apple. Add flour mixture to egg mixture about ⅓ at a time, alternating with milk; stir thoroughly after each addition. (Batter will be stiff and quite hard to stir.) Scoop mixture into loaf pan, filling to within ½″ of top; fill muffin pans almost to top. Bake at 350°: 45 min. for muffins, 1 hr. and 10 min. for loaf, or until a cake tester inserted in the center comes out clean. Remove pans from oven and place on a wire cake rack for 10 min. Remove loaf or muffins from pans and set on wire cake racks to cool completely. Makes twelve 2½″ muffins and one loaf bread. Serves 24.

Mrs. Charles McIntyre
Fayette County

AUSTRIAN OATMEAL BREAD

1¼ c. boiling water	½ c. margarine
	1 c. brown sugar
1 c. quick cooking oatmeal	1 t. cinnamon
	1 t. soda
	1½ c. flour
1 c. granulated sugar	2 eggs
	1 t. vanilla

Pour boiling water over the oatmeal and margarine. Let it cool. Combine dry ingredients and mix with oatmeal mixture. Add eggs and vanilla and mix well. Pour into greased loaf pan. Bake at 350° for 50–60 min.

Mrs. Rod Beheler
Rush County

BANANA BREAD

1¾ c. flour, sifted	1 c. banana, mashed
¼ t. soda	2 t. baking powder
⅔ c. sugar	½ t. salt
2 eggs at room temperature, unbeaten	⅓ c. shortening
	½ c. nuts

Sift together dry ingredients then add rest of ingredients. Put everything in bowl before you start to mix, then beat for 1 min. only. Bake in greased 8½×4½×3″ loaf pan at 350° for 35–40 min.

Mrs. Tom Hoffman
Dubois County

HOLIDAY BANANA BREAD

1¾ c. flour, sifted	2 eggs, slightly beaten
2¾ t. baking powder	1 c. bananas, mashed
½ t. salt	1 c. mixed candied fruits and peels
½ c. nuts, chopped	
⅓ c. shortening	¼ c. raisins
⅔ c. sugar	

Sift together flour, baking powder, and salt; add nut meats. Place shortening in a mixing bowl and beat until creamy and glossy. Gradually add sugar to shortening, beating until fluffy. Add eggs and beat until thick and lemon in color. Add flour mixture and bananas alternately. Blend thoroughly after each addition. Fold in fruits, peels, and raisins. Grease bottom only of 4½×8½×3″ loaf pan. Bake at 350° for 60–70 min. Serves 20.

Mable Shade
Fountain County

BRAN BREAD

3 c. bran flakes	2 c. sour milk
3 c. flour	(buttermilk)
1 lb. raisins	1 egg, beaten
2 t. baking	½ c. dark corn
powder	syrup
1 T. salt	1 c. sugar
1 T. soda	

Mix together sugar, egg, and syrup. Add buttermilk. Add sifted flour to which has been added salt, soda, and baking powder; mix well. Add bran flakes; mix well. Add raisins; mix well. Put in five greased and floured No. 2 or 303 tin cans. Fill about ⅔ full. Bake at 350° for 45 min.

Mrs. Martha Brady
LaPorte County

BOSTON BROWN BREAD

1 c. dates,	2 eggs
chopped	4 c. flour
2 c. boiling water	1 t. salt
2 t. soda	2 t. vanilla
2 T. butter	1 c. nuts,
2 c. sugar	chopped

Mix dates, boiling water, and soda. Set aside to cool. Cream butter and sugar; add

eggs. Mix and add to cooled date mixture. Mix flour and salt and add. Add vanilla and nuts. Bake in 4 or 5 (No. 2) tin cans that have been oiled well. Fill ½ full of batter. Bake 1 hr. at 350°.

Jean Thrush
Noble County

CARROT BREAD

1½ c. flour, sifted	2 eggs
1½ t. baking	¾ c. sugar
soda	1 c. salad oil
½ t. salt	1 t. vanilla
1½ t. cinnamon	1½ c. carrot
1 c. pecans	pieces

Grease a 9×5×3″ loaf pan. Sift flour, baking soda, cinnamon, and salt into a large mixing bowl. Set aside. Put nuts into blender container, cover, and chop. Add nuts to dry ingredients. Put eggs, sugar, oil, and vanilla into blender container, cover, and process until smooth. Stop blender, add carrot pieces, cover, and process. Pour over dry ingredients and mix only until dry ingredients are moistened. Pour into prepared pan and bake at 350° for 1 hr., or until tester comes out clean. Cool 5 min. in pan, then turn out on cake rack and cool before frosting with Lemon Glaze.

Lemon Glaze:

½ c. confection-	½ t. lemon juice
er's sugar	1 T. milk

Put all ingredients into blender container and process until sugar is liquefied. Pour over bread, spread with a spatula so glaze drizzles down the sides.

Mrs. Philip Burket
Tippecanoe County

CHERRY PECAN BREAD

¾ c. sugar	1 c. pecans,
½ c. butter or	chopped
margarine	1 10-oz. jar
2 eggs	maraschino
2 c. flour	cherries,
1 t. baking soda	drained and
½ t. salt	chopped
1 c. buttermilk	1 t. vanilla

In large mixer bowl, cream together sugar, butter, and eggs until light and fluffy. Sift together flour, soda, and salt; add to creamed mixture with the buttermilk. Beat until blended. Stir in nuts, cherries, and vanilla. Pour batter into greased 9×5×3″ loaf pan. Bake at 350° for 55–60 min. Remove from pan; cool. Glaze with confectioners' sugar icing, if desired.

Joan Perry
Vanderburgh County

DATE NUT LOAF

1 1-lb. pkg.	2 eggs, well
pitted dates	beaten
2 t. baking soda	4 c. cake flour
2 c. boiling	½ t. salt
water	½ t. nutmeg
½ c. butter	½ t. cinnamon
2 c. sugar	1 c. chopped nuts

Cut dates into pieces with scissors. Dissolve baking soda in water, pour over dates and let stand until water is cool, (about 15 min.). Cream the butter with the sugar. Add well-beaten eggs. Sift the flour, salt, nutmeg, and cinnamon. Take about ¼ c. of dry ingredients and mix with nuts. Add the rest to creamed mixture alternately with water on dates. Beat smooth. Add dates and floured nuts last. Mix thoroughly. Pour into 2 greased 9×5×2¾″ loaf pans and bake in moderate oven (350°) until done, about 1¼ hr. May also bake in greased and floured coffee cans, soup cans, etc. Fill cans only ½ full. Wrap in aluminum foil after it is cooled.

Mrs. Henry Wittman
Spencer County

GRAPE NUTS BREAD

2 c. buttermilk or	1 c. granulated
sour milk	sugar
1 c. Grape Nuts	1 egg
3 c. flour	1 t. vanilla
½ t. salt	1 c. crushed
1 t. cinnamon	pineapple, well
4 t. baking	drained
powder	1 c. raisins,
2 t. soda	plumped

Pour buttermilk over Grape Nuts and let stand 10 min. Sift together flour, salt, cinnamon, baking powder, and soda. Add sugar, egg, and vanilla to milk mixture and mix well. Add flour mixture to milk mixture and blend well. Add pineapple and raisins. Pour into two well-greased pans. Bake at 350° for 50–60 min.

Monica Ordway
Steuben County

GUMDROP BREAD

1 c. butter	½ c. white raisins
2 c. sugar	½ c. candied
5 eggs	fruits
1 t. vanilla	1 c. nuts
4 c. flour	1 can flaked
1 t. soda	coconut
1 t. salt	1 c. powdered
¾ c. buttermilk	sugar
1 pkg. dates	¼ c. frozen
1 lb. orange slices	orange juice
candy	

Cream butter and sugar; add eggs one at a time. Add vanilla, soda, salt, and flour (reserve ½ c. flour). Mix well and fold buttermilk into mixture. Chop or cut up dates, nuts, orange slices, and raisins. Mix with reserved flour and add to first mixture. Place into four small greased loaf pans and bake for 1 hr. at 375°. When baked, pour over the tops the powdered sugar dissolved in frozen orange juice.

Mildred Young
Daviess County

HOBO BREAD

2 c. raisins	pinch of salt
2 c. boiling water	2 eggs, well
4 t. soda	beaten
½ c. salad oil	4 c. flour
1½ c. sugar	1 c. black walnuts

Combine water, raisins, and soda. Put in refrigerator overnight. Next day add other ingredients. Grease three 1-lb. coffee cans well. Bake at 350° for 60 min. Cool on rack. Remove bread when cold. Wash cans thoroughly. Put back into cans and store for a week in refrigerator.

Muriel Reynolds
Perry County

IRISH COTTAGE BREAD

1 c. rolled oats	5 c. self-rising
2 c. milk	flour

Soak oats in milk 15 min. Add 1 c. flour to milk mixture. Work in remaining flour (dough will be very stiff). Turn onto floured surface and knead into smooth, firm ball for 1 min. Place on greased baking sheet. With a sharp knife slice dough into quarters without going through the bottom. Bake at 375° for 1 hr., or until

golden brown. Remove immediately from baking sheet.

Ellen Edmondson
Clay County

IRISH SODA BREAD

⅔ c. raisins	1½ t. caraway
2 c. flour, sifted	seeds
1½ t. baking	3 T. shortening
powder	1 c. buttermilk
¾ t. soda	melted butter and
1 t. salt	sugar for top
3 T. sugar	

Chop raisins coarsely, if desired. Resift flour with baking powder, soda, salt, and sugar. Add caraway seeds. Cut in shortening until in fine pieces. Make a well in center; pour in buttermilk and add raisins. Mix lightly to moderately soft dough. Turn out on floured board and knead gently a few strokes. Shape into a round and fit into a greased 8 or 9″ round layer cake pan. With a sharp knife or scissors, cut loaf crosswise into quarters about ⅔ way through dough. Brush top surface of loaf with melted butter and sprinkle with sugar. Bake at 350° for about 30 min.

Grandmother says this is what they took to the fields for the workers at teatime in Ireland.

Jean French
Brown County

LEMON BREAD

⅔ c. butter,	3 c. flour
melted	2 t. baking
2½ c. sugar	powder
4 eggs, one at a	1 t. salt
time	1 c. milk
1 t. almond	2 T. lemon rind
extract	1 c. nuts, chopped

Combine ingredients, except lemon juice

and powdered sugar, and mix well. Bake in loaf pan at 350° for 45 to 50 min. Take out of oven; let cool 5 min. Loosen edge of bread with a knife. Combine lemon juice and powdered sugar. Pour over bread.

Gayle Tellman
Bartholomew County

MARMALADE BREAD

3 c. all-purpose flour	1 1-lb. jar (1½ c.) orange marmalade
3 t. baking powder	¼ c. salad oil or melted shortening
1 t. salt	
¼ t. soda	
1 egg, beaten	1 c. California walnuts, broken
¾ c. orange juice	

Sift together dry ingredients. Reserve ¼ c. marmalade. Combine remaining 1¼ c. marmalade, egg, orange juice, and salad oil; add to flour mixture, stirring until moistened. Stir in nuts. Turn into greased 9½×5×3″ loaf pan. Bake in moderate oven (350°) about 1 hr., or until done. Remove bread from pan and place on baking sheet; spread top with reserved marmalade and return to oven 1 min., or until glazed. Cool on rack.

Mrs. Richard Petro
Bartholomew County

MOLASSES BREAD

¼ c. white sugar	1 egg
¼ c. shortening	1 t. soda
¾ c. sorghum or ¼ c. heavy syrup	½ c. hot water
	1 T. baking powder
2 c. white flour	pinch of salt

Cream sugar and shortening. Add egg and sorghum. Mix well. Dissolve soda in hot water. Add flour and salt, then water and soda. Mix all ingredients. Bake in two greased loaf pans at 325° for 1 hr., or until golden brown. Makes two 1-lb. loaf breads.

Betty Ratliff
Hendricks County

ORANGE LOAF

2 c. flour	½ c. grated fresh orange peel, shredded fine
2 t. baking powder	
⅛ t. salt	⅔ c. fresh orange juice
4 T. (¼ c.) butter or margarine	⅔ c. milk
1 egg, well beaten	1 c. sugar

Sift dry ingredients and cut in butter with a pastry blender until coarse (like corn meal). Mix peel with egg, milk, orange juice, and sugar. Stir into dry ingredients just enough to moisten. Spread in a well-greased loaf tin. Bake 50–60 min. at 350°.

Mrs. Kenneth Boyd
Allen County

PEANUT BUTTER BREAD

1¾ c. flour	⅓ c. peanut butter
1 t. soda	
½ t. salt	1 egg, well beaten
1 c. brown sugar, packed	1 c. buttermilk

Sift flour, measure, and resift 3 times with soda and salt. Blend sugar into peanut butter. Stir in well-beaten egg and beat until smooth. Add flour mixture and buttermilk alternately, beating until smooth after each addition. Turn into buttered loaf pan. Bake in moderate oven (350°) 1 hr., or until well browned.

Genieva Shipley
Wayne County

PUMPKIN BREAD

3⅓ c. flour
2 t. soda
½ t. baking powder
1½ t. salt
1 t. cinnamon
1 t. pumpkin pie spice

1 1-lb. can pumpkin
⅔ c. water
⅔ c. soft shortening or oil
2⅔ c. sugar
2 eggs

Mix dry ingredients. Beat eggs, add to pumpkin, then add liquids. Mix dry ingredients into pumpkin mixture. Bake about 1 hr. at 350°, or until done, in two greased loaf pans. When cool, wrap in film or cloth until serving. Can serve with golden spread: ½ c. margarine, beaten smooth; gradually add ½ c. dark corn syrup, mix well.

Goldie Jones
Pike County

RHUBARB NUT BREAD

1½ c. brown sugar
⅔ c. liquid shortening
1 egg
1 c. sour milk
1 t. salt
1 t. soda
1 t. vanilla

2½ c. flour
1½ c. fresh rhubarb, diced
½ c. nuts, chopped

Topping:
½ c. sugar
1 T. butter

Stir in the ingredients in the order given. Pour into two well-greased and floured loaf pans. Fill pan ⅔ full. Sprinkle topping evenly over each. Bake at 325° for 40 min.

Pat Neal
Boone County

SPANISH NUT LOAF

1¾ c. flour
1 t. cinnamon

3 t. baking powder

¼ t. salt
1 c. sugar
⅔ c. nuts, chopped

2 eggs
½ c. butter, melted
½ c. milk

Sift dry ingredients into bowl. Add nuts. Separate eggs, beating whites until stiff. Add melted butter to beaten egg yolks and milk. Add this mixture to dry ingredients and mix well. Fold in beaten egg whites. Bake in greased 8½×4½" loaf pan at 350° for 1 hr. May sprinkle with powdered sugar or cover with a soft chocolate frosting.

Nancy Steward
Greene County

STRAWBERRY NUT BREAD

3 c. flour
1 t. soda
1 t. salt
2 10-oz. pkg. frozen strawberries, not drained

3 t. cinnamon
2 c. sugar
4 eggs
1¼ c. pecans, chopped
1¼ c. cooking oil

Sift dry ingredients together into large mixer bowl. Add other ingredients, mixing on medium speed and scraping bowl to mix well. Pour into two greased loaf pans. Bake at 350° for 1 hr. Cool in pans 10 min.; then turn out. May be served with strawberry butter, spread between two thin slices.

Strawberry Butter: Thaw one 10-oz. pkg. frozen strawberries and soften 1 c. butter or margarine. In blender container, combine strawberries, butter, and 1¼ c. sifted confectioners' sugar. Cover and blend until smooth. Makes 2½ cups.

Mrs. Donnetta Ratliff
Henry County

ZUCCHINI BREAD

3 eggs	1 t. salt
1 c. oil	3 t. cinnamon
2 c. sugar	¼ t. baking
2 c. zucchini,	powder
peeled and	½ c. nuts,
grated	chopped
3 c. flour	2 t. vanilla
1 t. soda	

Mix eggs, oil, sugar, and grated zucchini. Add the rest of the ingredients. Divide batter into two greased 9×5×2″ loaf pans. Bake for 1 hr. at 325°. Freezes well.

Mrs. Evelyn Mousa
Jennings County

COFFEE CAKES

SOUR CREAM COFFEE CAKE

1 c. butter	1 t. baking
2 eggs	powder
½ t. vanilla	
¼ t. salt	Topping:
2 c. sugar	1 c. nut meats
1 c. sour cream	1 t. cinnamon
2 c. flour	8 T. brown sugar

Cream butter, sugar, and eggs. Fold in sour cream and vanilla. Sift in dry ingredients. Mix topping ingredients. Spoon half of batter into greased, floured pan, cover with half the topping and repeat. Bake at 350° for 45–50 min.

Mrs. Gail Spegal
Shelby County

STREUSEL

¾ c. sugar	2 t. baking
¼ c. soft	powder
margarine	Topping:
1 egg	½ c. brown sugar
½ c. milk	2 T. flour
1½ c. flour	2 T. margarine
½ t. salt	1½ t. cinnamon

Cream sugar and margarine until smooth. Add egg and milk. Sift flour, baking powder, and salt. Add liquid ingredients to dry ingredients and mix well. Spread ½ of batter into greased 9″ cake pan. Mix topping ingredients. Sprinkle ½ of topping onto batter. Add other half of batter and remainder of topping. Bake at 375° for 35 min.

Josephine Neukam
Franklin County

CORN BREADS

FRESH CORN CORN BREAD

1 c. flour, sifted	1 c. fresh corn cut
1 c. cornmeal	from cob
½ t. soda	1 c. sour milk
¾ t. salt	½ c. water
1 T. sugar	¼ c. shortening,
2 eggs	melted

Sift together all the dry ingredients. Add eggs, fresh corn, milk, and water; mix only until all dry ingredients are moistened. Stir in shortening. Pour batter into hot, well greased 9×9″ baking pan. Bake at 425° for 35 min.

Fern B. Keller
Martin County

PERFECT CORN BREAD

1 c. flour	1 c. corn meal
½ c. sugar	2 eggs
4 t. baking	1 c. milk
powder	¼ c. shortening,
¾ t. salt	melted

Sift flour, sugar, baking powder, and salt. Stir in corn meal; add eggs, milk, and shortening. Beat until smooth (do not overbeat). Pour batter into greased 9″ pan or iron skillet. Bake at 425° for 20–25 min.

Mary Ashcraft
Switzerland County

HUSH PUPPIES

1 c. cornmeal	½ t. salt
1 c. flour	1 small onion,
2 t. baking	finely chopped
powder	2 eggs, beaten
1 t. red pepper	¼ c. sugar

Combine dry ingredients. Add beaten eggs and finely chopped onion. Add enough milk to make a stiff batter. Drop by table-spoonfuls into hot grease, preferably a deep fryer. Hush puppies are done when they turn golden brown and float to the top. Remove from grease and drain on paper towel.

Carol Mills
Morgan County

MICHIGAN ROAD CORN CAKE

1½ c. white corn-	1 t. baking soda
meal (prefer-	2 eggs, well
ably water	beaten
ground)	2 c. buttermilk
1 T. sugar	1½ T. butter
1 t. salt	

Grease 12″ iron skillet or iron spider and put over coals to heat. Put cornmeal, sugar, salt, and baking soda into bowl. Combine eggs and buttermilk and stir into the corn-meal mixture; keep it smooth. Last of all, stir in the butter, melted. Pour into hot spider and bake over coals for thirty min. or so.

"Blue River Pioneer Cookin' "
Shelby County Historical Society

MOTHER'S CORN PONE

Use 4 T. of burr ground meal for each person. Add a pinch of salt and enough boiling water to make a batter that will slip freely from the spoon. Stir until all the meal is well dampened, then cover the bowl and let set for 2 or 3 hr.; this seems to sweeten the batter. To fry, heat iron griddle, add bacon grease, spoon the batter onto the griddle, pressing it to about ½″ thickness, brown well on one side, turn and brown on the other side. It is good served hot with butter, and with greens or turnips.

Dorothy Rice
Putnam County

REAL PLANTATION JOHNNY CAKE

One pint of Indian meal, half a cup of sugar, three eggs, a tablespoon of lard, or butter, a small teaspoon of soda, the same of cream tartar, and enough buttermilk, or sweet milk to make a thick batter. Grease your pan well, and pour the batter into it. Bake in a slow, steady oven, for at least five hours. This is the real Plantation Johnny, or Hoe Cake which has become so celebrated, the recipe for which was obtained from a former slave of Governor Poindexter, of Georgia.

Mrs. Allan Rogers
Dearborn County

SOUTHERN SPOON BREAD

1 c. plain	1 t. salt
cornmeal	1 t. baking
2 c. boiling milk	powder
2 T. cooking oil	1 c. cold milk
or melted butter	3 eggs, separated

Pour meal into boiling milk. Cook approximately 2 minutes, until the consistency of mush. Cool. Add salt, baking powder, butter, and cold milk. Add well-beaten egg yolks. Fold in stiffly-beaten egg whites. Bake in greased 2-qt. baking dish at 325° for about 1 hr. Spoon onto plates while hot; top with butter.

Florence Asher
Harrison County

VIRGINIA ASH CAKE

Add a teaspoonful of salt to a quart of sifted corn meal. Make up with water and knead well. Make into round, flat cakes. Sweep a clean place on the hottest part of the hearth. Put the cake on it and cover it with hot wood ashes. Wash and wipe dry, before eating it. Sometimes a cabbage leaf is placed under it, and one over it, before baking, in which case it need not be washed.

Mrs. Loys Rees
Rush County

CRACKERS

CRACKERS

3 c. flour	1 c. creamed
½ t. salt	cottage cheese
1 c. margarine	

Mix flour and salt. Add oleo and cottage cheese. Cut with pastry blender until well blended. Wrap dough in waxed paper and chill 1 hr. On well-floured board, roll out ⅛″ thick. Cut out dough with 2″ cookie cutter and place on ungreased baking sheet. Prick each cracker with a fork. Bake at 450° for 12–15 min. until lightly brown Makes 100 crackers.

For variations add to dough: 4 t. caraway seeds for caraway crackers. 4 t. sesame seed and 4 t. grated onion for sesame-onion crackers. 2 t. poppy seed for poppy seed crackers. 4 t. chopped parsley, 4 t. chopped chives, and ½ t. dried dill weed for herb crackers.

Marilyn Small
Boone County

HOMEMADE CRACKERS

2 c. flour	1 t. salt
½ t. baking powder	½ c. milk
¼ c. butter	1 large egg

Sift the flour, salt, and baking powder into a bowl. Cut in the butter until very fine. Add the milk and egg and mix to make a stiff dough. Knead thoroughly and then roll the dough very thin. Cut into squares or rounds and place on lightly buttered cookie sheets. Prick the crackers with a fork and then bake at 400° for 10 min., or until very lightly browned. If desired, crackers may be sprinkled with coarse salt. Makes about 3 dozen.

Mrs. Harry Kyle
Dearborn County

LEMON CRACKERS

3½ c. sugar	1 oz. baking
1 c. lard	ammonia
2 eggs, beaten	8–10 c. flour, for
1 pint sweet milk, warm	a very stiff dough
3 t. oil of lemon	

Cream first three ingredients; add next three ingredients. Gradually add flour to mixture. Knead and roll very, very thin. Cut. Bake in hot oven until browned on bottom only.

Beulah Reeves
Sullivan County

DOUGHNUTS

BUTTERMILK DOUGHNUTS

3 eggs	4 c. flour,
1¼ c. sugar	approximately
¼ c. butter, melted	2 t. baking powder
1 c. buttermilk	½ t. salt
1 t. soda	1 t. vanilla

Beat eggs thoroughly; beat in sugar and melted butter. Stir in buttermilk. Sift together flour, baking powder, soda, and salt; add to egg-buttermilk mixture. Add vanilla and chill at least 1 hr. Roll to about 1/3" thick, cut and fry in deep hot fat at 375°. Drain and place on absorbent paper. Makes 3 dozen.

Mary Bryant
Harrison County

DROP DOUGHNUTS

1 egg	1½ c. flour, sifted
½ c. mashed	½ t. baking soda
potatoes	½ t. salt
½ c. sour cream	¼ t. baking
¼ c. sugar	powder
1 t. vanilla	

Beat egg until light and fluffy. Add sugar, potatoes, sour cream, and vanilla; beat until smooth. Sift flour with soda, salt, and baking powder; add to egg mixture, beating until blended. Drop from a teaspoon into deep hot fat at 360°; fry until golden brown, turning once. Drain on paper toweling. Cool. Roll in sugar and cinnamon mixed, or in powdered sugar. Makes about 2½ dozen.

Mrs. Harold Oman
LaPorte County

QUICK DOUGHNUT BALLS

1/3 c. sugar	½ t. cinnamon
1½ c. flour, sifted	½ c. milk
½ t. salt	1 egg
2 t. baking	2 T. shortening,
powder	melted
½ t. nutmeg	

Drop by spoonfuls and fry in deep fat. Roll in sugar when brown, if desired, or shake in paper bag.

Mrs. Cleora Morgan
Brown County

OLD-FASHIONED POTATO DOUGHNUTS

1 c. mashed pota-	1 t. vanilla
toes (may use	extract
leftovers)	¼ t. nutmeg
1 T. lard	5 t. baking
1 c. sugar	powder
3 eggs, beaten	¼ t. soda
1 c. milk	3¾ c. flour

Sift flour, salt, baking powder, soda, and nutmeg. Cream mashed potatoes and lard with sugar; add beaten eggs and mix well. Add dry ingredients alternately with milk and vanilla. Roll to ½" thickness. Dough will be soft and sticky but can be handled with care. Cut with medium to large doughnut cutter. Fry in deep fat at 375° for 1½ min. on each side, or until nicely browned and done. Drain on absorbent paper. May be dusted with confectioners' sugar or rolled in granulated sugar or left plain. Makes approximately 3 dozen.

Mrs. Lloyd Mason
Fayette County

MUFFINS

SPICED APPLE MUFFINS

¼ c. shortening	1 t. cinnamon
½ c. sugar	½ c. milk
1 egg	1 c. apple,
1½ c. flour	chopped fine
1 T. baking	1/3 c. brown sugar
powder	1/3 c. nuts, finely
½ t. salt	chopped

Cream shortening and sugar. Add egg and blend well. Sift flour, baking powder, salt and ½ t. cinnamon. Alternately add milk and flour mixture to shortening mixture. Fold in apple. Fill muffin cups ½ full. Make topping by mixing brown sugar, ½ t. cinnamon, and nuts. Top each muffin with topping mixture. Bake at 350° for approximately 30 min. Makes 18.

Mrs. John Clark
LaPorte County

RUSSETT'S BLUEBERRY MUFFINS

½ c. shortening	2 T. baking
½ c. plus 2½ T.	powder
sugar	1 t. salt
2 large eggs	¾ c. canned blue-
1 c. milk	berries, drained
2 c. flour	

Beat shortening; add sugar and cream well. Add eggs and a little yellow food coloring; beat on medium speed of mixer for about 10 min. Stir in milk. Measure out about ½ c. flour; add baking powder to this and stir. Sprinkle about 2 T. of the remaining flour over the well-drained blueberries. Sift remaining flour with salt; stir into creamed mixture. When well mixed, add the flour and baking powder combination and beat only 3 or 4 times (if top of batter is still floury, stir in gently).

Fold in floured blueberries. Pour into greased muffin pans. Bake at 425° for 18–25 min. (15 min. for small muffin pans). Makes 18. ·

Janet Krumme
Lawrence County

REFRIGERATOR BRAN MUFFIN
MASTER MIX

2 c. boiling water	1 qt. buttermilk
2 c. seedless	4 c. all bran
raisins	cereal
5 t. soda	2 c. 40% bran
1 c. shortening	flakes
2 c. sugar	1 c. nuts,
5 c. flour	chopped and
1 t. salt	mixed with
4 eggs, beaten	½ c. flour

Pour water over raisins; add soda, mix, and let cool. Sift flour and salt together. In very large mixing bowl cream shortening with sugar. Add eggs. Blend buttermilk into this mixture. Fold in raisin mixture. Add cereal. Add all at once to flour and salt. Fold in nuts. Cover tightly and store in refrigerator. Pour into muffin cups in quantity needed. Bake 20–25 min. at 375°. Master Mix will keep 3 or more weeks in refrigerator.

Katheryn F. Weinhold
Fayette County

CRANBERRY MUFFINS

½ c. powdered	2 T. sugar
sugar	3 t. baking
½ c. cranberry-	powder
orange purée	1 egg
2 c. sifted flour	1 c. milk
¾ t. salt	

Combine cranberries and powdered sugar and let stand. Mix flour, baking powder, salt, and sugar together. Combine egg and milk and add to dry ingredients. Stir just enough to moisten dry ingredients. In the last few strokes of mixing, stir in cranberry mixture. Fill each muffin cup ⅔ full. Greased muffin tins or cupcake papers may be used. Bake at 425° for 30 min. Makes 12.

Mrs. Barbara Dorton
Delaware County

SHREDDED WHEAT AND ALL BRAN
MUFFINS

2 large or 3 small	⅓ c. plus 1 T.
shredded wheat	shortening
biscuits	1¼ c. sugar
¼ c. raisins	2 eggs
(or more)	2½ c. unsifted
1 c. boiling water	flour

1 pt. (2 c.)	2½ t. soda
buttermilk	2 c. all bran cereal
1 t. salt	

Pour boiling water over shredded wheat biscuits and raisins. Cool. Cream shortening and sugar. Combine with first mixture and add eggs and flour. Add buttermilk, salt, soda, and all bran. Store in refrigerator and use as desired. Will keep up to 6 weeks. Spoon into muffin cups and bake at 425° for 15 min., or until done.

Mabel Ehrhardt
Porter County

PANCAKES AND WAFFLES

PANCAKES

1 c. plus 2 T. milk	½ t. salt
2 T. shortening	2 T. sugar
or lard	2 T. baking
1 egg, beaten	powder
1 c. flour	

Mix lard, egg, and 1 c. milk. Add dry ingredients; add 2 T. milk. Fry on hot griddle. Serve with butter and syrup.

Cecile Nicoll
Carroll County

HOTCAKES ALASKA

⅔ c. warm water	1 egg
2 pkg. dry yeast	2 c. biscuit mix
¼ t. salt	1 c. milk

Measure warm water into bowl. Sprinkle in dry yeast and stir until dissolved. Add remaining ingredients. Beat with rotary beater until smooth. Let stand 10–15 min. (this gives the yeast time to work). Bake pancakes on a hot, lightly greased griddle. Turn only once when bubbles appear and the edge becomes dry. Serve with butter and syrup. Makes about twelve 4" pancakes.

Mrs. Edward Leonard
Pulaski County

OATMEAL PUFFERS

1 c. quick or old-	½ c. flour
fashioned	1 t. salt
rolled oats	2 T. sugar
1 c. milk	1 T. baking
¼ c. (½ stick)	powder
melted butter	1 egg
or vegetable oil	

Combine oats and milk in mixing bowl which will hold entire mixture; let stand 5 min. Sift flour, salt, sugar, and baking powder together; set aside. Beat egg, then beat in shortening. Add to milk and oats; mix well. Stir in dry ingredients only until moistened. Cover and let stand in refrigerator a few hours or overnight. Bake on ungreased or lightly greased griddle. Makes about twelve 4" pancakes.

Mrs. Freeman Phillips
Switzerland County

STIR-A-BOUT (1820)

Prepare a medium to thick pancake batter and pour into a hot well-greased skillet. With a spoon stir and cut constantly until the batter forms small balls. Serve with butter and syrup.

This recipe has been a favorite for six generations. My great-great grandmother used this method to serve pancakes to a very large family.

Harriet S. Cutshall
Monroe County

PECAN WAFFLES

2⅔ c. flour, sifted	2⅔ c. milk
3 T. sugar	½ c. plus 1 T.
4 t. baking	butter, melted
powder	⅓ c. pecans,
1 t. salt	chopped
4 eggs, separated	

Sift dry ingredients. Beat yolks until thick. Combine yolks with milk and butter and stir into dry ingredients. Add pecans. Beat egg whites until stiff and fold into batter. Bake in hot waffle iron. Makes 6–8.

Nancy Hewitt
Wells County

Yeast Breads

LOAF BREADS

OLD-FASHIONED WHITE BREAD

2 cakes yeast	4 T. sugar
1 c. lukewarm	4 t. salt
water	4 T. melted
2 c. evaporated	shortening
milk (diluted	12 c. sifted flour
with 2 c. water)	

Soften yeast in lukewarm water. Scald milk; add sugar, salt, and shortening. Cool to lukewarm. Add 2 c. flour, mixing well. Add yeast. Add 2 c. flour at a time, until 11 cups have been added, mixing well each time. Turn out on floured board using the 12th cup of flour to knead with. Knead until satin smooth (5–8 minutes). Shape into ball; place in lightly greased bowl. Grease surface of dough lightly. Cover dough. Let rise 1½ hours in warm place (80–85°) or until double in bulk. Punch down and divide into 4 equal portions, forming smooth balls. Cover dough and let rest 10 minutes. Shape into loaves or rolls. Place in greased bread pans and let rise 1 hour more. Bake loaves at 400° for 50 minutes; rolls at 350° for 25–30 min. Remove from oven, brush melted shortening or butter on top and place damp towel around bread. Makes 4 loaves or 24 medium size rolls.

Note: Yeast must have plenty of worked foam on top or this bread will fail.

Marium Bourlard
Boone County

BUTTERMILK BREAD

2 c. buttermilk	2 pkg. yeast
¼ c. sugar	½ t. baking soda
1 T. salt	7–7½ c. flour
½ c. warm water	¼ c. shortening

Combine buttermilk, sugar, salt, and shortening in pan. Heat until bubbles appear on edges. Cool. Measure water in large bowl, put yeast in, and add lukewarm milk mixture. Sift baking soda with 3 c. flour and add. Beat hard until smooth. Add remaining flour to make soft dough, turn out on floured board. Knead 5 minutes or until smooth. Let rise about 1½ hr., then punch down, and let rise 30 min. Knead to distribute bubbles. Divide into 2 loaves and bake at 350° for 25–30 min.

Mrs. Oscar Hoffman
Dubois County

BUSY DAY BATTER BREAD

2 pkg. yeast	½ c. instant dry
½ c. lukewarm	milk
water	4 T. soft
4 c. sifted flour	shortening
¼ c. sugar	1 c. water
1½ t. salt	

Stir to dissolve yeast in ½ c. lukewarm water. Sift flour onto waxed paper. Put into a bowl: sugar, salt, dry milk, shortening, and 1 c. water. Mix in yeast mixture. Add ½ of flour (2 c.) and beat with electric mixer at medium speed for 2 min. Stir in remaining flour and beat for 3 min. Cover with waxed paper and cloth. Allow to double in bulk (about 1½ hr.). Stir down about 50 strokes. Put in well-greased 9×5×3″ pan. Smooth top with lightly floured finger. Allow to double in bulk (about 45 min.). Bake at 375° for 45 min. or until well browned and bread pulls away from sides. Dough may also be placed in greased muffin tins, filling tins ½–⅔ full. Let rise and bake at 400° for 15–20 min.

This batter bread also makes good sweet rolls by putting butter, brown sugar, and halves of nuts into muffin tins and filling tins ½–⅔ full with batter. Let rise and bake at 400° for 15–20 min.

Marjorie Dierdorf
Knox County

ANADAMA BREAD

1½ c. water	1 cake compressed
1 t. salt	yeast or 1 pkg.
⅓ c. yellow	dry yeast
cornmeal	¼ c. lukewarm
⅓ c. molasses or	water
sorghum	4–4½ c. flour
1½ T. shortening	

Bring 1½ c. water and salt to boil in a saucepan; remove from heat and add cornmeal, then molasses and shortening. Let it just come to boil and immediately remove from heat. Cool slightly, then add yeast which has been dissolved in ¼ c. lukewarm water. Mix in flour, first with large spoon and then with hands. Dough will be

slightly sticky. Lightly grease large bowl and round up dough. Cover with damp warm cloth, let rise in warm area for 1–1½ hr. Knead well, then shape into loaf and place in 9×5×3″ loaf pan. Let rise until double (about 1 hr.). Bake at 375° for 40–45 min.

You may brush top with melted butter and sprinkle cornmeal mixed with a little salt over top before baking for a nice crusty top.

Mildred Clifford
Boone County

EARLY COLONIAL BREAD

½ c. yellow	½ c. lukewarm
cornmeal	water
5 T. dark brown	¾ c. stirred
sugar	whole-wheat
1 T. salt	flour
2 c. boiling water	½ c. stirred rye
½ c. cooking oil	flour
2 pkg. active dry	4¼–4½ c. sifted
yeast	all-purpose
	flour

Combine thoroughly cornmeal, brown sugar, salt, boiling water, and oil. Let cool to lukewarm, about 30 min. Soften yeast in ½ c. lukewarm water. Stir into the cornmeal mixture. Add whole wheat and rye flours and mix well. Stir in enough all-purpose flour to make a moderately stiff dough. Turn out on lightly floured surface and knead until smooth and elastic, 6–8 min. Place in greased bowl, turning once to grease surface. Cover and let rise in warm place until double, 50–60 min. Punch down. Turn out on lightly floured surface and divide in half. Cover and let rest 10 minutes. Shape into 2 loaves and place in greased 9×5×3″ loaf pans. Let rise again until almost double, about 30 min. Bake at 375° for 45 min., or until done. Cap loosely with foil after first 25 min. if bread browns too much. Remove from pans. Cool on rack.

Mrs. Harold Oman
LaPorte County

PIONEER BREAD

½ c. yellow cornmeal	4 T. molasses
⅓ c. cold water	2 t. salt
1 c. boiling water	2 c. tomato juice
4 T. vegetable oil	2 pkg. dry yeast
	10 c. flour

Stir cornmeal into cold water. Add this mixture to boiling water, stirring constantly while boiling 5 min. Add to the mush mixture vegetable oil, molasses, and salt. Set aside to cool to lukewarm. Heat tomato juice to lukewarm; add dry yeast and stir until dissolved. Combine with the lukewarm mush mixture. Stir into the mixture 4 c. of flour, until smooth. Knead 6 c. of flour into the batter. Set dough in a warm place until double in bulk. Then knead down and let rest 15 min. Grease 3 bread pans with shortening. Divide bread dough into 3 equal portions. Let dough rise again until double in size. Bake at 325° for 30 min., or until done.

Albertamae Stanley
Hendricks County

BEER BREAD

¼ c. very warm water	¼ c. sugar
3 T. yeast	1½ T. salt
2¾ c. warm beer	5 T. oil
	6–8 c. flour

Combine water and yeast; add beer, sugar, and salt. Beat in 3–4 c. flour, then knead in 3–4 c. more flour. Add oil. Knead 5–10

min. Cover; let rise 45 min., or until doubled. Punch down, divide, and place in two greased 9×5" pans. Let rise for 30 min. Bake at 375° for 35–40 min.

Marie Reineke
Posey County

DILLY BREAD

1 pkg. active dry yeast	1 T. instant minced onion
¼ c. warm water	1 T. butter
1 c. creamed cottage cheese, heated to lukewarm	2 t. dill seed
	1 t. salt
	¼ t. soda
	1 egg
2 T. sugar	2¼–2½ c. flour

Soften yeast in water. In large bowl, combine cottage cheese, sugar, onion, butter, dill seed, salt, soda, egg, and yeast. Gradually add flour to form a stiff dough, beating well after each addition. Cover; let rise in warm place until doubled, 50–60 min. Stir down dough with a spoon. Place in a well-greased 8" round (1½–2 qt.) casserole. Let rise again in warm place until doubled, about 30–40 min. Bake at 350° for 40–50 min. until golden brown. Brush with butter and sprinkle with coarse salt.

Anita Haddix
Wells County

FRENCH BREAD

2 pkg. yeast	2 c. boiling water
1 T. sugar	6½ c. flour
½ c. lukewarm water	1 egg
2 T. sugar	2 T. milk
2 T. shortening	sesame or poppy seeds
2 t. salt	(optional)

Dissolve yeast and 1 T. sugar in lukewarm water. Dissolve 2 T. sugar, shortening, and salt in boiling water; cool. Pour mixtures together and mix in flour. Put in warm place and stir down 5 times within an hour. Divide into 2 or 3 loaves. Roll out to less than ½″ thick. Roll like jelly rolls and put on greased cookie sheet. Slit tops ¼″ deep. Let rise 20–30 min. Beat egg and milk. Brush tops and sides of loaves. Sprinkle seeds on tops of loaves, if desired. Bake 20–30 min. at 400°.

Mrs. Hugh Umbaugh
Marshall County

HERB BREAD MIXTURE

1 t. thyme	½ t. salt
½ t. rosemary	2 dashes of
1 t. marjoram	cayenne
1 t. basil	¼ lb. butter,
½ t. savory	softened
½ t. paprika	

Combine ingredients. Take one loaf of French bread and cut slices ¾ of the way through. Spread each slice with mixture. Wrap bread in foil and bake at 350° for approximately 15 min., or until butter is melted into bread and bread is good and hot.

Carol Mills
Morgan County

GRANOLA BREAD

2 T. butter or	1 c. granola
margarine	½ c. wheat germ
2 c. water	2 t. salt
¼ c. molasses	2 pkg. active dry
½ c. orange	yeast
marmalade	4 c. all-purpose
2 c. whole-wheat	flour
flour	

Put water, butter, molasses, and marmalade in saucepan over low heat until very warm (120–130°). Stir together in large

mixer bowl the next 5 ingredients and 1 c. flour. Pour heated liquid over flour mixture and beat 3 min. at medium speed, scraping sides of bowl occasionally. Stir in enough flour to make a moderately stiff dough. Turn out on floured board and knead, adding more flour as needed, for 8 min., or until smooth and elastic. Put in greased bowl and turn to grease top. Cover and let rise in warm place free from drafts for 1¼ hr., or until doubled in bulk. Punch down and divide into 2 equal parts. Roll each in a rectangle about 9×14″. Shape in 2 loaves by rolling dough from short end. Seal ends and put in 2 greased 9×5×3″ loaf pans. Cover and let rise in warm place 1½ hr., or until doubled in bulk. Bake at 375° for 40 min. Cool on wire racks.

Anna Lee
Parke County

OATMEAL YEAST BREAD

½ c. warm water	2 T. shortening
1½ pkg. dry	(part butter)
yeast	1 T. salt
2 c. milk, scalded	2 c. quick oats
¼ c. brown	5½ c. sifted flour
sugar, packed	

Dissolve yeast in warm water. Add sugar, salt, and shortening to scalded milk. Cool. Stir in yeast liquid. Add oats and flour. Let stand 10 min. Knead until smooth and elastic. Place in a greased bowl. Let rise until double in bulk. Shape into loaves and place in two greased 5×9×3″ loaf pans or three greased 7⅜×3⅝×2¼″ pans. Let rise until almost to top of pans. Bake at 350° for about 40 min., or until browned on top. When done, turn out on rack, butter top, and cool.

May Brown
Rush County

CASSEROLE ONION BREAD

1 c. milk	2 pkg. yeast
1 T. salt	½ c. onion,
3 T. sugar	minced
1½ T. margarine	4 c. unsifted flour
¾ c. warm water	

Scald milk; stir in sugar, salt, and margarine. Cool to lukewarm. Measure water into large bowl; add yeast, and stir. Add milk mixture, onions, and flour. Stir until well blended (about 2 min.). Cover; let rise until more than doubled (about 45 min.). Stir batter down. Beat vigorously (about ½ min.). Turn into greased 1½-qt. casserole or two 9×5×3″ pans. Bake uncovered at 375° for 45 min. to 1 hr.

Barbara Cloud
Rush County

RAISIN BREAD

1 c. milk	2 pkg. yeast
½ c. sugar	1 egg
1 t. salt	4½ c. unsifted
¼ c. (½ stick)	flour
margarine or	1 c. seedless
butter	raisins
½ c. warm water	2 t. cinnamon

Scald milk; add sugar, salt, and shortening. Cool. Dissolve yeast in warm water. Stir yeast liquid, egg, and 3 c. flour into milk mixture. Beat until smooth. Stir in remaining flour to make a stiff batter. Cover; let rise till double (about 1 hr.). Stir batter down. Beat in plumped raisins and cinnamon. Turn into two greased 1-qt. casserole dishes and bake at 375° until done. Ice, if desired. May also be baked in angel food cake pan with icing drizzled over.

Jan Heiny
Pulaski County

GRANDMA ESTHER'S SWEDISH RYE BREAD

2 c. milk, scalded,	½ c. molasses
or potato water	1 cake yeast
2 heaping T.	¼ c. warm water
shortening	2 c. rye flour
2 t. salt	4 c. white flour
½ c. brown sugar	

Dissolve yeast in water. Scald milk and while cooling add salt, sugar, molasses, and shortening. When cool, add yeast and flour. Pour onto floured board and knead; add flour as needed. Let rise in greased bowl until double in size. Punch down and form into two large loaves. Place in greased loaf pans. Let rise again. Bake at 375° for 45–50 min.

Marlene O'Bryan
Marion County

HERB SOUR CREAM BREAD

½ c. warm water	½ t. marjoram
(105–115°)	leaves
2 pkg. dry yeast	½ t. oregano
1 c. warm sour	½ t. thyme
cream	2 eggs at room
6 T. margarine	temperature
⅓ c. sugar	3¾–4¾ c.
2 t. salt	unsifted flour

Measure warm water into large warm bowl. Sprinkle in yeast; stir until dissolved. Add sour cream, margarine, sugar, salt, marjoram, oregano, thyme, and eggs. Beat in 3 c. flour until well blended (about 1 min.). Stir in enough additional flour to make soft dough. Cover and let rise in warm place until it has doubled in bulk (about 50 min.). Then stir or punch down. Turn into two greased 1-qt. casserole dishes. Cover and let rise 1 hr. Bake at 375° for about 35 min. Remove from casserole; cool on wire racks. This is very good served with herb butter spread on it.

Herb Butter:

1 stick of butter	1 t. marjoram
2 T. fresh chives, chopped	leaves

Mix or beat together.

Mrs. Joseph Haas
Shelby County

WHEAT GERM BREAD

2¾ c. water	¾ c. instant
¼ c. honey	nonfat dry milk
2 T. margarine	1 pkg. dry yeast
1 c. plain yogurt	5 t. salt
8–9 c. flour	1 c. wheat germ

Combine water, honey, margarine, and yogurt in saucepan and heat until very warm (120–130°). (Margarine does not need to melt.) In a large bowl mix thoroughly 3½ c. flour, dry milk, dry yeast, and salt. Gradually add warm liquid, scraping bowl occasionally. Stir in wheat germ and enough additional flour to make a stiff dough. Turn out onto a lightly floured board; knead until smooth and elastic (about 8–10 min.). Place in greased bowl, turning to grease top. Cover and let rise in a warm place free from draft until doubled in bulk (about 1 hr.). Punch down dough and form into two large loaves (using large bread pans) or into three medium loaves (using medium bread pans). Cover the loaves and let rise until doubled (about 1 hr.). Brush with beaten egg and sprinkle with wheat germ. Bake at 350° for 30–35 min., or until done. Remove from baking pans and cool on wire racks.

Dough may be formed into braided loaves and baked on cooky sheets.

Mrs. Donald R. Wolf
Allen County

MOLASSES WHEAT BREAD

2 envelopes active dry yeast	4 t. salt
	⅓ c. light or dark molasses
1 c. lukewarm water	1 c. wheat germ
⅓ c. sugar	2 c. sifted whole wheat flour
⅓ c. vegetable shortening	6 c. (about) all-purpose flour
2 c. lukewarm milk	

Dissolve yeast in lukewarm water. Stir in sugar, shortening, salt, milk, and molasses. Beat in wheat germ, whole wheat flour, and enough white flour to make a stiff dough. Turn out on floured board and knead 10 to 15 min. until smooth and elastic. Cover dough and let rise in a warm place until double in bulk. Grease two 9×5×3″ pans. Cut dough in two equal pieces. Shape into loaves and place seam side down in two greased pans. Let dough rise until double in bulk. Bake at 375° 40–45 min. Unmold and cool thoroughly before slicing. After cooling, the loaves may be wrapped in foil and frozen. To thaw, unwrap and let stand at room temperature for 30 min. For crisp crust, brush loaves with water or beaten egg white before rising. For soft crust, brush loaves before rising with melted butter.

Mrs. Charles McIntyre
Fayette County

WHOLE WHEAT BREAD

1 yeast cake	2 T. blackstrap molasses
1 c. lukewarm water	1 t. salt
1 c. milk, scalded	6 c. sifted whole-wheat flour
2 T. butter	
2 T. honey	

Dissolve yeast in lukewarm water. Add

milk to butter, molasses, honey, and salt with yeast water. Add flour until dough can be handled without sticking to hands. It will not require all the flour. Place in greased bowl; cover until doubled in size. Divide in half. Shape and place in greased pans. Cover with towels. Let rise again. Bake for 45 min. at 375°.

Wilma Hudson
Pike County

YEAST BISCUITS

ANGEL BISCUITS

1 cake yeast	3 t. baking
5 c. flour	powder
¾ c. shortening	3 T. sugar
(scant)	½ c. lukewarm
1 t. salt	water
1 t. baking soda	2 c. buttermilk

Dissolve yeast in lukewarm water. Sift together dry ingredients. Cut in shortening, add buttermilk and dissolved yeast. Mix well with large spoon until all flour is moistened. Cover bowl and place in refrigerator. When ready to use, take amount out that is needed and roll on floured board to ½" thick. Cut out with cutter and bake on greased cookie sheet at 400° for 12 min. Yields 6 dozen. Dough will keep several weeks in refrigerator.

Lola Adams
Pike County

QUICK YEAST BISCUITS

1 pkg. yeast	¼ c. shortening
1 c. warm water	3 c. self-rising
1 egg	flour
2 T. sugar	½ t. salt

Mix shortening and flour. In another bowl put remaining ingredients; beat with mixer until egg is well mixed. Add to flour mixture and stir just until dough goes together. Cover and put in the refrigerator. Roll out like biscuits and bake at 400° for 10–15 min.

Muriel Reynolds
Perry County

NASHVILLE HOUSE FRIED BISCUITS

½ c. shortening	½ c. lukewarm
1 qt. milk	water
½ c. sugar	6 t. salt
3 pkg. dry yeast	7–9 c. flour

Dissolve yeast in lukewarm water. Add other ingredients. Let rise covered, until about double, in warm place. Work into biscuits and drop into hot grease at 375°. Makes about 7 dozen.

Mrs. Fred Cole
Steuben County

YEAST BUNS AND MUFFINS

BUTTERMILK BUNS

4½ c. flour	1¼ t. salt
2 pkg. dry yeast	¼ c. sugar
¾ c. warm water	½ c. butter or
(105–115°)	margarine
2 t. baking	1¼ c. buttermilk
powder	

Heat oven to 350°. Turn off and let cool 10 min. Place flour in warm oven for 15 min. Dissolve yeast in warm water, set aside. Place heated flour, baking powder, salt, and sugar in large bowl. Cut in butter until mixture looks like meal. Make well in center and pour in buttermilk and dissolved yeast. Stir well, then knead to blend well. Add more flour if necessary until dough does not adhere to side of bowl. Dough will be soft and slightly sticky.

Knead gently in bowl for 2 min. Let rise in warm place until double (about 1 hr.). Punch down, divide into 24 equal parts. Shape each piece into a smooth ball, place about 3″ apart on lightly greased pan. Let rise until double (about 45 min). Bake at 375° until brown (15–20 min.). Makes 2 dozen.

Mrs. Cecil Austin
Hendricks County

FEATHER BUNS

2 pkgs. dry yeast	4 T. butter
1 c. warm milk	1 c. warm water
1 t. sugar	4 c. flour, plus
1 t. salt	enough to
½ c. sugar	make soft
3 eggs	dough

Beat the first 3 ingredients with mixer and let stand 20 min. Then add remaining ingredients. Beat with mixer. Knead in enough flour to make a soft dough. Put in a greased bowl and let rise twice, punching in each time. When it has risen the third time, shape into buns and let rise. Bake at 350° for 25 min. Makes 2 dozen buns.

Many variations can be made from this dough: braided coffee cakes, doughnuts stuffed with cooked prunes (with the pit in) and covered with the dough and fried in deep shortening, and buns. Coffee cakes may be frosted with powdered sugar icing and covered with chopped nuts.

Stella Schnepf
Adams County

HAMBURGER ONION BUNS

1 pkg. active dry yeast	2 T. instant minced onion
1¼ c. warm water	4 c. Bisquick
2 T. sugar	shortening

In large mixing bowl, dissolve yeast in water. Add sugar and half the Bisquick. Beat 2 min. with mixer at medium speed, scraping sides and bottom of bowl frequently, or 300 vigorous strokes by hand. Add remaining Bisquick and the onion. Blend well with spoon. Scrape batter from sides of bowl. Cover with cloth. Let rise in warm place (85°) until double, about 30 min. Stir down by beating 25 strokes. Drop dough by spoonfuls, forming 12 mounds, about 2″ apart on greased baking sheet. With floured fingers, flatten mounds into rounds about ½″ thick. Let rise in warm place (85°) for 40 min. Bake at 400° for 12–15 min., or until browned. While hot, brush top of bun with shortening.

Mrs. Homer Johnson
Steuben County

ENGLISH MUFFINS

¾ c. scalded milk, cooled to lukewarm	1 pkg. yeast
	1 T. honey
	1 egg (optional)
¼ c. shortening, melted and cooled to lukewarm	1 t. salt
	3 c. wheat flour
	½ c. (about) cornmeal

Add lukewarm shortening (test on wrist) to the lukewarm milk. Add honey, egg, and salt to this mixture; stir. Add the softened yeast. Stir in about half the flour. Knead in rest of flour. Let rise until double. Punch down and knead. Pat dough on floured surface to a thickness of about ½″. Cut into rounds with cup or jar and let rise 1 hr. Sprinkle cornmeal in frying pan or griddle with about a tablespoon (more, if needed) lard. Bake 7 min. Cover pan before and after turning, so they bake as well as fry. Yield 1 dozen.

Shirley Kuhn
Pulaski County

YEAST DOUGHNUTS

YEAST DOUGHNUTS

1 c. milk	½ c. sugar
1 pkg. yeast	½ c. butter
2 c. flour, plus	3 eggs, beaten
approximately	1 t. vanilla
4 to 5 c.	pinch of salt

Scald milk and cool to lukewarm. Add yeast to milk; stir in 2 c. flour. Let set for ½ hr. Add the rest of the ingredients except flour. Stir and add enough flour (approximately 4 to 5 c.) to make soft dough. Let rise until doubled in bulk. Roll out to ¼–½″ thick and cut with doughnut cutter. Let rise for 15 min. Fry in medium-hot grease. Drain. Glaze while hot.

Glaze:

1 lb. powdered	1 T. cream
sugar	vanilla
1 T. corn starch	

Mix with cream and enough vanilla to make a paste.

Mrs. Eugene Wilson
Wabash County

YEAST POTATO DOUGHNUTS

1 c. sieved cooked	1 T. salt
potatoes	1 pkg. dry yeast
1 c. liquid from	2 eggs
potatoes	5–6 c. flour
¾ c. vegetable	¾ c. warm water
shortening	(105–115°)
½ c. sugar	

Dissolve yeast in warm water. Stir in mixture of potatoes, water from potatoes, shortening, sugar, and salt. Stir in eggs. Add enough flour to make dough. Turn onto lightly floured surface; knead 5–8 min. Place in greased bowl. Lightly grease top of dough. (Do not punch down.) Cover; let rise 1–1½ hr. Pat dough on lightly floured surface to ¾″. Cut with 2½″ cutter. Let rise 1 hr. Heat oil or shortening to 375°. Fry doughnuts 2–3 min. each side. Drain on paper towels. Glaze while warm.

Glaze:

6 c. powdered	1 c. boiling
sugar	water

Mix powdered sugar, and boiling water until consistency of gravy.

Dough may be kept for 3 days if covered with damp towel immediately after kneading and stored in refrigerator. If dough rises, punch down, and re-cover with damp towel.

Mrs. Charles Coughlin
Vanderburgh County

MEXICAN DOUGHNUTS
(*Sopaipillas*)

¼ c. lukewarm	⅓ c. melted
water	margarine
1 pkg. yeast	⅓ c. sugar
1 egg	5 c. flour
1½ c. milk	1 T. cornmeal
1¼ t. salt	

Mix water and yeast in blender until thoroughly mixed. Blend in remaining ingredients and 2 c. flour. Put dough in large bowl, cover, and let stand in warm place 1 hour. Add remaining flour. Knead into soft dough. Cover and let rise until double in size. Punch down and store in a plastic bag in refrigerator until ready to use. Dough will keep in refrigerator for a few days. Roll dough about ⅛″ thick. Cut into 4 to 5″ squares or triangles. Heat oil in deep pan. It is hot enough when dough sinks to the bottom and rises quickly. Fry pieces until they are puffy and golden brown. Serve with honey or covered with powdered sugar. Serves 12.

Mrs. Reid Keffer
Boone County

YEAST ROLLS

HOT ROLLS

2 cakes yeast	1 egg
2 c. warm water	4 T. melted
½ c. sugar	shortening
1 t. salt	7 c. flour

Mix all ingredients together. Knead on floured board. Shape into loaves or make individual rolls. Place in greased pans. Let rise (they do not have to rise twice). Bake at 375° until golden brown. Remove from oven; spread butter on tops.

Mary Rose Strosnider
Lawrence County

QUICK YEAST ROLLS

1 c. warm water	1 t. salt
1 pkg. dry yeast	1 egg
2 T. sugar	2 T. soft
2¼ c. flour	shortening

Dissolve yeast in water. Stir in sugar, ½ the flour & salt. Beat with spoon until smooth. Add egg and shortening. Beat in rest of flour until smooth. Cover with cloth and let rise in warm place until double (30 min.). Grease 12 large muffin cups. Stir dough. Spoon into cups until ½ full. Let rise to top of cup (20–30 min.). Bake 15–20 min. at 400°.

Judith Leitch
Noble County

RICH REFRIGERATOR ROLLS

2 pkg. dry yeast	3 eggs
1 c. warm water	1 t. salt
½ c. margarine	5 c. sifted flour
½ c. sugar	

Add yeast to warm water and let stand. Set aside. Measure margarine, sugar, salt, and eggs in large bowl. Blend with mixer at low speed. Add 1 c. flour to bowl, then the yeast mixture. Beat until smooth. Add more flour, beating first with mixer, then by hand. Blend well. Cover with waxed paper, then with foil. Refrigerate 2 hr. to 3 days. Punch down occasionally as it rises. Shape as desired. Place on greased baking sheets. Cover and let rise 1–1½ hr. Place in cold oven and turn it on to 400°. Bake about 25 min. Makes about 3 dozen.

Marsha Boyd
Daviess County

COTTAGE CHEESE YEAST ROLLS

1 pkg. yeast	Filling:
¼ c. warm water	
2½ c. flour	3 T. butter,
¼ c. sugar	melted
1 t. salt	¾ c. brown sugar
½ c. butter or	¼ t. salt
margarine	½ t. almond
1 c. small-curd	extract
cottage cheese	½ t. vanilla
1 egg, beaten	½ c. nuts,
	chopped

Dissolve yeast in warm water. Sift flour, sugar, and salt. Cut in butter or margarine. Add cottage cheese, egg, and dissolved yeast. Knead dough and roll into 14″ square. Combine ingredients for filling. Spread filling on dough square and roll up. Cut in slices, 8 or more, and place on greased cookie sheet. Let rise until double in size. Bake at 400° for 10–15 min., until lightly browned. Glaze with mixture of confectioners' sugar and milk.

Mrs. Wesley R. Goss
Allen County

MUSH ROLLS

From a 1923 Cookbook:

½ c. sugar	1 qt. warm mush
½ c. butter or other shortening	1 t. salt
	1 yeast cake
	flour

Mix thoroughly and add yeast cake previously well soaked. When well raised, add flour to make a dough. Let rise and mold into rolls, two in one gem pan. Make in morning for supper or at night for breakfast. Bake about 40 min. in moderate oven.

Mrs. Lewis Wiley
Jay County

OATMEAL YEAST ROLLS

¾ c. milk, scalded	1½ T. shortening
1½ t. salt	2 T. molasses
2 T. brown sugar	1 c. rolled oats
1 pkg. yeast	⅓ c. warm water
1 egg, beaten	2¾–3 c. flour

Combine scalded milk, salt, shortening, molasses, brown sugar, and oats and stir well. Cool to lukewarm. Dissolve yeast in warm water. Add yeast, egg, and 1 c. flour to milk mixture; beat until smooth. Gradually add remaining flour; stir. Turn onto lightly floured board and knead for 10 min. Place dough in greased bowl, turn, and cover with damp cloth. Let rise until double in bulk. Punch down. Shape dough into balls sized to ½ fill greased muffin pans. Cover and let rise until double in size. Bake at 400° for 15–18 min. Makes 18 rolls.

Ruby H. Lough
Parke County

PARKER HOUSE WHEAT ROLLS

2 c. all-purpose flour, sifted	½ c. boiling water
1 c. whole-wheat flour	1 cake compressed yeast or 1 pkg. dry granular yeast
½ c. shortening	
¼ c. sugar	
½ t. salt	½ c. lukewarm water
1 egg, well beaten	

Combine flours. Cream shortening, sugar, and salt in large bowl. Blend in ½ c. boiling water; cool to lukewarm. Dissolve yeast in ½ c. lukewarm water. Add to shortening-sugar liquid. Blend in egg and combined flours. Mix well. Place in greased bowl. Cover. Let rise in warm place (85–90°) until double in bulk, about 1–1¼ hr. Roll out on lightly floured board to ¼″ thickness. Cut into rounds with 3″ cutter and brush with melted butter. Mark a crease with dull edge of knife to one side of center of each round. Fold small part over large, press edges to seal, and place in greased pan. Tops may be brushed with butter. Let rise in warm place until double in bulk, about 1 hour. Bake in moderately hot oven (400°) 12–15 min. Makes 24 rolls.

Eleanor Lowe
Marion County

POPPY SEED ROLLS

2 pkg. yeast	½ c. shortening
½ c. very warm water	2 t. salt
½ c. plus 1 T. sugar	3 eggs, beaten
	6 c. flour
1 c. scalded milk	poppy seeds

Sprinkle yeast and 1 T. sugar into very warm water and stir until dissolved. Mix scalded milk, ½ c. sugar, salt, and shortening until shortening is melted. Cool until lukewarm. Add beaten eggs and 2 c. flour to milk mixture. Beat at medium speed with mixer for about 4–5 min. Add yeast mixture. Stir in the rest of the flour by hand. Stir until smooth. Put in greased bowl and let rise until double in bulk. Punch dough down and divide into two parts. (Dough may be divided into three parts and rolled in the same way to make smaller rolls.) Roll each part into a 9 to 10″ circle and cut into 12 (pie) wedges. Roll wedges up starting at wide end. Place on greased cookie sheet. Brush with milk and sprinkle on poppy seeds. Let rise until double in bulk. Bake at 400° for 10 min., then at 375° for 15 min., or until brown. Makes 2–3 dozen.

Susann Wendel
Franklin County

MASHED POTATO ROLLS

2 cakes granular yeast	1½ t. salt
1½ c. lukewarm potato water	2 eggs, well beaten
⅔ c. sugar	7–7½ c. sifted flour
1 c. mashed potatoes	⅔ c. melted shortening

Put yeast in crock; add a little lukewarm potato water. When dissolved, add mashed potatoes, remaining potato water, sugar, salt, and eggs. Add about half of flour; beat well. Add shortening; then add rest of flour. Turn out on board and let stand 10 min. to tighten up. Knead until smooth. Place in greased crock to rise and double in bulk. Shape into rolls or store in refrigerator. Dough will keep several days. Bake at 425° for 15 min. Makes 50 rolls.

Mrs. Anna Wells
Clark County

YEAST SWEET BREADS

BASIC SWEET DOUGH

½ c. warm water	½ c. soft
2 pkg. active dry yeast	shortening or 1 stick margarine
1½ c. milk	flour as needed,
½ c. sugar	approximately
2 eggs	7 c.
2 t. salt	

Scald milk. Remove milk from heat; add sugar, salt, butter or margarine. While milk is cooling to lukewarm, dissolve yeast in warm water. When milk mixture is cool, add beaten eggs and dissolved yeast. Add 3 c. flour and stir (with mixer) until flour is blended. Add enough flour (approximately 4 c.) until mixture leaves sides of mixing bowl. Turn on floured board or countertop and knead until smooth and elastic. Put in greased mixing bowl. Cover bowl with cloth. Let rise in a warm place until double, about 1½ hours. Punch down. Let rise 30 min. Shape, let rise in greased pans and bake.

Goldie Miller
Crawford County

ALMOND COFFEE PUFFS

1 cake compressed yeast	½ t. salt
¼ c. lukewarm water	2–2½ c. flour
	2 eggs
½ c. milk	1 c. almonds,
¼ c. shortening	blanched and
5 T. sugar	chopped

Soften yeast in lukewarm water. Scald milk; add shortening, 1 T. sugar, and salt. Cool to lukewarm. Add flour, beating thoroughly. Add softened yeast, and then add unbeaten eggs, one at a time. Beat until mixture is smooth. Cover and let rise until double, about 1 hour. Stir down and add ½ c. chopped almonds. Fill greased muffin pans ½ full. Sprinkle with remaining almonds which have been mixed with 4 T. sugar. Cover and let rise until doubled (about 30 min.). Bake at 375° for 15–20 min. Makes 2 dozen 2″ puffs.

Karen Merkel
Dearborn County

CHRISTMAS BREAD (*Yule Kaga*)

2 cakes yeast	½ c. citron,
¼ c. sugar	chopped
1 c. milk, scalded	½ c. raisins,
4½ c. flour	chopped
1 t. salt	½ c. currants,
¼ c. shortening	chopped
2 eggs, beaten	

Make as bread, mixing all together and let rise twice before putting in pan for baking. Use any 8″ round cake pan. Serves 12–15.

Vivian Saxton
Marion County

CHRISTMAS DANISH ROLLS

3½–4 c. unsifted	¼ c. (½ stick)
flour	margarine
½ c. sugar	2 eggs at room
1½ t. salt	temperature,
2 T. cornstarch	separate
1½ t. lemon peel,	1½ c. (3 sticks)
grated	margarine
2 pkg. active dry	1 T. water
yeast	confectioners′
¾ c. milk	sugar frosting
½ c. water	colored sprinkles

In a large bowl, thoroughly mix 1¼ c. flour, sugar, salt, cornstarch, lemon peel, and undissolved dry yeast. Combine milk, water, and ¼ c. margarine in saucepan. Heat over low heat until liquids are warm; margarine does not need to melt. Gradually add to dry ingredients and beat for 2 min. at medium speed with electric mixer, scraping bowl occasionally. Add 2 egg yolks, 1 egg white (reserve remaining egg white), and ¾ c. flour, or enough flour to make a thick batter. Beat at high speed for 2 min., scraping bowl occasionally. Add enough flour to make a stiff dough; stir just until blended. Cover tightly with aluminum foil; chill about 1 hr. On waxed paper, spread 1½ c. margarine into 10× 12″ rectangle. Chill 1 hr. On a lightly floured board, roll chilled dough into 12× 16″ rectangle. Place margarine slab on ⅔ of dough. Fold uncovered third over middle section; cover with remaining third. Give dough a quarter turn; roll into 12× 16″ rectangle; fold as above. Turn, roll, and fold once more. Chill 1 hr. Repeat procedure of 3 rollings, foldings, turnings, and chillings two more times. Refrigerate overnight. On a lightly floured board, divide dough in half. Roll ½ of dough into 15×6″ rectangle. Cut 12 strips, 15×½″. Twist each strip and form into a circle, sealing ends well. Place on greased baking sheets. Repeat with remaining piece of dough. Cover lightly with plastic wrap. Refrigerate overnight. Combine reserved egg white with 1 T. water. Brush rolls with egg white mixture. Bake in moderate oven (375°) about 15 to 20 min., or until done. Remove from baking sheets and cool on wire racks. Frost with confectioners′ sugar frosting and decorate with colored sprinkles. Makes 2 dozen rolls.

Marie L. Mapel
St. Joseph County

CHRISTMAS STOLLEN

2½ c. warm milk	4 eggs, beaten
1 stick butter or margarine	1 t. nutmeg
grated rind of 3 lemons and 1 orange	1 c. raisins, scalded and floured
1 t. salt	3 c. flour, plus enough to make soft dough
4 cakes or pkg. yeast	
½ c. warm water	Topping:
2½ c. sugar	confectioners' sugar frosting
1 pkg. red, green, and yellow gumdrops, cut in pieces and floured (optional)	1 drop of oil of cinnamon red and green sugar (optional)

Dissolve yeast in warm water. Put ingredients (except raisins and gumdrops) and 3 c. flour into bowl. Beat with electric mixer until well blended. Stir in prepared raisins and gumdrops; add extra flour to make soft dough. Knead a few minutes. Place in greased bowl to rise. When light, turn out on floured board and knead until elastic. Return to bowl and let rise again. When light, divide into two 8×8" pans or one 9×13" pan. Score top with a sharp knife from corner to corner, so top will remain more even; brush with melted butter, and let rise again. Bake at 350° about ½ hr. Cool on wire rack. Frost with confectioners' sugar frosting to which oil of cinnamon has been added. Red and green sugar may be sprinkled on top for holiday appearance.

Anna Fisse
Ripley County

COFFEE STICKS

½ c. shortening	½ c. plus 1 t. sugar
1 c. boiling water	2 well-beaten eggs
1 c. condensed milk	1 t. nutmeg
3 pkg. dry yeast	1 t. cinnamon
½ c. warm water	2 t. salt
8–9 c. flour	

Dissolve shortening in boiling water; cool to lukewarm. Add condensed milk. Dissolve yeast in water with 1 t. sugar. Add to milk; mix thoroughly. Add eggs, nutmeg, cinnamon, remaining sugar, salt, and flour. Knead for 5 min. Rest for 10 min. Roll out ¼" thick. Cut into strips. Let rise until double in bulk. Fry in deep fat at 420°. Makes 6 dozen sticks.

Frosting:

¼ c. butter	powdered sugar
½ c. brown sugar	few drops maple flavoring
2 T. cream	

Melt butter and brown sugar; boil for a few minutes. Add maple flavoring, cream, and enough powdered sugar to spread easily. Spread over sticks.

Mrs. James Bryan
Montgomery County

FILLED BUNDT KUCHEN

1 c. plain yogurt	¼ c. lukewarm water
1½ t. salt	
1 c. sugar	Filling:
1 c. butter	¾ c. sugar
1 T. lemon peel	½ c. flour
1 T. orange peel	½ c. butter
½ c. egg yolks, beaten	1 t. almond extract
1½ pkg. yeast	1 t. brandy extract
6 c. flour	

1 c. mixed	1½ c. coconut
candied fruit	¾ c. candied
1½ c. almonds,	cherries
ground	1 c. raisins

Dissolve yeast in lukewarm water. Pour scalded yogurt over salt, sugar, butter, and grated peels. Stir to melt butter. Let cool to lukewarm. Add egg yolks and dissolved yeast. Beat well. Gradually work in flour. Knead. Place in bowl, brush with fat, cover, and let rise until double. Mix ingredients to make filling. Punch dough down. Roll out dough and cover with filling. Roll like a jelly roll. Butter bundt pan, arrange almonds in a decorative pattern on bottom of pan, and place tightly rolled dough on top. Cover; let rise. Bake at 350° for 1 hr. Turn out and drizzle with confectioners' sugar icing. Makes 24 servings.

Maria Crosman
Marion County

LINCOLN LOGS

4–5 c. unsifted	¼ c. margarine
flour	2 eggs at room
½ c. sugar	temperature
1½ t. salt	
2 pkg. active dry	Filling:
yeast	8-oz. pkg. cream
½ c. milk	cheese, softened
½ c. water	1 egg yolk
	¼ c. sugar

In a large bowl, thoroughly mix 1¼ c. flour, ½ c. sugar, salt, and undissolved dry yeast. Combine milk, water, and margarine in saucepan. Heat over low heat until liquids are warm; margarine does not need to melt. Gradually add to dry ingredients and beat 2 min. at medium speed with electric mixer, scraping bowl occasionally. Add eggs and ½ c. flour, or enough flour to make a thick batter. Beat at high speed for 2 min., scraping bowl occasionally. Stir in enough additional flour to make a soft dough. Turn onto lightly floured board, knead until smooth and elastic (about 8–10 min.). Place in greased bowl, turning to grease top. Cover; let rise in warm place, free of drafts, until doubled in bulk, about 1 hour. Meanwhile prepare filling. Cream cheese with ¼ c. sugar until light and fluffy. Blend in egg yolk. Punch dough down; turn onto lightly floured board. Divide dough in half. Roll ½ of dough into 10×14" rectangle. Spread with ½ of filling. Roll up like jelly roll into 14" roll. Seal edges. Place on greased baking sheet. Cut slits ¾ through the log at 1" intervals. Repeat with remaining dough and filling. Cover; let rise in warm place until doubled in bulk (about 1 hr.). Bake in moderate oven (350°) about 20–25 min., or until done. Remove from baking sheets and cool. Frost with Browned Butter Frosting.

Browned Butter Frosting:

1 c. confectioners'	1½ T. milk
sugar	⅛ c. browned
1 t. vanilla	butter

Nancy Jackson
Elkhart County

MAPLE NUT COFFEE TWIST

3½ c. flour	2 eggs
1 pkg. yeast	6 T. butter,
¾ c. milk	melted
¼ c. butter	
1 t. salt	Filling:
1 t. honey	¾ c. sugar
1 t. maple	1 t. cinnamon
flavoring	1 c. pecans,
1 T. sugar	chopped

In large mixing bowl, combine 1½ c. flour and yeast. Heat milk, honey, butter, 1 T. sugar, salt, and flavoring to 115°, stirring to melt butter. Let cool to lukewarm. Add to dry mixture in bowl; add eggs. Beat at low speed with mixer for ½ min., scraping bowl. Beat 3 min. at high speed. Stir in rest of flour. Knead on floured surface. In greased bowl, let rise until doubled. Punch down, cover, and let rise 10 min. Mix together ¾ c. sugar, cinnamon, and pecans to make filling. Divide dough into 3 balls of equal size. Roll one ball out to edge of 12″ pizza pan. Brush with 2 T. melted butter. Sprinkle ⅓ of filling over dough. Continue with second ball of dough; place on top of first layer in pan. Brush with 2 T. butter and sprinkle ⅓ of filling. Do the same with the third ball, using the last of butter and filling. Place a glass in center of pizza pan. Cut from outside edge of pan to form 16 pie-shaped wedges. Twist each 3-layer wedge 3 times. Remove glass. Let rise until double. Bake at 350° for 20–25 min. Drizzle while warm with glaze. Makes 18 servings.

Glaze:

1½ c. powdered sugar	1 t. maple flavoring
3 T. milk	

Mix together until creamy. Drizzle over warm twist.

Mrs. Leo Bowman
Carroll County

NUT ROLLS

6 c. sifted flour	½ c. warm milk
1 t. salt	½ lb. butter
5 T. sugar	1 c. sour cream
2 small cakes yeast	3 eggs, slightly beaten

Filling:

1 c. sugar	1 lb. walnuts, finely ground

Mix walnuts and sugar to make filling. Mixture will make 3 c. filling—enough to fill a number of nut rolls. Sift flour into large bowl and add sugar, salt, and butter. Crumble as for pie dough. Dissolve yeast in warm milk and add to flour mixture with beaten eggs and sour cream. Knead well and remove dough to floured board. Divide into 4 equal parts. Roll dough into rectangles as for jelly roll and fill with nut mixture. Roll and place on greased baking sheets. Let rise for 1 hr. Brush with mixture of 1 egg and 1 T. water. Bake at 350° for 35 min.

Ruby Brown
Porter County

YEAST NUT TORTE

1 pkg. dry yeast	3 egg yolks, slightly beaten
¼ c. lukewarm water	
	Filling:
1 c. butter, melted	3 egg whites, beaten stiffly
1 t. salt	1 c. sugar
⅓ c. sugar	1 c. nuts, finely
4 c. flour	chopped

Dissolve yeast in water. Mix milk, butter, egg yolks, salt, and sugar in a large bowl. Add yeast. Add flour and beat thoroughly. Cover tightly with waxed paper and place in refrigerator overnight, or at least 4–5 hr. On a floured pastry cloth, roll into a rectangle about 12×18″. Beat sugar into egg whites gradually. Fold in nuts. Spread on dough. Roll like jelly roll. Place in buttered 10″ tube pan. Bake in moderate oven 1 hr. at 350°.

Mrs. Victoria Novy
LaPorte County

PLUCKETTS

1 pkg. yeast	⅓ c. butter,
1 c. milk, scalded	melted
⅓ c. sugar	
½ t. salt	Dipping mixture:
½ c. warm water	½ c. nuts,
3 eggs	chopped
4 c. flour	1 c. brown sugar
	3 t. cinnamon

Dissolve yeast in warm water. Add sugar, butter, and salt to scalded milk. When lukewarm, add dissolved yeast, eggs, and flour to milk mixture. Beat thoroughly. Let rise until double; stir down. Take teaspoonfuls of dough and make balls. Dip each ball in melted butter, then in mixture of nuts, brown sugar, and cinnamon. Pile balls loosely in ungreased angel food pan. Let rise 30 min. Bake at 400° for 10 min., then at 350° for 30 min. Turn pan upside down immediately. Serve warm. Everyone plucks his own roll.

Norma Cross
Randolph County

RAISIN TOWER BREADS

1 c. raisins	1 egg
¾ c. milk	3½ c. sifted flour
½ c. orange	½ c. soft butter
marmalade	1 c. powdered
1 T. sugar	sugar
1 t. salt	½ c. chopped
2 pkg. yeast	pecans
¼ c. warm water	1 T. orange juice

Chop raisins slightly. Heat milk to boiling and pour over raisins. Stir in marmalade, sugar, and salt. Cool to lukewarm. Dissolve yeast in water; add to raisin mixture. Add beaten egg and pecans. Beat in 2 c. flour thoroughly. Add softened butter and rest of flour. Beat or knead quite smooth. Cover

and refrigerate at least 2 hr. Divide dough into 12 equal balls. Press firmly into well-greased 6-oz. juice cans. Cover and let rise till doubled. Bake at 375° about 25 min. Mix powdered sugar and orange juice to spreading consistency. Ice when breads are cool. Sprinkle with nonpareils if desired.

Linda Honegger
Wells County

PIZZAS

AMERICAN PIZZA

Dough:	1 can mush-
2 c. Bisquick	rooms, drained
½ c. water	½ t. oregano
	1 c. grated cheese
Sauce:	or several slices
1½ lb. ground	of cheese, cut in
beef	small pieces
¼ c. chopped	¾ c. tomato sauce
onion	

Mix Bisquick and water; knead lightly. Place in 14″ round pizza pan and roll out to edge of pan making a slight rim. Fry ground beef and onions until almost done. Drain off grease. Place mushrooms on the dough, then ground beef and onions; sprinkle oregano over meat, then pour tomato sauce over the top. Bake for 20 min. at 425°. About five min. before it's done, sprinkle cheese over top and return to oven until cheese is melted.

Mrs. Marie Meyer
Dubois County

CRAZY CRUST PIZZA

Batter:	1 t. salt
1 c. flour	⅓ t. pepper
1 t. oregano	⅔ c. milk
2 eggs	

Topping:
1½ lb. ham-
  burger or
  sausage
¼ c. chopped
  onion
  (optional)
1 c. pizza sauce

1 4-oz. can mush-
  room stems and
  pieces, well
  drained
  (optional)
1 c. (4 oz.)
  shredded moz-
  zarella cheese

Brown hamburger or sausage, seasoning to taste. Drain; set aside. Lightly grease pan and dust with flour or cornmeal. Combine flour, salt, oregano, pepper, eggs, and milk. Pour batter into pan. Arrange topping of meat, onion, and mushrooms over batter. Bake on low rack in oven at 425° for 25–30 min. until pizza is deep golden brown. Remove from oven, drizzle with pizza sauce and sprinkle with cheese. Return to oven for 10–15 min.

If desired, use 8 oz. tomato sauce, 1–2 t. oregano, and ¼ t. pepper as a substitute for pizza sauce.

Lois Shroyer
Delaware County

GOOD 'N EASY PIZZA

Dough:
1 pkg. active dry
  yeast
1 c. warm water
1 t. sugar
1 t. salt
2 T. salad oil
2½ c. flour

Sauce:
½ c. onion,
  chopped
1 8-oz. can
  tomato sauce
¼ t. salt
¼ t. instant
  garlic
½ t. pepper

Dissolve yeast in warm water. Stir in remaining dough ingredients; beat vigorously, about 20 strokes. Allow dough to rest about 5 min. while preparing sauce. Mix sauce ingredients; set aside. Divide dough in half. On lightly greased baking sheets pat each half into 10″ circles. Continue to flour your fingers when patting dough into circles. Spread sauce onto each circle. Sprinkle alternately with grated Parmesan cheese and mozzarella cheese. Arrange slices of pepperoni or any other topping you like. Bake at 425° for 20–25 min., or until crust is brown and sauce is hot and bubbly. Makes two 10″ pizzas.

Mrs. Gordon D. Mason
St. Joseph County

KERSHNERS PIZZA DOUGH

2 t. powdered
  yeast
⅓ c. plus 2 T.
  warm water

1½ c. flour
4 T. olive oil
½ t. salt

Mix and press out on pizza pan. Use sauce and topping as preferred. Bake 20 min. at 400°.

Juamaine Stull
Noble County

SOURDOUGH BREADS

SOURDOUGH BASIC STARTER WITH YEAST

2 c. flour
2 c. warm water

1 pkg. dry yeast

Mix all ingredients. Let stand uncovered in a warm place overnight or up to 48 hours. The longer the mixture stands, the stronger the ferment will be. After fermenting, the starter is ready to use or to store in refrigerator. "Feed" once or twice a week with 1 c. milk, 1 c. flour, and ¼ c. sugar. After feeding, wait 3–4 days before using.

Mrs. Ruth Culler
Clay County

FRONTIER SOURDOUGH STARTER
(Without Yeast)

1 c. sugar	water in which
½ c. mashed	potatoes were
potatoes	cooked
4 c. flour	

Mix all ingredients together in a wide-necked crock or jar and set aside in a warm place for at least 48 hours. Use, or store in cold place.

The starter may also be made with other grain flours, such as rye, buckwheat, barley, millet, corn, oat, bran or rice. It was often important to conserve white wheat flour, for it was the most expensive and the most difficult to obtain.

Mrs. John Schneider
Posey County

SOURDOUGH BREAD

1 pkg. dry yeast	4 c. plus about
1 c. warm water	1 c. flour
1½ c. sourdough	2 t. salt
starter	2 T. sugar

Dissolve yeast in warm water and let set 5 min. Stir in sugar and sourdough starter. Gradually add flour and salt. Let rise 1–1½ hours. Turn dough out on floured board and work in about 1 c. more flour. Split dough in half and make 2 long loaves; cut across top diagonally. Sprinkle cornmeal on cookie sheets; put loaves on sheets. Bake at 325° for about 45 min. Butter tops of loaves upon removing from oven.

Nancy Callecod
Parke County

SOURDOUGH DROP BISCUITS

1 c. sourdough	¼ t. salt
1 c. flour	⅓ c. oil
¾ t. soda	

Combine ingredients. Drop by tablespoon on ungreased cookie sheet. Bake at 350° for 10–15 min. Do not let them get too brown. Yields 24 drop biscuits.

Shirley Rutherford
Orange County

SOURDOUGH CORN BREAD

1 c. sourdough	¾ t. soda
starter	¼ t. salt
⅓ c. oil	½ c. flour
1 egg	1 c. cornmeal

Mix starter, oil, and egg. Sift together dry ingredients and add to sourdough mixture. Mix until well blended. Pour into an 8″ greased square pan, and bake at 350° for 25–30 min. Yields 9 pieces.

Shirley Rutherford
Orange County

SOURDOUGH-CHEESE BUNS

1 pkg. dry yeast	¼ c. sugar
¾ c. warm water	¼ c. softened
(110°)	butter or
4¼–4½ c.	margarine
unbleached	1 egg
white flour	½ t. baking soda
1 c. sourdough	¾ c. grated sharp
starter, at room	cheddar cheese
temperature	2 t. salt

In large mixer bowl, soften yeast in warm water. Blend in 2 c. flour, sourdough starter, sugar, butter, egg, and salt. Beat 3–4 min. with mixer. Add soda to 1 c. flour; stir into flour-yeast mixture. Add cheese and enough of remaining flour to make a soft dough. Knead on floured surface until smooth (5–8 min.). Place in greased bowl; turn once. Cover; let rise until double (1½–2 hr.). Punch down. Cover; let rest 10 min. Divide into 12 pieces; shape into buns. Place on greased baking sheets. Cover; let rise until double (25–30 min.). Bake at 375° for about 20 min. Remove from baking sheets and cool on racks.

Mrs. Lawrence Wright
Madison County

SOURDOUGH COFFEE CAKE

1 c. sourdough with yeast	coconut, nuts, raisins, candied fruit, or dates (optional)
1 c. flour	
¾ t. soda	
¼ t. salt	Topping:
⅓ c. shortening, softened	1 c. brown sugar
¾ c. sugar	2 T. flour
½ t. cinnamon	½ stick margarine
1 egg	1 t. cinnamon

Mix ingredients for coffee cake dough. Pour into greased and floured 8×8" pan. Crumble together brown sugar and flour for topping; add margarine and cinnamon. Sprinkle over coffee cake. Bake at 350° for 40–50 min. until center is done. Cover as soon as baked.

Mrs. Ruth Culler
Clay County

SOURDOUGH SUGAR COOKIES

1 c. sugar	1 c. sourdough mixture
½ c. butter	1¾ c. flour
1 t. vanilla	¼ t. salt
1 egg	¼ t. baking soda
2 t. baking powder	

Combine all ingredients. Drop by spoonfuls on baking sheet. Bake at 350° for about 12 min. Sprinkle with sugar and cinnamon or frost.

Mrs. Argyl Mendenhall
Steuben County

SOURDOUGH MOCHA NUT BREAD

½ c. butter or margarine, softened	½ c. hot coffee
	1 T. instant coffee
1½ c. granulated sugar	1 c. sourdough starter
3 eggs	2 c. all-purpose flour
1 T. cocoa	1 c. pecans or walnuts, chopped
1 t. baking powder	
1 t. baking soda	powdered sugar
1 t. cinnamon	

Beat butter, sugar, and eggs until light and fluffy. Beat in cocoa, baking powder, baking soda, and cinnamon. Dissolve instant coffee in hot coffee. Beat flour, coffee mixture, and sourdough starter alternately into batter. Beat until smooth. Stir in pecans. Pour into well-greased and floured 12-c. bundt pan. Bake at 350° until wooden pick inserted in bread comes out clean (40–45 min.). Cool on wire rack 10 min. Remove from pan; cool thoroughly. Sprinkle with powdered sugar.

Mrs. John Hensel
Hamilton County

Sandwiches

APRIL FOOL SANDWICHES

¼ lb. (1 c.) American cheese, cubed	3 hard-cooked eggs, chopped
1 7-oz. can tuna	2 T. green pepper, chopped
2 T. onion, chopped	2 T. stuffed olives
2 T. sweet pickles, chopped	½ c. mayonnaise
	8 buns

Put mixture on buns. Wrap in aluminum

foil. Prick with fork. Bake in slow oven (250°) 30 min. Serves 8.

Harriet Teboe
Hamilton County

BAR-B-QUED BEEF SANDWICHES

1 lb. beef, cut in ½″ pieces	1 t. chili powder
1 T. fat	1 c. catsup
1½ c. water	¼ c. brown sugar
1 med. onion, chopped	2 T. vinegar
½ c. celery, diced	2 T. Worcestershire sauce
⅓ c. green peppers, diced	1 t. salt
	12–16 hamburger buns

Brown beef in hot fat, add water and simmer in covered skillet for 1½ hr. or until tender. Reserve broth, adding enough water to make ¾ c. Break beef into small pieces. Cook onion, celery, and pepper in fat until tender. Add beef, broth, and remaining ingredients. Simmer uncovered 20–30 min. Serve on toasted buns.

Kay Kyler
Whitley County

CORNED BEEF BARBECUES

1 green pepper, chopped	1 c. water
1 onion, chopped	1 large bottle catsup
2 cans corned beef, shredded with fork	1 t. cinnamon
	½ t. ground cloves

Cook 15 min. Serves 12–14.

Mrs. Clarence Downey
Lake County

CREOLE BEEF SANDWICHES

1 lb. ground beef	2 T. green pepper, chopped
¼ c. onion, chopped	¾ t. salt

1 can (2 oz.) mushroom stems and pieces, drained	½ c. catsup
⅛ t. pepper	1 can (8 oz.) tomato sauce (tomato juice may be used)
¼ t. garlic salt	6 hamburger buns
¼ t. basil	

Brown onion, green pepper, and mushrooms in lard or drippings. Add ground beef and brown lightly. Pour off drippings. Add salt, pepper, garlic salt, basil, tomato sauce, and catsup. Cook slowly 15 min. Serve on hamburger buns.

Mary Ray
Whitley County

BATTER-FRIED BRAINS SANDWICHES

2 eggs	½ t. salt
⅓–½ c. milk	2 T. melted shortening
1 c. flour, sifted	1½ c. pork brains
1½ t. baking powder	

Clean brains and remove membranes. Beat eggs in small bowl of electric mixer at medium speed for one minute. Add milk, sifted flour, baking powder, and salt. Add to milk mixture. Add shortening. Beat at low speed until blended. Coat brains. Drop bun-sized amount of brains on hot greased griddle. Slide off into hot pre-heated shortening in deep fryer; fry until golden brown.

Mrs. Charles Coughlin
Vanderburgh County

BAKED CHEESE SANDWICHES

12 slices French bread ½″ thick, crust removed	1 6-oz. pkg. sliced Monterey Jack cheese
½ c. Parmesan cheese	3 eggs
	1¾ c. milk

3 T. onion,   ⅛ t. pepper
  minced   2 t. parsley,
1½ t. mustard   minced
¾ t. salt

Arrange half of bread in a baking pan. Cover with sliced cheese. Sprinkle with all but 2 T. Parmesan cheese. Cover with remaining bread and sprinkle with remaining Parmesan cheese. Beat eggs with milk, onion, mustard, salt, pepper, and parsley. Pour over bread mixture. Bake uncovered in 350° for 45 min. Serves 4. For two servings use 2 eggs, ⅔ c. milk, and less bread.

Jeannette Fenton
Noble County

PIMIENTO CHEESE SPREAD

1 egg   ⅓ c. cream
1 T. butter   1 c. cheese, grated
¼ t. mustard   1 small can
¼ t. salt   pimientoes

Cook all ingredients except pimientoes over low fire or in double boiler until smooth. Remove from heat and add pimientoes. Can be served warm or refrigerated and served cold. Makes 20 sandwiches.

Jackie Nentrup
Jennings County

EGG SALAD SANDWICHES

12 slices whole   ⅔ c. carrots,
   wheat bread   grated
butter   ½ c. celery,
8 hard-cooked   chopped
   eggs   1 T. pimiento,
1 c. greens (violet   chopped
   leaves, lambs   2 T. onion,
   quarters, or   chopped
   plain old spin- 1 t. salt
   ach), chopped   ½ t. pepper
½ c. mayonnaise   lettuce leaves

Combine all ingredients except bread, butter, and lettuce. Divide on 6 slices bread. Top with lettuce leaves. Cover with remaining 6 slices of bread, which you have buttered.

This may also be served as a salad.

Mrs. Joseph O'Bryan
Floyd County

GOOEY BUNS

1 lb. bologna   ⅓ c. salad
¼ c. mustard   dressing
1 t. minced onion 2 T. chopped
¾ lb. cheese   pickle

Grind meat and cheese, add remaining ingredients and mix. Cut buns in half. Spread with butter and then fill with mixture. Wrap in aluminum foil and bake in low oven (325°) for 25 min. Makes about 24.

Mrs. Kathryn Dean
Randolph County

GREEN TOMATOES SANDWICH
SPREAD OR DIP

1 dozen green   ½ c. white sugar
   tomatoes   1 c. prepared
1 dozen red or   mustard
   green peppers   1 T. celery seed
1 dozen onions   1 quart salad
2 T. salt   dressing

Grind tomatoes, peppers, and onions together. Drain off juice, add salt. Let stand 20 min. Add sugar, mustard, and celery seed. Mix well and cook 10 min. Cool. Stir in salad dressing. Put in small sterilized jars and store in refrigerator or cool place. Will keep for a long time. Pickle relish may be substituted for green tomatoes, but it should not be cooked with other ingredients, if used.

Mabel Collins
Washington County

HAM BUNWICHES

½ lb. boiled or baked ham	1 (2¾ oz.) bottle stuffed olives, drained, or use sweet pickles
½ lb. sharp process cheese	
1 small onion, chopped	12 hamburger buns
½ c. ketchup	

Put ham, cheese, olives or pickles and onion through food chopper. Stir in ketchup. Wrap each sandwich in foil. Refrigerate until serving time. Heat in slow oven (300°) for 20 min. Makes 12.

Mrs. DeWayne Heagy
Miami County

GERMAN POPPY SEED
HAMWICHES

¼ c. soft margarine	2 t. poppy seed
2 T. prepared horseradish mustard	8 slices rye bread
	4 thin slices boiled ham
2 T. onion, finely chopped	4 slices Swiss cheese
	butter

Mix margarine, mustard, onion, and poppy seed together. Spread on 4 slices rye bread. Top each slice with thin slice of ham, a slice of cheese, then another slice of rye bread. Butter tops and bottoms of sandwiches. Grill on both sides at 300° on a preheated griddle until hot and cheese is melted.

Mrs. Max Tribbett
Montgomery County

Mrs. Jerry Gaerke, Adams County, suggests adding 1 t. Worcestershire sauce to this recipe and wrapping sandwich in foil and baking at 400° for 10 min. Omit buttering outside of sandwich if baking it.

MEAT BOAT

1 loaf Vienna bread	1 10¾-oz. can tomato soup
¼ c. onion, chopped	1 egg
¼ c. green pepper, grated	1 T. salt
	1 T. pepper
1 T. butter	1 lb. hamburger
	garlic salt

Beat egg slightly and add tomato soup. Hollow out loaf of bread. Add bread taken from inside of loaf to mixture. Brown onion and green pepper in butter in skillet. Add browned onion mixture to bread mixture. Add beef, salt, and pepper to the mixture. Butter the inside of the bread loaf that has been hollowed out. Sprinkle garlic salt over it. Add meat mixture to loaf. Cover with the top crust of bread. Bake at 350° for 1 hr. Remove lid from bread and bake 15 min. more.

Directions for hollowing out bread: Cut the top of the loaf off as if making a Jack-o-Lantern. Save the crust lid. Cut along the sides of the loaf and then pull the bread out with your fingers.

Dorothy Haberle
Sullivan County

PARTY SANDWICH LOAF

1 loaf French bread	¾ c. uncooked quick oats
1½ lbs. ground beef	½ c. onion, chopped
½ lb. American cheese, grated	1 T. horseradish (optional)
⅔ c. (small can) undiluted evaporated milk	1 T. mustard
	1 t. garlic salt
1 egg	½ t. salt

Cut French bread in half lengthwise. Wrap each piece in aluminum foil, leaving top uncovered. Combine remaining ingredients in mixing bowl. Mix until blended. Spread evenly over top of bread. Place on cookie sheet. Bake in moderate oven (350°) for 25 min. Garnish with strips of cheese. Bake 5 min. longer. Cut slices diagonally to serve. Serves 6–8.

Ruth Stolte
Noble County

PIZZA BURGERS

1 lb. hamburger	¼ c. onion,
⅓ c. grated Par-	chopped
mesan cheese	12 oz. tomato
1 t. garlic salt	paste
1 pkg. sliced moz-	1 loaf French
zarella cheese	bread, sliced
1 t. salt	

Brown hamburger in skillet. Combine ingredients except mozzarella cheese in skillet and simmer. Spread meat sauce on slice of French bread. Place a slice of cheese on top of meat sauce. Broil on ungreased cookie sheet for 3 min. or more. Serves 15 or more, depending on how much meat sauce is placed on each bread slice.

Mrs. Carl L. Thomas
Delaware County

MOLLY'S PIZZA SANDWICH

1 lb. ground beef	8 slices American
2 8-oz. cans	cheese
tomato sauce	1 can (2 oz.)
1 t. oregano	sliced mush-
2 c. Bisquick	rooms, drained
baking mix	¼ c. grated Par-
1 egg	mesan cheese
⅔ c. milk	

Cook and stir ground beef until brown; drain. Mix in 1 can tomato sauce and the oregano. Simmer uncovered 10 min. Stir Bisquick, egg, and milk to a soft dough.

Spread half of the dough in greased 9× 9×2″ pan. Pour remaining can of tomato sauce over dough, spreading evenly. Layer 4 slices cheese, the meat mixture, mushrooms, remaining cheese slices and Parmesan cheese. Cover with remaining dough. Bake at 400° for 20–25 min., or until golden brown. Serves 4–6.

Dorothy Waltz
Parke County

SCHEIMANN SANDWICHES

12 hamburger	½ c. catsup
buns	1 t. salt
1 lb. ground beef	¼ t. pepper
2 T. fat	1 T. Worcester-
1 onion, chopped	shire sauce
¼ green pepper,	1 c. Velveeta
chopped	cheese,
½ c. celery,	shredded
chopped	

Melt fat in skillet. Add onion, green pepper, and celery. Cook and stir 5 min. Add ground beef and cook until redness is gone. Add catsup, Worcestershire sauce, salt, pepper, and cheese. Cook slowly 10 min. Chill. Add filling to buns and wrap individually in foil. Bake at 350° for 10–15 min.; 20–30 min. if frozen. If mixture is too juicy after cooking, add 1 T. oatmeal. Makes 12–16 sandwiches.

Sandy Kiess
Allen County

SLOPPY JOES

7 lbs. hamburger	2 t. salt
1 lb. chopped	1 No. 10 can
celery	tomatoes
1 lb., 5 oz.	½ No. 10 can
chopped onions	tomato paste
1 t. garlic powder	1 t. pepper
1 t. chili powder	

Brown meat and celery, onions, and seasonings. Simmer. Add tomatoes and tomato paste. If mixture is too thin, thicken with a little flour. Serve on a toasted bun. Makes 50 servings.

Mrs. Margaret A. Neal
Steuben County

STRINGY BAR-B-Q SANDWICHES

4 c. cooked meat (beef, pork, or combination)	½ c. bar-b-q sauce
¼ c. brown sugar	½ c. catsup
½ c. onion, chopped	¼ c. vinegar
1 c. pickle relish	1 T. mustard
	1 T. Worcestershire sauce

Tear meat into strings. Cook meat, brown sugar, and onion until onion is clear, about 10 min. Add rest of ingredients and simmer 1 hr. Very good to freeze for later use. Makes 12 large bun sandwiches.

Mrs. Marilyn Cramer
Marshall County

TAVERNS

1 or 2 lb. hamburger, fried and drained	1 T. ketchup
1 onion, chopped	1 T. prepared mustard
1 can chicken gumbo soup	salt and pepper to taste

Fry hamburger and onion together. Drain grease. Add remaining ingredients. Simmer for 20 min. Serve on hamburger bun halves. Serves 4.

Marcia Powers
Greene County

BAKED TUNA FISH SANDWICHES

12 slices white sandwich bread	⅔ lb. sharp cheese, shredded
butter as needed	
2 small cans tuna, drained	3 c. milk
4 eggs	1 can cream of mushroom soup

In 9×13″ Pyrex dish thickly butter 6 slices of bread and place butter side down. Cover the 6 slices with tuna, spreading evenly. Over tuna, spread cheese. Cover with remaining 6 slices of thickly buttered bread, buttered side up. Beat eggs and milk. Pour over sandwiches and refrigerate overnight. Bake next day at 350° until set. Pour hot undiluted mushroom soup over sandwiches after removing from oven.

Meta Sanders
Marion County

TUNA CHEESE BUNS

¼ lb. American cheese, cubed	3 T. stuffed olives, chopped
3 hard-cooked eggs, chopped	2 T. pickled relish
1 c. chunk style tuna, drained	½ c. mayonnaise
1 T. onion, minced	6 hamburger buns

Combine ingredients. Spoon between buttered split buns. Wrap in aluminum foil. (May be refrigerated until ready to bake.) Bake at 300° for about 15 min., when ready to use. Chicken or turkey may be substituted for the tuna.

Mrs. Earl Dawson
Dearborn County

Cakes and Cake Frostings

Since a cook's skill can truly be measured by her cake baking abilities, making one from scratch is worthwhile for at least two reasons—pride in a job well done and the joy of deserved compliments. Back in the days when women always beat up their own cakes, their creations were usually three layers instead of the modern two. An old-fashioned cook always tested a cake with a broom straw—a clean one, of course—taken from the top of the broom! Today's cook uses a wire cake tester or a wooden pick.

Since cake cell walls are fragile, try to keep the kitchen peaceful, at least during the first quarter of the baking period. Cakes rise more in the center, so for an even cake, gently push the batter up the sides of the pan, leaving a slight depression in the center.

There are at least two explanations for the name angel food cake. Some say it was because of its pure white color, while others claim it was because of its light airiness and heavenly taste.

Pound cake quite logically came by its name since original recipes listed the main ingredients by pounds: one pound of flour, one pound of eggs, one pound of sugar, etc.

Cakes from Scratch

OLD-FASHIONED SCRIPTURE CAKE
With Bible in hand you can easily bake this cake.

2 c. Jeremiah 6:20	2 c. Nahum 3:12	
6 Jeremiah 17:11	2 T. I Samuel 14:25	

4½ c. I Kings 4:22	2 t. Luke 13:21
1 c. Judges (last clause) 5:25	½ c. Judges (last clause) 4:19
2 c. I Samuel 30:12	pinch of Leviticus 2:13
2 c. Numbers 17:8	season to taste with II Chronicles 9:9

Mix and bake in large tube pan about 2 hr. in a slow oven (250°), with about 2″ of water in a pan in the oven with the cake.

In case you do not have time to look up the ingredients, they are:

2 c. sugar	2 t. soda
6 eggs	½ c. milk
2 c. figs	pinch of salt
2 T. honey	(about ½ t.)
4½ c. flour	about 2 t. spices—
1 c. butter	cinnamon,
2 c. raisins	cloves, and
2 c. almonds	nutmeg

Cream shortening and sugar together, add eggs and beat mixture smooth. Dissolve soda in milk, and add to mixture. Reserve part of flour to coat fruit and nuts. Add sifted flour with spices and salt and beat until smooth. Then fold in fruit and nuts, and bake as above.

Mrs. Royal B. Grant
Randolph County

ANGEL FOOD CAKE

For 9″ cake pan:

1 c. egg whites	¾ t. vanilla
1¼ c. sugar	3 drops almond flavoring
1 c. cake flour, sifted	
¼ t. salt	
1 t. cream of tartar	For 10″ cake pan:
	1½ c. egg whites
	1⅞ c. sugar
	⅓ t. salt

1½ c. cake flour, sifted	1 t. vanilla
1½ t. cream of tartar	4 to 5 drops almond flavoring

Separate eggs and let egg whites warm to room temperature before beating. Beat egg whites until frothy on high speed of mixer. Add cream of tartar and salt and continue beating at high speed (about 1 min.), until the soft peak stage. Add sugar gradually on low speed (about 2½ min.). Add flavoring and beat at low speed for about 30 seconds. Fold in flour, ⅕ at a time, with 10 strokes for each addition, plus an extra 5 strokes at the end. Scrape bowl several times while folding in flour. Pour into ungreased tube pan, turning the pan as you pour. For a loose bottom pan, cut through the mixture several times to remove large air bubbles. For a one-piece pan, drop the pan from a height of 6″ 3–4 times. Bake at 375° for 30–40 min. Turn pan upside down on funnel or long-necked bottle until cooled. Loosen edges before removing.

Betty H. Sendmeyer
Putnam County

SPONGE CAKE

2 eggs	½ t. salt
1 c. sugar	½ c. milk (hot)
1 c. sifted flour	1 T. butter
2 t. baking powder	1 t. vanilla

Beat eggs 8 to 10 min. with mixer. Add sugar gradually, continue beating until blended. Add vanilla, add sifted flour, baking powder and salt to eggs and sugar. Put butter in milk and heat until hot and butter is melted. Be sure milk is very hot. Pour at once in other mixture and beat well until smooth. Pour into 8×8×2″ pan and bake 35 or 40 min. at 325°.

Mary Richhart
Brown County

LEMON SPONGE CAKE

6 egg whites	¼ c. fresh lemon
1¾ c. sifted all	juice
purpose flour	2 T. water
½ t. salt	1 t. grated lemon
1½ c. granulated	peel
sugar	confectioners'
6 egg yolks	sugar

In large bowl of electric mixer, let egg whites warm to room temperature (about 1 hr.). Preheat oven to 350°. Sift flour with salt; set aside. With mixer at high speed, beat egg whites until foamy. Gradually beat in ½ c. sugar, beating after each addition. Continue beating until soft peaks form when beater is slowly raised. Set aside. In small bowl of mixer, at high speed and with same beater, beat egg yolks until thick and lemon colored. Gradually beat in remaining sugar, continue beating until mixture is smooth and well blended. At low speed, blend in flour mixture, guiding it into beater with rubber scraper. Add lemon juice, water, and the lemon peel, beating just until combined (about 1 min.). With wire whisk or rubber scraper and using an under-and-over motion, gently fold egg yolk mixture into egg white mixture just until blended. Pour batter into ungreased 10×4″ tube pan or decorative 3-qt. pan; bake 40 min., or until cake tester inserted in center comes out clean. Invert pan over neck of bottle; let cake cool completely (about 1 hr.); with spatula, carefully loosen cake from pan. Sprinkle with confectioners' sugar.

Brittie Baker
Noble County

ORANGE SPONGE CAKE

6 egg yolks	1⅓ c. sifted cake
1 T. grated	flour
orange peel	6 egg whites
½ c. orange	1 t. cream of
juice	tartar
1 c. sugar	½ c. sugar
¼ t. salt	

Beat egg yolks until thick and lemon-colored. Add orange peel and orange juice; beat until very thick. Gradually beat in 1 c. sugar and salt. Fold in flour a little at a time. Beat egg whites with the cream of tartar until soft peaks form. Gradually add ½ c. sugar (about 1 T. at a time), beating until stiff peaks form. Thoroughly fold whites into egg yolk mixture. Bake in ungreased 10″ tube pan in slow oven (325°) about 55 min., or until done. Invert pan to cool. When completely cool, split into three layers, spread filling between layers, frost with orange frosting and cover with shredded coconut.

Filling: Beat together 1 envelope Dream Whip, 1 small package French vanilla instant pudding mix, and 1½ c. milk until peaks are formed. Add about 1 t. orange extract and about 1 t. grated orange peel. Beat. Mix in chopped maraschino cherries.

Frosting: Cream ¼ c. margarine or shortening with 1 egg yolk. Gradually stir in 3 c. sifted confectioners' sugar alternately with 3 T. orange juice. Blend in 1 T. grated orange peel.

Mildred Rogers
Rush County

FRESH APPLE CAKE (1)

2 c. apples, diced	1 c. sugar
2 t. melted	1 egg
margarine	1 c. flour

1 t. soda	½ c. nutmeats
1 scant t. cinnamon	½ c. dates or raisins

Chop apples and mix with sugar; let stand 10 min. Stir in beaten egg. Add flour, soda, cinnamon, nuts, and dates or raisins. Bake 35–40 min. at 375°.

Sauce:

½ c. white sugar	1 c. water
½ c. brown sugar	¼ c. margarine
2 rounded T. flour	1 t. vanilla

Cook sugars, flour, and water until clear and add margarine and vanilla. Pour over cake while still warm.

Irene E. Blair
Vigo County

FRESH APPLE CAKE (2)

1 c. oil	1 t. cinnamon
3 eggs	1 T. vanilla
2 c. sugar	3 c. apples, sliced
2 c. self-rising flour	1 c. nuts, chopped
1 t. nutmeg	

Mix and beat oil, eggs, and sugar into stiff batter. Add flour and rest of ingredients. Bake at 325° until toothpick comes out clean (about 45 min.).

Maple Cream Frosting:

⅓ c. soft margarine	3 c. confectioners' sugar
1½ t. maple flavoring	8-oz. softened cream cheese
2 T. milk (about)	

Ledra Holden
Monroe County

IRISH APPLE CAKE

3 c. sifted flour	½ t. salt
¾ c. sugar	3 egg yolks

1 c. butter or margarine	2 No. 303 cans applesauce
grated rind of 1 lemon	1 t. cinnamon
	½ t. cloves

Mix together flour, sugar, salt, egg yolks, butter or margarine, and lemon rind. Pat ½ of mixture into bottom of 9×13×2″ cake pan. Mix together applesauce, cinnamon, and cloves. Spread mixture over dough in pan. Sprinkle remaining dough mixture over applesauce. Bake 40–45 min. at 350°. Top with whipped cream or lemon sauce.

Mrs. Dean Hupp
Elkhart County

JEWISH APPLE CAKE

5 medium apples, peeled and sliced thin	4 unbeaten eggs
	½ t. salt
	⅓ c. orange juice
2 t. cinnamon	2½ t. vanilla
5 T. sugar	3 t. baking powder
3 c. unsifted flour	
2¼ c. sugar	½ c. raisins
1 c. oil or shortening	½ c. nuts

Put cinnamon and sugar in bowl with apples and set aside. Combine flour, sugar, oil or shortening, eggs, salt, orange juice, vanilla, and baking powder. Beat until smooth. Add apple mixture, raisins, and nuts. Pour into greased tube pan. Bake at 350° for 1½–2 hr.

For fruit cake: Instead of apples mix 1½ c. pineapple, peaches, and cherries together. Add cinnamon and sugar.

Stella Jester
Jefferson County

SUGARLESS APPLE CAKE

2 c. water	2 T. liquid sweetener
2 c. raisins	

1 c. unsweetened applesauce
2 c. flour
½ t. salt
2 eggs
1 t. soda
1¼ t. cinnamon
¾ c. cooking oil
½ t. nutmeg

Cook raisins in water until soft; drain off water. Add applesauce, eggs, sweetener, and oil to raisins and mix well. Blend in baking soda and flour. Add remaining ingredients and mix well. Bake in 13×9×2″ pan at 350° for 45 min., or until tester comes out clean.

Mary E. Bolinger
Randolph County

APRICOT BRANDY CAKE

3 c. sugar
1½ c. margarine
6 eggs
3 c. flour
¼ t. soda
½ t. salt
1 c. sour cream
½ t. rum flavoring
1 t. orange flavoring
¼ t. almond flavoring
½ t. lemon flavoring
1 t. vanilla
½ c. apricot brandy

Heat oven to 350°. Cream butter and sugar. Add eggs and beat thoroughly. Sift flour, soda, and salt. Combine brandy, sour cream, and flavorings. Add flour alternately with sour cream mixture to egg mixture. Beat until just blended. Pour into bundt pan and bake 70 min., or until done. Cool 15 min.

Melt ½ c. apricot preserves; thin with brandy. Pour over cake.

Jean Carter
Vanderburgh County

BANANA CAKE

1 stick margarine
2 eggs
1 c. banana pulp

1 c. sugar
1 t. vanilla
2 c. flour
1 t. baking powder
1 t. soda
½ t. salt
1 c. nuts
½ c. buttermilk

Cream margarine, sugar. Add eggs, banana pulp, vanilla. Combine flour, salt, baking powder, soda; blend with egg mixture. Add nuts and buttermilk. Pour into well greased, floured pans. Bake at 350° for 30–35 min. Serves 12–15.

Cream Cheese Frosting: Cream ½ stick margarine with small pkg. cream cheese. Add 2 heaping c. powdered sugar and enough milk for spreading consistency.

Mrs. Rex Goings
Whitley County

FLUFFY BANANA CAKE

2¼ c. unsifted cake flour
1¼ t. baking powder
1¼ t. baking soda
½ t. salt
⅔ c. shortening
1⅔ c. sugar
3 large eggs
1 c. mashed bananas (2 medium)
1 t. vanilla
1¼ c. milk

Grease and flour pans. Sift flour, baking powder, baking soda, and salt together. Set aside. In large bowl, beat ⅔ c. shortening, sugar, and eggs until light and fluffy. Gradually add ¾ c. mashed bananas and vanilla. Add flour mixture and milk, beginning and ending with flour. Bake at 350° for 35–40 min. Cool completely.

Frosting: Prepare 1 pkg. creamy vanilla white frosting mix according to directions on pkg. Add ¼ c. bananas. Beat until smooth and creamy.

Linda Gulley
Spencer County

BANANA SPLIT CAKE

2 c. crushed graham crackers	1 can crushed pineapple, drained
5 T. margarine, melted	3 c. bananas, sliced
2 c. powdered sugar	1 large container Cool Whip
2 eggs	chopped nuts
½ c. margarine	maraschino cherries
1 t. vanilla	

Combine graham cracker crumbs and melted margarine. Pat in 9×13″ pan. Chill until firm. Combine powdered sugar, eggs, margarine, and vanilla and beat with mixer for 10 min. Place on top of graham cracker crust. Add next layer of pineapple and bananas. Top with Cool Whip, nuts, and maraschino cherries. Chill 2 hr. Serves 10–12.

Mrs. David Thomas
Marshall County

RED BEET CAKE

1½ c. red beets	1½ c. sugar
1 c. oil	1¾ c. flour
2 sqs. chocolate, melted	1½ t. soda
	½ t. salt
3 eggs	1 t. vanilla

Blend red beets, oil, and melted chocolate in blender until smooth. Set aside. Beat eggs and sugar. Add blender mixture and other ingredients. Mix well and pour into two 8″ pans. Bake at 350° for 25–30 min., or until done. This cake usually takes longer to bake.

Ruth Newenschwander
Adams County

BLACKBERRY CAKE

½ c. butter	1 unbeaten egg
1 c. sugar	2 c. flour

1 t. cinnamon	1 c. blackberries and juice
1 t. soda	
½ c. sour milk	

Blend butter and sugar. Add egg. Add flour, cinnamon, and soda alternately with sour milk. Add berries. Bake at 350° for 25–30 min.

Joan Jones
Lawrence County

BURNT SUGAR CAKE

2 c. brown sugar	1 t. baking powder
½ c. shortening	
2 eggs	2 T. burnt sugar
1 c. sour cream or buttermilk	1 t. soda
	½ c. hot black coffee
2½ c. flour	

Cream sugar and shortening, add eggs, well beaten, and beat mixture. Add milk and beat well. Add sifted flour and baking powder and beat. Dissolve burnt sugar and soda in hot coffee, add and beat thoroughly. Bake in 10×8×2½″ pan at 325°.

To make burnt sugar: Place 1 c. granulated sugar in iron skillet. Using wooden spoon, stir until sugar is melted and brown. While still over heat, pour in 1 c. boiling water, stirring constantly. Boil until thick like heavy syrup.

Ann Cull
Jay County

BUTTER CAKE

⅔ c. soft butter or margarine	3 c. sifted cake flour
1¾ c. sugar	2½ t. baking powder
2 eggs, at room temperature	1 t. salt
1½ t. vanilla	1¼ c. milk

Beat butter or margarine, sugar, eggs, and vanilla in mixer at high speed for 5 min.

Sift flour, baking powder, and salt. Starting with flour, add flour and milk alternately. Blend on low speed until smooth. Pour into greased and floured pan. Bake at 350° for 30–35 min.

Mrs. Milo Green
Jay County

CARROT CAKE

2 c. grated carrots	2 t. salt
2 c. sugar	2 t. cinnamon
1 c. Mazola oil	3 c. cake flour
2 t. baking	4 eggs
powder	1 c. chopped nuts
2 t. soda	

Cream carrots and sugar, add oil and cream again. Sift together dry ingredients, add to creamed mixture. Add beaten eggs. Add nuts. Pour into two greased and floured layer pans. Bake at 325° for 1 hr. Serves 12–16.

Frost with cream cheese frosting. Top frosted cake with tinted (orange) coconut.

Ladies Nite Out EH Club
Wabash County

CHEESE CAKE

Crust:

½ lb. crushed	1 c. boiling water
graham	1 8-oz. pkg.
crackers	cream cheese
½ lb. margarine,	1 c. sugar
melted	1 t. vanilla
	1 can chilled
	Milnot,
Filling:	whipped
1 3-oz. pkg.	1 can crushed
Lemon or Lime	pineapple,
Jello	drained

Mix graham crackers and margarine. Press mixture in 2×9×12″ cake pan. Save small amount to sprinkle on top. Dissolve Jello

in water and cool; let it set to consistency of egg white. Cream cheese, sugar, and vanilla together. Add Jello and mix well. Fold in whipped Milnot and then drained pineapple. Pour into graham cracker crust. Sprinkle remainder of crumbs on top. Refrigerate. Serves 15.

Mrs. Lois Brown
Greene County

CHEESE CAKE SUPREME

Crust:

1 c. graham	3 egg yolks
cracker crumbs	1 t. vanilla
¼ c. ground	extract
pecans	½ c. sugar
¼ c. sugar	3 egg whites,
¼ c. melted	beaten
butter	
¼ t. cinnamon	Topping:
	¼ c. sugar
Filling:	2 c. sour cream
1 lb. cream cheese	1 t. vanilla

Mix together crumbs, pecans, sugar, butter, and cinnamon. Press into 10″ spring form pan or 9×13″ pan. Refrigerate. Beat cheese, egg yolks, and vanilla until smooth. Add sugar and beat until well blended. Fold in beaten egg whites. Pour onto graham cracker crust and bake for 20 min. at 375°. Remove from oven and cool for 15–20 min. Blend together sugar, sour cream, and vanilla. Spoon over filling. Increase oven temperature to 475° and bake 10 min. longer. Cool.

Mrs. Raymond Katter
Dubois County

CHOCOLATE CAKE

1 c. mayonnaise	pinch of salt
1 c. sugar	2 t. soda
2 c. flour	1 c. warm water
4 T. cocoa	1 t. vanilla

Combine mayonnaise and sugar in large mixing bowl. Sift flour, cocoa, and salt together. Add flour mixture, alternating with water in which soda was dissolved, to mayonnaise mixture. Add vanilla. Pour into 9×13″ pan or two 8″ layer pans. Bake at 375°.

Mrs. Kathryn Carr
Bartholomew County

EGGLESS CHOCOLATE CAKE

3 c. flour	2 T. vinegar
2 c. sugar	2 t. vanilla
⅓ c. cocoa	⅔ c. salad oil
2 t. soda	2 c. cold water
1 t. salt	

Mix dry ingredients, then add rest of ingredients and mix well. Pour into prepared pan and bake at 350° for 30 min.

Muriel Reynolds
Perry County

GERMAN CHOCOLATE CAKE

1 4-oz. pkg.	1 t. vanilla
German sweet	2½ c. sifted cake
chocolate	flour
½ c. boiling	1 t. soda
water	½ t. salt
1 c. butter	1 c. buttermilk
2 c. sugar	4 egg whites,
4 egg yolks	stiffly beaten

Melt chocolate over boiling water; cool. Cream butter and sugar until fluffy. Add yolks, one at a time, beating well after each addition. Blend in vanilla and chocolate. Sift flour with soda and salt. Add alternately with buttermilk to chocolate mixture until smooth. Fold in beaten egg whites. Line bottom of three 8″ or 9″ layer pans with waxed paper. Pour cake mixture into pans. Bake at 350° for 35–40 min. Cool. Frost tops only.

Frosting:

1 c. evaporated	½ c. butter
milk	1 t. vanilla
1 c. sugar	1⅓ c. coconut
3 egg yolks,	1 c. pecans,
slightly beaten	chopped

Combine first 5 ingredients. Cook and stir over medium heat until thickened (about 12 min.). Add coconut and chopped pecans. Cool until thick enough to spread. Beat occasionally. Makes 2½ cups.

Mrs. Hazel Grimm
Jay County

GRANDMA'S CHOCOLATE CAKE

1 c. shortening	1 t. baking soda
2 c. sugar	1 c. water,
2 eggs, beaten	boiling
1 t. vanilla	¾ c. cocoa
1 c. buttermilk	3 c. flour

Cream shortening and sugar. Add eggs. Mix buttermilk and soda together in cup. Stir over mixing bowl and add to first mixture. Mix water and cocoa together and add. Add flour one cup at a time. Bake at 350° for 35–45 min. Makes three 8″ layers or two layers and 12 cupcakes.

Mrs. Edna Malcomb
Jennings County

CHOCOLATE APPLESAUCE CAKE

1½ c. sifted flour	¾ c. sugar
¼ c. cocoa	1 t. soda
½ t. salt	1 c. applesauce
½ c. water	⅓ c. cooking oil
1 T. vinegar	1 t. vanilla

Sift flour, sugar, cocoa, soda, and salt into mixing bowl. Add remaining ingredients; stir until dry ingredients are moistened. Pour into greased 8″ square pan. Bake in moderate oven (350°) until done (30–35 min.). Serve cake squares topped with sour cream or whipped cream and a dab of applesauce. Serves 9.

Eloise McDonald
Posey County

CHOCOLATE "COOKIE SHEET" CAKE

2 c. flour	3 T. cocoa
2 c. sugar	2 eggs
1 stick margarine	1 t. vanilla
½ c. vegetable oil	1 t. cinnamon
	1 t. soda
1 c. water	½ c. buttermilk

Mix together flour and sugar. Combine margarine, oil, water, and cocoa. Bring to rapid boil. Pour over flour mixture and blend well. Stir in eggs, vanilla, cinnamon, soda, and buttermilk. Pour batter onto oiled cookie sheet and bake at 400° for 20 min.

Icing:

1 stick margarine	box of powdered sugar
6 T. milk	
3 T. cocoa	1 c. nuts, chopped
1 t. vanilla	

Bring margarine, milk, and cocoa to a rapid boil. Remove from heat. Add vanilla, nuts, and powdered sugar. Blend well. Spread on cake as soon as it is removed from oven.

Pauline Snell
Noble County

CHOCOLATE FUDGE CAKE

½ c. shortening	2 c. dark brown sugar
3 eggs, beaten	
1 t. vanilla	2 sq. melted chocolate
1 c. buttermilk	
1 t. soda	⅓ t. salt
2 c. flour	

Cream shortening and sugar. Add remaining ingredients; beat 2 min. Half fill 2 layer cake pans which have been lined with wax paper, greased and floured. Bake in moderate oven 25 min.

Della Hoggatt
Lawrence County

CHOCOLATE KRAUT CAKE

2¼ c. sifted all purpose flour	⅔ c. shortening
	1½ c. sugar
1 t. baking powder	1¼ t. vanilla
	3 eggs
1 t. baking soda	1 c. water
¼ t. salt	½ c. well-drained sauerkraut
½ c. cocoa	

Sift together flour, baking powder, soda, salt, and cocoa in bowl. Cream shortening with sugar. Beat well. Add eggs, one at a time, beating well after each addition. Add vanilla. Add dry ingredients alternately with water. Blend. Fold in sauerkraut. Spoon into greased 13×9″ pan. Bake at 375° for 35–40 min., or until done.

Betty Hilton
Pulaski County

CHOCOLATE MACAROON CAKE

1 egg white	¾ c. hot coffee
2 t. vanilla	3 eggs, separated
2¼ c. sugar	1 t. soda
2 c. grated coconut	½ c. sour cream
	½ c. shortening
1 T. flour	1 t. salt
½ c. cocoa	2 c. flour

Beat 1 egg white with 1 t. vanilla until soft mounds form. Add ½ c. sugar gradually, beating until stiff peaks form. Stir in coconut and 1 T. flour. Set aside. Dissolve cocoa in hot coffee. Beat 3 egg whites until soft mounds form. Add ½ c. sugar gradually, beating until meringue stands in stiff peaks. Add soda to sour cream. Beat 1¼ c. sugar, shortening, egg yolks, ½ t. salt, 1 t. vanilla, and half of cocoa mix, until light and creamy, about 4 min. Add 2 c. flour, sour cream, and remaining cocoa mix; blend well. Fold in egg whites. Turn one third of batter into 10″ tube pan, greased on bottom. Add one half of coconut mix. Cover with one half of remaining chocolate batter. Top with rest of coconut mix, then chocolate batter. Bake at 350° for 55–65 min. Cool completely before removing from pan. Frost top and sides.

Marietta Bailiff
Lawrence County

CHOCOLATE POUNDCAKE RING

2¾ c. cake flour
¾ t. cream of tartar
½ t. baking soda
1½ t. salt
1¾ c. granulated sugar
⅔ c. milk
1 c. vegetable shortening
1 t. vanilla
3 whole eggs
1 egg yolk
4 sq. unsweetened chocolate, melted

Grease bundt cake pan. Into large bowl sift flour, cream of tartar, baking soda, salt, and sugar. Drop in shortening, milk, and vanilla. Beat at low speed until well blended. Beat in whole eggs and egg yolk along with melted chocolate. Beat until well blended; do not overbeat. Turn into bundt pan. Bake at 350° for 1 hr. and 10 min.

Glaze: In double boiler melt ½ c. semi-sweet chocolate pieces. Remove from heat and stir in 2 T. white corn syrup and 1 T. water until smooth. Drizzle glaze over warm cake.

Diana Shafer
Gibson County

CHOCOLATE PUDDING CAKE

2 c. sifted flour
4 t. baking powder
½ t. salt
4 T. cocoa or 1 sq. chocolate
1½ c. sugar
½ c. nuts
4 T. margarine
1 c. milk

Topping:
1½ c. brown sugar
¼ c. cocoa
2½ c. boiling water

Sift together flour, baking powder, and salt; add cocoa, sugar, and nuts. Melt margarine and add milk. Add to dry ingredients; blend well. Pour into ungreased long pan. Mix brown sugar with cocoa, blend well, and sprinkle over top of batter. Pour over all 2½ c. boiling water. Bake 40 min. at 350°.

Shirley Tobey
Fulton County

CHOCOLATE "WACKY" CAKE

1½ c. flour
3 level T. cocoa
1 c. sugar
1 t. soda
¼ t. salt
1 T. vinegar
1 t. vanilla
5 T. melted shortening or oil
1 c. warm water

Use 10×7×1½″ oblong pan, the pan you are baking the cake in. Sift into ungreased pan flour, cocoa, sugar, soda, and salt. Make a dent in one corner, add vinegar. In opposite corner, add vanilla. Draw line through middle, add melted shortening. Over all pour warm water. Mix all together. Bake at 350° for 30–35 min.

Icing:
2 T. dark brown sugar
2 T. Milnot
2 T. melted butter
powdered sugar

Mix brown sugar, butter, and Milnot. Thicken with powdered sugar.

Mrs. Wayne Powers
Clay County

CHOCOLATE ZUCCHINI CAKE

½ c. soft margarine	½ t. baking powder
½ c. vegetable oil	1 t. soda
1¾ c. sugar	½ t. cinnamon
2 eggs	½ t. cloves
1 t. vanilla	2 c. zucchini, finely grated
½ c. sour milk	
2½ c. flour	½–1 c. chocolate chips
4 T. cocoa	

Cream margarine, oil, and sugar. Add eggs, vanilla, and sour milk; beat. Mix in flour, cocoa, baking powder, soda, cinnamon, and cloves. Stir in zucchini. Pour into 9× 12″ greased pan. Sprinkle top with chocolate chips. Bake at 325° for 45 min. Serves 12.

Lola Mae Taylor
Greene County

WHITE CHOCOLATE CAKE

¼ lb. white chocolate	1 t. soda
½ c. hot water	1 t. salt
1 c. butter or margarine	1 c. buttermilk
1 c. sugar	4 egg whites, stiffly beaten
4 egg yolks	1 c. flaked coconut
1 t. vanilla	
2½ c. sifted cake flour	1 c. chopped pecans

Melt chocolate in hot water; cool. Cream together butter and sugar until fluffy. Beat in egg yolks, one at a time, beating well after each addition. Add cooled chocolate mixture and vanilla. Sift flour, soda, and salt together and add alternately with buttermilk. Do not overbeat. Fold in stiffly beaten egg whites. Gently stir in pecans and coconut. Bake in three greased and floured or paper-lined 9″ layer pans at 350° for 25–30 min. Do not overbake. Cool the layers completely before frosting.

Icing:

⅔ c. evaporated milk	3 egg yolks
1 c. sugar	1 c. flaked coconut
¼ c. butter	1 c. chopped nuts
1 t. vanilla	

Combine milk, sugar, butter, vanilla, and egg yolks. Cook over low heat, stirring often (about 15 min.). Remove from heat and add coconut and chopped nuts. Beat until creamy.

Mrs. Eva Willis
Rush County

COLA CAKE

2 c. flour	2 beaten eggs
2 c. sugar	1 t. soda
2 sticks butter	1½ c. tiny marshmallows
3 T. cocoa	
1 c. cola drink	1 t. vanilla
½ c. buttermilk	

Combine sugar and flour. Heat butter, cola, and cocoa to a boil. Pour flour and sugar mixture, add buttermilk, eggs, soda, and vanilla, then add marshmallows. Pour into shallow baking pan. Bake at 350° for 30–40 min.

Icing:

½ c. butter	1 box powdered sugar
3 T. cocoa	
6 T. cola drink	1 c. chopped nuts

Combine butter, cocoa, and cola; heat to a boil. Pour over powdered sugar and nuts. Spread over cake while hot.

Dora Erwin
Spencer County

CRUMB CAKE

2 c. brown sugar	1 t. soda
2 c. flour	1 egg
½ c. shortening	dash of salt
1 c. sour milk or	dash of cinnamon
buttermilk	(optional)

Mix brown sugar, flour, and shortening to coarse crumbs with pastry blender. Reserve ½ c. of mixture for topping. To the remander add sour milk, soda, egg, and salt. Pour mixture into 13×9″ pan. Sprinkle reserved crumb mixture over top before baking. Dash of cinnamon may be added to reserved mixture. Bake at 350°.

Claudene Gross
Daviess County

DATE NUT CAKE

1 lb. pitted dates,	3½ c. flour
cut	1 t. cinnamon
2 c. boiling water	1 t. salt
2 c. sugar	2 level t. soda
1 c. shortening	1 c. chopped nuts
2 eggs	

Combine dates and water; set aside to cool. Cream sugar and shortening. Add dry ingredients. Then add date mixture. Bake in well-greased tube pan or bundt cake pan at 325° for 50–60 min., or until top is golden brown and springs back when touched. Cool and glaze.

Mrs. Quentin Elbrecht
Dearborn County

FIG CAKE

1 c. raisins	2 eggs
6 figs	2 c. flour
1 c. hot water	½ c. nuts,
1 t. soda	chopped (use
1 c. sugar	in cake or
½ c. shortening	frosting)

Put raisins and figs through food chopper.

Pour water in which soda has been dissolved over chopped raisins and figs. Mix sugar, shortening, eggs, and flour. Mix with raisin-fig mixture; stir well. Bake in 2 layer pans at 300° for 30 min. Cool and frost.

Marie Waldron
Noble County

FRUIT CAKE

½ c. butter	½ t. ground
1 c. sugar	cloves
1 egg	½ t. vanilla
½ t. salt	1 c. chopped
2 t. soda	dates
1½ c. unsweet-	1 c. raisins
ened applesauce	1 c. nuts
1 t. baking	2 c. flour (reserve
powder	some for flour-
1 t. cinnamon	ing fruit and
½ t. allspice	nuts)

Cream together butter and sugar, add egg, then add applesauce, mixing well. Add dry ingredients; mix. Add vanilla. Then add dates, raisins, and nuts which have been lightly floured. Bake at 350° in loaf pan or layer pan until done. Makes fifteen ½″ slices.

Mrs. Alma Galliher
Jennings County

INDIANA CHRISTMAS FRUITCAKE

2 c. mincemeat	½ c. butter or
2 c. diced	margarine
candied fruits	2 eggs
and peels	1 t. vanilla
(1 lb.)	2 c. all purpose
1 c. red candied	flour
cherries,	1½ t. baking
chopped	powder
2 c. walnuts,	½ t. soda
chopped	½ t. salt
1 c. brown sugar	

Combine mincemeat, fruits and peels, and nuts in a large bowl. Combine butter or margarine and sugar in a smaller bowl. Beat until fluffy. Add eggs and vanilla, mixing well. Sift together flour, baking powder, soda, and salt. Blend into the sugar mixture. Fold into fruit mixture. Oil and line 5 small loaf pans (or one large tube pan) with brown paper. Spoon batter into pans, bake at 325° for 1 hr. and 20 min. Cool cakes in pans; remove. Wrap in foil or clear plastic wrap and store in a cool place.

Mrs. Clarence W. Gunter
Kosciusko County

FRUIT COCKTAIL CAKE

2 c. sugar	2 c. fruit cocktail
2 c. flour	with juice
2 eggs	1 t. soda
1 t. cinnamon	

Blend sugar and eggs, add other ingredients, and beat. Bake in loaf pan at 350° for about 30 min.

Genevieve Cummings
Crawford County

GINGERBREAD (Old Recipe)

½ c. shortening	1 c. sour milk
(partly bacon	3 c. flour
drippings)	1 t. soda
1 c. sugar	1 t. cinnamon
2 eggs	½ t. ginger
1 c. molasses	1 t. cloves
(preferably	⅛ t. nutmeg
sorghum)	

Mix first 5 ingredients in order given. Add soda and spices to flour and add to first mixture. Pour into two 7×11″ pans. Bake at 325° for 40 min.

Doris Winn Sodrel
Perry County

GRANNY CAKE

2 c. flour	apple (not
1½ c. sugar	drained)
1 t. salt	¼ c. brown
1 t. soda	sugar
2 eggs	½ c. pecans,
1 No. 2 can	chopped
crushed pine-	

Mix together flour, sugar, salt, soda, eggs, and pineapple. Pour into 9×13″ pan. Sprinkle with brown sugar and pecans. Bake at 325° for approximately 1 hr.

Topping:

1 stick butter	½ c. sugar
1 c. evaporated	1 t. vanilla
milk	

Boil and pour over hot cake. Serve with whipped cream.

Mrs. Glen Hardwick
Miami County

SHELLBARK HICKORY NUT CAKE

One cup of butter, two of sugar, three of flour, one of sweet milk. The whites of seven eggs and yolks of two eggs, three teaspoons of baking powder, one pint of hickory nuts, chopped fine and sprinkled with flour. Put cake together in the usual fashion and fold in the egg whites and nuts last. Bake until you judge it lightly brown and done.

"Blue River Pioneer Cookin' "
Shelby County Historical Society

JAM CAKE

2½ c. sugar	4 c. flour
1 c. butter	1 t. soda
5 eggs	1 t. allspice
2 c. jam	1 t. cinnamon
1 c. buttermilk	½ t. black
pinch of salt	pepper

Cream sugar, butter, and eggs. Add jam and buttermilk; then add all the dry ingredients. Beat the batter with a mixer at least 2 min. or until smooth. Pour into three well-greased 9″ cake pans. Bake at 350°.

Jennie Staples
Posey County

JELLY ROLL

3 eggs	1 t. baking
1 c. sugar	powder
3 T. cold water	⅓ t. salt
1 c. flour	

Sift flour, salt, and baking powder together twice. Beat eggs and sugar until quite thick. Add water, then flour mixture. Line shallow 17×11″ pan with waxed paper, pour in batter evenly, and bake at 375° for about 12 min. Turn out on cloth or waxed paper sprinkled with sugar and tear off first paper. Spread with jelly or jam. Roll up quickly. Serves 10–12.

Mrs. Roscoe Stewart
Boone County

LEMON QUEEN CAKE

1½ c. margarine	2 c. thin milk
3 c. sugar	(half water)
4½ c. cake flour,	1 t. almond
sifted	flavoring
6 t. baking	2 t. vanilla
powder	9 egg whites,
1½ t. salt	stiffly beaten

Sift flour once, measure, add baking powder and salt and sift three times. Cream butter and sugar, beating until light and fluffy. Add flour mixture alternately with milk, beginning and ending with flour. Beat after each addition until smooth. Add flavorings; fold in beaten egg whites.

Bake in three greased, waxed paper-lined 9×1½″ round layer pans at 350° for 35–45 min. While cake is baking, toss 2 c. flaked coconut with 2 T. lemon juice and tint with several drops of yellow food coloring. Set aside.

Lemon Filling:

1½ c. sugar	½ c. lemon juice
6 T. cornstarch	9 egg yolks,
½ t. salt	beaten
2½ c. water	

Mix sugar, cornstarch, and salt in top of double boiler. Slowly stir in water and lemon juice. Cook, stirring constantly, until mixture thickens and boils. Blend about 1 c. of hot mixture into bowl of beaten egg yolks, return to heat and cook, stirring constantly until mixture thickens and boils. Chill until cold.

Lemon Butter Icing:

3 c. confectioners'	1 large egg or 2
sugar	small eggs
6 T. butter	2 t. lemon rind,
1 t. vanilla	grated

In a small bowl, blend about 1 c. confectioners' sugar with butter, beating well until creamy. Beat in egg, lemon rind, and vanilla. Gradually add remaining sugar and beat well until creamy. Assemble cake in layers with the lemon filling. Frost with lemon butter icing and press the coconut around sides of the cake.

Mrs. Bruce M. Smith
Scott County

MISSISSIPPI MUD CAKE

2 c. sugar	3 t. vanilla
1 c. shortening	1 c. chopped nuts
1½ c. flour	½ of 10-oz. pkg.
4 eggs	miniature
⅓ c. cocoa	marshmallows
¼ t. salt	

Cream shortening and sugar. Add eggs and beat by hand. Sift flour, cocoa, and salt and add to mixture. Add vanilla and nuts. Pour into greased and floured 9× 13″ pan. Bake 35 min. at 300°. Remove from oven and pour marshmallows over top. Return to oven for 10 min. at 350°. Cool cake 1 hr. before icing. Serves 24.

Icing:

1 box powdered sugar	1/3 c. cocoa
2 sticks margarine, melted	1/3 c. evaporated milk
1 t. vanilla	1 c. chopped nuts

Sift sugar and cocoa and stir into melted margarine. Add milk, vanilla, and nuts; spread on cake.

Mrs. Elizabeth Marshall
Washington County

FRANKLIN NUT CAKE

1 lb. butter	1/4 t. salt
2 c. sugar	1/2 lb. candied pineapple
2 t. vanilla	
1 t. baking powder	1/2 lb. candied cherries
6 eggs	1 lb. pecans
4 c. flour	

Cream butter and sugar. Add beaten eggs. Add 3 c. flour sifted with baking powder and salt. Mix remaining flour with cherries, nuts, and pineapple. Stir into batter. Add vanilla. Pour into tube cake pan. Bake at 250° for 3 hr. Let cool in pan. Serves 20–25.

Mrs. Bell Friddle
Delaware County

OATMEAL CAKE

1 rounded c. quick oats	1 1/4 c. boiling water

1 stick butter or margarine	pinch of salt
1 1/2 c. flour	1 t. soda
1 c. white sugar	1 t. vanilla
1 c. brown sugar	2 eggs, beaten
1 t. cinnamon	3/4 c. raisins (optional)

Pour boiling water over oats and stir at once. Add butter or margarine, flour, cinnamon, salt, soda, vanilla, sugars, and eggs. Add raisins, if desired. Mix thoroughly and put in greased, floured large cake pan. Bake for 30–35 min. at 350°. Serves 12–15.

Frosting:

1/2 c. butter, melted	1 c. brown sugar
	4 oz. coconut
1/2 c. evaporated milk	1/2 c. nuts (optional)

Mix ingredients and spread on top of cake. Broil until brown.

Mrs. Carl J. Sharp
Union County

ORANGE SLICE CAKE

1 c. margarine	1 8-oz. pkg. pitted dates
3 1/2 c. flour	
4 eggs	1 8-oz. jar maraschino cherries
1 lb. candy orange slices	
	1 c. drained pineapple chunks
1 can shredded coconut	1/2 c. buttermilk
1 c. chopped nuts	1 t. soda
1 lb. raisins	2 c. sugar

Prepare fruit, candy, and nuts by cutting into small pieces and rolling in 1/2 c. flour. Cream margarine and sugar. Add eggs, one at a time, blending well. Add buttermilk. Sift together remaining flour with soda and add to mixture. Fold in chopped nuts, dates, raisins, cherries, pineapple chunks, orange slices, and coconut. Bake in greased, floured 9″ tube pan for 3 hr. at 250°. Leave cake in pan to cool. While still hot, glaze.

Glaze:

2 c. powdered sugar	1 c. orange juice

Mix sugar and juice well. Pour over cake while still hot.

LouAnna Taylor
Daviess County

FRESH PEACH CAKE

2¾ c. sugar	¾ c. evaporated
2 c. flour	milk
2 t. baking soda	1 t. vanilla
2 eggs	1 c. chopped
2½ c. mashed	nutmeats
ripe peaches	1 c. shredded
1 stick butter or	coconut
margarine	

Sift together 2 c. sugar, flour, and baking soda. Beat eggs and add with peaches to dry ingredients. Turn batter into greased, floured 13×9×2″ cake pan. Bake at 350° for 30 min., or until done. Combine remaining ¾ c. sugar and the rest of the ingredients in heavy saucepan and cook over medium heat, stirring frequently, until thickened, approximately 6–8 min. Spread over warm cake.

Mrs. Hurley Fletcher
Lawrence County

PIE FILLING CAKE

2 c. flour	1 c. raisins
1 c. sugar	1 c. nuts
1½ t. soda	(optional)
1 t. salt	1 can pie filling,
1 t. vanilla	apple or
2 eggs, beaten	pineapple
⅔ c. cooking oil	

Stir together with spoon; do not beat. Put in ungreased 13×9×2″ pan and bake at 350° for 40–50 min. Serves 15–20.

Frosting:

1 3-oz. pkg. cream cheese	1 t. vanilla
1 c. powdered sugar	½ stick margarine

Beat together and spread over cooled cake.

Mrs. Howell Hemminger
Marshall County

PINEAPPLE CAKE

2 c. flour	1 t. vanilla
1½ c. sugar	No. 2 can crushed
2 eggs	pineapple (do
½ t. salt	not drain)
2 t. soda	½ c. brown sugar

Mix together, except brown sugar, and pour into greased oblong pan. Sprinkle top with brown sugar and bake 30 min., or until done, at 350°. When cake is taken out of oven, boil ¾ c. sugar, ½ c. evaporated milk and 1 stick margarine for 2 min. and pour over top of warm cake.

Dena McKown
Whitley County

PINEAPPLE UPSIDE-DOWN CAKE

3 T. butter or margarine	1 c. sugar
½ c. brown sugar	2 t. baking powder
5–6 pineapple rings, drained	½ t. salt
maraschino cherries	⅓ c. shortening
	⅔ c. milk
Batter:	1 t. vanilla
1½ c. cake flour or 1⅓ c. all-purpose flour	½ t. lemon flavoring (optional)
	1 egg

Prepare the pan: Melt butter or margarine in 8×8×2″ pan. Sprinkle brown sugar evenly over butter. Arrange pineapple rings over butter-sugar mixture, adding maraschino cherry to each pineapple ring. Make the batter: Sift together cake flour, sugar, baking powder, and salt. Add shortening, milk, vanilla, and lemon flavoring. Beat 2 min. Add egg and beat for 2 min. more. Pour batter over fruit. Bake at 350° for 45 min., or until done. Cool for 3–4 min. Turn upside down on cake rack or serving plate. Serves 16.

Elva Harmon
Harrison County

POPPY SEED CAKE
Batter:

1½ c. sugar	¼ c. poppy seeds
1 c. butter	1 c. buttermilk
4 egg yolks	1 t. vanilla
2½ c. flour	4 egg whites,
1 t. soda	beaten
½ t. salt	Filling:
2 t. baking	½ c. sugar
powder	1 t. cinnamon

Cream sugar, butter, and egg yolks. Sift together flour, soda, salt, and baking powder. Add alternately with poppy seeds soaked in buttermilk. Add vanilla. Fold into beaten egg whites. Pour ½ of batter in greased bundt pan, sprinkle some filling on batter, and continue until batter and filling are used. Bake at 350° for 1 hr. Drizzle on glaze of powdered sugar and milk. Serves 10–12.

Betty Hall
Monroe County

PORK CAKE

1 c. ground pork fat	2½ c. brown sugar
1 c. boiling water	1 c. nuts, floured
1 c. raisins, floured	1 t. cinnamon
pinch of salt	½ t. allspice
1 scant T. soda, dissolved in ¼ c. warm water	¼ t. cloves
	5 eggs
	2½ c. flour

Pour boiling water over ground pork fat. Stir until almost dissolved, then add brown sugar. Add rest of ingredients. Pour into 2 medium loaf pans. Bake at 275° to 300° for about 30 min.

Maureen Rogers
Allen County

POUND CAKE

4 c. sifted cake flour	1 lb. butter or margarine (or ½ lb. each)
3 c. sifted sugar	⅔ c. milk
6 eggs	

Sift flour once, measure, and sift 3 more times. Cream butter and sugar until light and fluffy. Add eggs, one at a time, beating well after each addition. Add flour and milk alternately, beating well. Pour into greased and floured 10″ tube pan. (Can also be baked in two 9×5×2½″ loaf pans that have been greased, waxed paper lined, and greased again.) Bake at 350° for 1 hr. and 15 min., or until done. Frost with any desired frosting or just sprinkle with powdered sugar.

Mrs. Jerry Krueger
Fayette County

TENNESSEE PRUNE CAKE

2½ c. flour	1 c. cooked prunes, chopped
1 t. cinnamon	
1 t. nutmeg	
1 t. soda	1 c. corn oil
1 c. buttermilk	1 c. nuts, chopped
3 eggs	
1½ c. sugar	pinch of salt

Mix together and add prunes last. Pour into tube pan. Bake 1 hr. at 350°.

Glaze:

1 c. sugar	1 stick margarine
½ c. buttermilk	3 T. white syrup
½ t. soda	pinch of salt

Mix soda with buttermilk until it fizzes. Cook together in large pan until thick and brown. Pour warm glaze over cake.

Kay Schoen
Floyd County

RICE CAKE

1 c. rice (raw)	rind of 1 orange,
1 qt. milk	grated
¾ c. butter	½ c. raisins
3 egg yolks	(optional)
1 c. sugar	3 egg whites

Wash the rice and put into a 4-qt. pan. Add just enough water to cover. Bring to a boil and drain. Add milk and cook rice until done. Cream butter and sugar well. Beat egg yolks until thick and lemon colored. Add to butter and sugar mixture. Add to warm rice along with orange rind and raisins. Blend well. Fold in stiffly beaten egg whites. Put into a 10″ tube pan, buttered and dusted with cracker crumbs. Bake at 350° for 50 min. Cool 20 min. Loosen with a knife, invert pan, remove cake, and sprinkle with powdered sugar. Serves 12–16.

Mrs. Pauline Menyhart
St. Joseph County

SPANISH CREAM CAKE

2 c. sugar	1 t. vanilla
1¼ c. shortening	1 c. buttermilk
½ c. butter	2 c. flour, sifted
5 egg yolks	1 t. soda

½ t. salt	2 c. coconut
1 c. chopped	5 egg whites,
pecans	beaten stiff

Cream first 3 ingredients until fluffy. Add yolks, one at a time, beating well after each addition. Add vanilla. Add sifted ingredients alternately with buttermilk to mixture. Stir in coconut and pecans. Fold in egg whites. Bake in three 9″ cake pans at 350° about 30 min.

Frosting:

½ c. butter	1 t. vanilla
1 8-oz. pkg.	1 lb. powdered
cream cheese	sugar
2 T. coconut	

Beat together and spread over cooled cake.

Mrs. Albert Pfaffenberger
Jackson County

SQUASH (PUMPKIN) CAKE

½ c. shortening	3 c. sifted cake
1 c. brown sugar,	(or all-pur-
firmly packed	pose) flour
1 c. white sugar	4 t. baking
2 beaten eggs	powder
1 c. cooked,	¼ t. soda
mashed squash	½ c. milk
or canned	1 c. chopped
pumpkin	walnuts
	1 t. maple extract

Cream shortening. Slowly add brown sugar, white sugar, eggs, and squash or pumpkin. Sift together flour, baking powder, and soda. Add to creamed mixture alternately with milk. Fold in walnuts and maple extract. Pour into three waxed paper-lined 8″ layer pans. Bake at 350° for 30 min. Cool and frost.

Mary Fleenor
Randolph County

CANADIAN WAR CAKE (No Sugar, No Milk, No Eggs)

2 c. hot water	1 t. cinnamon
2 T. butter	1 t. cloves
1 scant t. salt	3 slightly
2 c. light cook-	rounded c. flour
ing molasses	2 t. soda
1 pkg. raisins	2 t. hot water

Combine water, butter, salt, molasses, raisins, cinnamon, and cloves and boil for 5 min., after bubbles start. Take from stove and cool. Dissolve soda in hot water and with flour add to mixture. Bake in 2 loaf pans for 45 min. in moderate oven.

This recipe was obtained from a Canadian chef during the First World War.

Frieda Shoultz
Posey County

WHITE CAKE

1½ c. sugar	½ t. salt
2½ c. cake flour,	1 t. white vanilla
sift before	1 c. cold water
measuring	3 egg whites,
3 t. baking	beaten to soft
powder	peaks

½ c. plus 1 T.	¼ t. almond
shortening	extract

Sift sugar, flour, baking powder, and salt 3 times. Cream shortening with white vanilla and almond extract. Add sifted mixture alternately with water. Beat until fluffy. Gently fold in egg whites. Push batter into 2 greased, floured layer cake pans. Bake at 320° for 25–30 min., or until cake leaves side of pan. Cool 5 min. and turn out on cake rack to cool.

Frosting:

1 c. sugar	2 unbeaten egg
¼ t. salt	whites
2 T. white corn	1 t. white vanilla
syrup	1½ c. confec-
3 T. water	tioners' sugar

Mix first 5 ingredients in top of double boiler; beat well. Place over boiling water; cook until mixture stands in peaks (about 4–5 min.), beating constantly. Remove from heat; add vanilla and confectioners' sugar. Beat until smooth. Makes about 3½ cups.

Mrs. William H. Shrack
Jay County

Cakes from Mixes

A CAKE MIX AND . . .

White Cake Mix Variations:

WALNUT CAKE—Add 2 eggs, 1½ c. water, 2 T. cooking oil, ⅔ c. chopped nuts, and ½ t. walnut extract. Blend and bake as directed on box.

STRAWBERRY CAKE—Add 2 eggs, 1 c. mashed berries, ⅓ c. water. Blend and bake as directed on box.

Yellow Cake Mix Variations:

BANANA CAKE—Add 2 eggs, 1 c. mashed ripe bananas, ⅓ c. water, ½ c. chopped walnuts or ½ t. walnut extract. Blend and bake as directed on box.

CHOCOLATE CAKE—Add 2 eggs, ¾ c. cocoa, 2 T. sugar, 1½ c. water, 3 T. cooking oil (and optional: ½ c. chopped nuts). Blend and bake as directed on box.

PUMPKIN CAKE—Add 2 eggs, 1 c. mashed pumpkin, 1 t. pumpkin pie spice, 1 T. molasses, ½ c. water, 2 T. cooking oil. Blend and bake as directed on box.

Dearborn County

ALMA'S DREAM CAKE

1 pkg. cake mix (white, yellow, or chocolate)	4 eggs, whole 1 c. cold water flavoring for
1 envelope Dream Whip	yellow or white mix

Combine cake mix, dry Dream Whip, eggs, and water in large mixer bowl. Blend until moistened. Beat 4 min. at medium speed. Pour into two greased and floured 9" layer pans or three 8" pans. Bake at 350° for 30–35 min. Cool for 10 min. in pans. Remove from pans and cool on cake racks. Ice as you wish, or slice fresh strawberries on top of each piece and top with Dream Whip. Serves 16–18.

Mrs. Alma Galliher
Jennings County

LEMON CAKE

1 pkg. Lemon Supreme cake mix	1 c. boiling water ⅓ c. cold water
1 pkg. Lemon Jello	½ c. Wesson oil 3 eggs

Dissolve Jello in boiling water. Add to rest of ingredients and beat about 3 min. Put in greased and floured 9×13" pan and bake at 350° until done. Remove from oven, punch holes in top with fork. Make glaze of lemon juice and powdered sugar and pour over cake while still hot.

Dona Jackson
Spencer County

TURTLE CAKE

Batter:	Filling:
1 pkg. fudge cake mix	28 light caramels 1⅓ c. (14-oz.
1 c. water	can) sweetened
1 T. shortening	condensed milk
3 eggs	1 T. butter

Melt filling ingredients in top of double boiler, stirring often. Blend cake ingredients. Pour ½ of cake batter in greased and lightly floured 9×13" pan. Spread filling evenly over batter. Add rest of cake batter. Bake at 350° for 30–35 min. Frost.

Nettie Coughlin
Delaware County

YELLOW CAKE MIXES

APRICOT NECTAR CAKE

1 pkg. yellow cake mix	½ c. sugar ½ c. shortening
1 c. apricot nectar	4 eggs

Mix ingredients, adding the eggs one at a time. Bake in a tube pan at 350° about 50–55 min., or until done. Cool for 15 min. before removing from pan. Ice with powdered sugar mixed with apricot nectar. It takes 1½ cans nectar for cake and icing. Serves 16.

Mrs. Maurice Kimick
Scott County

BUNDT CAKE

1 18.5-oz. pkg. yellow cake mix	1 pkg. coconut and pecan frosting mix
4 eggs	4 T. melted margarine
1 12-oz. pkg. sour cream	

Mix cake mix, eggs, and sour cream until smooth. In another bowl, mix melted margarine and frosting mix until crumbly. Pour ⅓ of cake batter mixture into greased and floured 10″ tube pan or bundt pan, then ½ of frosting mixture, ⅓ of cake batter mixture, ½ of frosting mixture, ending with ⅓ of cake batter mixture. Bake 55–60 min. at 350°. Cool 10 min.; remove from pan. May be dusted with powdered sugar.

Judy Bathke
Pulaski County

BUTTERSCOTCH PUDDING CAKE

1 3¾-oz. pkg. butterscotch pudding pie mix (not instant)	1 1-lb., 2-oz. pkg. yellow cake mix
2 c. milk	1 small pkg. butterscotch morsels
chopped nuts	

Prepare pudding with milk as directed on package. Cool. Stir in cake mix until well blended. Grease 9×13×2″ pan. Sprinkle top with butterscotch morsels and nuts. Bake at 350° for 35–40 min. Serves 15 or more.

Loretta Roberts
Parke County

DUMP CAKE

1 No. 2 can crushed pineapple	1 lb. can cherry pie filling
1 box of yellow or white cake mix	2 sticks of butter or margarine
	1 can chopped pecans

Put pineapple in greased pan; cover with cherry pie filling. Sprinkle the cake mix from the box over the filling. Add chopped nuts over the cake mix. Cut the butter and arrange evenly over the top. Do not mix layers together. Bake at 350° for 1 hr. Serves 10.

Aldine Smith
Switzerland County

GOOEY BUTTER CAKE

1 pkg. yellow cake mix	1 8-oz. pkg. cream cheese, softened
4 eggs	1 lb. confectioners' sugar
1 stick butter, melted	

Mix cake mix with 2 eggs and butter. Spread in greased 9×13″ pan or two 8×8″ pans. Beat cream cheese with 2 eggs and confectioners' sugar. Reserve a few tablespoons of sugar for later. Spread over first mixture. Sprinkle with nuts, if desired. Bake at 350° for 35–40 min. Cake will be puffed up when taken from oven. Cool and sprinkle with reserved confectioners' sugar.

Juanita Fuller
Knox County

HARVEY WALLBANGER CAKE

1 pkg. yellow cake mix	4 eggs, at room temperature
1 small pkg. vanilla instant pudding	¼ c. vodka
	¼ c. galliano liqueur
1 c. oil	¾ c. orange juice

Mix and beat 4 min. Pour into greased and floured tube or bundt pan. Bake at 350° for 55 min.

Frosting: Mix powdered sugar and orange juice and drizzle over top. Can be topped with candy orange slices.

Karen Monroe
Allen County

NO NAME CAKE

1 pkg. yellow cake mix	¾ c. boiling water
1 large pkg. Jello (red)	1½ c. of red pop

Bake mix as directed in greased and floured 9×13″ pan. While cake is baking, dissolve Jello in boiling water. When dissolved, add red pop and blend together. When cake is done, punch holes in top with fork. While cake is still hot, pour the Jello mixture over cake, letting it soak into cake. Place in refrigerator until cool.

Frosting:

2 pkg. Dream Whip	1 6-oz. pkg. instant vanilla pudding
2 c. cold milk	

Prepare Dream Whip according to directions on box. Set aside. Mix pudding and milk until blended. Fold pudding into Dream Whip. Stir until well blended. Spread over cake. Keep cake in refrigerator.

Beverly Richardson
Putnam County

WHITE CAKE MIXES

PISTACHIO NUT CAKE (Watergate Cake)

1 pkg. white cake mix	1 c. Wesson oil
1 pkg. instant pistachio nut pudding	½ c. chopped nuts
	3 eggs
	1 c. club soda

Mix cake mix and pudding mix dry. Add eggs, nuts, oil, and club soda. Mix well.

Bake in 9×13″ pan at 350° for 45–50 min. Cool.

Frosting:

1 pkg. instant pistachio nut pudding	2 envelopes Dream Whip
1½ c. cold milk	nuts, coconut, or cherries

Mix pudding according to directions. Beat Dream Whip and milk at high speed until peaks form. Gradually add pudding; continue to beat until light and fluffy (about 2 min.). Sprinkle nuts, coconut, or cherries over frosting.

Mrs. Elco Eichhorn
Wells County

President, Indiana Extension
Homemakers, 1976

STRAWBERRY CAKE

1 3-oz. pkg. Strawberry Jello	4 eggs
	1 c. strawberries (or ½ c. strawberries and ½ c. water)
1 pkg. white cake mix	
1 c. Wesson oil	

Combine in the order given. Beat well. Bake in greased 9×13″ pan at 325° for 45–55 min. When cool, ice cake with Strawberry Icing.

Strawberry Icing:

1 lb. powdered sugar	1 stick margarine
	½ c. strawberries

Beat until smooth.

Mrs. Lawrence Cavin
LaPorte County

Cake Desserts

ANGEL FOOD CAKE DESSERTS

APRICOT NECTAR CAKE DESSERT

1 angel food cake, broken into pieces	2 12-oz. cans apricot nectar
1 c. sugar	4 T. cornstarch
	½ t. salt

Cook last 4 ingredients until pudding is clear; allow to cool. Spread over cake. Let stand overnight. Serves 10–12.

If desired: Whip 2 pkg. Dream Whip; add 1 small pkg. flaked coconut. Spread over cake.

Mrs. Betty Taylor
Ohio County

DELIGHTFUL CAKE

1 pkg. angel food cake mix	½ pt. whipping cream or Dream Whip
1 6-oz. pkg. Jello (red)	chopped nuts, if desired
3–4 bananas	

Mix cake according to directions. Place ½ of mixture in ungreased 13×9″ pan. Place other half in similar pan, or place in loaf pan. Bake. Leave in pan to cool. Mix Jello according to directions, minus ¼ c. cold water. Chill until syrupy. Cover cooled cake with slices of bananas. Pour Jello over bananas and cake. Cool until solid. Whip cream and cover Jello completely. Add nuts, if desired. Keep refrigerated. Serves 24.

Mary Ann Hofer
Allen County

ORANGE ANGEL DELIGHT

1 angel food cake	2 envelopes gelatin
1 c. cold water	
1 c. hot water	juice of 1 lemon
1 c. sugar	1 can of mandarin oranges, drained
1 c. orange juice	
grated rind of 1 orange	
	1 pint whipped cream or 1 pkg. Dream Whip
1 No. 2 can fruit cocktail, drained	

Soften gelatin in cold water. Add hot water and stir until dissolved. Add sugar, orange juice, grated orange rind, and lemon juice. Chill, but do not let it set. Add fruit cocktail, mandarin oranges. Fold in whipped cream or Dream Whip. Break angel food cake into small pieces and put in oblong or square dish and pour mixture over cake. Refrigerate until well set. Serves 10–12.

Mabel Detmer
Ohio County

PINEAPPLE ANGEL FOOD DESSERT

1½ T. gelatin	1 c. sugar
⅓ c. cold water	1 No. 2 can crushed pineapple, drained
2 c. milk	
2 eggs, separated	
1½ c. heavy cream, whipped	½ angel food cake, cubed

Soften gelatin in cold water for 20–30 min. Beat yolks slightly in double boiler. Gradually add milk. Add sugar and cook, stirring until mixture coats spoon. Add gelatin to hot custard. Cool until it starts to congeal. Fold in stiff egg whites and whipped cream. Add pineapple. Place cake pieces in bottom of baking dish. Pour mixture over cake. Refrigerate 2–3 hr.

Alta Gladish
Pike County

SNOWBALL CAKE

2 envelopes un-flavored gelatin	juice of 1 lemon
¼ c. cold water	1 No. 2 can crushed pine-apple, drained
1 c. boiling pine-apple juice, drained from No. 2 can crushed pineapple	1 large angel food cake
	3 pkg. Dream Whip
1 c. sugar	1 can flaked coconut

Soften gelatin in cold water, add boiling pineapple juice, and cool to lukewarm. Add sugar, lemon juice, and drained pineapple. Chill. Break cake into bite-size pieces. Prepare 2 pkg. Dream Whip and combine with chilled gelatin mix. Fold in cake a little at a time. Put in 9×13″ pan. Chill overnight, or 6 hr. Prepare third pkg. Dream Whip, spread on top of dessert, and top with coconut. Serves 12–15.

Katheryn F. Weinhold
Fayette County

STRAWBERRY DELIGHT

1 pkg. vanilla instant pudding	1 pkg. Straw-berry Jello
1 c. milk	2 c. strawberries, sliced
2 c. vanilla ice cream	½ angel food cake
1 c. hot water	

Break cake into 1″ pieces. Place in 9″ pan. Mix pudding with milk. Stir in ice cream. Pour over cake. Mix Jello with water. Stir in strawberries. Let set until slightly thickened. Pour over pudding and let set a few hrs.

Catherine Gady
Pulaski County

WHIPPED CREAM CAKE

1 angel food cake	1 pkg. Cool Whip
6 small Heath Bars	

Cut cake crosswise to make two layers. Put Heath Bars in plastic bag and hit with hammer until bars are in small pieces. Add to Cool Whip and frost cake.

Bea Helms
Marion County

LADYFINGERS CAKE DESSERTS

APRICOT REFRIGERATOR CAKE

1 11–12 oz. pkg. dried apricots	3 dozen lady-fingers
2 c. water	¾ c. heavy cream, whipped
1 c. soft butter	
2 c. sifted confec-tioners' sugar	⅓ c. pistachio nuts
4 eggs, separated	1 1-lb., 14-oz. can apricot halves, drained
1 lemon	
⅛ t. salt	
⅓ c. granulated sugar	

Stew dried apricots in water, covered, until tender and liquid is absorbed. Put through sieve or blender and cool. Cream butter, add confectioners' sugar, and beat until light. Beat in egg yolks, one at a time. Beat in apricot pulp and lemon juice. Beat egg whites with salt until stiff. Add granulated sugar and beat until dissolved. Fold into apricot mixture. Line bottom and sides of 3″ deep 9″ springform pan with split ladyfingers, split side up. Put in alternate layers of ⅓ of the mixture and ⅓ of remaining ladyfingers. Chill at least 12 hrs. To serve: remove ring, spread whipped cream on top of cake and garnish with apricot halves, then sprinkle with nuts. Serves 12.

Mrs. Kendel McCammack
Lake County

CHOCOLATE REFRIGERATOR CAKE

2 bars German sweet chocolate	4 eggs, separated
¼ c. cold water	1 pt. (2 c.) whipping cream
½ c. sugar	3 pkg. ladyfingers

Add water to chocolate and melt over low heat. Add sugar and mix well. Add egg yolks, one at a time, beating well after each addition. Cook for one minute, stirring constantly. Do not scorch. Cool. Beat egg whites until stiff and fold into chocolate mixture. Whip cream and fold into mixture. Line sides and bottom of 10″ springform pan with split ladyfingers. Pour in ⅓ of chocolate mixture. Top with a layer of ladyfingers, cover with another layer of chocolate mixture, repeat with ladyfingers and chocolate mixture. Top

with remaining ladyfingers. Refrigerate for 24 hr. Remove at least 1½ hr. before serving. Unmold. Serves 12–16.

Betty Weldon
Pulaski County

TIPSY CAKE

1 pkg. ladyfingers	1 large pkg. vanilla pudding
1 jar apricot preserves	½ pt. whipping cream
¾ c. sherry or brandy	½ c. sliced almonds
1 can apricots	

Place layer of ladyfingers in bottom of baking dish. Spread with apricot preserves. Pour sherry or brandy over this. Sprinkle ¼ c. almonds on top. Pour vanilla pudding, which has been prepared according to package directions and cooled, over this. Top with layer of apricots. Cover with whipped cream and sprinkle remaining almonds on top. Serves 8.

Mrs. Eugene Wakeland
Marion County

Cake Frostings and Icings

BEAT AND EAT FROSTING

1 egg white, unbeaten	¾ c. sugar
¼ t. cream of tartar	1 t. vanilla
	¼ c. boiling water

Mix first 3 ingredients in small deep bowl. Add boiling water and beat to stiff peaks. Makes 3 cups.

CARAMEL ICING

½ c. margarine	1½–2 c. powdered sugar
1 c. brown sugar	
¼ c. milk	

Melt margarine in saucepan. Add brown sugar and cook 2 min., stirring constantly. Add milk and bring to a boil. Remove from heat and cool. Add powdered sugar slowly until of consistency to spread.

Mrs. Catherine Ulch
Steuben County

PINEAPPLE FILLING (For White Cake)

1¼ c. crushed pineapple, undrained	¾ c. sugar
	1 egg yolk
	pinch of salt
1 T. cornstarch	½ c. coconut

Cook ingredients, except coconut, until thick. Cool. Add coconut.

Virginia Watson
Harrison County

CHOCOLATE ICING

1 stick margarine	1 box confec-
4 T. cocoa	tioners' sugar
7 T. milk	1 t. vanilla
1 c. chopped nuts	

Combine margarine, cocoa, and milk and bring to boil. Add sugar, vanilla, and nuts. Spread on cake while hot.

Mrs. Ruth Eckert
Crawford County

SOUR CREAM CHOCOLATE FROSTING

1 6-oz. pkg.	1 t. vanilla
semisweet choc-	¼ t. salt
olate pieces	2½–2¾ c. sifted
4 T. butter or	confectioners'
margarine	sugar
½ c. sour cream	

Melt chocolate pieces and butter or margarine over low heat. Remove. Blend in sour cream, vanilla, and salt. Gradually add sugar to make spreading consistency; beat well. Frosts one 13×9×2″ cake.

Pat Thom
Shelby County

CREAM CHEESE FROSTING

1 3-oz. pkg.	1 T. warm water
cream cheese	3 c. sifted confec-
1 t. vanilla	tioners' sugar
extract	

Mash cream cheese until softened. Add water and vanilla. Gradually add sugar, beat until smooth and of good spreading consistency. Makes 1½ cups.

Variation: To make Orange Cream Cheese Frosting, substitute fresh orange juice for the water and 1 t. grated orange rind for the vanilla.

Mrs. Wayne Miller
Kosciusko County

MOCK WHIPPED CREAM FROSTING

½ c. milk	2 T. flour
¼ c. butter	¼ c. shortening
½ c. sugar	1 t. vanilla

Cook milk and flour in small pan over low flame until thick. Cool. Blend butter and shortening with mixer. Add sugar gradually and mix for another 4 min. Add cooled milk paste. Mix for 2–4 min. Fold in vanilla.

Florence Wood
Pike County

AUNT LILA'S NEVER FAIL ICING

½ c. water	1 t. vanilla
3 c. sugar	(white, if
¼ c. corn syrup	possible)
½ t. cream of	1 scant c. pow-
tartar	dered sugar
4 egg whites	

Boil water, sugar, and corn syrup together until it spins a thread. Remove from heat. Add cream of tartar. Pour slowly over egg whites which have been beaten stiff but not dry. At high speed of mixer beat until smooth. Add vanilla. Gradually add powdered sugar. Continue to beat until consistency for frosting. Enough for two 8″ layer cakes.

Mrs. Lythia Armbrister
Jennings County

PRALINE FROSTING

¼ c. butter or margarine	2 c. miniature marshmallows
½ c. brown sugar, firmly packed	½ c. flaked coconut
2 T. cream or Milnot	¼ c. nuts

Cream margarine and sugar. Blend in cream. Stir in marshmallows, coconut, and nuts. Spread on 8 or 9″ baked cake while it is still warm in pan. Place under broiler until frosting is bubbly and lightly browned.

Mrs. Gerry Brown
Steuben County

PENUCHE ICING

1½ c. brown sugar, firmly packed	¼ c. plus 2 T. shortening
¼ c. plus 2 T. milk	¾ t. vanilla
¼ t. salt	1 t. cream
	½ c. nuts

Mix sugar, milk, shortening, and salt in saucepan. Bring slowly to a full rolling boil, stirring constantly, and boil 1 min. Remove from heat and beat until luke-warm. Add vanilla and continue beating until thick enough to spread. Add cream and nuts.

Maxine White
Steuben County

STRAWBERRY ICING (For Angel Food Cake)

| 1 c. strawberries, washed and drained | 1 c. sugar |
| | 1 egg white |

Place all ingredients in bowl of electric mixer and whip at high speed until of spreading consistency.

Catherine Miller
Floyd County

CONFETTI COCONUT

Put coconut in small jar. Drop 3 drops of food coloring of your choice. Shake well. Blend colors together.

Waneeta Daugherty
Sullivan County

Pies

In *Speak to the Earth* Rachel Peden said that "When a neighbor appears at a farmer's house at mealtime, and is, of course, invited to eat, he can get out of it by saying: 'Thanks, I just got up from the table.' After that the most the housewife can press on him is a cup of coffee or a glass of buttermilk. Unless there is pie. A man can always accept a piece of pie. On the farm, pie is the great common denominator."

For several generations standard pastry was made most often with lard, because most cooks had their own supply, and for those who had to purchase it, the price was low. Also, lard does make a superior, flaky pastry. However, it is not so much the ingredients as the way they are handled that insures a good pie. Avoid too much handling and use restraint in the amount of flour used during rolling. Pastry is easier to handle if chilled before rolling and using ice water helps to produce tender pastry.

Hickory nuts are enclosed in a hard wooden coating and the "meat" is the very devil "to pick out," but once you've tasted them in a cake, pie, or cookies, you'll be glad you "picked."

At its best a pumpkin pie should be a little "trembly" in consistency and delicately brown on top.

Rhubarb is sometimes called "pie plant." On old Indiana homesites it was found growing on the south side of a woodshed to encourage early growth. Always pull rhubarb when young instead of cutting it. Use as soon as possible after pulling, for it loses sugar. Both flavor and color are in the skin, so do not peel unless tough.

Whether dry- or wet-bottom, all varieties of shoofly pie contain molasses. Since flies are supposedly attracted to molasses, they had to be chased away while the cook made the pie.

FOOLPROOF PIE CRUST

4 c. unsifted	2 t. salt
flour	1 T. sugar
1¾ c. shortening	1 T. vinegar
½ c. water	1 egg

With a fork mix together flour, sugar, salt, and shortening. In separate bowl beat the remaining ingredients. Combine the two mixtures with a fork, until all are moistened. Then with hands mold in a ball. Chill at least 15 min. Makes two 2-crust pies and one 9″ shell.

Mrs. John Richardson
Dubois County

EGG YOLK PASTRY

5 c. flour, sifted	1½ c. lard
4 t. sugar	2 egg yolks
½ t. salt	1 scant c. cold
½ t. baking	water
powder	

Combine dry ingredients; cut in lard. Place egg yolks in measuring cup and stir with fork until smooth. Blend into flour mixture. Sprinle cold water gradually over flour mixture. Toss with fork to make soft dough. Roll. Makes three 9″ 2-crust pies.

Jean French
Brown County

HOT WATER PIE CRUST

2 c. flour	⅔ c. cooking oil
¼ c. sugar	¼ c. hot water
½ t. salt	

Mix with mixer. Roll out between waxed paper. Fill with berries, cherries, or any fruit. Bake at 450° until brown. Makes one 2-crust pie.

Mrs. Frank Reilly
Floyd County

QUICK AND EASY TWO-CRUST PIE DOUGH

½ c. vegetable	2 c. flour
oil (Crisco)	¼ t. salt
¼ c. milk	

Measure oil and milk in same glass measuring cup. Measure flour and salt and place in mixing bowl; add oil and milk mixture and mix together with a wooden spoon. Do not overmix. Divide dough in half and roll each between two pieces of waxed paper. Fit into pie pan. Makes one 8″ or 9″ 2-crust pie.

Mrs. Michael Marburger
Wabash County

MERINGUE HINTS

1. Have egg whites at room temperature.
2. Avoid overbeating the egg whites.
3. Beat egg whites until frothy, then start adding sugar, a little at a time, using no more than 2 T. per white. Beating time will be longer, but a more stable meringue will result.
4. Spread meringue on pie by spooning around edges to seal. Then pull toward the center.
5. Adjust oven temperature according to temperature of the filling. Ideally, one should use a warm, not hot, filling and bake meringue at 425° for about 4½ min. If the filling is cold, bake at 325° for 10 min. The higher temperature gives a more tender and less sticky meringue.

NEVER FAIL MERINGUE

1 T. cornstarch	3 egg whites
2 T. cold water	2 T. sugar
½ c. boiling	pinch of salt
water	1 t. vanilla

Dissolve cornstarch in cold water and add boiling water slowly, stirring constantly. Cook until clear over low heat. Put aside to cool. Beat egg whites until frothy; add salt. On high speed gradually add sugar until peaks form. Add vanilla. Switch to low speed. Gradually add cooled cornstarch mixture. On high speed beat well until peaks will not bend over or curl when beater is withdrawn. Pile on pie filling and bake at 375° or until slightly browned. Wheen the meringued pie is out of the oven, let it cool carefully on a rack for at least 1 hr. The meringue is much easier to cut if you will first dip your knife in cold water.

Mrs. George Fuhrman
Dubois County

MERINGUE THAT WON'T WEEP

8 T. sugar	3 egg whites
1 T. cornstarch	pinch of salt
½ c. water	

Cook together until clear cornstarch, 2 T. sugar, and water. Cool. Add egg whites and salt, which have been beaten until foamy and are standing in peaks. Continue beating until creamy; then add 6 T. of sugar gradually, beating until very creamy. Pile on pie and bake at 325° until golden brown.

Clema Perkins
Putnam County

AMBER PIE

2 T. flour	3 eggs, separated
1 c. sugar	1 whole egg
½ c. sour cream	6 T. sugar
½ c. tart plum jelly	¼ t. cream of tartar
½ c. soft butter	1 t. lemon juice

Cream butter and sugar until well blended. Add 3 egg yolks and 1 egg; beat well. Add flour, sour cream, and jelly; mix well. Put in a 10″ unbaked crust. Bake at 375° 10 min. Reduce heat to 325° and continue baking until silver knife inserted near center comes out clean. Remove from oven. Beat whites with sugar, cream of tartar and lemon juice until glossy peaks form. Spread over pie. Bake at 350° until brown.

Mrs. Esther Eggenspiller
Harrison County

ANGEL FOOD PIE

1 c. crushed pineapple and liquid	3 egg whites, stiffly beaten
1 c. sugar	½ pt. whipping cream (or Cool Whip)
1 c. water	
pinch of salt	1 small jar maraschino cherries, chopped
3 heaping T. cornstarch	

Bring first 4 ingredients to a boil. Dissolve the cornstarch in small amount of water; then stir into rapidly boiling mixture. Cook about 1 min., until cornstarch is well blended and clear. Cool. Fold in stiffly beaten egg whites. Add maraschino cherries. Pour into 9″ baked pie crust. Serves 6–8.

Mrs. Orville Fritcha
Allen County

APPLE PIE

4–5 tart apples, sliced (about 4 full c.)	1–1¼ c. sugar (depending on tartness of apples)
½ t. cinnamon	2 T. cornstarch
½ t. nutmeg	
1–2 T. butter	

Drop the apple slices in weak salt water while paring. Place apples, sugar, butter, and spices in saucepan and heat over low flame. Add no water; the sugar and juice will make enough liquid. As juice forms, pour off ½ c. liquid; let cool and add cornstarch. Let sliced apples heat through; remove from heat and add cornstarch mixture. Pour into unbaked pie crust and place circle of dough on top. Bake at 425° for 10–15 min., then reduce heat to 350° for 15–20 min. longer, or when juice boils up in pie, bubbly and thick and top is golden brown.

Ruth Clodfelter
Putnam County

APPLE PIE (With Cream)

Fill pie shell about ½ full of apples. Add 1 c. sugar and 1 T. flour. Fill with sweet cream, just so it doesn't quite cover the apples. Sprinke with cinnamon. Bake at 375° for about 45 min., or until center of pie starts to boil. Serves 6.

Marcia Powers
Greene County

APPLE MACAROON PIE

1 9" unbaked pastry shell	Coconut Topping:
½ c. sugar	1 egg, well beaten
½ t. salt	1 c. shredded coconut
4 c. apples, thinly sliced	½ c. sugar
1 T. flour	¼ c. milk
2 T. butter	

Line pie pan with pastry. Arrange apple slices in pan. Combine sugar, flour, cinnamon, and salt. Sprinkle on top of apples; dot with butter. Bake in hot oven (400°) for 10 min. Combine coconut topping.

Add to top and lower temperature to 350°. Bake 30 min. longer, or until topping is browned and crispy.

Cora Robling
Pike County

APPLE MINCE PIE WITH CHEESE CRUST

Crust:	Filling:
2 c. sifted flour	1 c. mincemeat
½ t. salt	4 c. apples, sliced
⅔ c. shortening	2 T. flour
½ c. shredded nippy cheese	¼ t. salt
	1 t. cinnamon
5–6 T. cold water	¾ c. sugar
	2 T. butter

Sift flour; measure; add salt and sift again. Cut in shortening and cheese until mixture resembles coarse meal. Add water, stirring with fork until dough forms. Roll ½ of dough to fit 9" pie tin. Spread mincemeat over bottom. Combine sugar, flour, cinnamon, and salt and mix into apple slices. Fit apple slices into pie shell on top of mincemeat. Dot with butter and moisten edge of crust with cold water. Roll out second half of dough; perforate; place over top of apples. Crimp edges together. Bake at 475° for 10 min.; reduce heat to 350° and bake an additional 45 min., or until apples are bubbling through perforations in top crust.

Gertrude Glasgow
Wells County

APPLE PIZZA PIE

1½ c. flour	½ c. shortening
1 t. salt	½ c. powdered non-dairy cream
1 c. shredded sharp cheese	

¼ c. ice water   ⅓ c. flour
½ c. brown sugar   ½ t. salt
6 c. pared apple   1 t. cinnamon
   slices   ½ t. nutmeg
½ c. sugar   ¼ c. butter

Mix flour and salt. Cut in shortening until crumbly. Add cheese. Sprinkle water over mixture gradually, and shape into a ball. Roll pastry into 15″ circle on floured surface. Place on pizza pan. Combine cream, sugars, flour, salt, and spices. Sprinkle ½ of mixture over pastry. Cut butter into remaining ½ until crumbly. Arrange apple slices, overlapping them in circles on crust. Sprinkle remaining sugar-flour-butter mixture on top. Bake at 450° for 30 min., or until apples are tender.

Patty Breeden
Monroe County

APPLE-RASPBERRY CHIFFON PIE

Crumb Shell: 1½ c. applesauce,
1¼ c. cheese   hot
   cracker crumbs   1 10-oz. pkg.
⅓ c. butter,   frozen red rasp-
   melted   berries, thawed
Filling: ¼ c. sugar
1 pkg. raspberry   1 c. whipping
   gelatin   cream, whipped

Combine cheese cracker crumbs and melted butter. Press evenly over bottom and sides of buttered 9″ pie pan. Chill thoroughly. Dissolve gelatin in hot applesauce; stir in undrained raspberries and sugar. Chill until partly set. Beat until fluffy. Fold in whipped cream. Spoon into crumb shell. Chill 2–3 hr., or until firm. Serves 6–8.

Mrs. Frank Mahlke, Jr.
Tippecanoe County

CARAMEL CRUNCH APPLE PIE

28 caramels   ¾ c. flour
2 T. water   ⅓ c. sugar
4 c. apples,   ½ t. cinnamon
   peeled and   ½ c. chopped
   sliced   walnuts
1 9″ unbaked pie   ⅓ c. butter
   shell

Melt caramels with water in saucepan over low heat, stirring occasionally until sauce is smooth. Layer apples and caramel sauce in pie shell. Combine flour, sugar, cinnamon, and nuts. Cut in butter until mixture resembles coarse crumbs. Sprinkle over apples. Bake at 375° for 40–45 min. Serves 8.

Barbara Brown
Parke County

DUTCH APPLE PIE

4–6 apples   ⅓ c. butter or
½ c. sugar   margarine
1 t. cinnamon   ½ c. brown sugar
¾ c. flour

Mix apples, sugar, and cinnamon and put into unbaked crust. Mix flour, butter or margarine, and sugar. Spread over apples. Bake in hot oven (375°) until done (about 1 hr.).

Kathryn Jensen
Porter County

DRIED APPLE PIES

dried apples   1 T. juice
pie dough   ¼ t. cinnamon
sugar to taste   ¼ t. nutmeg

Cook dried apples covered with water until done. Drain, reserving 1 T. juice, and cool. Make up favorite pastry for piecrusts; roll out half the dough. Using 6″ saucer for a measure, cut pastry circles. In medium bowl, mash apples with sugar to taste, juice, cinnamon, and nutmeg. Place about 2 T. fruit mixture on half of each circle; fold rest of pastry over filling. Dip fork in flour and press pastry edges firmly together to keep filling inside. Continue until all of pastry and fruit are used. Pour about 1″ salad oil in skillet; heat to about 375°. Fry pies, 2–3 at a time, until golden brown on both sides. Drain on paper towels. Serve warm to eat out of hand.

Donna Handley
Union County

SPICE 'N EASY APPLE CRUNCH PIE

Crust:	Topping:
1½ c. flour	½ c. Grape Nuts
2 t. sugar	or 1 c. Rice
1 t. salt	Krispies or corn
½ c. cooking oil	flakes
2 T. milk	⅓ c. flour
Apple Filling:	⅓ c. brown
⅔ c. sugar	sugar, firmly
¼ c. flour	packed
1 t. cinnamon	½ t. cinnamon
3–4 c. cooking	½ t. nutmeg
apples, sliced	¼ c. butter or
½ c. sour cream	margarine,
	softened

Combine crust ingredients in medium bowl; mix well. Pat in ungreased 9″ pie pan. Flute edges, if desired. Combine apple filling in large bowl; mix well. Spoon into unbaked crust. Combine topping in small bowl. Sprinkle over apples. Bake at 375° for 40–45 min. until topping is golden brown and apples are tender. Serves 8.

Thelma Hoagland
Allen County

FISHERMAN TARTS

People who go hunting and fishing like to fill their pockets with flat packets of food so that their hands are free to carry a gun or rod.

2 lb. apples	2 c. flour
1 c. sugar	1 t. salt
½ t. cinnamon	½ c. shortening
2 T. soft butter	½ c. cold water

Wash, core, and chop apples in large bowl. Mix with sugar and cinnamon. Set aside while making pastry. Sift together salt and flour in large bowl. Cut in shortening and blend thoroughly with water. Roll out on well-floured board. Cut pastry into small circles, using a saucer or small pan lid as a guide. Drain all liquid from chopped apples. Place ¼ c. apples on ½ of each pastry circle. Dot with butter. Fold other ½ of pastry over apple and seal securely on cut edge. Place on a cookie sheet and bake for 10 min. at 425°, then at 350° for additional 30 min.

Gertrude Glasgow
Wells County

JOHNNY APPLESEED PIE

⅓ c. sugar	½ c. semisweet
1 t. ground	chocolate pieces
cinnamon	1 c. biscuit mix
6 c. apples, pared	¼ c. sugar
and sliced	4 T. butter or
1 9″ unbaked	margarine
pastry shell	

Combine ⅓ c. sugar and cinnamon; mix with apples. Turn into unbaked pastry shell. Top with chocolate pieces. In small bowl, combine biscuit mix and ¼ c. sugar. Cut in butter or margarine until mixture resembles coarse meal. Sprinkle evenly over pie. Bake at 400° for 45 min., or until apples are tender. (If pastry browns too quickly, cap loosely with foil during last 5–10 min. of baking.) Garnish with poached apple slices if desired.

Ruth Gish
Dubois County

BANANA CREAM PIE

1 large pkg. Dream Whip	1 8-oz. pkg. cream cheese
2 pkg. vanilla instant pudding	¼ c. sugar fresh bananas

Mix pudding with about ¼ c. less liquid than directions call for. Cream sugar and cream cheese. Add pudding. Add Dream Whip which has been mixed with 1 T. less liquid than directions call for. Put into 2 baked 9″ pie crusts. Alternate layers of fresh banana slices and filling. Garnish with whipped topping, if desired. Chill well before serving.

Ann Stevens
Clay County

BANANA JEWEL PIE

1 9″ baked pie shell	1 10-oz. pkg. frozen straw-
1 3-oz. pkg. cream cheese	berries, thawed and mashed
1–1½ T. milk	2 large bananas,
½ t. nutmeg	sliced
1 box strawberry- flavored gelatin	whipped cream toasted coconut
½ c. hot water	

Mix cream cheese, milk, and nutmeg until well blended. Using the bottom of a spoon, spread over the sides and bottom of baked pie shell. Place in refrigerator to allow cream cheese mixture to become firm. Dissolve strawberry gelatin in boiling hot

water. To thawed, mashed strawberries, add enough cold water to make 1¼ c. Add to dissolved gelatin. Place in refrigerator until consistency of egg whites. To partially jelled mixture add sliced bananas. Pour into pie shell and let set in refrigerator until well jelled. Before serving, trim with an edging of whipped cream topped with toasted coconut. Serves 6–8.

Mrs. Max Tribbett
Montgomery County

BANANA SPLIT PIE

3 medium bananas	1 c. frozen whipped
1 T. lemon juice	dessert topping,
1 9″ baked pie shell	thawed whole maraschino
1 pt. strawberry ice cream (other flavors may be used)	cherries 2 T. chopped walnuts chocolate sauce

Thinly slice bananas, sprinkle with lemon juice, and arrange on bottom of pastry shell. Stir ice cream to soften; spread on bananas. Freeze firm. Spread whipped topping over ice cream layer. Top with cherries; sprinkle with nuts. Return to freezer. Before serving, remove pie from freezer and let stand at room temperature for about 30 min. Serve with chocolate sauce, if desired.

Mrs. Earl Epple
Dubois County

COFFEE BANANA PIE

½ lb. (32) marshmallows	1 c. heavy cream, whipped (or
2 T. instant coffee	Dream Whip)
½ c. hot water	1 9″ baked pie
2 c. sliced bananas	shell

Combine marshmallows, coffee, and water. Cook over low heat till marshmallows are dissolved. Cool until slightly thickened. Fold in whipped cream and sliced bananas. Pour into pastry shell. Chill. Garnish with banana slices and whipped cream.

Mrs. Ollie Rowls
Jay County

BLACKBERRY PIE

1 qt. frozen blackberries	pinch of salt
1 T. minute tapioca	few drops of lemon juice
2 T. and 2 t. cornstarch	1 c. sugar
	1 T. butter

Thaw the berries; drain juice. Mix juice with dry ingredients; cook until thickened and clear. Mix with blackberries, lemon juice, and butter; pour into pie shell. Bake at 400° for 15 min. Reduce heat to 350° and bake 30 min. more, or until crust is brown.

Mrs. Ben Seng
Dubois County

FRESH BLUEBERRY PIE

3 c. fresh blueberries	¼ t. salt
2½ T. quick tapioca	½ c. brown sugar, firmly packed
⅔ c. white sugar	1 T. margarine
1 T. lemon juice	

Mix berries, sugar, salt, lemon juice, and tapioca. Let stand. Make double crust for 9″ pie. Add berry mixture. Top with brown sugar. Dot with margarine. Add top crust. Bake at 425° until browned (about 30–40 min.).

Mrs. Matt Thrasher
Steuben County

BROWN SUGAR CREAM PIE

2 eggs, separated	dash of salt
4 level T. flour	2 c. milk
1 c. brown sugar	1 T. butter

Mix flour, sugar, and salt together. Beat egg yolks slightly. Add part of milk to egg, then stir into sugar and flour mixture, mixing well. Add remaining milk and butter. Cook over medium heat until thickened, stirring to keep mixture from sticking. Cool. Pour into baked pie crust. Top with meringue made from two egg whites. Brown at 350°.

Ruby Luhrsen
Dearborn County

BUTTER PIE

⅔ c. granulated sugar	1 egg
1½ T. butter	1 c. sweet milk
2 level T. flour	nutmeg

Cream sugar and butter well; add flour and mix again. Add egg and beat. Mix milk into this mixture and pour in unbaked pie shell. Sprinkle with nutmeg. Bake at 400° until filling is firm and brown.

A favorite in my family for several generations.

Mrs. Katherine Records
Monroe County

BUTTERMILK PIE

2 T. flour	1 T. butter
¼ t. nutmeg	¾ c. sugar
2 c. buttermilk	

Combine flour, sugar, and nutmeg and mix thoroughly in a mixing bowl. Beat in buttermilk gradually, beating until smooth. Pour mixture into unbaked pie shell. Dot with butter and sprinkle with nutmeg.

Bake at 350° for 40–50 min., or until filling is set and crust is golden.

Mrs. Leona Humbert
Dubois County

BUTTERSCOTCH PIE

1 c. dark brown sugar	3 egg yolks, slightly beaten
¼ c. cornstarch	1½ t. vanilla
1 c. water	⅓ c. butter or margarine
¼ t. salt	
1⅔ c. milk	

Mix brown sugar, cornstarch, and salt in saucepan or top of double boiler. Gradually stir in water, milk, and butter. Cook over low heat or in pan of water, stirring constantly until mixture thickens, boil 1 min. longer. Stir ½ of mixture into egg yolks, then blend in remaining mixture along with the vanilla. Pour into baked pie shell, top with meringue, and bake until brown. Serves 6.

Mrs. Alma Jane Simmons
Jennings County

CANDY BAR PIE

1 9″ baked pie shell	4½-oz. milk chocolate candy with almonds (6 bars weighing ¾-oz. each)
20 large marshmallows	
½ c. milk	
1 pt. whipping cream	

Combine marshmallows and milk in sauce pan. Cook over low heat, stirring occasionally, until marshmallows are melted. Add 5 candy bars and continue heating until chocolate melts. Cool thoroughly. Beat 1 c. whipping cream and fold into chocolate mixture. Spoon filling into baked pie shell. Chill 3–4 hr. Whip remaining cream and spread over filling. Grate remaining candy bar and sprinkle over whipped cream. Serves 6–8.

Penny Burns
Miami County

CARROT PIE

¾ c. sugar	½ t. lemon rind, grated
½ t. salt	2 eggs, lightly beaten
½ t. nutmeg	
1 t. cinnamon	1 c. evaporated milk, undiluted
1 t. ginger	
⅛ t. cloves	1 9″ unbaked pie shell
2 c. carrots, cooked and sieved	

Combine first 6 ingredients. Add remaining ingredients; mix well. Pour into pastry-lined pie pan. Bake at 400° for 40–45 min. or until filling is firm.

Mrs. Joseph O'Bryan
Floyd County

SARA SUE'S CHERRY PIE

Crust:	
	½ c. cherry juice
2 c. flour	1 c. sugar
1 t. salt	1 T. butter
⅔ c. lard	½ t. lemon juice
5 T. water	2 c. sour cherries
Filling:	¼ t. salt
4 T. cornstarch	

Sift flour and salt together. Blend in lard, using pastry blender. Sprinkle water over it slowly, turning with fork. Press together and transfer to board. Prepare for size of pan used. To make filling: Mix cornstarch and cherry juice in top of double boiler. Add sugar and cook 5 min. Add butter, lemon juice, salt, and cherries, stirring constantly. Bake at 375° for 45 min.

Sara Sue Phegley
Sullivan County

CHESS PIE

2 c. sugar	5 egg yolks,
2 T. flour	beaten
2 T. cornmeal	1 c. half & half
½ c. butter	

Cream together flour, cornmeal, sugar, and butter. Add beaten egg yolks and half & half. Bake in unbaked pie shell at 425° for 15 min. Reduce heat to 375° and bake for 30 min.

Mrs. Deane Wiggs
Jefferson County

GRANNY CHOCOLATE PIE

2 c. sugar	1 stick butter,
4 eggs	melted
4 T. cocoa	½ c. whole
2 t. vanilla	pecans

Sift sugar and cocoa. Add other ingredients and stir. Place pecans in bottom of unbaked 9″ pie shell, and pour remaining ingredients on top. Bake at 350° for 25–40 min. Serves 6.

Donalea Hastings
Ohio County

MARY ROSE'S CHOCOLATE PIE

1 c. milk	3 T. cocoa
1 c. sugar	1 t. vanilla
2 egg yolks	1 heaping T.
1 T. butter	flour

Mix flour and sugar; add rest of ingredients and mix well. Cook until thick. Put in a baked pie shell. Top with meringue.

Mary Rose Strosnider
Lawrence County

COCONUT CHIFFON PIE

1 baked 9″ pie	1 t. vanilla
shell	3 large egg
1 T. unflavored	whites
gelatin	¼ t. cream of
¼ c. cold water	tartar
½ c. sugar	½ c. sugar
4 level T. flour	½ c. whipping
½ t. salt	cream
1½ c. milk	1½ c. coconut

Soften gelatin in cold water. Mix sugar, flour, and salt and stir milk in gradually; cook over low heat until thickened. Remove from heat and stir in dissolved gelatin. Allow to partially set; beat until smooth and add vanilla. Beat egg whites with cream of tartar until stiff and glossy, gradually adding sugar. Beat whipping cream until stiff. Fold all 3 mixtures together; add coconut and put into pie shell. Chill. When ready to serve, top with whipped cream. Serves 5–6.

Mrs. Kenneth A. Willis
Orange County

COCONUT CUSTARD PIE

1 9″ pastry crust	½ t. lemon
¼ t. salt	extract
3 eggs, separated	¼ t. almond
½ c. sugar	extract
1½ c. milk	1½ c. flaked
2 T. butter or	coconut
margarine	

Beat egg yolks and salt until thick and lemon colored. Beat in sugar, milk, butter or margarine, and extracts. Fold in coconut and stiffly beaten egg whites. Turn into unbaked pie shell. Bake at 375° for 50 min. Serves 6.

Ruth Taylor
Spencer County

COCONUT MACAROON PIE

1½ c. sugar	¼ c. flour
2 eggs	½ c. milk
½ t. salt	1½ c. grated
½ c. soft butter	coconut
or margarine	

Beat sugar, eggs, and salt until lemon colored. Add butter or margarine and flour; blend well. Add milk. Fold in 1 c. coconut. Pour into 9″ pie shell. Top with ½ c. coconut. Bake at 325° for 60 min.

Jean French
Brown County

CORNMEAL PIE

1 c. granulated	½ t. almond
sugar	flavoring
1 c. brown sugar	1 T. vinegar
¼ c. butter or	2 T. cornmeal
margarine,	1 c. milk
softened	2 T. flour
2 eggs	

Combine all ingredients and mix well. Pour into 9″ unbaked pie shell. Bake at 375° for 40–45 min.

Edythe Price
Clay County

CORNSTARCH PIE

¾ c. sugar	1 c. cold milk
2 heaping T.	3 c. hot milk
cornstarch	1 t. vanilla
2 egg yolks	

Mix sugar, cornstarch, beaten egg yolks, and cold milk. Add to hot milk. Let come to boil. Remove and add flavoring. Fills 2 baked pie crusts. May be used with bananas, coconut, etc. Serves 6–8.

Jackie Nentrup
Jennings County

EXQUISITE CUSTARD PIE

⅓ c. butter	½ c. seedless
1 c. sugar	raisins
½ t. cinnamon	2 eggs, well
½ t. nutmeg	beaten
1 t. vinegar	1 unbaked pie
½ c. nuts,	shell
chopped	

Cream butter and sugar. Add cinnamon, nutmeg, vinegar, nuts, and raisins. Stir in eggs. Pour into pie shell. Place pie in cold oven. Bake for 1 hr. at 300°–325°. Serves 6.

Ella Rose Bredeweg
Greene County

VELVETY CUSTARD PIE

4 eggs, slightly	2½ c. milk,
beaten	scalded
½ c. sugar	1 9″ unbaked pie
¼ t. salt	shell
1 t. vanilla	

Thoroughly mix eggs, sugar, salt, and vanilla. Slowly stir in hot milk. Pour at once into pie shell. Sprinkle top with nutmeg. Bake at 475° for 5 min., then reduce heat to 425° and bake 10 min. longer, or until knife inserted halfway between center and edge comes out clean.

Wanda Couch
Clark County

ELDERBERRY PIE

1 unbaked pie	1 c. sugar
crust	6 T. milk or
2–2½ c. berries	cream (enough
3 rounded T.	to thin)
flour	

Put berries in pie crust. Cream sugar, flour, and milk or cream. Pour over berries. Bake at 350° for 30 to 45 minutes.

Helpful Hint: Wash elderberries with stems. Then pull off stems and measure.

Dorothy Overmyer
Marshall County

OLD-FASHIONED FRIED PIES

2 c. sifted flour	sweetened sieved
1 t. salt	fruit, dried or
¼ c. lard	fresh
⅓ c. cold water	

Sift flour and salt together; cut in lard until pieces are size of small peas. Gradually sprinkle water over mixture, mixing after each addition. Roll out on floured surface to about ⅛″ thickness. Cut into 4″ rounds. Spoon about 1 T. fruit on each round, moisten edges with water, fold to form semi-circle, and press edges together. Fry in deep fat at 365° until golden brown on each side. Drain on absorbent paper.

Canned pie fillings may be used for the fruit filling.

Ruth Ann Roach
Martin County

JAPANESE FRUIT PIE

2 sticks soft	1 c. pecans,
margarine	chopped
2 c. sugar	1 8-oz. can
2 T. vinegar	coconut
4 eggs	2 unbaked pie
1 c. raisins	shells

Mix margarine, sugar, and vinegar until creamy. Stir in pecans, raisins, and coconut. Spread in pie shells. Bake at 325° for 35–40 min.

Leona Hermansen and Martha Kittell
Pulaski County

WINTER FRUIT PIE

graham cracker crust	pineapple slices, drained
Devonshire Cream:	apricots
2 8-oz. pkg. cream cheese, softened	pears
	mandarin oranges
	green grapes
1 c. confectioners' sugar	cherries
½ c. light cream	Glaze:
Fruit Filling:	1 c. apricot preserves
peaches	

Line 14×10″ glass dish with graham cracker crust. In medium bowl, combine cream cheese, sugar, and cream. Beat until smooth. Spread Devonshire Cream evenly on graham crust. Overlap pineapple slices crosswise of rectangular dish. Add peaches, apricots, pears, mandarin oranges, and green grapes. Decorate with cherries. In small sauce pan, heat apricot preserves until preserves are melted. Spread over fruit. Serves 16.

Katheryn Rice
Jay County

FRESH GOOSEBERRY PIE

½ c. gooseberries, crushed	3 T. quick cooking tapioca
1½ c. sugar	2½ c. whole
¼ t. salt	gooseberries

Prepare pastry for 2-crust 9″ pie. Combine first 4 ingredients; cook and stir until mixture thickens and boils. Add whole berries. Fill pastry shell. Dot with butter. Adjust top crust, cutting slits; seal. Bake at 400° for 30–40 min., or until crust is brown. Serve warm.

Susan Robinson
Adams County

Note: If gooseberries are not available, substitute green grapes. They have the same inimitable flavor and aroma of gooseberries.

Evelyn Jarboe
Whitley County

GRAPE PIE

1¼ c. grapes, seeded, pulp and skins put together	2 T. butter, melted
	1 c. sugar
	2 T. flour
2 eggs	

Mix eggs, sugar, flour, and butter; combine with grapes. Pour into pie shell and bake in a moderate oven (350°) until a knife comes out fairly clean. Serves 6.

Mrs. Roy Lester
Greene County

FLUFFY GRAPE PIE

1 c. grape purée	1½ c. heavy cream, whipped
¼ c. water	
1 3-oz. pkg. Lemon Jello	1 baked 9″ pie shell
¾ c. sugar	

Bring purée and water just to a boil; stir in Jello until dissolved. Add sugar; mix well. Chill until mixture mounts when dropped from spoon. Beat until fluffy; fold in whipped cream. Pour into pie shell. Refrigerate at least 2 hrs. Serve topped with thin layer of whipped cream.

Catherine Current
Delaware County

SOUTHERN GRAPE NUTS PIE

½ c. Grape Nuts	¾ c. sugar
½ c. warm water	⅛ t. salt
3 eggs, well beaten	1 c. dark corn syrup

1 t. vanilla	1 unbaked pie shell
3 T. butter	

Combine Grape Nuts and warm water. Let stand until water is absorbed. Add remaining ingredients. Pour into pie shell and bake at 350° for 50 min., or until filling is puffed completely across the top. Serve plain or with whipped cream.

Donola Hysong
Fountain County

GREEN TOMATO PIE

6 medium green tomatoes	1 c. sugar
	⅛ t. salt
2 T. water	¼ t. cinnamon
1 lemon, sliced thin	2 T. butter
	2-crust pastry
2 T. cornstarch	

Wash, stem, and slice tomatoes. Cook with lemon slices in water until tomatoes are almost tender. Drain; keep liquid. When liquid is cooled, add cornstarch mixed with sugar and salt. Cook until thickened. Add tomatoes, cinnamon, and butter. Mix thoroughly. Pour hot mixture into baked pastry shell. Top with unbaked layer of pastry and bake at 375° until golden brown. Serves 8.

Edna Chambers
Switzerland County

HICKORY NUT PIE

1 c. hickory nuts (the more the better)	2 T. butter
	½ t. vanilla
	1 c. sugar
3 eggs	1 T. flour
1 c. light syrup	

Mix ingredients; place in unbaked pie shell. Bake at 350° for 45 min. Serves 6.

Kay Baugh
Hendricks County

ICE CREAM PIE

Crust:	Filling:
⅓ c. honey	vanilla or straw-
⅓ c. peanut	berry ice cream
butter	strawberries or
2 c. Rice Krispies	peach slices
	(optional)

Mix honey and peanut butter. Add Rice Krispies and mix again. Pat with spoon into pie pan to make crust. For filling: use ice cream. Put pie in freezer for 10–15 min. to set, then cover with Saran wrap and keep frozen until serving. Garnish with strawberries or peach slices, if desired. Serves 6–7.

Mrs. Catherine Bolinger
Marshall County

IMPOSSIBLE PIE

4 whole eggs	½ c. self-rising
½ stick butter,	flour
melted	¼ can shredded
1¾ c. sugar	coconut
2 c. milk	

Beat eggs thoroughly. Add melted butter, sugar, flour, and milk. Beat thoroughly. Stir in coconut. Bake in 2 ungreased pie pans at 350° for 35 to 40 min. Serves 12.

Mrs. W. G. Bufkin
Floyd County

IMPOSSIBLE PIE (Modern Version)

4 eggs	1 T. margarine
2 c. milk	½ c. Bisquick
⅔ c. sugar	4-oz. coconut
1 t. vanilla	

Put all ingredients except coconut into blender and mix for 5 min. Stir in coconut

and pour in greased pie plate. Bake at 350° for 35 to 40 min. Serves 6–8. Pie will come out with crust on bottom.

Mary Jane Westendorf
Allen County

LEMON PIE

| 2 large lemons | 4 eggs, beaten |
| 2 c. sugar | 2-crust pastry |

Slice the lemons paper thin; soak in sugar for 2 hr. Mix eggs with lemon mixture. Pour evenly into unbaked pie shell and put another pie shell on top. Bake at 425° for 15 min., then reduce heat to 350° and bake 40 min. longer, or until toothpick comes out clean.

Pat Inman
Putnam County

LEMON ANGEL PIE

4 eggs, separated	4 T. lemon juice
pinch of salt	1 t. grated rind
¼ t. cream of	½ pint whipping
tartar	cream, whipped
1⅓ c. sugar	

Beat egg whites: add salt and cream of tartar. Beat until stiff; add 1 c. sugar slowly. Bake in greased and floured 10″ pie pan for 20 min. at 275°, then 40 min. at 300°. Cool. Beat egg yolks until creamy. Add lemon juice and grated rind. Add ⅓ c. sugar and beat. Cook until thick, over low heat. Cool. Combine lemon mixture with whipped cream. Put into cooked meringue. Chill. Refrigerate at least 3 hr. or overnight.

Selma Lautner
Spencer County

LEMON ANGEL TART

1 pkg. pie crust mix	½ t. salt
1¼ c. sugar	½ c. lemon juice
6 eggs	¼ c. water
1 envelope unflavored gelatin	1 t. grated lemon peel
	whipped topping

Combine pie crust mix and 2 T. sugar in medium bowl. Beat 1 egg in small bowl; stir into pie crust mixture until well blended. Roll out to 13″ round on lightly floured pastry cloth. Fit into 9″ round layer cake pan. Trim even with rim of pan. Prick shell well all over with fork. Bake about 15 min., or until golden brown. Cool completely in pan. Remove shell and place on large, flat serving plate. Mix gelatin, ½ of remaining sugar, and salt in medium sauce pan. Separate remaining eggs into two bowls; beat yolks well. Stir in lemon juice and water; stir into gelatin mixture. Cook slowly, stirring constantly, until gelatin dissolves and mixture coats spoon. Remove from heat. Stir in lemon peel. Chill 30 minutes or until mixture mounds softly. While gelatin mixture chills, beat egg whites until foamy in medium bowl; slowly beat in remaining sugar until meringue stands in firm peaks; fold into thickened gelatin mixture until no streaks of white remain. Spoon into shell. Chill several hours until firm. Just before serving, prepare whipped topping. Spread over tart. Garnish with slices of lemon dipped in sugar, if desired. Serves 10–12.

Bev Parsley
Clay County

LEMON CHIFFON PIE

4 eggs, separated	1 t. salt
2 c. sugar	1 c. fresh lemon juice
½ c. butter or margarine	2½ c. milk
2 T. corn starch	1 unbaked deep pie shell
3 T. flour	

Whip egg whites until very stiff; set aside. Cream butter and sugar with mixer. Blend in egg yolks. Gradually add rest of ingredients. Fold in egg whites. Pour into pie shell. Bake at 400° about 1 hr., or until pie is done.

Evelyne Baldwin
Putnam County

BLACK BOTTOM LEMON PIE

baked 9″ pie shell	¼ c. lemon juice
2-oz. semisweet chocolate	3 T. water
4 eggs, separated	1 t. lemon peel
	1 c. sugar

Melt chocolate; spread evenly over bottom of baked, cooled pie shell. In top of double boiler, beat egg yolks until thick and lemon colored. Add lemon juice and water, mixing well. Then stir in lemon peel and ½ c. sugar. Cook over hot (not boiling) water, stirring constantly, until thick (about 12 min.). Remove from hot water. Beat egg whites until frothy. Add remaining ½ c. sugar gradually, beating until stiff glossy peaks form. Fold ½ of mixture into egg-yolk mixture. Pour over chocolate in pie shell. Spoon remaining egg-white mixture into pastry tube, make a lattice design on top of filling. Bake in slow oven (325°) for 10–15 min., or until lightly browned.

Viola Chrimes
Parke County

BLENDER LEMON PIE

1 unbaked crust	1 c. water
1 c. dry bread crumbs	2 whole eggs
	butter size of
1 whole lemon	walnut
1 c. sugar	

Place bread crumbs on crust. Wash and slice lemon (including rind) and put into blender. Add rest of ingredients. Blend and pour over crumbs. Bake for 15 min. at 450°, then turn to 350° and bake until set (about 20 min.). Serves 6.

Mrs. Burchell Hamill
Boone County

EASY LEMONADE FROZEN PIE

1 can frozen lemonade	1 can Eagle Brand milk
1 4½-oz. pkg. Cool Whip	graham cracker crust

Mix together well. Slowly pour into graham cracker crust. Put into refrigerator for about 6 hr. Serves 6–8.

Mrs. Clyde Goen
Washington County

LIME CHEESE PIE

Filling:

1 8-oz. and 1 3 oz. pkg. cream cheese	6 drops green food coloring
½ c. sugar	Crust:
3 eggs	1¼ c. chocolate cookie crumbs
1½ t. grated lime rind	2 to 3 T. sugar
2 T. lime juice	3 T. butter, melted

Combine sugar and melted butter with cookie crumbs; mix well. Press evenly on bottom and sides of 8″ pie plate. Chill while preparing filling. Cream cream cheese and sugar together until light and fluffy. Add eggs, one at a time, beating un-til smooth after each addition. Stir in lime rind and juice. Tint with food coloring. Pour into chilled chocolate crust. Bake at 350° for 30–35 min., or until filling is firm. Cool; chill several hours. Garnish with whipped cream, chocolate crumbs or grated lime rind, if desired. Serves 6–8.

Marlene Cotner
Monroe County

FLORIDA KEY LIME PIE

1 envelope (1 T.) unflavored gelatin	⅓ c. lime juice
	½ t. salt
¼ c. cold water	2 t. grated lime peel
4 eggs, separated	green food coloring
1 c. sugar, divided	

Soften gelatin in cold water. Beat egg yolks; add ½ c. sugar, lime juice, and salt. Cook over hot water, stirring constantly until thickened. Add grated peel and gelatin; stir until gelatin is dissolved. Tint pale green with food coloring. Cool. Beat egg whites stiff but not dry; add remaining sugar slowly. Beating after each addition, fold into lime mixture. Pour into 9″ baked pie shell; chill until firm. Garnish top with whipped cream and white grapes and mint sprigs to resemble grape clusters, if desired. Serves 6.

Kay Baugh
Hendricks County

MAPLE SYRUP PIE

1 unbaked 9″ pie shell	2 eggs
	2 T. flour
1–1½ c. maple syrup	¼ c. heavy cream

Mix maple syrup, eggs, flour, and cream. Bake for 45 min. at 375°.

Ruth Curry
Owen County

MILLIONAIRE PIE

1 baked graham cracker pie crust
1 can Eagle Brand milk
1/3 c. lemon juice
1 large carton Cool Whip
1 No. 2 can mandarin oranges, drained
1 pkg. coconut
1 No. 2 can crushed pineapple, drained

Mix the ingredients together. Pour into baked crust. Makes 2 pies.

Mildred McNay
Scott County

OATMEAL PIE

3 eggs, beaten
2/3 c. sugar
2/3 c. dark syrup
2/3 c. quick cooking oats
3 T. butter or margarine, melted
2/3 c. coconut
1 t. vanilla
1/2 c. nuts, chopped (optional)
1 unbaked pie shell

Mix all ingredients. Pour into unbaked pie shell and bake at 350° for 45 min.

Selma Kincade
Posey County

ORANGE PIE

1 baked pie shell
Filling:
1 c. sugar
3½ T. cornstarch
1⅓ c. frozen orange juice (diluted according to directions)
2 egg yolks, slightly beaten
2 T. butter

Meringue:
2 egg whites
1/4 t. cream of tartar
4 T. sugar

Mix sugar, cornstarch, and orange juice.

Cook over moderate heat, stirring constantly until mixture thickens and boils. Beat a little hot mixture into egg yolks. Return to heat and boil 1 min. Blend in butter. Let cool. Pour into baked pie shell. Top with meringue.

Ruth Officer
Jefferson County

OSGOOD PIE

Pastry Shell:
1 c. unsifted flour
1/2 t. salt
1/3 c. margarine
3–4 T. ice water

Filling:
2 c. sugar
2 T. margarine
1/4 t. cinnamon
4 egg yolks, well beaten
1/4 t. cloves
2 T. evaporated milk
1 t. vanilla
1 t. white vinegar
2 c. pecans
1 c. plump seedless raisins
4 egg whites, beaten to stiff peaks
brandy-flavored whipped cream

Combine flour and salt in bowl. Cut in 1/3 c. margarine until mixture resembles coarse meal. Stir in ice water; mix well. On lightly floured board, roll out dough and fit into 9″ pie plate; shape edge. Cream together sugar and 2 T. margarine. Add egg yolks, cinnamon, cloves, milk, vanilla, and vinegar; mix well. Stir in pecans and raisins. Fold in egg whites. Pour into unbaked pastry shell. Bake at 350° for about 45 min., or until done. Serve at room temperature with brandy-flavored whipped cream. Serves 5–6.

Osgood Pie is typical of early baking which relied heavily on nuts, raisins, and other dried fruits.

Mrs. Earl Stephens
Ripley County

TROPICAL PARFAIT PIE

Filling: Coconut Crust:

1 3-oz. pkg. lime	2 c. flaked
gelatin	coconut
1 c. boiling water	2 T. sugar
1 pt. vanilla ice	1 T. flour
cream	2 T. margarine,
2 c. miniature	melted
marshmallows	

Combine coconut, sugar, and flour; blend in margarine. Press mixture into 9″ pie plate; bake at 350° for 10 min. Chill. Dissolve lime gelatin in water. Add ice cream, stirring until melted. Chill until almost firm. Fold in marshmallows. Pour into coconut crust. Serves 6–8.

Mary Whitezel
Howard County

PEACH PIE

2-crust pastry	2 T. flour
dough	2½ c. peaches,
1 c. sugar	frozen or
½ c. cream	canned

Place unbaked pie crust in pan. Mix all ingredients together and place in pie crust. Cut pastry strips and make a lattice top. Bake at 400° for 15 min., then lower temperature to 375° and bake for 30–40 min. longer. Serves 6.

Mrs. Loren Logue
Union County

PEACH-APPLE PIE

2-crust pastry for	1 c. sugar
9″ pie	2–3 T. tapioca
3 c. fresh apples,	or flour
sliced	1 T. butter
3 c. fresh peaches,	(optional)
sliced	

Divide pastry almost in half. Using the larger half, roll out to fit 9″ deep-dish pan, about 1″ larger than pan. Transfer pastry to pan, patting down and avoiding stretching. Trim off overhang and make fluted edge. Make top slightly smaller than pan. Make several slits in it. Mix filling thoroughly and place in pastry-lined pan. Cover with pastry lid. Bake at 400° for 50–60 min. Serves 6–8.

Meta Fellerman
Ripley County

CRUMBLY PEACH PIE

1 c. sugar	6–8 large peach
¼ c. flour	halves, frozen,
⅛ t. nutmeg	fresh, or
¼ c. butter	canned (well
¼ c. water	drained)

Mix sugar, flour, and nutmeg; cut in butter until crumbly. Sprinkle half the crumbs in 9″ square pan. Arrange peach halves, cut side down over crumbs, and cover with remaining crumb mixture; add water. Bake at 450° for 10 min. and continue baking at 350° for 30 min.

Mrs. Marcus Luginbill
Adams County

GLAZED PEACH PIE

baked pie shell	5–6 drops yellow
1 c. water	coloring
1 c. sugar	fresh peaches,
2 T. cornstarch	sliced
1 pkg. Peach	whipped cream
Jello	

Boil water, sugar, and cornstarch until clear. Add Peach Jello; stir until dissolved. Add yellow coloring. Cool. Slice fresh peaches into pie shell. Pour glaze over and chill. Top with whipped cream.

Variation: Use fresh whole strawberries and Strawberry Jello.

Mrs. Cleo Baker
Vanderburgh County

PEANUT BUTTER PIE

1 baked pie shell	1 large container
1 c. confec-	Cool Whip
tioners' sugar	1 3-oz. cream
½ c. peanut	cheese, softened
butter	

Mix well sugar and peanut butter. Add Cool Whip and cream cheese. Place in baked pie shell and refrigerate. Serves 8.

Genieva Shipley
Wayne County

PEANUT BUTTER CHIFFON PIE

2 eggs, separated	2 c. (4½ oz.)
¼ t. salt	Cool Whip
½ c. sugar	½ c. peanut
1 envelope	butter
gelatin	1 10" baked pie
1 c. milk	shell

Beat egg yolks and add ¼ c. sugar, gelatin, salt, and milk. Cook and stir over medium heat until mixture comes to a boil. Remove from heat; stir in peanut butter until blended. Cool. Beat egg whites until foamy; gradually add ¼ c. sugar, beating until stiff. Fold into cooled peanut butter mixture. Add Cool Whip. Pour into pie shell and chill until firm.

Irene Pillman
Porter County

PEANUT BUTTER CREAM PIE

1 baked pie shell	3 T. cornstarch
¾ c. powdered	1 T. flour
sugar	pinch of salt
½ c. peanut	3 egg yolks
butter	3 c. milk
⅔ c. sugar	2 T. butter

3 egg whites,	1 t. vanilla
stiffly beaten	¼ c. granulated
¼ t. cream of	sugar
tartar	

Cream powdered sugar and peanut butter together until crumbly and set aside. Stir next 8 ingredients together in sauce pan. Cook over medium heat, stirring constantly; bring just to below boiling point and cook a few minutes. Sprinkle ⅔ of peanut butter mixture in bottom of baked pie shell. Pour custard over this. Make a meringue of egg whites, cream of tartar, and sugar. Spread on custard and sprinkle with remainder of peanut butter mixture. Bake at 350° until meringue is browned.

Mrs. George Wilson
Franklin County

SOUTHERN PECAN PIE

1 c. pecans	1 T. butter or
1 9" unbaked pie	margarine,
shell	melted
3 eggs	½ t. vanilla
1 c. light corn	¾ c. sugar
syrup	1 T. flour

Arrange nuts in pie shell. Beat eggs; add and blend corn syrup, butter, and vanilla. Combine sugar and flour. Blend with egg mixture and pour over nuts in pie shell. Let stand until nuts rise. Bake in moderate oven (350°) for 45 min. Serves 6–8.

Albertamae Stanley
Hendricks County

PERSIMMON PIE

2 c. persimmon	¼ t. ginger
pulp	½ c. sugar
1 egg, beaten	1 T. corn starch
1 c. milk	1 unbaked 9" pie
⅛ t. salt	shell
½ t. cinnamon	

Mix persimmon pulp, egg, and milk in a separate bowl. Combine thoroughly sugar, salt, cornstarch, and spices. Add to persimmon mixture and combine until well mixed. Line 9″ pie pan with pastry. Pour in persimmon filling. Bake at 450° for 10 min., then reduce temperature to 350° and bake for 50 min. longer. Serve with whipped cream. Serves 8.

Mrs. Esther Eggenspiller
Harrison County

PINEAPPLE ANGEL PIE

4½ T. cornstarch
¾ c. sugar
1½ c. boiling water
⅜ t. salt
3 egg whites
1 t. sugar
1 No. 2 can crushed pineapple, drained
1 t. vanilla

Mix cornstarch and ¾ c. sugar; add boiling water and cook until thick. Beat egg whites with 1 t. sugar, salt, and vanilla. Fold in egg whites. Add pineapple. When cool, pour into baked pie shell. Chill well before serving. Top with whipped cream.

Anna Jeanne Moorlag
Porter County

MOTHER'S PINEAPPLE CREAM PIE

1 baked pie shell
½ c. sugar
6 T. flour
⅛ t. salt
2–3 eggs
1 c. crushed pineapple, drained
2 T. butter
1¼ c. milk
2 T. lemon juice

Combine all ingredients except lemon juice. Stir and cook over low heat until thick. Then stir in lemon juice. Cool custard and pour into pie shell. Top with whipped cream and chill.

Marilyn Sater
Monroe County

PINEAPPLE FLUFF PIE

1 3¼ oz. pkg. vanilla pudding
1 c. milk
10 marshmallows, halved
1 can crushed pineapple, drained
2 c. Cool Whip
1 baked pie shell

Cook pudding. Add marshmallows to hot pudding and let cool. Add pineapple. Fold in Cool Whip and pour into baked shell.

Louise Pershing
Putnam County

GOLDEN TREASURE PIE (Pineapple)

2 8½-oz. cans undrained crushed pineapple
½ c. sugar
2 T. water
1 T. butter
1 c. cottage cheese
½ t. salt
1¼ c. milk
2 T. cornstarch
⅔ c. sugar
¼ c. sifted flour
1 t. vanilla
2 eggs, slightly beaten
10″ pie shell

Combine pineapple, ½ c. sugar, cornstarch, and water in small saucepan. Bring to a boil; cook 1 min., stirring constantly. Cool. Blend ⅔ c. sugar and butter; add flour, cheese, vanilla, and salt; beat until smooth. Slowly add eggs then milk to cheese mixture, beating constantly. Pour pineapple into crust, spreading evenly. Gently pour custard over pineapple, being careful not to disturb first layer. Bake at 450° for 15 min., then reduce heat to 325° and bake 45 min. longer. Serves 8–10.

Edna Parker
Morgan County

GRANDMA WINN'S PUMPKIN PIE

1½ c. sugar
1 T. flour
1 t. cinnamon
⅛ t. nutmeg
⅛ t. (or less) ginger

2 eggs 1 c. sweet milk
2 c. pumpkin

Put ingredients together in order given. Put mixture into unbaked pie crust. Bake as for custard pie.

This makes 2 small pies. For 9″ or larger pie, make 1½ times the recipe for 2 pies. Mashed sweet potatoes or mashed squash may be substituted for pumpkin.

Doris Winn Sodrel
Perry County

PUMPKIN PIE (With Brown Sugar)

1¼ c. mashed, cooked pumpkin 1½ T. white sugar
½ t. salt 1 t. cinnamon
1¼ c. milk ⅓ t. ginger
2 eggs ⅓ t. nutmeg
½ c. brown sugar ¼ t. cloves
 1 t. whisky

Beat together with rotary beater. Bake at 425° for 45–55 min. Serves 6,

For a pie with lighter color and milder flavor, use all white sugar and omit cloves.

Dorothy Burley
Switzerland County

PUMPKIN PIE (With Cream Cheese)

8-oz. cream cheese, softened 1½ c. sugar
¼ c. white sugar 1 t. cinnamon
½ t. vanilla ¼ t. ginger
1 egg ¼ t. nutmeg
1 9″ unbaked pie crust dash of salt
1¼ c. pumpkin 2 eggs, slightly beaten
 1 c. Milnot

Combine cream cheese, ¼ c. sugar, vanilla, and 1 egg. Mix well. Put mixture in bottom of unbaked pie crust. Combine the next 6 ingredients; mix well. Blend in 2 eggs and Milnot. Carefully pour over cream cheese mixture. Bake at 350° for 70 min. Serves 6.

Virginia Carpenter
Pulaski County

PUMPKIN ICE CREAM PIE

¾ c. canned pumpkin ¼ t. salt
¼ c. honey or brown sugar 1 qt. vanilla ice cream
½ t. cinnamon 1 baked pie shell

Combine pumpkin, spices, sugar, and salt. Heat, stirring constantly. Cool and beat into ice cream. Place in baked pie shell. Freeze. May be served with whipped cream. Serves 5.

Verona Lemmon
Daviess County

PUMPKIN PECAN PIE

3 eggs, slightly beaten ½ t. cinnamon
1 c. canned or mashed pumpkin ¼ t. salt
 1 c. chopped pecans (as little as ¼ c. may be used)
1 c. sugar
½ c. dark corn syrup 1 unbaked 9″ pastry shell
1 t. vanilla

In small mixing bowl, combine eggs, pumpkin, sugar, corn syrup, vanilla, cinnamon, and salt; mix well. Pour into unbaked pastry shell. Top with chopped pecans. Bake in moderate oven (350°) for about 40 min. Chill, serve topped with whipped cream.

Frances Barden
Greene County

PRALINE PUMPKIN PIE

⅓ c. ground pecans	⅔ c. brown sugar
⅓ c. brown sugar	½ t. salt
2 T. butter or margarine	½ t. mace
1 unbaked 9″ pie shell	½ t. cinnamon
2 eggs	½ t. ginger
1 c. canned pumpkin	¼ t. ground cloves
	1 c. light cream
	1 T. flour

Combine pecans, brown sugar, and butter or margarine. Blend well. Gently press mixture into bottom of pie shell with back of spoon. Beat eggs in medium bowl until frothy. Add remaining ingredients. Beat until well blended. Pour into prepared pie shell. Bake at 400° for 50–55 min. Serves 7 (425 calories in each slice).

Mrs. Katherine Barker
Jefferson County

SOUR CREAM PUMPKIN PIE

1 c. sugar	1 c. half & half cream
½ t. salt	
½ t. cinnamon	½ c. sour cream
3 eggs	1 9″ unbaked pie crust
1⅔ c. pumpkin	

Mix well and pour into pie crust. Sprinkle cinnamon on top of pie. Bake at 425° for 15 min.; lower temperature to 350° and bake for 35 min. more. Serves 8.

Lorene Sallee
Lawrence County

RAISIN PIE

¾ c. sugar	1½ c. water
1½ T. cornstarch	2 T. butter or margarine
½ t. cinnamon	
¼ t. salt	8″ 2-crust pastry
1½ c. raisins	

Mix first 4 ingredients in small bowl. Boil raisins and water in saucepan for 5–10 min. until puffed and tender. Gradually pour sugar mixture into raisins, stirring continually, and cook until thickened. Add butter or margarine. Cool. Use as filling for 2-crust pie. Bake at 425° for 10 min.; reduce temperature to 375° and bake 30 min. longer. Serves 6.

Mrs. Wayne Brown
Harrison County

RAISIN CRISSCROSS PIE

2-crust pastry	½ t. grated lemon peel
1 c. brown sugar	
3 T. cornstarch	⅓ c. orange juice
1½ c. water	3 T. lemon juice
2 c. raisins	½ c. broken walnuts (optional)
1 t. grated orange peel	

In sauce pan, combine sugar, cornstarch, water, raisins, orange and lemon peels, and orange and lemon juices. Cook, stirring constantly, over medium heat until mixture thickens and bubbles. Stir in nuts. Set aside to cool. Line a 9″ pie plate with pastry. Pour in raisin filling. Adjust lattice top; seal. Flute edge. Brush top with milk and sprinkle with sugar. Bake at 400° for 30–35 min. Serves 6.

Mrs. Charles McIntyre
Fayette County

SOUR CREAM RAISIN PIE

1 c. packed raisins	1 egg yolk, beaten
½ c. water	2–3 T. flour
1 c. sugar	1 c. sour cream
1 t. salt	1 baked pie shell

Cook raisins in water until tender. Add sugar, egg yolk, flour, salt, and sour cream. Cook until thick and pour into pie shell.

Sprinkle with vanilla wafer crumbs. Serves 6–8.

Mrs. William Rambo
Wayne County

RASPBERRY CHIFFON PIE

⅔ c. sugar	¼ t. cream of
1 envelope unfla-	tartar
vored gelatin	⅓ c. sugar
1 c. raspberries,	½ c. whipping
thoroughly	cream, whipped
crushed	1 9″ baked pie
3 egg whites	shell

Blend sugar, gelatin, and raspberries in saucepan and cook to a full rolling boil, stirring constantly. Place pan in cold water; cool until mixture mounds slightly when dropped from a spoon. Make meringue of egg whites, cream of tartar, and sugar. Fold into gelatin mixture. Carefully blend in whipped cream. Pile into baked pie shell. Chill until set. Garnish with whole raspberries, if desired.

Patricia Harmon
Harrison County

RASPBERRY VELVET PIE

1 9″ baked pastry	1 T. lemon juice
shell	White Layer:
Red Layer:	1 3-oz. pkg.
3-oz. raspberry	cream cheese
gelatin	⅓ c. confec-
¼ c. granulated	tioners' sugar,
sugar	sifted
1¼ c. boiling	1 t. vanilla
water	1 c. heavy cream,
10-oz. pkg. frozen	whipped
red raspberries	dash of salt

Dissolve gelatin and sugar in boiling water. Add frozen berries and lemon juice; stir until berries thaw. Chill until par-tially set. Blend cream cheese, confectioners' sugar, vanilla, and salt. Fold in small amounts of whipped cream and blend. Spread ½ of white cream cheese mixture on bottom of pastry shell. Cover with ½ of red raspberry mixture and repeat layers, ending with raspberry layer on top. Chill until thick.

Mrs. George Weaver
Putnam County

RHUBARB PIE

3½ c. rhubarb,	1¼ c. sugar
diced	½ t. cinnamon
1 3-oz. pkg.	¼ c. butter
Strawberry	pastry for 10″
Jello	2-crust pie
½ c. flour	

In a 2-qt. mixing bowl, mix rhubarb, flour, sugar, and cinnamon. Pour into pastry-lined pie pan. Dot with butter and sprinkle Jello evenly over rhubarb. Cover with top crust and place a few thin slabs of butter on top. Sprinkle lightly with sugar and bake at 350° for 50 min.

Virginia Watson
Harrison County

RHUBARB-CHERRY PIE

2 c. rhubarb,	¾ c. sugar
sliced	2½ T. quick-
1 21-oz. can	cooking tapioca
cherry pie	pastry for 2-crust
filling	lattice-top pie

Combine sliced rhubarb, cherry pie filling, sugar, and tapioca. Let mixture stand 15 min. Line 9″ pie plate with pastry. Fill with rhubarb mixture. Carefully adjust top lattice crust; seal and flute edges. Bake at 400° for 40–45 min.

Lorene Rice
Shelby County

RHUBARB CREAM PIE

2½ c. rhubarb, finely cut	2 egg yolks
1½ c. brown sugar	½ t. vanilla
1 heaping T. flour	½ c. seedless raisins, soaked and drained

Pour into unbaked shell. Bake at 350° for about 45 min. When baked, cover with meringue from egg whites, and bake until browned. Serves 6–8.

Mrs. Grace Burch
Starke County

RHUBARB HONEY PIE

3 c. rhubarb, cut up	2½ T. tapioca
1 c. honey	butter
	2-crust pastry

Mix honey and tapioca together and pour over rhubarb. Pour into pastry-lined pie pan. Dot with butter; put on top crust. Rub milk over top and sprinkle with sugar. Bake at 350° for 50 min.

Mrs. Roy Hackman
Jackson County

RHUBARB SPONGE PIE

2 c. rhubarb, diced	2 T. melted butter or margarine
2 egg yolks	2 egg whites, stiffly beaten
1 c. sugar	
1 c. milk	
1 t. lemon juice	1 9″ unbaked pie crust
2 T. flour	

Beat egg yolks in a bowl. Add sugar, milk, lemon juice, butter, and flour. Fold in stiffly beaten egg whites. Arrange rhubarb in bottom of pie shell. Pour mixture over it. Bake at 450° for 10 min. Reduce heat to 350° and bake for about 30 min. more. Serves 6.

May be used as a baked dessert by omitting the pie crust.

Edna Hood
Rush County

SHAKER SHOOFLY PIE

¾ c. dark molasses	¼ c. butter
¾ c. hot water	½ t. soda
1½ c. flour	½ c. brown sugar
	1 pastry crust

Mix molasses with hot water and blend well. Blend flour, sugar, and soda and cut in butter to form coarse crumbs. Line pie dish with pastry. Pour in ⅓ of molasses mixture and top with ⅓ of crumb mixture. Repeat, adding alternate layers with crumbs on top. Bake for 35 min. at 375°.

Clarice Phegley
Sullivan County

SOUR CREAM PIE

2 egg yolks	1 c. thick sour cream
1 whole egg	
½ c. sugar	1½ t. lemon juice (optional, depending on cream's acidity)
¼ t. cloves	
½ t. cinnamon	
½ c. seeded raisins, finely chopped	baked pie shell

Cook and stir ingredients in double boiler until thick. Cool slightly. Pour into pie shell. Cover with meringue. Bake in a slow oven (300°) for 15–20 min.

Henryetta Ferguson
Orange County

STRAWBERRY GLAZE PIE

1 pt. strawberries	2 T. lemon juice
Filling:	baked pastry shell
8-oz. cream cheese	Glaze:
2 eggs	⅓ c. sugar
½ c. sugar	3 T. cornstarch

¾ c. water
1 T. lemon juice

¼ t. red food
coloring

Soften cream cheese in small mixing bowl; beat eggs, one at a time, beating well after each addition. Blend in sugar and lemon juice. Mix well. Pour into baked pastry shell. Bake at 350° for 15 min. until slightly firm. Cool. Top with strawberries. Combine sugar and cornstarch in small saucepan. Gradually add water, lemon juice, and food coloring. Cook over medium heat until thick and clear. Cool to lukewarm. Spread strawberries with glaze. Chill several hours before serving.

Linda Dudley
Elkhart County

STRAWBERRY-PINEAPPLE CHIFFON PIE

3 eggs, slightly
  beaten
1 c. sugar
1 8-oz. can
  crushed
  pineapple
1 small pkg.
  Strawberry
  Jello

1 large can evap-
  orated milk
  (put in freezer
  1 hr. before
  using)
2 9″ baked pie
  crusts

Mix eggs, sugar, and pineapple in saucepan. Cook until thick; remove from heat. Stir in Strawberry Jello. Place mixture in refrigerator to cool. Pour milk into bowl and beat until stiff. Fold into cooked mixture. Pour into baked pie crusts and place in refrigerator until set (about 20 min.). Serves 6.

Whipping cream may be substituted for evaporated milk, if desired.

Gladys Brown
Switzerland County

STRAWBERRY SHORT PIE

¾ c. flour
1 c. cold milk
6 T. margarine
1 small pkg.
  instant vanilla
  pudding
½ c. pecans,
  finely chopped

1 c. whipping
  cream
1 T. granulated
  sugar
3 T. brown sugar
1 c. fresh straw-
  berries, sliced

Combine flour, margarine, pecans, and brown sugar. Mix with hands until crumbly. Press mixture firmly against sides and bottom of 9″ pie pan. Bake for 15 min. at 425°. Place an 8″ pan on top of pie crust while it is baking. Remove top pan and cool. Whip cream and sugar until soft peaks form. Set aside. Pour milk in mixing bowl. Add pudding and beat 1 min. Immediately fold whipped cream and strawberries into pudding. Pour into cooled pie shell. Chill until firm. Garnish with whole strawberries. Serves 6.

Mrs. Kay Rouse
Jennings County

FRENCH STRAWBERRY PIE

1 baked 9″ pie
  shell
1 3-oz. pkg.
  cream cheese
3 T. cream
2 T. cornstarch

few drops of
  lemon juice
1 qt. strawberries
1 c. sugar
1 c. whipping
  cream

Blend cream cheese and cream. Spread over the cooled pie shell. Wash and hull berries. Select ½ of best ones and, if large, slice in half. Add sugar to the rest and let stand until juicy. Mash and rub through sieve. Mix purée with cornstarch; add lemon juice. Cook until thick and clear, stirring constantly. Pour ½ over cheese filling, add rest of berries to sauce and chill. Top with whipped cream. Serves 6–8.

Mrs. Walter Zinkan
Knox County

GLAZED STRAWBERRY PIE

1 qt. strawberries	2 T. Strawberry
1 c. sugar	Jello
2 T. cornstarch	1 baked pie shell
1 c. boiling water	

Wash strawberries, cut in half, and drain. Mix sugar, corn starch, and boiling water in pan. Cook until thick and clear. While hot, stir in Strawberry Jello; let cool. Stir in strawberries and put in baked pie shell. Serve with whipped cream. Serves 4–6.

Mrs. Diana Sturm
Montgomery County

SUGAR CREAM PIE (200-year-old Recipe)

1½ c. sugar	2 t. vanilla
⅓ c. flour	1 T. butter,
½ t. salt	melted
2½ c. cream	unbaked pie shell

Blend together sugar, flour, and salt.. Stir in cream, vanilla, and butter. Pour thoroughly beaten mixture into unbaked pie shell. Bake for 10 min. at 450° and then at 325° for 35 min.

Mrs. Kenneth D. Hahn
Miami County

AMISH VANILLA PIE

½ c. brown sugar, packed	½ c. brown sugar, packed
1 T. flour	½ t. cream of tartar
¼ c. dark corn syrup	½ t. baking soda
1½ t. vanilla	⅛ t. salt
1 egg, beaten	¼ c. butter
1 c. water	1 9″ unbaked pie shell
1 c. unsifted flour	

Combine first 5 ingredients in 2-qt. saucepan. Slowly stir in water. Cook over medium heat, stirring, until mixture comes to a boil. Let cool. Combine remaining ingredients; mix until crumbly. Pour cooled mixture into pie shell; top with crumbs. Bake at 350° for 40 min. or until golden brown. Serves 6.

Mrs. Leo Knust
Dubois County

VINEGAR PIE

1 c. sugar	½ c. water
2 eggs	⅛ t. salt
2 T. flour	2 t. lemon extract
½ c. cider vinegar	¼ t. nutmeg
	unbaked pie shell

Beat sugar, eggs, and flour together. Combine vinegar, water, salt, and nutmeg. Gradually add to egg mixture, mixing well. Flavor with lemon extract. Pour into pie shell. Sprinkle with nutmeg. Bake at 300° for 30 min., then at 350° until done.

Cecile Webb
Martin County

Desserts

Desserts are often rightfully described as "terrible temptations" that offer nothing to a meal but pleasure. Certainly dessert is the one course at a meal that nobody wants to miss.

Ice cream was probably "invented" by the Chinese some 3,000 years ago. The hand-cranked portable ice cream freezer was invented by a Nancy Johnson in 1846. According to some sentimental accounts, the ice cream cone originated at the St. Louis Fair in 1904. An ice cream soda, without the soda, was developed and called a sundae in order to get around a law prohibiting the sale of "stimulating beverages" on Sunday.

The trifle was brought to America by British colonists. It is sometimes known as tipsy squire and tipsy parson—compliments of the wine-soaked cake that is its base.

Persimmons grow wild over much of southern Indiana. They are prized as a real delicacy, both fresh and in prepared dishes. Many varieties lose their "pucker power" as they become ripe, long before the first frost. The pulp is prepared from fully ripened, washed persimmons with the calyx removed. Crush the fruit through a colander or food mill to separate the pulp from the seeds and skin. Use immediately or freeze for use at a later date.

Persimmon pudding is a favorite in southern Indiana, and Mitchell, Indiana, has an annual Persimmon Festival. A recipe that would suit all persimmon pudding lovers is as scarce as hens' teeth. Whatever is in the pudding—sweet milk, buttermilk, eggs, no eggs, coconut, etc.—developing an appreciation for persimmon pudding takes a few "tastings." It's easier to appreciate if you've been "raised on it."

APPLE BROWN BETTY

⅓ c. sugar
½ t. cinnamon
¼ t. salt
2 c. fine dry crumbs

4 tart apples, pared and diced
3 T. butter or margarine, melted

Mix sugar, cinnamon, and salt. Put layer of crumbs in greased baking dish. Cover with layer of apples. Sprinkle with sugar mixture. Continue until all ingredients are used. Have layer of crumbs on top. Pour melted butter over crumbs. Cover dish. Bake at 375° for 40 min. Remove cover the last 10 min. to brown the top. Serves 4.

Odelia Lohman
Ripley County

APPLE CRISP

4 c. apples, sliced
1 T. brown sugar
1 t. cinnamon
1 c. flour

1 c. sugar
2 t. baking powder
1 egg

Slice apples thin and put in casserole; sprinkle with brown sugar and cinnamon. Mix flour, sugar, and baking powder. Stir egg into dry mix until crumbly; then pour over apples. Bake at 350°–400° for about 45–60 min. Serve hot or cold with cream.

Janet G. Meyer
Pulaski County

APPLE DUMPLINGS

Dough:
2 c. flour
2 t. baking powder
½ c. milk
¾ c. shortening
1 t. salt

Filling:
2 c. apples, chopped
½ c. brown sugar
1 c. nuts (pecans)

Syrup:
2 c. white sugar
½ c. margarine
2 c. water

¼ t. nutmeg
¼ t. cinnamon
1 t. vanilla

Mix dough and roll out flat. Mix apples, brown sugar, and nuts. Spread on dough. Roll up like jelly roll and cut ½″ thick. Place in buttered pan sliced side down. Mix syrup. Pour over dumplings. Bake at 400° for 40 min. Makes 12 dumplings.

Mrs. Chester Cawein
Shelby County

BAKED APPLE DUMPLINGS

Syrup:
2 c. sugar
2 c. water
2 T. butter
¼ t. nutmeg
1 t. cinnamon
¼ c. red hots candy

Filling:
8 apples, cored and sliced

sugar
cinnamon
butter

Dough:
2½ c. flour
½ c. shortening, softened
4 t. baking powder
¾ t. salt
¾ c. milk

Mix dough. Roll out as pie dough but not too thick. Cut into eight 6″ square pieces. Put sliced apples, 1 t. sugar, dash of cinnamon, and dot of butter in middle of each square of dough. Fold up and turn upside down in large baking dish, placing them close together. Mix ingredients for syrup. Bring to boil. Pour all of hot syrup over dumplings. Bake for 10 min. at 425° and then 30 min. at 375°, basting once with syrup from between dumplings. Serves 8.

Mrs. Joe Braun
Pulaski County

AMISH BAKED APPLES

12 apples, peeled and sliced	1 t. cinnamon
	½ t. salt
3 T. cornstarch	2 c. boiling water
1½ c. sugar (or less)	

Slice apples into large greased baking dish. Mix remaining ingredients in saucepan and cook until clear. Pour over sliced apples and bake in a moderate oven. Serve either hot or cold. Top with whipped cream.

Mrs. Robert Jacob
Noble County

SOUR CREAM BAKED APPLES

¾ c. brown sugar	½ c. hot water
¾ c. white sugar	6–8 apples,
2 T. cornstarch	peeled and
½ c. sour cream or sweet cream	cored

Mix sugars, cornstarch, cream, and water in deep baking dish. Add apples and bake for 30–40 min. at 375°. Serves 6–8.

Gwen Graber
Daviess County

BUTTERSCOTCH APPLES

8 medium tart apples, pared and cored	½ c. white sugar
	2 T. butter
2 c. water	2 T. cornstarch
2 c. brown sugar	vanilla

Make a syrup of 1 c. water and brown sugar. When boiling, put in apples and cook slowly until well done. Lift apples out carefully and place on large flat dish. To the syrup add 1 c. water, white sugar, butter, and cornstarch. Cook until thick;

flavor with vanilla; pour over apples. (There should be almost 2 c. syrup.) Serve cold. Serves 8.

Mrs. Arby Prentiss
Boone County

CARAMEL APPLES

6 medium red apples	1 c. light cream
	2 T. butter
1 c. sugar	1 t. vanilla
¾ c. dark corn syrup	½ c. nuts, chopped

Stick wooden skewers into stem-end of apples. Combine corn syrup, cream, and butter; cook over low heat until sugar is dissolved and small amount of mixture forms hard ball when dropped in cold water. Remove from heat; add vanilla. Dip apples into syrup quickly; roll in chopped nuts. Place on well-buttered cookie sheet to cool.

Mrs. George Romney
Steuben County

BANANA FRITTERS

1 c. flour, sifted	1 T. butter, melted
½ t. salt	
1 t. baking powder	3 bananas, cut or mashed
2 eggs	powdered sugar
½ c. milk	

Preheat frying pan with 6 c. shortening or oil to 400°. Sift dry ingredients together. Add unbeaten eggs, milk, and melted butter. Stir bananas into batter. Stir well. Drop by spoonfuls into hot fat and cook until golden brown. Roll in powdered sugar.

Marie Elkins
Dubois County

BANANA SPLIT DESSERT

First Layer:

2 c. graham crackers, crushed

1 stick margarine

Second Layer:

2 sticks margarine

2 c. powdered sugar

2 eggs

Third Layer:

4 bananas, sliced

Fourth Layer:

1 c. crushed pineapple, drained

Fifth Layer:

2 small pkg. frozen strawberries, thawed and drained

Sixth Layer:

1 large carton Cool Whip

chopped nuts

maraschino cherries

Mix graham cracker crumbs and 1 stick margarine as pie crust. Place in 9×13″ pan. Mix 2 sticks margarine, powdered sugar, and eggs. Beat with electric mixer for 20 min. Add to bottom layer. Refrigerate for a short time. Add third, fourth, and fifth layers. Spread with Cool Whip; sprinkle with chopped nuts, and decorate with maraschino cherries. Serves 24.

Mrs. Earl Ballinger
Union County

BANANA SPONGE DESSERT

3 bananas, mashed (about 1 c. pulp)

1 T. gelatin

2 T. water

½ c. boiling water

½ c. sugar

2 t. lemon juice

3 egg whites, stiffly beaten

¼ t. salt

whipped cream

½ t. vanilla

Soak gelatin in water; dissolve in boiling water. Stir in sugar until dissolved; cool. Stir in banana pulp and lemon juice. Chill until mixture begins to thicken. Whip it. Fold stiffly beaten egg whites and salt into gelatin mixture. Fill sherbets. Top with whipped cream to which vanilla has been added.

Sarah Emma Striebeck
Boone County

CHERRY CHEESE DESSERT

24 graham cracker squares

¼ c. plus 1 t. soft butter

Filling:

½ c. powdered sugar

1 3-oz. pkg. cream cheese

1 c. whipping cream

1 can cherry pie filling

Roll crackers very fine; add soft butter and mix well. Pour crumbs into 8″ square pan and press firmly. Bake at 350° for 5 min. Let cool. Cream powdered sugar and cream cheese until smooth. Whip cream and fold into creamed mixture. Pour into cooled crust. Cover with cherry pie filling. Refrigerate for at least 8 hr. before serving.

J. Nugnis
Porter County

CHERRY CREAM FREEZE

1 can sweetened condensed milk

¼ c. lemon juice

1 can cherry pie filling

¼ t. almond extract

1 9-oz. can crushed pineapple, drained

2 9-oz. pkg. Cool Whip

Combine first 5 ingredients; then gently fold in Cool Whip. Place in 9×13×2″ pan. Cover with foil. Freeze 24 hr. Serves 8.

Benita Basham
Marshall County

CHERRY DUMPLINGS (19th Century Recipe)

1 c. flour	scant ½ c. milk
1 t. baking powder	1 No. 2 can sour cherries or blackberries
¼ t. salt	1⅓ c. sugar
1 T. sugar	

Sift first 4 ingredients together. Stir in milk, just until blended. Put sour cherries in saucepan; add 1⅓ c. sugar and boil 5 min. Drop dumplings on boiling fruit by tablespoonfuls. Turn down fire so fruit is barely boiling. Cover pan with lid and cook 8–10 min. without removing lid. Serve warm with cream, ice cream, or whipped topping. Serves 4–6.

Mrs. Wayne Brown
Harrison County

CHERRY MERINGUE DESSERT

Cookie Pastry:

- 1¼ c. flour
- 1 t. baking powder
- ¼ t. salt
- ⅓ c. shortening
- ⅓ c. sugar
- 2 unbeaten egg yolks
- 1 T. milk
- ¼ c. chopped nuts

Meringue:

- 2 egg whites
- ¼ c. sugar
- small amount of chopped nuts

Cherry Filling:

- 1 No. 2 can cherries, drained, reserving juice
- 2 T. cornstarch
- ½ c. sugar
- ¾ c. cherry juice
- ¼ t. almond extract

Sift flour, baking powder, and salt. Cut in shortening and sugar, creaming well. Blend in egg yolks and milk. Beat well. Mixture will form a ball. Press into well-greased 9″ or 11″ round baking dish. Sprinkle chopped nuts over top, pressing down slightly. Bake at 375° for 12–15 min. until golden brown. Cool. Beat egg whites until slight mounds form. Add sugar gradually. Continue beating until stiff peaks form. Transfer cooled cookie circle to baking sheet. Drop meringue around edges of circle until a ridge is formed. Sprinkle with small amount of chopped nuts. Bake at 350° for 12–15 min., or until slightly browned. Cool. Combine cornstarch, sugar, and cherry juice. Cook over low heat until thick and clear. Remove from heat and add almond extract and cherries. Cool. Fill circle center with cooled cherry filling. Serves 8–10.

Margaret Fulford
Noble County

CHOCOLATE-NUT FONDUE

6-oz. chocolate chips	½ c. milk
½ c. sugar	½ c. chunk style peanut butter

In saucepan combine chocolate chips, sugar, and milk. Cook, stirring constantly, until chocolate is melted. Add peanut butter. Mix well; pour into fondue pot. Keep warm. Serves 6–8. Suggested dippers: pound cake, bananas, cherries, marshmallows.

Kay Baugh
Hendricks County

CHOCOLATE NUT CRUNCH

1 pkg. graham crackers, crumbed	3 sq. unsweetened chocolate, melted
1 c. nuts, ground	1 t. vanilla
1½ c. butter	6 egg whites, stiffly beaten
2 c. (1 box) powdered sugar	½ gal. vanilla ice cream, softened
6 egg yolks	

Combine graham cracker crumbs, nuts, and ½ c. butter. Bake ½ of mixture in foil-lined large Pyrex dish at 400° for 5 min. Cream 1 c. butter and sugar. Add yolks; beat well. Add chocolate and vanilla; mix well. Fold in egg whites. Spread ½ of chocolate mixture over baked crumbs. Chill 1 hr. Add ice cream. Add other ½ of chocolate mixture. Top with remaining crumbs. Freeze. Serves 15.

Patricia Frey
Carroll County

CHOCOLATE PEPPERMINT DESSERT

2 c. vanilla wafer crumbs (56 wafers)	3 c. powdered sugar, sifted
⅔ c. butter or margarine	1 t. vanilla
1 sq. unsweetened chocolate	¾ c. pecans
2 sq. semisweet chocolate	½ gal. peppermint ice cream, softened to room temperature
3 eggs, separated	

Cover bottom of ungreased 9×13″ pan with ½ c. wafer crumbs. Melt butter and chocolate together over lowest heat. With electric mixer, beat egg yolks. Add powdered sugar, chocolate mixture, and vanilla. Beat egg whites and blend into chocolate mixture with pecans. Spread mixture over the crumbs in pan. Spread softened ice cream over chocolate mixture. Sprinkle remaining wafer crumbs over ice cream. Cover with foil and freeze.

Mrs. Willard Lehman
Adams County

VIENNESE CHOCOLATE DESSERT

2 8-oz. pkg. chocolate bits	3 heaping T. sugar
2 c. whipping cream	dash of salt
4 eggs, separated	1 angel food cake, torn into bite-size pieces
1 t. vanilla	

Melt chocolate bits in double boiler. Add vanilla and salt. Cool. Beat egg yolks; add to chocolate mixture. Beat egg whites until stiff, adding sugar. Fold whites into cooled mixture. Make layers of cake pieces and chocolate mixture, starting with cake (2 layers of each). Let stand 12 hr. in refrigerator. Serves 16.

Note: The chocolate will harden if the vanilla is added too fast. Add later for best results, or very slowly to melted chocolate.

Mrs. Perry More
Whitley County

CRANBERRY FLUFF

1 lb. cranberries, coarsely ground (use blender)	1 can mandarin oranges, well drained
1 can crushed pineapple, well drained	2 c. miniature marshmallows
1 c. pecans, chopped	1 c. sugar
	1 large container Cool Whip

Combine first six ingredients. Chill overnight. Drain well; add Cool Whip.

May omit Cool Whip and use as a relish, or may use Cool Whip and put in baked pie shell.

Dorothy Drew
Pike County

CREAM PUFFS

½ c. shortening (lard)	1 c. boiling water
⅛ t. salt	1 c. sifted flour
	4 unbeaten eggs

Add lard and salt to boiling water; bring

to a boil. Add flour all at once; stir vigorously until mixture forms a ball in pan and leaves side of pan. Remove from heat; add 1 egg at a time, beating well after each addition. Mixture will be thick and shiny. Break from spoon on cookie sheet. Bake at 450° for 20 min.; reduce to 350° for 20 min. Remove from oven and cool. Cut ½″ circle in top. Fill with lemon cream pudding or any you choose. Dust with powdered sugar. Top with whipped cream if desired. Makes 12 puffs.

Velda S. Helton
Tippecanoe County

CROWN JEWEL DESSERT

1 3-oz. pkg. Orange Jello	½ c. pineapple juice
1 3-oz. pkg. Cherry Jello	1½ c. graham cracker crumbs
1 3-oz. pkg. Lime Jello	⅓ c. butter, melted
4 c. boiling water	2 envelopes Dream Whip or 2 c. whipping cream, whipped
1½ c. cold water	
1 3-oz. pkg. Lemon Jello	
¼ c. sugar	

Prepare Orange, Cherry, and Lime Jellos separately, using 1 c. boiling water and ½ c. cold water for each. Pour each flavor into 8″ square pan. Chill until firm. Combine Lemon Jello, sugar, and remaining 1 c. boiling water; stir until gelatin and sugar are dissolved. Stir in pineapple juice. Chill until slightly thickened. Meanwhile, mix crumbs and melted butter. Press into bottom of 9″ spring form pan or 13×9× 2″ pan. Cut firm Orange, Cherry, and Lime Jellos into ½″ cubes. Prepare whipped topping mix as directed on package. Blend with Lemon Jello. Fold in gelatin cubes. Pour into pan. Chill at least 5 hr. Serves 16.

Ruth Silver
Switzerland County

CRUNCHY FREEZE

½ gal. vanilla ice cream	¾ c. brown sugar
1 stick margarine	1 can flaked coconut
2½ c. Rice Krispies	1 c. broken pecans

Soften ice cream. Melt margarine at 300° in 13×9″ pan for 10 min. Stir in brown sugar, Rice Krispies, coconut, and pecans. Bake in oven for 30 min., stirring occasionally. Cool. Remove ½ of mixture, spreading remainder evenly over bottom of pan. Spread ice cream over mixture. Sprinkle other ½ of mixture over the ice cream. Freeze at least 2 hr. Serves 15–20.

Mrs. Marilyn Beesley
Jennings County

CUSTARD

1 qt. hot milk (not boiled)	2 t. vanilla
4 eggs	¼ t. salt
5 t. sugar	¼ t. nutmeg

Beat eggs; add hot milk, sugar, vanilla, and salt. Pour custard into 8 individual custard cups. Sprinkle with nutmeg. Arrange custard cups in a pan with 1½ c. of water in bottom. Bake at 225° for 12 min., or until custard is firm. If glass or ceramic custard cups are used, bake 17 min. Serves 8.

Mrs. Marcia Baird
LaPorte County

BAKED CUSTARD (Low Calorie)

4 egg whites,   ¾ t. vanilla
 beaten   ½ c. dry pow-
1¼ t. powdered   dered milk
 Sweet & Low   few drops of
2 c. hot water   yellow food
⅛ t. salt   color

Bake at 300° in pie shell or custard cups in pan of water until set.

Mrs. Ida Flick
Orange County

FLAN

1 c. flour   ⅓ stick butter or
¾ c. sugar   margarine,
1 t. nutmeg   melted
4 eggs   2 t. vanilla
4 c. milk

Mix flour, sugar, and nutmeg together in large bowl. Add eggs and melted butter. Mix well. Add milk and vanilla. Pour into greased 9×13″ pan. Bake at 325° for 1 hr.

Betty Wilz
Daviess County

FRUIT COCKTAIL FLUFF

20 graham   ½ c. sweet milk
 crackers, rolled   1 medium can
 fine   fruit cocktail,
½ c. melted   drained
 butter   pinch of salt
1 t. sugar   ½ pt. whipping
½-lb. marsh-   cream, whipped
 mallows   stiff

Mix graham cracker crumbs, butter, and sugar. Pat into 8×8″ pan, saving some for topping. Heat milk and marshmallows in pan, stirring constantly. Add salt and let cool. When mixture is cool, add drained fruit cocktail and whipped cream. Mix

lightly and put in pan. Sprinkle remaining crumbs over top. Refrigerate overnight.

Helene Tichenor
Gibson County

HEAVENLY HASH

1 large can   1 c. sugar
 crushed pine-   1 t. vanilla
 apple, drained   1 pkg. small
2 T. flour   colored
1 egg   marshmallows
½ c. pineapple   1 large bottle
 juice or water   maraschino
1 pt. whipping   cherries, well
 cream, whipped   drained and cut
 stiff   in small pieces

Combine pineapple, flour, egg, sugar, and juice. Cook until thick. Cool. Mix whipped cream, vanilla, marshmallows, and cherries. Add to cooled mixture. Let stand in refrigerator a few hours. Serve with angel food or white cake.

Inez Blaize
Pike County

MANDARIN ORANGES IN A CLOUD

1 envelope unfla-   3 eggs, separated
 vored gelatin   1 c. mandarin
3 c. milk   oranges
½ c. sugar   1 t. grated lemon
¼ t. salt   rind

Day before in top of double boiler: Mix gelatin, ¼ c. sugar, and salt. Stir in egg yolks, then slowly stir in milk. Cook over boiling water, stirring constantly, until mixture coats spoon; remove from fire. Stir in lemon rind. In large bowl beat egg whites until they form moist peaks; gradually add ¼ c. sugar; continue beating until egg whites are stiff. Fold in hot gelatin mixture. Refrigerate. Before serving next day: Spoon ½ of mixture into serving portions. Add orange sections, then add more mixture. Top each portion with 1–2 orange sections.

Friendly Neighbors Club
LaPorte County

FROSTY MANDARIN DESSERT

1 11-oz. can mandarin oranges, drain and reserve syrup	2 3-oz. pkg. Orange Jello
2 c. boiling water	1 pt. orange sherbet

Measure drained syrup; add water to make 1 c. Dissolve gelatin in boiling water. Add measured liquid. Add sherbet by spoonfuls, stirring until melted. Chill until thickened. Fold in oranges, reserving a few to garnish with. Put into individual serving dishes and chill until set, at least 1 hr. Makes 5 cups or 8 servings.

Trudy Schmuck
Posey County

PARTY DESSERT

First Layer:	reserve rest of carton
1 c. flour	Third Layer:
1 stick margarine	
½ c. pecans, chopped	2 pkg. instant strawberry or lemon pudding
Second Layer:	3 c. milk
1 8-oz. pkg. cream cheese	Fourth Layer:
1 c. powdered sugar	remainder of Cool Whip
1 c. Cool Whip,	

Combine flour, margarine, and pecans. Spread in 9×13″ pan. Bake at 375° for 15 min. Cool. Combine cream cheese, pow-

dered sugar, and 1 c. Cool Whip. Spread over cooled crust. Combine instant pudding and milk; beat for 2 min. Pour over second layer. Spread rest of Cool Whip over third layer. Refrigerate. Serves 12–15.

Sheryl Newkirk
Montgomery County

PINEAPPLE PARTY LOAF

1 8½-oz. can crushed pineapple, drain and reserve syrup	1 3½-oz. pkg. vanilla pudding and pie filling
1 3½-oz. pkg. ladyfingers, split	1 envelope unflavored gelatin
	1 pt. vanilla ice cream, softened

Measure drained pineapple syrup; add water to make 2 c. Combine pudding mix, gelatin, and measured liquid in large saucepan. Cook over medium heat, stirring constantly, until pudding comes to a full boil (usually about 5 min.). Remove from heat and stir in ice cream. Chill until mixture begins to thicken; fold in pineapple. Line bottom and sides of 8×4″ loaf pan with 2 layers of waxed paper. Place split ladyfingers in bottom and along sides of pan. Pour in pineapple mixture. Refrigerate. To serve: Lift out of loaf pan and slice to desired serving size. Serves 8.

Mrs. Melvin Bookout
Allen County

SCALLOPED PINEAPPLE

3 eggs, beaten	1 large can crushed pineapple and juice
1 qt. fresh bread crumbs, packed	½ c. whipping cream
1 pt. or 2 c. sugar	
½ c. butter	

Mix dry ingredients and butter. Add beaten

eggs, pineapple, and cream. Bake at 350° for 45 min., or until brown. Serves 10.

Grace Spohr
Noble County

PRUNE WHIP

- 1 12-oz. pkg. pitted prunes or 1 16-oz. pkg. whole prunes
- 2 oz. pkg. Dream Whip (or whipped cream)
- ¼ c. shredded coconut
- ¼ c. pecans, finely chopped
- few drops of vanilla

Cook prunes until tender. Remove pits if using whole prunes; chop. Beat Dream Whip according to directions on package. Combine with prunes. Mix with remaining ingredients. Keep refrigerated until ready to use.

Mrs. Elizabeth Ramsey
Posey County

PUMPKIN SQUARES

First Layer:

- 1¾ c. graham cracker crumbs
- ⅓ c. sugar
- ½ c. butter, melted

Second Layer:

- 2 eggs
- ¾ c. sugar
- 1 8-oz. pkg. cream cheese

Third Layer:

- 3 egg yolks
- ½ c. sugar
- 1 16-oz. can pumpkin (about 2 c.)
- ½ c. milk
- ½ t. salt
- 2 t. cinnamon
- 1 pkg. unflavored gelatin
- ¼ c. cold water
- 3 egg whites
- ¼ c. sugar

Mix graham cracker crumbs, sugar, and melted butter. Put in buttered 13×9×2″ dish. Mix eggs, sugar, and cream cheese; beat until light and fluffy. Carefully pour over crumbs and bake 20 min. at 350°. Mix pumpkin, egg yolks, sugar, milk, salt, and cinnamon; beat well. Cook, stirring frequently, in double boiler until thick (about 5 min.). Sprinkle gelatin in cold water; stir over low heat until dissolved. Stir into hot pumpkin mixture. Cool. Beat egg whites; gradually beat in sugar. Beat until very stiff. Gently fold into cooled pumpkin mixture. Pour over baked layers. Top with additional graham cracker crumbs. Refrigerate. Serve with whipped cream.

Ruby Shatz
Porter County

CREAM CHEESE-PUMPKIN ROLL

- 3 eggs
- 1 c. sugar
- ⅔ c. pumpkin
- 1 t. lemon juice
- ¾ c. flour
- 1 t. baking powder
- 2 t. cinnamon
- 1 t. ginger
- ½ t. nutmeg
- 1 t. pumpkin pie spice
- ½ t. salt
- 1 c. pecans, chopped

Filling:

- 1 c. powdered sugar
- 8 oz. pkg. cream cheese
- 4 T. butter or margarine
- ½ t. vanilla

Beat together eggs, sugar, pumpkin, and lemon juice. Mix flour, baking powder, cinnamon, ginger, nutmeg, salt, and pumpkin pie spice. Fold dry ingredients into wet ingredients. Spread onto greased cookie sheet lined with greased wax paper. Top with pecans. Bake for 15 min. at 375°. Place nut side down on towel sprinkled with powdered sugar. Remove waxed paper and roll into towel while still warm. Roll tightly and refrigerate overnight. Mix filling ingredients and spread on unrolled cake. Roll back up, wrap in waxed paper, and refrigerate. Serves 8–12.

Mrs. Lucille Mueller
Marion County

RHUBARB CRUNCH

1 c. rolled oats, uncooked	1 stick margarine
1 c. flour	1 c. nuts, chopped
1 c. brown sugar, packed	3 c. rhubarb, cut and uncooked

Put rhubarb in a deep baking dish. Mix rest of ingredients together. Cut in margarine until crumbly. Sprinkle over rhubarb. Bake at 350° for 45–60 min. Serves 6–8.

Mrs. Doris Keely
Noble County

RHUBARB DESSERT

½ c. granulated sugar	½ c. shortening
½ c. nuts, chopped	1 egg
1 T. butter or margarine, melted	2 c. flour
	1 t. soda
	½ t. salt
1 t. cinnamon	1 c. sour cream
1½ c. brown sugar	1½ c. rhubarb, cut into ½" pieces

Mix sugar, nuts, butter or margarine, and cinnamon until crumbly; set aside. Cream together brown sugar, shortening, and egg. Thoroughly stir together flour, soda, and salt. Add to creamed mixture alternately with sour cream. Stir in rhubarb. Turn into greased 13×9×2" pan. Sprinkle with reserved topping. Bake at 350° for 45–50 min. Cut in squares. Serve warm or cool.

Jean Montgomery
Scott County

GLORIFIED RICE

4 c. cooked rice, cooled	½ c. sugar
2 c. crushed pineapple, drained	1 c. whipped cream or whipped topping
½ lb. miniature marshmallows	1½ t. vanilla

Gently mix pineapple, marshmallows, sugar, and rice. Add vanilla to whipped cream; fold into rice mixture. Chill. Serves 8.

Mrs. Meyer Carlisle
Pulaski County

STRAWBERRY DESSERT

Filling:	Crumble Topping:
2 egg whites, beaten stiff	½ c. brown sugar
	1 c. flour
1 pkg. Dream Whip	1 stick butter, melted
1 1-lb. pkg. frozen strawberries, thawed	1 c. pecans, chopped

Mix topping ingredients. Bake at 325° for 20 min. Cool, then crumble. Mix filling ingredients. Put ½ of crumble topping on bottom; add filling; put remaining topping on top. Freeze for several hours. Serves 15.

Mrs. Richard Kyler
Whitley County

STRAWBERRY-PINEAPPLE CHIFFON

3 eggs, lightly beaten	1 small pkg. Strawberry Jello
1 c. sugar	½ pt. whipping cream, whipped stiff
1 8-oz. can crushed pineapple	

Mix eggs, sugar, and pineapple in saucepan. Cook until thick. Remove from heat. Stir in Strawberry Jello. Place mixture in refrigerator to cool. Fold whipped cream into cooked mixture. Pour into 6×10″ dish and chill until set. Serves 6–8.

Mrs. Orlando Lehman
Adams County

SOUR CREAM BAVARIAN

2 envelopes unfla- vored gelatin	Fruit Sauce:
1⅓ c. sugar	16 oz. frozen red raspberries,
1½ c. boiling water	strawberries, or blueberries,
2 c. sour cream	thawed, drain
2 t. vanilla	and reserve
1 9-oz. pkg. Cool Whip, thawed	syrup
	2 T. sugar
	2 T. cornstarch

Combine gelatin and sugar. Add boiling water and stir until dissolved. Blend in sour cream and vanilla. Chill until slightly thickened. Blend in Cool Whip. Pour into 9½″ diameter mold, which has been thoroughly sprayed with Pam. Chill at least 3 hr. Unmold and serve with Fruit Sauce. To make sauce: Measure drained syrup; add water to make 1½ c. liquid. Mix sugar and cornstarch, then mix with 1 T. liquid. Add to remaining liquid and cook over medium heat until mixture is thickened and clear. Add fruit. Chill. Serves 12.

Mrs. Charles E. Flannagan
Perry County

SMALL PEARL TAPIOCA DESSERT

5 c. hot water	1 3-oz. pkg.
¾ t. salt	Strawberry
½ c. plus 1 T. small pearl tapioca	Jello
	1 c. pineapple bits, drained
1 c. sugar	1 large box Cool
3 sliced bananas	Whip

Cook tapioca, salt, and water for 15 min. Add Jello and sugar. Cool. When starting

to set, fold in bananas and pineapple; lightly fold in Cool Whip. Chill. Serves 16.

Mrs. Charles Whiteman
Marshall County

ENGLISH TRIFLE

1 pkg. Jello (any flavor)	1 16-oz. can fruit cocktail, well
5 ladyfingers (or equal amount of plain cake)	drained
	½ pint whipping cream
1 pkg. instant vanilla pudding	

Put ladyfingers in bottom of glass bowl. Make Jello according to directions, using ¾ c. cold water. Pour Jello over cake or ladyfingers and allow to set. Make vanilla pudding according to directions but use ½ c. less milk. Spread well-drained fruit cocktail over set Jello. Spread pudding mix over fruit and top with whipped cream. Decorate with slivered almonds. Chill. Serves 6–8.

Note: One-half c. sherry may be poured over cake if desired.

Gayle Tellman
Bartholomew County

VINEGAR DUMPLINGS (Very Old Recipe)

1 c. light brown sugar	1 T. butter or margarine
¾ c. water	1 t. cinnamon
½ c. vinegar	

Put in pan and place on low fire. When syrup is boiling, drop in dumplings. Cook until done, about 10 min. Serves 6.

Use any good dumpling recipe you prefer.

Mrs. Thomas Callahan
Floyd County

COBBLERS

BLACKBERRY COBBLER

5 c. fresh or frozen blackberries	4 t. baking powder
1 c. sugar	½ t. cream of tartar
3 T. sifted flour	2 T. sugar
butter or margarine	½ t. salt
Pastry Top:	½ c. butter or margarine
2 c. flour	½ c. milk

Toss blackberries with sugar. Pour into well-buttered 1½-qt. oblong baking dish. Sprinkle sifted flour over berries; dot with butter. Set aside. Put flour, baking powder, cream of tartar, sugar, and salt in bowl. With a fork stir in butter until mixture resembles coarse meal. With fork stir in milk. Form mixture into a ball. Roll dough ¼″ thick on a floured board. Cover blackberries with dough; trim edges. Cut a vent in the center of dough and sprinkle top generously with sugar. Bake cobbler at 400° for 40 min., or until crust is golden. Serve warm with cream or plain.

Rose Bauernfiend
Martin County

BLUEBERRY BUCKLE

Batter:	2 c. fresh blueberries
¾ c. sugar	
¼ c. soft margarine	Crumb Topping:
1 egg	½ c. sugar
½ c. milk	⅓ c. flour
2 c. flour	½ t. cinnamon
2 t. baking powder	¼ c. margarine or soft butter
½ t. salt	

Mix sugar, shortening, and egg thoroughly. Stir in milk and salt. Sift flour with baking powder into mixing bowl. Stir in well. Fold in berries carefully so you don't crush them. Grease and flour lightly 9″ square baking pan. Spread batter evenly. Preheat oven to 375° while you make topping. Combine ingredients and sprinkle over batter. Bake at 375° for about 45–50 min. Serve warm.

Karen Merkel
Dearborn County

CHERRY COBBLER

1 No. 303 can unsweetened cherries, not drained	Batter:
	1 c. flour, sifted
	¼ t. salt
½ can water	¾ c. sugar
1 c. sugar	1 t. baking powder
¼ t. almond flavoring	⅓ c. margarine
	½ c. milk

In saucepan, heat to boiling undrained cherries, water, sugar, and almond flavoring. In bowl, mix flour, salt, sugar, and baking powder. Cut in margarine and add milk. Beat well. Pour batter into well-greased 9″ square pan. Pour cherry mixture over batter. Bake at 350° for 35–40 min. Batter will rise to top. Serves 6.

Ruth McDaniel
Pike County

CHERRY COBBLER (Lazy Day)

1 stick margarine	¼ t. salt
1½ c. sugar	¾ c. milk
1 c. flour	1 can unsweetened cherries, not drained
1½ t. baking powder	

Put margarine in deep dish and place in oven to melt. Beat together 1 c. sugar, flour, baking powder, salt, and milk. Pour this over melted margarine, but do not stir. Empty undrained cherries over batter and sprinkle with ½ c. sugar. Bake at 350° for 30 min.

Dottie Isbell
Posey County

QUICK FRUIT COBBLER

1 can fruit pie filling	⅔ c. pancake mix
½ t. nutmeg	2 eggs, beaten
⅔ c. brown sugar, firmly packed	½ c. raisins, *if* apple pie filling used

Empty pie filling into baking dish. Mix brown sugar, pancake mix, and nutmeg with beaten eggs. Pour over pie filling; dot with butter. Bake at 350° for about ½ hr. Serve plain or with ice cream.

Mrs. Douglas Lowes
Rush County

PEACH COBBLER

2 c. fresh peaches, sliced (or other fruit)	1 c. flour
	½ t. salt
4 T. butter	
¾ c. sugar	Topping:
½ c. milk	1 c. sugar
1 t. baking powder	1 T. cornstarch
	¼ t. salt
	1 c. boiling water

Place sliced peaches in bottom of 8×8×2″ pan. Combine sugar and butter. Add other dry ingredients, alternating with milk. Spread over fruit. Mix sugar, cornstarch, and salt. Sift over batter. Pour boiling water over all. Bake at 325° for 50 min. Serve warm with cream or ice cream.

Martha Renschler
Jefferson County

RHUBARB COBBLER

3 c. rhubarb, diced	3 t. baking powder
1 c. sugar	¼ t. salt
3 T. margarine	¾ c. sugar
Topping:	¼ c. margarine
1½ c. flour	1 egg, beaten
	½ c. milk

Grease 9×13″ pan with margarine. Put diced rhubarb, sugar, and margarine into pan. Sift together flour, baking powder, salt, and sugar. Mix margarine, beaten egg, and milk. Add to sifted ingredients; cut in like pie dough. Mixture will be thick. Spoon evenly over rhubarb and spread to cover rhubarb. Bake 45 min. at 375°. Serves 12.

Mrs. Clyde Dawson
Wabash County

RHUBARB-PEAR COBBLER

3 c. rhubarb, diced	1 3-oz. pkg. Lemon Jello
1-lb., 13-oz. can pears, sliced, drain and reserve 1 c. juice	1 pkg. yellow cake mix
	1 stick butter

Line bottom of large pan with rhubarb and pear slices. Sprinkle Jello over fruit. Pour reserved pear juice over fruit and Jello. Cut butter into cake mix; sprinkle over all. Bake at 350° for 35–45 min. Serves 15–18.

Mrs. Sarah Jean
Owen County

GRANDMA ROW'S STRAWBERRY COBBLER

Filling:	sliced, or preferred fruit
3½–4 c. fresh strawberries,	1½ c. sugar

Dough:

2 c. flour, sifted
4 t. baking
  powder
6 T. sugar
¾ t. salt
⅓ c. shortening

⅔ c. milk
1 large egg,
  beaten

Topping:

¼ c. soft butter
¼ c. sugar
3 T. flour

Sprinkle sugar over strawberries. Set aside. Sift together flour, baking powder, sugar, and salt. Blend with shortening. Combine milk and beaten egg. Blend with flour mixture. Spread dough into well-greased 7×12″ pan. Cover with sweetened fruit. Combine butter, sugar, and flour. Sprinkle topping over fruit. Bake at 350° for 35–40 min. Serves 6–8.

Jane Row
Orange County

ICE CREAMS, ICES, AND SHERBETS

BANANA ICE CREAM

2½ qt. whole
  milk
¾ pt. cream
2 Junket tablets
2 T. water

2 c. sugar
3–4 ripe bananas,
  mashed
2 T. vanilla

Dissolve Junket tablets in water. Warm milk to lukewarm; put in 1 gal. freezer can with sugar, vanilla, and dissolved Junket tablets. Let stand until mixture thickens; add cream and mashed bananas to the top but *do not stir*. Freeze at once.

Mrs. John McAuley
Monroe County

EASY ICE CREAM

4 eggs
2 c. sugar
1 can Milnot
1 t. vanilla

½ gal. milk
1 small-size pkg.
  instant pud-
  ding, any flavor

Beat eggs and sugar well. Add remaining ingredients. Mix thoroughly and freeze in ice cream freezer. Makes 1 gallon.

Estelee Clark
Hamilton County

HERITAGE CUSTARD ICE CREAM

1½ c. sugar
¼ c. flour
½ t. salt
1 qt. milk

4 eggs, beaten
1 qt. cream or
  half & half
3 T. vanilla

Combine sugar, flour, and salt. Gradually stir in milk. Cook over low heat, stirring until thickened. Stir a small amount of hot mixture into beaten eggs and add to hot mixture. Cook 2 min. over low heat, stirring constantly. Chill. Stir in cream and vanilla. Freeze in ice cream freezer. Yields 2½ quarts.

JoAnn Wyatt
Wayne County

INDIANA PERSIMMON ICE CREAM

⅔ c. persimmon
  pulp (about
  20 persimmons,
  or 1 pt.)
1¾ c. sugar
1½ T. flour
4 eggs

⅛ t. salt
1½ c. heavy
  cream
2 T. fresh lemon
  juice
3½ c. milk

Remove seeds from persimmons, but do not skin. Purée persimmons in electric blender on medium speed. Combine sugar, flour, eggs, salt, cream, persimmon pulp, lemon juice, and milk. Beat with wire whip until well blended. Churn-freeze. Makes ½ gallon.

Maria Crosman
Marion County

STRAWBERRY ICE CREAM

1 qt. strawberries	2 egg whites,
1 c. granulated	beaten stiff
sugar	1 c. Milnot,
2 egg yolks, well	beaten to soft
beaten	peaks

Clean, stem, and mash strawberries. Add sugar and let stand 10 min. Add egg yolks. Fold beaten egg whites and Milnot into strawberry mixture. Place in 8×8×2″ pan and freeze.

Joanie Smith
Rush County

TROPICAL ICE CREAM

4 egg yolks,	1 c. whipping
well beaten	cream, whipped
1 c. sugar	1 8¾-oz. can
¼ t. salt	crushed
1½ c. milk,	pineapple
scalded	¼ c. maraschino
3 ripe bananas,	cherries
mashed (1½ c.)	½ c. walnuts
	(optional)

Combine egg yolks, sugar, and salt. Slowly stir in slightly cooled milk. Cook and stir over low heat until mixture coats metal spoon. Add mashed bananas. Cool and pour into one 6-c. or two 3-c. refrigerator trays and freeze firm. Break frozen mixture into chunks and beat until fluffy. Fold in pineapple, cherries, and whipped cream. Return to trays; freeze firm. Makes 2 quarts.

Mrs. Mary M. Good
Pulaski County

BANANA ICE MILK

3 bananas,	2 qt. milk
crushed	2 T. vanilla
6 eggs, beaten	⅛ t. salt
2 c. sugar	

Blend bananas and eggs thoroughly. Add sugar gradually and continue beating until mixture is very stiff. Stir in remaining ingredients. Freeze in 4-qt. electric freezer according to directions on the freezer. Let ice milk ripen for 3–4 hr. Makes 4 quarts.

Marianna Roth
Spencer County

ORANGE ICE

1½ c. sugar	2 egg whites,
1 c. water	beaten
2 T. sugar	(optional)
2 t. gelatin	2 c. orange juice
2 T. water	¼ c. lemon juice

Boil 1½ c. sugar and 1 c. water for 5 min. Cool. Soften gelatin in 2 T. water. Add 2 T. sugar to beaten egg whites. Add orange juice, lemon juice, egg whites, gelatin in water to hot syrup. Mix together and freeze without stirring.

Mrs. Paul A. Smith
Randolph County

STRAWBERRY MILK SHERBET

¾ c. sugar	2 T. lemon juice
2 c. water	2 t. grated orange
1 pkg. Strawberry	rind
Jello	2 c. milk

Add sugar to 1 c. water. Boil 2 min. Dissolve Jello in hot liquid. Add 1 c. water, lemon juice, and grated orange rind. Freeze in refrigerator trays or 13×9″ sheetcake pan. When partly frozen, beat with rotary beater until fluffy. Add milk; blend. Continue freezing, stirring once after 30 min. Freezes in 5 hr. Makes 1½ quarts.

Karen Merkel
Dearborn County

1–2–3 STRAWBERRY SHERBET

4 c. fresh ripe strawberries	2 c. sugar
	2 c. buttermilk

Rinse, drain, and hull strawberries. Add sugar to berries and mash. Stir in buttermilk. Pour into refrigerator trays; freeze firm. Break in chunks; place in blender and blend until smooth. Freeze firm. Can be kept frozen in plastic containers in freezer. Serves 10.

Eunice Gigstead
Lake County

POPSICLES

Basic Mixture:	To 6 T. of mixture add:
1 3-oz. pkg. Jello	
2 pkg. Kool-Aid	¾ c. hot water
1¼ c. sugar	¾ c. cold water or fruit juice

Combine ingredients to make basic mixture, using flavors of your choice. Store. To make popsicles: Add hot water and cold water or fruit juice to 6 T. of mixture. Fill molds and freeze.

Mrs. Forrest Meyers
Hamilton County

FUDGESICLES

1 pkg. instant chocolate pudding	¼ c. sugar
	3 c. milk
	1 c. ice cream

Beat and let stand for 5 min. Fill molds and freeze.

June Hendrix
Martin County

PUDDINGS

ANGEL PUDDING

2 c. milk, scalded	1 T. unflavored gelatin
½ c. sugar	
3 egg yolks	¼ c. cold water
1 c. whipping cream, whipped	3 egg whites, beaten stiff, but not dry
1 t. vanilla	½ c. graham cracker crumbs
¼ c. sugar	

Combine milk, ½ c. sugar, and egg yolks. Let come to boil; remove from heat. Soften gelatin in cold water. Add to custard mixture. Let cool. Combine whipped cream and beaten egg whites. Add vanilla and ¼ c. sugar. Fold into custard. Put graham cracker crumbs in bottom of dish. Add pudding on top. Chill in refrigerator. Serves 8–10.

Lovina Fruchey
Noble County

APPLE PUDDING

1 c. sugar	1 c. flour
½ c. shortening	¼ t. nutmeg
1 egg	¼ t. salt
1 c. apples, chopped	½ t. soda
½ t. baking powder	½ t. cinnamon
	¼ t. cloves

Cream sugar, shortening, and egg. Add chopped apples. Sift together remaining ingredients. Combine all. Bake in 9×9″ pan at 350° for 25–30 min. Cut in squares. Cool. Top with whipped cream.

Mary Stenger
Franklin County

BLACKBERRY PUDDING

1 c. sugar	1 t. cloves
1 c. blackberries	1 t. nutmeg
1 egg	Topping:
2 T. butter, melted	2 egg yolks
3 T. sour milk	1 c. sugar
1 c. flour	1 T. butter
1 t. soda	1 T. flour
1 t. cinnamon	1 t. vanilla
	½ c. water

Mix together first 10 ingredients. Bake in oblong pan. Bake in slow oven (300°). Combine topping ingredients. Cook until thickened. When cake is cool, pour over top. Serves 6–8.

Mrs. Henry Duncan
LaPorte County

BRANDYWINE BLACKBERRY PUDDIN'

Three cupfuls of flour, one cupful of molasses, half a cupful of milk, a teaspoon of salt, a little cloves, a little cinnamon, a teaspoon of soda, dissolved in a little of the milk. Then stir in a quart of the berries, floured. Bake in a buttered Dutch oven for about two hours. Serve hot or cold with thick cold cream. Eat with a spoon.

"Blue River Pioneer Cookin' "
Shelby County Historical Society

BREAD PUDDING

2 slices bread	Sauce:
1½ pt. milk	
1 c. brown sugar	1 c. brown sugar
2 c. cooked	1 t. butter
raisins	1 T. flour
1 T. butter	small amount cold
1 t. cinnamon	water
2 eggs, well	2 c. boiling water
beaten	

Soak bread in milk; add sugar, raisins, butter, cinnamon, and eggs. Bake in greased pan at 350° for 45 min. Serve with sauce: Make paste of brown sugar, butter, flour, and cold water. Add to boiling water. Cook until thick. Serves 8.

Mrs. Esther McConnaughey
Jay County

GRANDMA WIGMORE'S BREAD PUDDING

2 eggs	1 t. cloves
2 c. brown sugar	Sauce:
butter, size of egg	
1 c. raisins	1 c. brown sugar
8 slices toast,	1½ T. flour
cubed	1 t. vanilla
1 qt. milk	½ c. cold water
1 t. cinnamon	1 c. boiling water
	1 T. butter

Beat eggs in 2-qt. casserole; add remaining ingredients. Stir until thoroughly blended. Bake at 350° until raised in center. Mix brown sugar, flour, and vanilla with cold water. Add boiling water and butter. Cook until thick and pour over pudding. Serves 8.

Mrs. Nelson Retter
Randolph County

BROWN SUGAR PUDDING

1 c. brown sugar	⅔ c. milk
1½ c. flour	Syrup:
3 t. baking	
powder	1 c. brown sugar
1 t. butter	1 T. butter
1 c. raisins	3 c. boiling water

Mix together pudding ingredients in 9" baking pan. Make syrup of brown sugar, butter, and boiling water. Pour syrup over pudding mixture and bake until brown at 350°. Serves 6.

Goldie Humphrey
Putnam County

BUTTERSCOTCH PUDDING

1 c. brown sugar	2 T. butter
⅓ c. boiling	⅛ t. salt
water	¼ t. vanilla
2 egg yolks	few drops of
3 T. flour	maple flavoring
1½ c. milk	(optional)

Boil sugar and water for 2 min. Stir flour to a paste with a little of the milk, then add the egg yolks, salt, and the rest of the milk. Stir this into the sugar syrup and cook until thick and smooth.

Gladys Gill
Porter County

CHERRY PUDDING

⅓ c. butter
⅔ c. sugar
2 eggs, separated
⅓ t. salt
⅔ c. water
1½ c. flour
3 t. baking
   powder

½ t. vanilla

Cherry Topping:
1 c. water
1½ c. sugar
2 T. butter
2 c. cherries,
   drained

Cream butter; add sugar, beaten egg yolks, and vanilla. Add flour mixture and water alternately. Fold in beaten egg whites. Pour in 9×13″ pan. Bring water to boil. Add sugar, butter, and cherries. Spoon mixture over cake batter. Bake at 375°.

Mrs. Kathryn Carr
Bartholomew County

CINNAMON PUDDING

Syrup:
2 c. brown sugar,
   packed
2 c. water
2 t. butter

Batter:
1 c. sugar

2 t. soft butter
2 c. flour
2 t. baking
   powder
1 t. cinnamon
1 c. milk
dash of salt

Make syrup: Combine brown sugar, water, and butter and cook over medium heat for 5 min. Pour into 9″ square baking pan. Mix rest of ingredients as cake batter. Pour over syrup. Bake at 350° for 30 min.

Mrs. James Bryan
Montgomery County

COTTAGE PUDDING

2 T. butter
½ c. sugar
¾ c. sweet milk
2 egg yolks
¼ t. salt
1½ c. flour
2 t. baking
   powder
vanilla to taste

Sauce:
1½ c. sweet milk
1 T. butter
½ c. sugar
2 T. flour
2 egg whites,
   beaten
vanilla to taste

Mix ingredients as for cake batter. Bake at 350° and add sauce. Sauce: Cook first 4 ingredients until thick; add beaten egg whites and vanilla. Serves 10.

Blanche C. Rusk
Fountain County

DATE PUDDING

1 c. brown sugar,
   packed
1 c. flour
1 c. dates,
   chopped
½ c. milk
¼ t. salt
1 T. baking
   powder

2 c. brown sugar,
   packed
2½ c. boiling
   water
1 T. vanilla
1 T. butter
1 c. nuts,
   chopped

Mix first 6 ingredients and put into buttered 9×13″ pan. Mix remaining ingredients and pour over mixture in pan. Bake at 350° for about 1¼ hr. Serves 15. This date pudding makes its own "sauce."

Myla Nixon
Rush County

FRESH FRUIT PUDDING

1⅔ c. sugar
1 c. flour
2 T. butter
1 t. baking
   powder

½ c. milk
1½–2 c. fresh
   sliced peaches
   or cherries
1 c. cold water

Mix 1 c. sugar, flour, butter, baking powder, and milk. Spread this thick batter in pan. Place peaches or cherries on top of batter, sprinkle ⅔ c. sugar over fruit, add water over all. Bake at 350°.

Mrs. Garold Mills
Jay County

GOOSEBERRY PUDDING

1 c. sugar	1 c. floured
1 T. shortening	gooseberries
2 eggs	1 t. soda dissolved
1 c. flour or a	in 3 T. hot
little more	water

Mix and bake at 325°–350°. Serve with milk to which a little nutmeg has been added.

Virginia L. Bosstick
Sullivan County

GRAPE NUTS PUFF PUDDING

⅓ c. butter	2 c. milk
2 c. sugar	juice and grated
4 egg yolks, well	rind of 2
beaten	lemons
4 T. flour	4 egg whites,
6 T. Grape Nuts	stiffly beaten

Cream butter and sugar thoroughly. Add egg yolks, flour, Grape Nuts, milk, lemon juice and rind. Fold in egg whites. Pour into greased baking dish; place in pan of hot water. Bake at 375° for 50–60 min. When done, pudding will have crust on top, jelly below. Serve hot or cold, plain or with whipped cream. Serves 6.

Mrs. Floyd Chapman
Spencer County

HOOVER PUDDING

1 c. sugar	2 t. baking
1 c. buttermilk	powder
1 t. soda	1 t. vanilla

3 c. flour	2 T. flour
pinch of salt	3 T. cocoa
Topping:	lump of butter
1 c. sugar	2 c. boiling water

Mix batter ingredients. Pour into oblong pan and bake at 350° until done. Mix topping ingredients and cook until thick. Pour over pudding. Serves 6–8.

Mrs. Henry Duncan
LaPorte County

HOT FUDGE PUDDING

1 c. flour	2 T. butter,
2 t. baking	melted
powder	Topping:
¼ t. salt	1 c. brown sugar
¾ c. sugar	4 T. cocoa
1½ T. cocoa	1¾ c. hot water
½ c. milk	

Sift together first 5 ingredients. Stir in milk and melted butter. Spread mixture in 9×9″ dish. Mix brown sugar and cocoa and spread over batter. Pour hot water on top. Bake at 375° for 35–40 min., or until cake is done and pudding is thick.

Mrs. Fred Burk
Randolph County

INDIAN PUDDING

4 c. milk	1 t. salt
½ c. yellow	1 t. cinnamon
cornmeal	¼ t. ginger
2 T. butter,	2 T. sugar
melted	2 eggs
½ c. molasses	

Scald milk. Pour slowly on corn meal, stirring constantly. Cook over hot water for 20 min. Combine butter or margarine, molasses, salt, cinnamon, and ginger. Beat eggs well; add with molasses mixture to cornmeal. Pour into greased baking dish. Place in pan of hot water. Bake at 350° for 1 hr. Serve hot with sauce, whipped cream, or vanilla ice cream.

Mrs. R. C. Anderson
Marion County

LEMON SNOW PUDDING

1 c. vanilla wafers or graham cracker crumbs	1 13-oz. can Milnot
	3 T. lemon juice
	1 c. sugar
1 small box Lemon Jello	1 c. hot water

Dissolve Jello in hot water and cool. Whip until foamy; add sugar and lemon juice; beat until thick. Beat Milnot until thick. Fold in lemon mixture. Cover bottom of a 9×13″ pan with crumbs. Pour in lemon mixture. Sprinkle few crumbs on top. Chill. Serves 12.

Mrs. Stanley F. Sears
Putnam County

ORANGE PUDDING

1 c. sugar	1 c. washed raisins
½ c. shortening	
2 c. flour	1 whole orange peel
1 t. soda	
¼ t. salt	Orange Syrup:
1 c. buttermilk or sour milk	juice of 2 large oranges
2 whole eggs	1½ c. sugar
1 c. nuts	

Grind raisins, orange peel, and nuts. Cream sugar and shortening. Combine with flour, soda, salt, buttermilk, and egg. Add ground mixture. Bake in greased

12×8″ pan at 350° for about 40 min. While cake bakes, put orange juice and sugar on stove and bring to a boil. When cake is done, pour this liquid over it.

Barbara Snyder
Pike County

PEACH PUDDING

1 stick butter	1 large can peaches, drained
1 c. flour	
1 c. sugar	
2 t. baking powder	juice of canned peaches
¾ c. milk	

Melt butter in 8×12×2″ pan. Mix flour, sugar, baking powder and milk. Pour over melted butter. *Do not stir.* Place canned peaches on top of butter mixture. Pour juice over all. Bake at 350°. Serves 8.

Mary Ashcraft
Switzerland County

PERSIMMON PUDDING (With Buttermilk)

2 c. persimmon pulp	1 t. cinnamon
2 c. buttermilk	2 c. sugar
½ c. butter or margarine	2 c. flour
	2 eggs, beaten
1 t. vanilla	1 t. soda

Mix soda in buttermilk and dissolve. Cream sugar and butter; add pulp and then eggs. Add salt and cinnamon to flour. Add flour mixture alternating with buttermilk. Bake in 9×13″ pan for 30 min. at 350°. Do not overbake. Serves 12–15.

Hazel Parks Russell
Lawrence County

PERSIMMON PUDDING (With Sweet Milk)

1 c. sugar	1 T. baking
1 T. butter	powder
1 t. cinnamon	1 c. persimmon
1 c. flour	pulp
1 egg	1 c. sweet milk
pinch of salt	

Put all ingredients into large bowl and mix well with electric mixer. Pour into 9× 13″ greased pan. Bake for 20 min. at 350°. Cut into squares and serve with whipped cream.

Betty Ratliff
Hendricks County

PLUM PUDDING

1 c. chopped suet	1 t. soda
2 eggs	1 t. baking
½ c. sour milk or	powder
buttermilk	1½ c. flour
1 c. raisins	citron (optional)
1 c. currants	

Combine first 7 ingredients. Sift in flour. Put in cloth bag and steam 3 hr. Be sure bag is wet and floured. Serve with hard sauce or Garrity's Christmas Custard.

Hard Sauce:

1 pt. water	cinnamon to taste
1 c. sugar	cornstarch to
lump of butter	thicken

Combine and cook until thick.

Mrs. Eleanor Beal
Jennings County

GARRITY'S CHRISTMAS CUSTARD

1 T. flour	2 qt. milk,
1 c. sugar	scalded
salt	1½ T. vanilla
6 eggs	

Mix flour, sugar, and salt. Add eggs and milk. Cook in double boiler over medium heat until mixture coats the spoon. Remove from heat. Strain. Add vanilla. Serve with plum pudding.

Mrs. Wilma Binford
Jennings County

CREAMY RICE PUDDING

½ c. sugar	1 c. cooked rice
2 rounded T.	⅓ c. raisins
cornstarch	pinch of salt
2 eggs	dash of nutmeg
2 c. milk	1 t. vanilla

Mix sugar and cornstarch together in saucepan; add eggs and beat thoroughly. Add milk, rice, raisins, and salt and cook until thick. Add vanilla and nutmeg. Serve warm or chilled. Serves 6.

Irene Stoller
Wayne County

GRANDPA'S SUET PUDDING

½ c. ground suet	1 t. nutmeg
¾ c. seedless	1 t. allspice
raisins	1 t. soda
½ c. (6-oz. jar)	1 t. salt
citron, chopped	1 c. soft bread
2 medium apples,	crumbs
chopped (about	1 c. sugar
1 c.)	3 eggs, beaten
2 c. flour	lightly
1 t. cinnamon	½ c. molasses

Mix together the first 11 ingredients. Mix together sugar, eggs, and molasses in another bowl. Pour liquid mixture over dry mixture, making sure all of dry mixture is saturated. Pour two well-greased qt. molds ¾ full. Cover with lid or foil. Place in steamer. Steam 3–3½ hr. Serve with hard sauce.

Mary Graham
St. Joseph County

TRANSPARENT PUDDING

pie dough	1 heaping T.
2 egg yolks	butter
1 heaping c.	⅔ c. milk
brown sugar	2 egg whites,
cinnamon	beaten

Line muffin tins with pie dough. Mix together egg yolks, brown sugar, butter, cinnamon, and milk. Divide into muffin tins and bake until brown. Add meringue made from egg whites flavored to suit taste. Brown in oven.

This recipe is at least 75 years old.

Marguerite Gaiser
Wells County

VANILLA PUDDING

1½ c. milk	2 egg yolks,
¾ c. sugar	beaten
2 T. cornstarch	pinch of salt
1 t. vanilla	

Mix cornstarch and ¼ c. of milk together and set aside. Combine the remaining 1¼ c. milk and sugar together and place over medium heat. When just warm, add cornstarch mixture, egg yolks, and pinch of salt. Continue heating and stirring until mixture thickens. Remove from heat and add vanilla. Cool and serve.

Recipe may be combined with bananas or coconut for pie fillings.

Carolyn Frey
Putnam County

WOODFORD PUDDING

½ c. shortening	1 t. cinnamon
1 c. sugar	1 t. soda
3 eggs	½ c. sour milk
1 c. blackberry	1 c. flour
jam	

Butterscotch Sauce:

1½ c. dark	1 c. boiling water
brown sugar	4 T. butter
4 T. flour	2 T. cream

Cream sugar and shortening; add eggs and beat. Add jam and cinnamon. Dissolve soda in sour milk. Add flour and milk alternately to mixture. Beat well; Bake in 9×13″ pan at 325° for 40 min. Sauce: Mix brown sugar and flour. Add boiling water. Cook for 6–8 min., stirring constantly. Remove from heat; add butter and cream. Serve warm over pudding. Serves 9.

Hazel Russell
Lawrence County

SHORTCAKES

STRAWBERRY SHORTCAKE

1½ c. flour, sifted	½ c. brown
3 t. baking	sugar, packed
powder	1 egg
¼ t. soda	¾ c. buttermilk
½ t. salt	½ t. vanilla
⅓ c. shortening	

Grease one 9″ round cake pan. Combine first 5 ingredients—stir together or sift. Combine shortening and dry ingredients by cutting in as for pie dough. Combine egg, buttermilk, and vanilla and stir into dry mixture only until blended. Bake at 350° for 20–25 min. Cut layer crosswise, making two layers. Fill and top with sweetened strawberries. Garnish with whipped cream or pour half & half or milk over and serve.

Mrs. Barbara R. Endress
Elkhart County

STRAWBERRY SHORTCAKE
(Biscuit Type)

2 c. flour	few grains of
1/3 c. sugar	nutmeg
4 t. baking	1 egg, well beaten
powder	1/2 c. butter
1/2 t. salt	1/3 c. milk

Sift dry ingredients into bowl. Cut in butter as for pie crust. Add well-beaten egg and milk. Mix and roll lightly as for pie crust on lightly floured pastry cloth. Dough will be sticky. Leave about 1/2" thick. Will make two 8" cakes or about twenty 4" individual cakes. Bake at 425° until lightly browned (about 10 min.). Split in middle and add sweetened berries.

Jesse Colbert
Daviess County

STRAWBERRY SHORTCAKE
(Cake Type)

1 c. sugar	3 t. baking
4 T. shortening	powder
1 egg	1 c. milk
2 c. flour	1 t. vanilla
1/8 t. salt	1 qt. strawberries

Cream sugar and shortening thoroughly. Add egg and beat well. Add sifted dry ingredients alternately with milk. Add flavoring. Pour in greased shallow pan and bake in moderate oven for 20–30 min. To serve, split in half and spread crushed sweetened berries between layers and on top. Serves 9.

Dorothy M. Collahan
Pulaski County

TORTES

BUTTERSCOTCH TORTE

6 eggs, separated	1 t. baking
1 1/2 c. sugar	powder
1 t. almond	Butterscotch Sauce:
extract	1/4 c. butter
2 c. graham	1/4 c. water
cracker crumbs	1 c. brown sugar
1 c. chopped	1 T. flour
nuts	1 egg, well
1/2 pt. whipping	beaten
cream, whipped	1/4 c. orange juice
2 t. vanilla	1/2 t. vanilla

Beat egg yolks well; add sugar slowly, then baking powder and flavorings. Beat egg whites until stiff and fold into yolk mixture. Fold in crumbs and nuts. Bake in two greased and waxed paper-lined 9" pans. Bake at 325° for 30–35 min. Cool and frost with whipped cream between layers and on top and sides. Butterscotch Sauce: Melt butter in water. Add rest of ingredients except vanilla. Bring to a boil and cook until fairly thick. Remove from heat; add vanilla and cool. Drizzle over top and sides. Serves 8.

Mrs. Eugene Wakeland
Marion County

SAUCY CHERRY TORTE

2 eggs, beaten	1 c. nuts,
1 1/2 c. sugar	chopped
1 1/2 c. flour, sifted	2 T. butter,
1 t. soda	melted
1/4 t. salt	Cherry Sauce:
1 t. cinnamon	1/2 c. sugar
1 No. 2 can sour	1 1/2 T. cornstarch
cherries, drain	reserved cherry
and reserve	juice with wa-
juice	ter to make 1 c.

Combine eggs and sugar. Sift dry ingredients together and add to egg mixture. Add cherries, nuts, and butter and stir until cherries are well mixed. Pour into greased

11×7×1½″ baking pan. Bake at 350° for about 40 min. Cherry Sauce: Mix sugar with cornstarch in saucepan; slowly add cherry juice and water. Cook until thick, stirring constantly. Serve torte with sauce and vanilla ice cream. Serves 12.

Kathleen Rader
Daviess County

LEMON ANGEL TORTE DESSERT

4 egg whites
½ t. cream of tartar
1 c. sugar

Lemon Pudding:

4 egg yolks
2 T. lemon juice
2 t. grated lemon rind
½ t. salt
½ pt. whipped cream, or Dream Whip

Beat egg whites until frothy. Add cream of tartar and beat into stiff peaks. Add sugar gradually until glossy and stiff. Spread in greased 13×9″ pan and bake for 1 hr. and 20 min. at 275°, then at 300° for 40 min. Cool on rack. Lemon Pudding: Put first 4 ingredients in top of double boiler and cook until thick. Cool completely. Spread thin layer of whipped cream over baked meringue. Spread lemon pudding on top. Spread rest of whipped cream over top. Serves 12–15.

Mrs. A. W. McClure
Marion County

PUMPKIN TORTE

24 graham crackers, crushed
⅓ c. sugar
½ c. margarine, melted
2 eggs, beaten
¾ c. sugar
8 oz. pkg. cream cheese

Pumpkin Filling:

2 c. pumpkin
3 egg yolks
½ c. sugar
½ c. milk
½ t. salt
1 T. cinnamon
1 pkg. unflavored gelatin
¼ c. water
3 egg whites
¼ c. sugar
2 pkg. Dream Whip, mixed according to directions

Combine graham crackers, ⅓ c. sugar, and margarine. Press into bottom of 9×13″ pan. Beat cream cheese until light and fluffy. Add ¾ c. sugar and eggs; beat until smooth. Pour over graham cracker mixture and bake for 20–30 min. at 350°. Cool. Filling: Combine pumpkin, egg yolks, ½ c. sugar, milk, salt, and cinnamon. Cook over medium heat, stirring constantly, until very thick. Remove from heat. Dissolve gelatin in water and add to pumpkin mixture. Beat egg whites, gradually add ¼ c. sugar. Fold into pumpkin-gelatin mixture. Pour over baked mixture and refrigerate until firm. Completely cover with Dream Whip and refrigerate for at least 2 hr.

Sharon Coffey
Rush County

RHUBARB TORTE

Torte Crust:

1 c. flour
2 T. sugar
¼ t. salt
½ c. butter or margarine

Rhubarb Filling:

2½ c. rhubarb, cut up
1¼ c. sugar
2 T. flour
2 egg yolks, slightly beaten
⅓ c. cream or half & half

Meringue Topping:

2 egg whites
6 T. sugar
½ t. cream of tartar
1 t. lemon juice

To make crust: Combine ingredients. Work with 2 forks or pastry blender until mixture is crumbly. Press into bottom of 8×10″ baking pan. Bake at 325° for 25 min. To make filling: Combine ingredients. Cook over medium heat, stirring often, until thickened. (Watch carefully as it scorches easily.) Cool slightly and pour over baked crust. To make meringue: Beat egg whites with cream of tartar until soft peaks form. Gradually add sugar and lemon juice. Beat until stiff. Spread on top of rhubarb filling. Bake at 350° for 10–15 min., or until meringue is color desired. Serves 8–10.

Mrs. Esther Eggenspiller
Harrison County

SODA CRACKER TORTE

3 egg whites	1 t. vanilla
¼ t. cream of tartar	1 c. crushed pineapple, well drained
1 c. sugar	
16 soda crackers, crushed	½ c. (or more) whipping
1 c. pecans, chopped	cream, whipped

Beat egg whites until slightly foamy. Add cream of tartar; continue beating until stiff. Gradually add sugar. Fold crackers into egg whites. Add nuts and vanilla. Pour mixture into greased 9″ pie plate. Bake at 325° for 35 min. Remove from oven and let cool. Fold pineapple into whipped cream. Pour over cooled pie crust. Refrigerate overnight.

Mrs. Ray Davenport
Elkhart County

SODA CRACKER LEMON TORTE

3 egg whites	1 c. sugar
½ t. cream of tartar	16 soda crackers, broken

½ c. nuts, chopped	2 cans or 2 pkg. lemon pie filling
2 pkg. Dream Whip	¾ c. coconut, browned
1 8-oz. pkg. cream cheese	

Beat egg whites with cream of tartar. Add sugar. Beat until sugar is dissolved. Add soda crackers and nuts. Spread in greased 9×13″ pan. Bake at 325° for 25–30 min. Cool. Whip Dream Whip and add cream cheese. Beat until smooth. Spread ½ of cream cheese filling over baked crust. Spread lemon pie filling (if using pkg., prepare according to directions) over cream cheese filling. Spread other ½ of cream cheese filling over lemon pie filling. Sprinkle browned coconut over top. Chill overnight.

Betty Hilton
Pulaski County

SAUCES, SYRUPS, AND TOPPINGS

BUTTERSCOTCH SAUCE

1 c. brown sugar, firmly packed	⅓ c. light cream or evaporated milk
⅓ c. dark corn syrup	⅛ t. salt
¼ c. water	½ t. vanilla
¼ c. butter	

Combine brown sugar, corn syrup, water, and butter. Bring to boil and cook, stirring occasionally, to soft-ball stage (236°). Remove from heat. Let cool slightly. Add remaining ingredients. Beat well. Serve warm or cold over ice cream. Makes 1 cup.

Lillian Hague
Noble County

HOT FUDGE SUNDAE SAUCE

1 T. butter	1 small (4-oz.)
1 sq. chocolate,	can evaporated
cut up	milk
⅔ c. sugar	½ t. vanilla

Combine ingredients in heavy saucepan and cook until mixture begins to thicken. Spoon over ice cream and top with chopped nuts.

Mrs. Max Tribbett
Montgomery County

CHOCOLATE SYRUP

2 c. sugar	1 pt. white syrup
4–5 T. cocoa	1 c. hot water
pinch of salt	1 t. vanilla

Boil all ingredients, except vanilla, in large kettle to soft-ball stage. Add vanilla. If too thick when cool, thin with hot water. Makes 4 cups.

Mrs. Donald Jones
Boone County

CORN COB SYRUP

6 dried corn cobs	3 c. sugar
1 qt. water	

Boil together until syrupy. Strain well. If not as thick as desired, boil syrup longer. Tastes somewhat like maple syrup.

Arphelia Ann Sheetz,
in memory of Arzona Noyes
Fulton County

PANCAKE SYRUP

1 c. brown sugar	1 c. water
1 c. granulated	¾ t. maple
sugar	flavoring
1 c. white syrup	

Heat all ingredients, except flavoring, to boiling point; then add maple flavoring. Keeps in refrigerator and will not sugar.

Mrs. Paul Wyatt
Steuben County

LOW CALORIE TOPPING

½ c. instant dry	½ c. ice water
milk	1 t. liquid
2 T. unsweetened	sweetener
lemon juice	

Combine ingredients in small mixing bowl. Beat at high speed until stiff peaks form. Serve immediately as topping for desserts, cakes, or salads.   *Elsie Senn*
Crawford County

WHIPPED TOPPING (Evaporated Milk)

Pour contents of 1 large (13-oz.) can evaporated milk into freezing tray. Freeze until tiny ice crystals begin to form around edges. Turn into chilled bowl and whip with rotary egg beater until stiff enough to hold its shape. If milk does not whip well, it is not cold enough; just chill and whip again. Sugar and vanilla may be added and whipped in at this stage, if desired. Makes 4 cups.

Mrs. Dorothy Selzer
Spencer County

Cookies and Candy

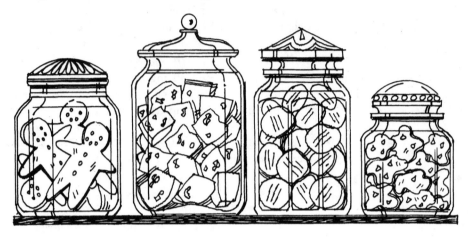

A filled cookie jar helps make home a happy place the world around. Our cookie heritage is as delicious as it is varied. All cookies are made from either a soft or a stiff dough. Soft cookies are dropped from a spoon. Soft dough may be baked in cake pans and cut into squares or bars. Any stiff dough may be sliced, as for refrigerator cookies, or shaped into balls instead of being rolled and cut. Store soft cookies with an orange, a lemon, or an apple to help keep them soft. Baked cookies made with butter will keep a week; those made with non-refrigerated shortening will last up to three months.

Making candy is a fun activity guaranteed to satisfy the most demanding sweet tooth. Although fudge leads the candy-making popularity list, the creative cook easily finds many recipes to add variety to her candy-making efforts. Anyone can have an occasional failure when making fudge, and some failures can be saved. When fudge fails to "set," pour it back into the pan, add ¼ cup of milk and cook; cool and beat again. Failures will also make great toppings for ice cream. If fudge hardens in the cooking pan, work it with your hands until it can be patted onto a buttered plate.

Cookies

TINY FRUIT CAKES

1 lb. pitted dates, chopped	1 c. candied fruits and peels, diced	1 c. candied red and green cherries, cut up	1 c. English walnuts, chopped

1 14-oz. can sweetened condensed milk	1 c. coconut

Combine all ingredients except the milk. Stir together with a wooden spoon. Then add milk and mix well. Mixture will be very sticky. Drop from spoon onto greased cookie sheet or put in bonbon or muffin foil cups. Put cups very close together on an ungreased cookie sheet and place in oven. Bake about 20 min. at 300°, and start checking. They are ready when the coconut starts to brown. Remove from oven and cool. They will be very sticky and if they fall apart they can be pressed back together easily. Store in tightly covered container and let age or mellow for about 2 weeks. These can be frozen after aging. Makes about 3 dozen.

Joan Koch
Franklin County

TEXAS TEATIME TASSIES

½ c. plus 1 T. butter	1 egg
1 3-oz. pkg. cream cheese	¾ c. brown sugar
	¾ c. nuts
1 c. sifted flour	1 t. vanilla
	dash of salt

Blend butter with cheese and flour; chill. Shape chilled dough into 2 dozen 1" balls; press into tiny ungreased tins. Beat together remaining ingredients. Pour small amounts of mixture into tins without completely covering dough shells. Bake at 325° for 25 min. Cool in tins. Makes 24 tiny cupcakes.

Doris Dressler
Spencer County

NO-BAKE COOKIES

BOURBON BALLS

2½ c. vanilla wafer crumbs, finely crushed	1 c. walnuts, finely chopped
2 T. cocoa	⅓ c. bourbon or rum
1½ c. confectioners' sugar	3 T. light corn syrup

Combine crumbs, cocoa, sugar, and nuts. Add bourbon and corn syrup. Mix well. Shape into 1" balls. Roll in sugar. Store in loosely covered container about 2 days.

Mrs. Lee J. Welp
Dubois County

DATE NUT BALLS

1 stick butter	2 c. Rice Krispies
1 c. sugar	½ c. nuts, chopped
1 egg	coconut
1 c. dates, chopped	

Cook butter, sugar, egg, and dates until thick. Let cool. Add Rice Krispies and nuts. Form into balls and roll in coconut.

Minnie Root
Lawrence County

ORANGE PECAN BALLS

½ c. (1 stick) butter or margarine, softened	1 11–12 oz. box vanilla wafers, crushed
1 1-lb. box confectioners' sugar	1 6-oz. can frozen orange juice, undiluted
1 c. pecans, chopped	

Mix butter, sugar, orange juice, and vanilla wafers. Roll into ¾" balls. Roll balls in chopped nuts. Refrigerate. Makes about 80 balls.

Loretta Roberts
Parke County

NO-BAKE SKILLET COOKIES

2 c. sugar	1 c. quick-cook-
1 stick margarine	ing oatmeal
½ c. milk	2 c. Granola
½ c. peanut	(cereal)
butter	1 t. vanilla

Combine sugar, margarine, and milk and cook 2 min. after it starts to boil. Remove from heat. Add rest of ingredients. Stir and drop on buttered pan. Makes about 4 dozen.

Mrs. Barbara Krueger
Jennings County

YANKEE DOODLE COOKIES

1 6-oz. pkg.	2 3-oz. cans chow
semisweet choc-	mein noodles
olate bits	½ c. peanuts or
1 6-oz. pkg.	cashews,
butterscotch	chopped
bits	

Melt chocolate and butterscotch bits in top of double boiler. Remove from heat. Stir in noodles and nuts until evenly coated. Drop by teaspoon onto waxed paper. Chill. Store in refrigerator until ready to serve. Makes 36.

Karen Taylor
Jefferson County

YUMMIES

1 stick butter or	¾ c. dates,
margarine	chopped
1 c. sugar	½ c. pecans,
¼ t. salt	chopped
1 egg, beaten	2–3 c. shredded
2 c. Rice Krispies	coconut

Melt butter, add sugar, salt, and egg. Cook until thick. Add dates and continue cooking about 4–5 min., stirring constantly. Pour over Rice Krispies and nuts. Stir un-

til well blended. Drop by teaspoonfuls into a bowl of coconut. Roll ball to cover with coconut and place on waxed paper. Cool 30 min. Store in an airtight metal container. Cookies may be rolled in chopped pecans instead of coconut. Makes 50.

Fay Daugherty
Parke County

DROP COOKIES

APPLE BUTTER DROP COOKIES

½ c. sugar	1 t. soda
1 c. apple butter	2¼ c. flour
½ c. milk	1 t. baking
½ t. salt	powder
½ t. vanilla	½ c. nuts
½ c. shortening	

Cream together sugar and shortening. Add apple butter and soda. Add flour, salt, and baking powder alternately with milk. Mix well. Add vanilla and nuts. Drop by teaspoon on cookie sheet. Bake for 10–12 minutes at 350°. Makes 4 dozen.

Mrs. Judy Carter
Rush County

APPLESCOTCH COOKIES

1¼ c. brown	1 t. nutmeg
sugar, packed	1½ c. apples,
½ c. butter	diced
3 T. milk	1 c. nuts,
1 egg	chopped
2 c. flour	1 c. white raisins
1 t. baking	1 6-oz. pkg.
powder	butterscotch
1 t. soda	bits
1 t. cinnamon	

Cream brown sugar, butter, milk, and egg. Sift together flour, baking powder, soda, cinnamon, and nutmeg. Add to creamed mixture. Add apples, nuts, white raisins, and butterscotch bits. Drop by teaspoonfuls on greased cookie sheet. Bake in 375° oven for 12–15 min.

Geraldine Leatherock
Bartholomew County

ARCHWAY COOKIES

3 c. brown sugar	1 c. nuts,
2 c. shortening	chopped
6 eggs	2 t. cinnamon
½ c. crushed	2 t. nutmeg
pineapple	2 t. ground cloves
½ c. white sugar	2 t. soda, dis-
1 c. strawberry	solved in 2 t.
jam	molasses
1 lb. chopped	1 t. salt
dates	8 c. flour
1 lb. raisins	

Combine pineapple with white sugar. Cook to thick syrup. Let cool. Cream shortening and brown sugar. Add eggs one at a time, beating after each addition. Add pineapple, jam, dates, raisins, nuts, and soda-molasses mixture. Sift flour, spices, and salt together. Mix with above. Chill 1 hr. Drop by spoon on cookie sheet. Bake at 350° for 15 min. Makes 12 dozen.

Peggy Buck
Lawrence County

BANANA DROP COOKIES

1½ c. sifted flour	1 c. sugar
¾ c. shortening	1 egg, well
1 c. (2–3 large,	beaten
extra ripe)	1¾ c. rolled oats
bananas,	½ t. baking soda
mashed	1 t. salt
¼ t. nutmeg	¾ t. cinnamon
½ c. nuts,	1 c. raisins
chopped	(optional)

Sift flour and baking soda. Cream shortening and sugar. Add well-beaten egg, mashed bananas, flour, soda, salt, and spices. Stir in rolled oats and nuts. Drop by teaspoon on baking sheet. Bake at 400° for 15 min., or until done.

Variation: Substitute 1 c. canned pumpkin for bananas.

Mary Mathias
Whitley County

BLACK WALNUT TREATS

½ c. butter	1 egg
1 c. light brown	1½ c. sifted flour
sugar, firmly	½ t. soda
packed	½ t. salt
1 t. black walnut	½ c. black wal-
flavoring	nuts, broken

Cream butter; add sugar gradually. Cream until light and fluffy. Add egg and extract. Beat well. Sift flour, soda, and salt together. Add to creamed mixture. Add walnuts; blend. Drop by teaspoonfuls onto greased cookie sheet. Bake at 350° for 10 min. Makes 5 dozen 2″ cookies.

Edith Yagel
Whitley County

BUCKAROON COOKIES

2 c. flour	2 eggs
1 t. soda	2 c. rolled oats
½ t. salt	1 t. vanilla
½ t. baking	1 pkg. chocolate
powder	chips
1 c. shortening	½ c. nuts,
1 c. white sugar	chopped
1 c. brown sugar	

Sift flour, soda, salt, and baking powder together and set aside. Blend sugars and shortening. Beat eggs until light and fluffy and add to shortening mixture with flour mixture. Add the rest of the ingredients. Drop on greased cookie sheet. Bake for 15 min. at 350°.

Mrs. George Briesacker
Elkhart County

Drop by teaspoon on greased baking sheet. Bake at 350° until lightly browned. Makes 3 dozen.

Mrs. Danny Young
Marshall County

CHERRY WINKS

2½ c. flour	1 c. dates,
1 t. baking	chopped
powder	⅓ c. maraschino
½ t. soda	cherries,
½ t. salt᾿	drained and
¾ c. butter	chopped
1 c. sugar	maraschino cher-
2 eggs	ries, cut in
2 T. milk	fourths
1 t. vanilla	2½ c. corn flakes,
1 c. pecans,	coarsely
chopped	crushed

Sift together flour, baking powder, soda, and salt. Cream butter. Gradually add sugar and cream well. Add eggs, milk, and vanilla and beat well. Add pecans, dates, and cherries. Drop by rounded teaspoonfuls into corn flakes. Toss lightly to coat. Shape into balls and place on greased cookie sheet. Top each with ¼ maraschino cherry. Bake 12–15 min. at 375°.

Mary Roberts
Steuben County

CORNMEAL COOKIES

¾ c. shortening	1 t. baking
¾ c. sugar	powder
1 egg	¼ t. salt
1½ c. flour	1 t. vanilla
½ c. yellow or	½ c. raisins
white cornmeal	(optional)

Mix shortening, sugar, and egg; beat well. Add rest of ingredients and mix well.

CRY BABY COOKIES (200-Years-Old Recipe)

½ c. sugar	1 t. soda
½ c. sorghum	½ c. strong coffee
molasses	1 t. ginger
½ c. shortening	2½ c. flour
½ c. raisins	1 t. cinnamon
½ c. chopped	¼ t. salt
nuts	

Cream sugar and shortening; add sorghum. Dissolve soda in coffee; add to shortening, sugar, and molasses. Stir together flour, cinnamon, ginger, and salt; add to liquid mix. Add sugar and nuts. Drop by teaspoonfuls on greased cookie sheets. Bake at 375° for 15 min. Cool 5 min. Remove with spatula.

Edith Wiseman
Crawford County

FORGOTTEN COOKIES

2 egg whites	½ c. broken
¾ c. sugar	pecans
1 c. chocolate bits	

Beat egg whites, adding sugar very gradually. Beat until very stiff. Do not *under* beat. Fold in chocolate and nuts. Drop by teaspoonfuls on foil-covered cookie sheets. Put in preheated 325° oven. Turn off heat immediately, and go to bed. Leave in oven at least 4 hr.

Louise Schuman
Noble County

MOTHER'S FRUIT COOKIES

1½ c. brown sugar	4 c. flour
1 c. shortening	½ box raisins
½ c. molasses	1 t. soda
¼ c. warm water	½ t. nutmeg
	2 eggs

Cream sugar and shortening; add eggs. Dissolve soda in warm water and add molasses; add to cream mixture. Mix in dry ingredients and raisins. Drop by spoonfuls on greased cookie sheet. Flatten out and bake at 375°. Makes 8 dozen.

Mrs. Noah Graber
Adams County

SOFT MOLASSES COOKIES

1½ c. unsifted flour	⅓ c. brown sugar, firmly packed
½ t. baking soda	
¼ t. salt	⅓ c. dark molasses
½ c. (¼ lb.) butter	3 T. apple butter
1 large egg	6 T. buttermilk

On waxed paper or in bowl, stir together the flour, baking soda, and salt. In small mixer bowl cream butter and sugar; thoroughly beat in egg, molasses, and apple butter. Stir in flour alternately with buttermilk. Drop by level tablespoonfuls on greased cookie sheets. Bake at 350° until edges are browned. About 15 min. Makes 3–4 dozen.

Mrs. Wandalee Bonnewell
Owen County

PUMPKIN COOKIES

1 c. sugar	1 t. vanilla
1 c. shortening	1 t. soda
1 c. pumpkin	1 t. baking powder
1 egg	
1 t. cinnamon	
½ t. salt	
2 c. flour	
½ c. chopped nuts	

Icing:
3 T. butter
4 T. milk
½ c. brown sugar
powdered sugar

Cream sugar and shortening; add pumpkin, egg, and vanilla. Add sifted dry ingredients and nuts. Drop by teaspoonfuls onto baking sheet. Bake at 350° for 10–12 min. Cool and ice. Combine butter, milk, and brown sugar. Boil for 3 min. Cool. Add enough powdered sugar for spreading consistency. Spread on cookies. Makes 5 dozen.

Marie Shelp
Ripley County

PECAN DREAMS

⅛ t. salt	3 T. flour
2 egg whites	1½ t. vanilla
1 c. brown sugar, firmly packed	2 c. pecans, chopped

Add salt to egg whites and beat until very stiff and dry. Mix together brown sugar and flour. Fold into beaten egg whites. Add vanilla and nuts. Drop on ungreased cookie sheet and bake at 350° for 10 min. Let cool before removing from cookie sheet. Makes 2–3 dozen.

Mrs. Lloyd Miller
Boone County

PERSIMMON COOKIES

1 c. white sugar	2 c. flour
1 c. brown sugar	1 t. cinnamon
½ c. margarine	½ t. nutmeg
1 egg	½ t. ginger
1 t. vanilla	1 c. dates, chopped
1 c. persimmon pulp	1 c. nuts, chopped
1 t. baking soda	

Cream sugars with margarine. Add egg and vanilla. Add persimmon pulp mixed with soda. Sift flour with spices and add, blending well. Stir in dates and nuts. Drop by teaspoonfuls onto greased cookie sheets. Bake at 350° for 10–12 min. Will be cake-like. Makes 6–8 dozen.

Patricia Harmon
Harrison County

PINEAPPLE DROP COOKIES

1 c. brown sugar	2 eggs
1 c. white sugar	½ t. salt
1 c. shortening	1 t. baking soda
1 c. crushed pineapple	2 t. baking powder
1 c. nuts, finely ground	4 c. flour
	1 t. vanilla

Cream sugars and shortening together. Add pineapple, eggs, nuts, salt, soda, baking powder, and vanilla; mix well. Slowly add flour. Drop by teaspoon onto greased cookie sheets. Bake at 375° for 12–15 min. Makes 5 dozen.

Barbara Helfrich
Dearborn County

SORGHUM COOKIES

¾ c. shortening	¼ t. salt
1 c. sorghum	1 t. cinnamon
2 eggs	½ t. ginger
3½ c. flour	½ c. milk
4 t. baking powder	½ t. soda
	1 c. raisins

Combine ingredients. Drop from spoon on greased baking sheet. Bake 15 min. at 350°.

Wilma Dayhuff
Owen County

AMISH SUGAR COOKIES

2½ c. sugar	1 T. soda
2 eggs	1½ t. baking powder
1 c. milk	
½ c. buttermilk	1 t. vanilla
1½ c. lard	7 c. flour

Combine all ingredients except flour and mix well. Then add enough flour for soft-drop consistency. Drop by tablespoonfuls on ungreased cookie sheet; press down with a glass and sprinkle with sugar. Bake for 10–12 min. at 350°. Makes 4 dozen.

Janet Lortie
Noble County

OLD-FASHIONED WINE COOKIES

1 c. butter	1 t. salt
1 c. sugar	3 c. flour
2 T. preserves or jelly	3 c. oats
1 t. soda	1 pony whiskey or wine
2 t. cinnamon	4 eggs, beaten

Cream butter, sugar, jelly, and eggs. Add flour, soda, cinnamon, and salt. Mix thoroughly. Add oats and wine. Drop by teaspoonfuls onto ungreased cookie sheet. Bake at 375° until set.

Janice Winiger
Posey County

BAR COOKIES

APPLE SQUARES

½ c. soft margarine	½ t. baking powder
1 c. sugar	1 t. cinnamon
1 egg	2 c. apples, thinly sliced
1 c. flour	
½ t. soda	½ c. walnuts, chopped
¼ t. salt	

Cream margarine and sugar. Add egg and

dry ingredients. Mix in apples and walnuts. Bake in 8" or 9" square pan at 350°
for 35–40 min.

Mrs. Wayne Matz
Marshall County

BROWNIES

2 c. flour	Brownie Frosting:
2 c. sugar	1 stick margarine
½ t. salt	3 T. cocoa
2 sticks marga-	6 T. milk
rine	1 1-lb. pkg.
1 c. water	powdered
3 T. cocoa	sugar
2 eggs, well	½ c. chopped
beaten	nuts
1 t. soda	1 t. vanilla
½ c. buttermilk	
1 t. vanilla	

Sift flour, sugar, and salt. Put margarine,
water, and cocoa in saucepan; bring to
boil. Pour boiling mixture over flour-sugar
mixture. In another bowl put eggs, buttermilk, soda, and vanilla. Add to above mixture and mix well. Bake at 350° in
greased, floured 10×15" pan for 20–25
min. or 9×13" pan for 25–30 min. Pour
Brownie Frosting over hot brownies as
soon as they come from oven. Mix frosting
ingredients in saucepan. Heat over low
flame. Bring to boil, but do not boil. Remove from stove and add powdered sugar,
nuts, and vanilla. Pour over brownies.
Makes 1 dozen.

Marcia Powers
Greene County

HONEY BROWNIES

½ c. butter or	1 c. sugar
margarine	1 c. plus 2 T.
4 eggs	flour, sifted

4 oz. unsweetened	1 c. honey
chocolate	1 c. chopped nuts
½ t. salt	

Melt butter and chocolate over low heat in
heavy saucepan. Beat eggs and salt in mixing bowl until light. Add sugar and honey
gradually and continue beating mixture
until very light. Add melted chocolate and
butter. Stir in flour, then add nuts. Pour
into 9" square pan. Bake at 325° for 50–
60 min.

Mrs. Ken Blessinger
Dubois County

MINT BROWNIES

1 c. butter	1 T. cream
4 sq. chocolate	dash of salt
2 c. sugar	1½ t. mint
4 whole eggs	flavoring
1½ c. flour	green food
½ c. nuts	coloring
2 t. vanilla	
	Fudge Frosting:
Mint Topping:	2 sq. semisweet
1 egg white	chocolate
2 c. confection-	3 T. butter
ers' sugar	1 box confection-
2 T. butter,	ers' sugar
melted	cream, as needed

Melt butter and chocolate. Cool. Add
sugar and eggs. Mix well. Add flour, nuts,
and vanilla. Pour into buttered 9×13"
pan. Bake 20–25 min. at 350°. Cool.
Spread with mint topping and fudge frosting. Mint Topping: Beat egg white, adding sugar gradually. Add melted butter,
cream, salt, mint flavoring, and coloring.
Spread on brownies. Fudge Frosting: Melt
chocolate and butter. Mix with sugar and
enough cream to make a soft frosting.
Makes 2 dozen.

Mrs. Cecil Austin
Hendricks County

CHEESECAKE COOKIES

1 c. flour	1 8-oz. pkg.
⅓ c. butter, softened	cream cheese, softened
⅓ c. brown sugar, firmly packed	¼ c. sugar
	1 egg
	2 T. milk
½ c. walnuts, chopped	2 T. lemon juice
	½ t. vanilla

In large bowl combine flour, butter, and brown sugar. Blend with mixer until particles are fine. Stir in walnuts. Reserve 1 c. for topping. Press remainder in ungreased 8″ square pan. Bake at 350° for 12–15 min. In same mixer bowl combine remaining ingredients. Blend well. Spread over partially baked crust. Sprinkle with reserved crumb mixture. Bake at 350° for 25–30 min. Cool. Cut into 16 squares.

Mrs. Tom Tillison
Rush County

CHERRY COCONUT BARS

Pastry:	½ t. baking powder
1 c. sifted flour	¼ t. salt
½ c. butter	1 t. vanilla
3 T. confectioners' sugar	¾ c. walnuts, chopped
	½ c. coconut
Filling:	½ c. maraschino cherries, quartered
2 eggs, beaten	
1 c. sugar	
¼ c. flour	

With hands mix flour, butter, and powdered sugar until smooth. Spread thin with fingers in greased 9×9″ pan. Bake at 350° for 15 min. Filling: Stir rest of ingredients into eggs. Spread over top of baked pastry while hot and bake 25 min. longer. Cool and cut into squares. Makes 20.

Anna Belle Wever
Lawrence County

CONGO SQUARES (Butterscotch Brownies)

1 6-oz. pkg. chocolate bits	2¼ c. flour
	2½ t. baking powder
¾ c. shortening or butter	½ t. salt
2¼ c. brown sugar	1 c. nuts, chopped
3 eggs	

Melt shortening; add brown sugar. Cool. Add eggs one at a time. Sift flour and other ingredients in saucepan and mix well. Add nuts and chocolate pieces. Pour into well-greased 7½×11×1½″ pan. Bake at 325° for 25 min. Makes 16 squares.

Beverly Shoemaker
Boone County

LEMON BARS

Crust:	4 T. lemon juice
½ lb. margarine	1 t. baking powder
2 c. flour	
½ c. confectioners' sugar	¼ t. grated lemon peel
	2 c. sugar
Filling:	4 T. flour
4 eggs, beaten slightly	

Mix crust ingredients with electric mixer until dough is crumbly. Press into ungreased 9×13″ pan. Bake at 350° for 20 min. Turns lightly brown. Mix filling ingredients and pour over baked crust. Bake 25 min., or until top is brown and filling is set. Sprinkle with confectioners' sugar.

Ann Apple
Orange County

MEXICAN MUD-HEN BARS

½ c. shortening (part butter)	1 c. sugar
	1 whole egg

2 eggs, separated
1½ c. flour
1 t. baking powder
¼ t. salt
1 c. nuts, chopped
½ c. chocolate bits
1 c. miniature marshmallows
1 c. light brown sugar, packed

Preheat oven to 350°. Cream shortening and sugar. Beat in the whole egg and 2 egg yolks. Sift flour, baking powder, and salt together; combine the two mixtures; blend thoroughly. Spread batter in 9×13″ pan. Sprinkle nuts, chocolate bits and marshmallows over the batter. Beat the 2 egg whites stiff; fold in brown sugar. Spread over top of cake. Bake 30–40 min. Makes 32 bars.

Mrs. Penn Peek
Wells County

MINCEMEAT PIE BARS

2½ c. sifted flour
1 t. salt
1 c. shortening
5–6 T. water
2 c. prepared mincemeat
2 T. sugar, for top

Combine flour and salt; cut in shortening until crumbly. Add enough water to make dough moist enough to hold together. Divide dough in half. Roll ½ on floured surface to make 14×9″ rectangle. Place on ungreased baking sheet. Spread mincemeat to within ½″ of edges. Roll remaining ½ of dough to 14×9″ rectangle. Place on mincemeat; seal edges with fork. Prick top with fork. Sprinkle with sugar. Bake at 400° for 30 min., or until golden. Cut in 2″ squares. Makes 28.

Margueriette Lowe
Randolph County

PEANUT BREAKFAST BARS

½ c. butter
½ c. light brown sugar, firmly packed
½ c. white sugar
2 eggs
½ t. vanilla
1½ c. quick-cooking oats
¾ c. whole wheat flour
½ t. soda
¼ t. salt
1 c. peanuts, coarsely chopped
½ c. seedless raisins

Icing:
½ c. confectioners' sugar
2 T. milk
2 T. peanut butter
½ t. vanilla

Cream butter, sugars, eggs, and vanilla. Mix oats, flour, soda, peanuts, and raisins. Pat mixture evenly into greased 8″ square pan. Bake 30 min. at 350°. Cool in pan. Icing: In a small saucepan, combine sugar, milk, and peanut butter. Cook over medium heat, stirring constantly, until it reaches a full boil. Continue boiling and stirring for 2 min. Remove from heat and add vanilla. Immediately drizzle icing over bars and cool. Makes 16 2″ bars.

Mrs. Bess Study
Jennings County

PUMPKIN BARS

2 c. flour
2 t. baking powder
1 t. soda
½ t. salt
1 t. pumpkin pie spice
2 c. sugar
4 eggs
1 16-oz. can pumpkin
1 c. salad oil
1 c. chopped nuts

Frosting:
3 oz. cream cheese
6 T. margarine
1 t. vanilla
1 T. milk
2 c. sifted powdered sugar, or until desired consistency

Sift together the first 6 ingredients. Add the next 4 ingredients. Mix together well. Pour into greased 17×11″ pan. Bake at 350° for 20–25 min. Cool. Make frosting. Frost and cut into bars. Makes 20–24 bars.

Carole Moore
Union County

RAISIN NUT BARS

1 c. raisins	1 t. baking
2 c. water	powder
½ c. shortening	1 t. soda
1½ c. sugar	1 t. salt
2 eggs, beaten	½ c. nuts,
3 c. flour, sifted	chopped

Boil raisins in water until it boils down to a little more than ½ c. Cream shortening and sugar. Add eggs. Sift baking powder, soda, and salt with flour. Add this to the other ingredients and blend well. Add nuts and raisins. Spread on lightly greased and floured cookie sheet. Bake 25 min. at 350°. Ice while hot with powdered sugar frosting.

Mrs. Sam Lehman
Kosciusko County

TOFFEE BARS

½ c. soft butter	½ c. uncooked
or margarine	rolled oats
¼ c. granulated	1 6-oz. pkg. semi-
sugar	sweet chocolate
¼ c. brown sugar	bits
¼ t. salt	¼ c. flaked
1 t. vanilla	coconut
1 egg, unbeaten	¼ c. walnuts,
½ c. flour, sifted	chopped

Mix first 6 ingredients until light and fluffy. Add flour and rolled oats; blend well. Spread in 11×7×1½″ pan. Bake at 350° for 30 min., or until done. Cool 10

min. Melt chocolate over hot water, stir until smooth; spread over baked layer. Sprinkle with nuts and coconut. Cool in pan. Cut into bars.

Mrs. Norman Gray
Noble County

SHAPED COOKIES

BROOMSTICK COOKIES

6 c. sugar	1 pt. water
3 c. lard	5 eggs
1 pt. sorghum	1 lb. roasted
molasses	peanuts
15 c. unsifted	2 lb. raisins
flour (less to	9 t. soda
make very soft	2 t. salt
dough)	

Mix altogether; chill a few hours or overnight. Make into rolls the diameter of a broomstick and place on greased cookie sheet lengthwise a few inches apart. Bake at 350°. Cut when baked. Makes about 20 dozen.

Nettie Singleton and Sue King
Adams County

CHOCOLATE CHEWS

½ c. shortening	2 c. flour
4 sq. chocolate	⅛ t. salt
2 c. sugar	½ c. nuts,
2 t. vanilla	chopped
4 eggs	powdered sugar,
2 t. baking	sifted
powder	

Melt together shortening, chocolate, sugar, and vanilla. Beat in eggs, one at a time. Sift together flour, baking powder, and salt, and add to mixture. Add nuts. Chill dough. Then form into small balls and roll in sifted powdered sugar. Bake on greased cookie sheet at 350° for 10 min. Makes 5 dozen.

Mrs. Gaylord Cole
Morgan County

OATMEAL REFRIGERATOR COOKIES

1 c. shortening or butter	3 c. quick-cooking oats
1 c. granulated sugar	1½ c. flour
1 c. brown sugar	1 t. soda
2 eggs	1 t. salt
	1 t. vanilla

Cream shortening and sugar. Beat in eggs; then add rest of ingredients and mix. Put dough in refrigerator at least 1 hr. Then roll dough into small balls and put onto greased cookie sheet. Flatten with a glass. Bake 8–10 min. at 400°. Do not overbake. Makes 3 dozen.

Connie Martin
Clay County

PEPPER NUTS

1 lb. brown sugar	1 t. soda to which
4 eggs	a little vinegar
1 T. cinnamon	has been added
3 T. syrup or honey	1 t. nutmeg
1 t. vanilla	1 t. black pepper
	about 3 c. flour

Mix all ingredients and add enough flour (about 3 c.) to make a stiff dough. Chill. Roll into small balls and press flat. Bake at 300° for 10–12 min. on lightly greased cookie sheet.

Mrs. Hilbert Fischer
Dubois County

ROYAL COCONUT COOKIES

1¼ c. sifted flour	½ t. salt
1 t. baking powder	½ c. granulated sugar

1 t. soda	½ t. almond or
½ c. brown sugar	vanilla extract
½ c. butter or shortening	1 c. oats, uncooked
1 egg	1 c. coconut

Sift together flour, baking powder, soda, and salt into bowl. Add sugars, butter, egg, and flavoring. Beat until smooth (about 2 min.). Fold in oats and coconut. Shape dough into small balls; place on greased baking sheet. Bake at 350° for 12–15 min. Makes 3 dozen.

Emma Sommer
Jefferson County

SHORTBREAD COOKIES

1 c. butter	2 c. flour
¼ c. granulated sugar	1 c. pecans, chopped
¾ t. salt	½ c. confectioners' sugar
1 t. vanilla	

Mix thoroughly butter, granulated sugar, and vanilla. Work in flour, salt, and nuts until the dough holds together. Shape the dough into 1″ balls and place them on an ungreased baking sheet. Bake at 400° for 10–12 min., or until set but not brown. While warm, roll in confectioners' sugar. Cool and roll in sugar again. Makes 40.

Betty McDill
Union County

SNICKER DOODLES

1 c. shortening	2 t. cream of tartar
1½ c. sugar	½ t. salt
2 eggs	4 T. sugar
2¾ c. flour	2 t. cinnamon
1 t. soda	

Combine shortening, 1½ c. sugar, and eggs and mix well. Add flour, cream of tartar, soda, and salt. Roll into balls and then roll in mixture of 4 T. sugar and cinnamon. Place 2″ apart on ungreased cookie sheet. Bake 8–10 min. at 375°.

Kathleen Ingle
Crawford County

TRIPLET COOKIES

Basic Cookie	2 eggs
Recipe:	2½ c. flour
1 c. brown sugar	1 t. salt
1 c. sugar	1 t. soda
1 c. shortening	

Cream sugar, shortening, and eggs. Spoon flour into measuring cup and level. Add salt and soda to flour and stir to blend. Add blended dry ingredients to creamed mixture and mix well.

Variations: ⅓ c. chocolate bits; ½ c. powdered sugar. Melt chocolate bits over hot water. Add to 1 portion of dough. Shape dough into 1″ balls and roll in powdered sugar. Place on greased baking sheet. Bake at 350° for 15–18 min.

Or: ½ c. cut-up dates; ½ c. chopped nuts. Add to basic dough. Make 1″ balls and bake at 350° for 15–18 min.

Or: Add ½ c. chocolate bits to basic dough. Make 1″ balls and bake at 350° for 15–18 min.

Mary Lou Decker
Wells County

REFRIGERATOR COOKIES

OLD-FASHIONED ICE-BOX COOKIES

2 c. brown sugar,	2 t. baking
packed	powder
½ c. lard	3–4 c. flour, or
½ c. butter	enough to make
2 eggs	a firm dough
1 t. soda	

Cream sugar and shortening; add eggs and beat. Add dry ingredients and mix well. Shape into rolls. Wrap in waxed paper. Store overnight in ice box. Slice ¼″ thick. Bake in moderate (375°) oven until browned.

Edith Wiseman
Crawford County

DATE-NUT REFRIGERATOR COOKIES

¼ c. (½ stick)	½ t. cream of
butter	tartar
1 c. brown sugar	½ t. cinnamon
½ t. vanilla	¼ c. dates, finely
1 egg, unbeaten	chopped
1¼ c. flour	¼ c. nuts, finely
⅛ t. salt	chopped
½ t. soda	

Combine butter, sugar, vanilla, and egg; beat until light and fluffy. Sift flour, salt, soda, cream of tartar, and cinnamon. Stir into first mixture. Stir in dates and nuts. Shape dough into long roll about 1½″ in diameter. Wrap in foil or freezer paper. Chill in refrigerator overnight. Slice thin; bake on greased baking sheet at 375° for 7–10 min., or until done. Makes 4 dozen crisp cookies.

Mrs. Leon Phillips
Fountain County

PEANUT WHIRLS

½ c. shortening	1¼ c. flour
1 c. sugar	½ t. salt
½ c. chunky-style	½ t. soda
peanut butter	2 T. milk
1 egg	1 pkg. chocolate
1 t. vanilla	chips

Cream shortening, sugar, peanut butter, vanilla, and egg. Add sifted dry ingredients alternately with milk. Roll out dough to rectangle ¼″ thick. Melt chocolate chips over hot water and cool slightly. Spread on rolled dough. Roll jelly-roll fashion and chill at least ½ hr. Slice and bake at 350° for 8–10 min.

Mrs. Lewis Wallace
Martin County

ROLLED COOKIES

ANGEL WINGS (Polish *Chouscik*)

5 egg yolks	1 T. brandy or
½ t. salt	rum
3 T. sugar	1 T. lemon juice
5 T. sour cream	1 t. lemon rind
2½ c. flour	confectioners'
1 t. vanilla	sugar

Add salt to eggs and beat until thick. Add sugar and all flavorings and continue to beat. Add sour cream and flour alternately, mixing well after each addition. Knead on floured board until dough blisters (about 15 min.). Using only part of dough at a time, roll out thin and cut each cookie 3×1½″. Cut a slit in middle, pull one end through slit. Fry in deep oil, about 3 seconds on each side. It should be tan color, not brown. Place on paper towel. Put on plate; sprinkle with confectioners' sugar.

Helen Carr
Owen County

CHERRY FILLED COOKIES

Dough:	2½ c. flour
½ c. shortening	¼ t. soda
1 c. sugar	½ t. salt
2 eggs	
2 T. thick cream	Cherry Filling:
1 t. vanilla	1 c. sugar

5 T. (⅓ c.) flour	1 qt. cherries and
½ t. cinnamon	juice
1½ T. butter	

Dough: Mix shortening, sugar, and eggs. Stir in rest of ingredients. Filling: Heat ingredients in saucepan. To make cookies: Roll out dough and cut with a cookie cutter. Line miniature muffin pans with circles of dough. Fill with cherry filling. Top with small circle of dough from doughnut cutter. Bake at 400° for 8–10 min. Makes 50–60.

Dorothy Overmyer
Marshall County

DUTCH KNEE PATCHES

4 eggs	pinch of salt
¼ t. soda	5–6 c. flour, to
½ c. milk	make stiff
butter, the size	dough
of an egg	

Mix flour into milk, eggs, soft butter, soda, and salt. Mix and divide into parts, 1½″ in diameter. Roll out and put between waxed paper. When all have been rolled out, heat fat to deep fry. Stretch the rolled-out pieces over your hand until very thin. Drop into hot fat. Fry a few seconds and turn over, fry a few seconds longer. Drain on paper towels. Makes 2½ dozen. Sprinkle with sugar when cool.

Mrs. Gilbert Stucky
Adams County

GREEK COOKIES

1 lb. unsalted	1 shot of whiskey
margarine	juice of ½
1 c. sifted pow-	orange
dered sugar	cake flour, about
2 egg yolks	¾ of box

Cream margarine with mixer 20–30 min. Add sugar; beat well. Add whiskey, egg yolks, and orange juice. Add enough flour to make a soft dough. Roll dough ¾" thick; cut with cutters. Slightly grease cookie sheet. Bake at 350° for 20–30 min. While cookies are still hot, sprinkle with powdered sugar.

Anne M. Novosel
Lake County

ITALIAN FRUIT CRUNCH COOKIES

Dough:	
½ c. soft butter	4 dried figs
½ c. sugar	6 dried peaches
1 t. vanilla	¼ c. candied
3 c. flour	cherries
1 t. baking	¼ c. citron
powder	⅔ c. honey
1 t. salt	⅛ t. allspice
¼ c. milk	⅛ t. cinnamon
1 egg	
	For Top:
Fruit Filling:	1 egg yolk
⅓ c. pitted dates	1 T. water
¾ c. dried	almonds, finely
apricots	sliced
	tiny colored
	candies

Dough: Cream butter; add sugar, egg, and vanilla. Beat until light. Add dry ingredients and milk. Mix well. Chill several hours or overnight. Filling: Force the fruits and citron through chopper. Add honey and spices. Mix well. Refrigerate while dough chills. To make cookies: Roll dough thin on floured board and cut in 2½" squares. Put 1 t. of filling down center of each square and roll up. Brush with mixture of egg yolk and water. Sprinkle with almonds and candies. Bake at 375° for 10 min.

Mrs. Roy Barnes
Elkhart County

KIEFLIES (Hungarian Filled Cookies)

Dough:	Filling:
1 lb. butter	3 lb. shelled
16 oz. sour cream	English walnuts
4 egg yolks,	2 c. sugar
slightly beaten	1 t. vanilla
4 T. sugar	1 c. warm water
8 c. flour, sifted	powdered sugar

Dough: Mix all ingredients together thoroughly; cover and refrigerate at least 2 hr. Prepare filling: Grind walnuts. Mix sugar, vanilla, and water. Stir into walnuts. Place in warm oven (300°), stirring often until sugar melts. To make cookies: Pinch off piece of dough the size of a walnut and roll very thin (⅛") on slightly floured board. It will make a 4–6" circle depending on size of dough ball. Place a heaping tablespoon of filling on dough, close to one edge, shaping filling into a "finger." Begin rolling dough over filling and bring ends of dough in over filling to seal. Continue rolling to opposite edge, shaping cookie into a crescent. Dough will make a double-layered covering over filling. Cookies will be approximately 3" in length and slightly bigger around than your thumb. (Size is determined by dough ball and amount of filling.) Space cookies about 1" apart on slightly greased cookie sheet. Bake 10 min. at 375°, until they just turn light gold around edges. Remove onto paper towels. Sprinkle with powdered sugar. Cool. Makes 12 dozen medium-sized kieflies.

Mrs. Albert E. Wilson
St. Joseph County

LOLLIPOP COOKIES

1 c. butter	½ t. almond
1 egg	flavoring

1½ c. sifted confectioners' sugar
1 t. vanilla
2½ c. flour
1 t. soda
1 t. cream of tartar

Easy Creamy Frosting:
4 c. confectioners' sugar
1 t. salt
2 t. vanilla
about 6 T. cream

Mix sugar and butter. Add egg and flavorings; mix thoroughly. Stir dry ingredients together and blend in. Refrigerate 2–3 hr. wrapped in Saran Wrap. Divide dough in half and roll ³⁄₁₆″ thick on lightly floured pastry cloth. Cut with 3″ cookie cutter. Place on lightly greased baking sheet. Bake at 375° for 7–8 min., or until delicately golden. Cool. Frosting: Blend sugar, salt, and vanilla. Add enough cream for spreading consistency. To make lollipop: Spread frosting on plain baked cookie with spatula or pastry brush. Place a flat wooden stick across the middle, letting one end extend beyond edge of cookie. Place another cookie on top; press down slightly. Decorate with faces of tinted icing. Makes 18 lollipops.

Mrs. Homer Allbright
Orange County

SORGHUM MOLASSES COOKIES

1 c. lard
1 c. brown sugar
½ t. salt

2 c. sorghum molasses
3 level T. soda

1 c. buttermilk
3 t. ginger
1 t. cinnamon

flour to make a stiff dough

Cream lard and brown sugar. Add molasses, soda dissolved in buttermilk, and ginger, salt, and cinnamon sifted with flour. Put in refrigerator overnight. Work with small amount of dough at a time, keeping balance refrigerated. Roll out (adding a little more flour if necessary), cut (sprinkle with sugar, if desired), and bake at 375°.

Viva Moore
Martin County

SOUR CREAM SUGAR COOKIES

3 eggs
2 c. sugar
1 c. shortening
¼ t. nutmeg
¼ t. salt
1 c. thick sour cream

1 t. soda
2 t. baking powder
5½ c. flour, reserve 1 c. for dusting

Beat eggs to creamy froth. Add sugar and mix well. Add shortening. Add nutmeg and salt. Add soda and baking powder to sour cream. Beat vigorously with a spoon until mixture doubles in bulk. Add this to first mixture, then blend in 4½ c. flour. Roll on floured board and cut out cookies. Place on cookie sheet; sprinkle with sugar before baking. Bake at 375°.

Evelyn Jarboe
Whitley County

Candy

MRS. MEEK'S OLD-FASHIONED BOURBON BALLS

1 lb. powdered sugar

1 c. pecans, finely chopped

1 stick butter
10 sq. semisweet chocolate

¼ c. bourbon
3 T. paraffin, melted

Beat sugar, bourbon, and butter until light

and fluffy. Add pecans. Shape in a ball and place in bowl. Cover with wet cloth and chill overnight. Roll into balls the size of walnuts. Put on cookie sheet and freeze. Melt chocolate and melted paraffin in top of double boiler. Bring a few balls at a time from freezer and dip in chocolate. (Ice tea spoon coats balls best. Don't use fingers; it leaves chocolate without gloss.) Put balls in waxed paper and return to freezer. Makes 2 dozen.

Mrs. H. K. Ulreich
Hamilton County

CARAMELS

2 c. heavy or	2 c. sugar
whipping	1 c. milk
cream	2 t. vanilla
1½ c. light corn	extract
syrup	

In 4-qt. heavy saucepan heat cream, sugar, and corn syrup to boiling, stirring frequently. Continue cooking until temperature reaches 234°, or soft-ball stage. Gradually add milk, stirring constantly. Continue cooking and stirring until temperature reaches 246°, or firm-ball stage. Remove pan from heat. Stir in vanilla. Pour into 13×9″ greased pan on wire rack and cool completely. Invert mixture from pan onto cutting board and cut into ¾″ squares. To store, wrap each piece in plastic wrap, if desired, and keep tightly covered in cool place. Makes about 2 pounds.

Barbara Musgrave
Monroe County

EASY CARAMELS

1 c. butter or	dash of salt
margarine	1 15-oz. can (1⅓
1 lb. (2¼ c.)	c.) sweetened
brown sugar	condensed milk

1 c. light corn	1 t. vanilla
syrup	

Melt butter in heavy 3-qt. saucepan. Add brown sugar and salt, stirring thoroughly. Blend in corn syrup; gradually add milk, stirring constantly. Cook and stir over medium heat until candy reaches firm-ball stage (245°). Remove from heat; stir in vanilla. Pour into buttered 9×9×2″ baking dish. Cool thoroughly. Cut in small squares. Wrap each piece in clear plastic wrap, if desired. Makes 2½ pounds.

Mrs. Virgil Dixon
Pulaski County

CARAMEL CLUSTERS

2 c. nuts	½ c. light corn
1 c. sugar	syrup
⅓ c. brown sugar	½ c. butter
¾ c. milk	¼ t. salt
1 t. vanilla	

In 2-qt. saucepan combine sugars, milk, corn syrup, butter, and salt. Over medium heat bring to a boil, stirring constantly until sugar dissolves and butter melts. Continue to cook, stirring occasionally, until mixture reaches 248° on candy thermometer. Remove from heat; add vanilla and nuts. Stir lightly until mixture just starts to hold shape. Drop by tablespoonfuls onto buttered baking sheets. Cool at room temperature (might have to shape some with hands as candy cools.) Wrap individually, if desired, and store in tightly covered container. Makes 48.

Roselyn McKittrick
Ripley County

CHOCOLATE BALLS

1 can Eagle	1 pkg. flaked
Brand milk	coconut
¼ lb. margarine	8 t. vanilla

2 lb. powdered sugar
1 c. nuts

1 12-oz. pkg. chocolate chips
½ cake paraffin

Mix first 6 ingredients and drop by teaspoon on cookie sheet. Chill overnight. Roll into balls and chill again. Melt chocolate chips and paraffin and dip the balls. Makes about 100.

Mary H. Smith
Lawrence County

CHRISTMAS DAINTIES

4 c. sugar
¼ t. salt
1½ c. boiling water
4 T. plain gelatin
1 c. cold water

red and green food coloring
½ t. peppermint extract
1 t. cinnamon extract

Heat sugar, salt and 1½ cups boiling water to boiling point. Meanwhile pour 1 c. cold water over gelatin. Add to hot syrup and stir until dissolved. Boil slowly 15 min. Take from fire and divide into 2 equal parts. Color ½ red and flavor with peppermint extract. Color other ½ green and flavor with cinnamon extract. Pour into two 4×8″ pans. Let stand overnight, or at least 12 hr. Turn out on granulated sugar and cut into squares with wet sharp knife. Roll in sugar.

June Harbison
Putnam County

CREAM CANDY

⅛ t. cream of tartar
4 c. sugar
2 c. cream
2 T. light corn syrup
1 t. vanilla
food coloring (optional)

chopped nuts, crushed peppermint candy, coconut, or cinnamon drops (optional)
chocolate (optional)

Mix cream of tartar with sugar in heavy 1½-gal. pan. Add cream and syrup. Place over medium heat; wipe sides of pan with damp cloth. Boil to 240°; remove immediately from heat. Add vanilla. Put candy in Pyrex dish rinsed in cold water. Let cool until lukewarm (about 1 hr.). Beat until candy becomes hard; cover with wet towel for 1 hr. Take small amount of candy at a time and knead until free of lumps. Shape candy in rolls or pieces and wrap in Saran Wrap. Food coloring may be added when candy is lukewarm. Nuts, peppermint candy, coconut, or cinnamon drops may be added while candy is being kneaded. After candy has been shaped, chocolate may be melted and drizzled over rolls. Makes 2½–3 pounds.

Note: Do not use more cream of tartar than recipe calls for or candy will never harden. Do not use evaporated milk, which has a tendency to boil over more than cream, and this candy boils over easily.

Avis Risk
Putnam County

CINNAMON HARD CANDY

2 c. sugar
⅔ c. light corn syrup
1 c. water

½ T. red food coloring
¼ t. oil of cinnamon

Combine sugar, syrup, and water in saucepan. Stir over heat until dissolved. Cook without stirring until hard-crack stage or brittle thread forms in cold water. Add cinnamon oil and coloring. Pour into shallow buttered pan. When hard, break into pieces.

Edith Hanha
Floyd County

DIP CANDY

1 stick butter, softened	1 t. vanilla
1 small pkg. cream cheese	1 can flaked coconut
2 boxes powdered sugar	1 c. pecans, chopped
1 can Eagle Brand milk	1 12-oz. pkg. chocolate chips
	1 stick paraffin

Cream butter and cream cheese. Add sugar and milk gradually. Add coconut, pecans, and vanilla. Let chill thoroughly, then form into small balls. Shave paraffin into top of double boiler to melt. Add chips. Stir until melted. Dip balls into chocolate mixture. Cool on waxed paper.

Donna Overton
Posey County

DIVINITY PUFFS

2 egg whites	¾ c. nuts, chopped (optional)
2½ c. sugar	
½ c. water	
½ c. light corn syrup	½ t. vanilla

Beat egg whites until stiff. Combine sugar, water, and corn syrup. Cook to thin stage or 234° on candy thermometer. Pour half of syrup mixture over egg whites. Stir constantly while pouring. Cook remaining half of syrup mixture to 260°. Pour over egg whites, beating constantly. Beat until mixture holds shape. Add vanilla and nuts, if desired. Swirl from teaspoon onto waxed paper. Makes 24 pieces.

Lillian Freschly
Spencer County

EASY DIVINITY

¾ c. light corn syrup	4 c. sugar
	¾ c. water

2 egg whites	1 c. nuts
1 pkg. flavored Jello	½ c. grated coconut

Grease 9″ square pan thoroughly. Then mix sugar, corn syrup, and water in a saucepan and cook to boiling point, stirring constantly. Reduce heat and continue cooking, stirring occasionally, until few drops in cold water form a hard ball (252°). Meanwhile, beat egg whites until they fluff up, then add the dry Jello gradually, beating until mixture holds a definite peak. Pour the syrup into the egg white mixture in a thin, thin stream, beating constantly until candy holds its shape and loses its gloss. Stir in nuts and coconut, and quickly pour into pan. Divinity cuts more satisfactorily if you keep dipping knife into hot water during cutting process. Makes 5 dozen pieces.

Carol Sargent
Pulaski County

NO-FAIL DIVINITY

1 box Betty Crocker Seven Minute Icing mix	⅔ c. white corn syrup
	¼ c. water
	1 t. vanilla
2 c. granulated sugar	1 c. nuts, chopped

Prepare icing mix according to directions. Mix sugar, corn syrup, and water. Boil together with occasional stirring until syrup mixture reaches 280°. Add syrup mixture to icing mixture. Beat until smooth and so stiff it is hard to handle. Add flavoring and nuts. Turn into buttered pan and press out smooth. When set, cut into squares. Makes about 2 pounds.

Wanda Perkins
Allen County

OLD-FASHIONED FUDGE

4 c. sugar	2 t. light corn
⅔ c. cocoa	syrup
1½ c. milk	6 T. butter
¼ t. salt	2 t. vanilla

Mix first 5 ingredients in 4-qt. heavy pan. Cook over medium heat and stir until sugar is melted. Boil to 234°. Remove from heat; let cool to 110°. Add butter and vanilla. Beat until it loses gloss. Pour into pan.

For plain fudge, leave out cocoa; for peanut butter fudge, omit cocoa and add ½ c. peanut butter.

Mrs. George Conrad, Sr.
Miami County

EASY FUDGE

1 12-oz. pkg. chocolate bits	dash of salt
1 6-oz. pkg. butterscotch bits	⅓ c. sour cream
	1 c. nuts, chopped

Melt bits in double boiler or over hot water. *Stir often.* When melted, remove from heat. Add cream and nuts. Stir until smooth and pour into greased pan. Refrigerate 24 hr.

Almira Downing
Porter County

GOLDEN FUDGE

1 lb. (2¼ c.) brown sugar, packed firmly	2 6-oz. pkg. butterscotch morsels
1 c. granulated sugar	1 7½-oz. jar marshmallow creme
½ stick butter or margarine	1 c. walnuts, chopped
1 c. evaporated milk	
½ c. golden raisins	1 t. rum or vanilla flavoring

Combine sugars, butter, and milk. Place over medium heat, stirring occasionally until it forms soft ball in cold water (about 15–18 min.). Remove from heat and stir in morsels and marshmallow creme. Blend well. Add walnuts, raisins, and flavoring. Pour into two greased 8″ square pans. When cool, cut in 1″ squares.

Mary Johnson
Rush County

MARSHMALLOW PUFFS (Fudge)

marshmallows, halved, to fill 8″ square pan	1½ c. sweet or semisweet chocolate pieces
½ c. chunky peanut butter	2 T. margarine or butter

In foil-lined 8″ square pan, place halved marshmallows with cut side up, so they touch but are not tight. Mix together chocolate pieces, peanut butter, and margarine or butter. Stir over hot water until melted. Pour over marshmallows and work in between them. Chill, turn out, and cut. Makes 36–56, depending on size of marshmallows.

Mrs. Robert L. Mueller
Marshall County

COBBLESTONE FUDGE

3 6-oz. pkg. chocolate chips	1 c. walnuts, coarsely chopped
2 c. miniature marshmallows	

Melt chips in double boiler. Add marshmallows and nuts. Pour into foil-lined 8× 8×2″ pan.

Mrs. Ruth Neff
Jefferson County

NUT FUDGE

2¼ c. sugar	1 c. evaporated
¼ c. butter or	milk
margarine	1 t. vanilla
16 marshmallows	1 6-oz. pkg. (1 c.)
or 1 c. marsh-	sweet chocolate
mallow creme	morsels
¼ t. salt	1 c. broken nuts

In a heavy 2-qt. saucepan mix sugar, butter or margarine, marshmallows or creme, salt, and milk. Cook and stir over medium heat until mixture boils and is bubbly all over top. Boil and stir for 5 min. more. Remove from heat. Stir in vanilla and chocolate until melted. Stir in broken nuts. Spread in buttered 8″ or 9 ″ square pan. Press nut halves on top if desired. Cool thoroughly. Cut into about 30 pieces.

Mrs. Velma Bowman
Crawford County

VARIATION from *Mrs. Robert Wendel, Wabash County:* After spreading in buttered pan, sprinkle ¼ c. crushed peppermint candy over mixture.

NEVER-FAIL QUICK NUT FUDGE

1 lb. powdered	1 T. vanilla
sugar	extract
½ c. cocoa	1 c. pecans or
¼ t. salt	walnuts,
6 T. butter	chopped
4 T. milk	

Combine all ingredients except nuts in top of double boiler. Place over simmering water and stir until smooth. Add nuts and mix. Spread candy quickly in buttered 9× 5″ loaf pan. Cool. Cut in 24 squares.

Karen Merkel
Dearborn County

PEANUT BUTTER FUDGE

1 pt. marsh-	1 t. vanilla
mallow creme	2 c. sugar
1 c. chunk-style	⅔ c. milk
peanut butter	

Combine in large warm mixing bowl marshmallow creme, peanut butter, and vanilla. Combine sugar and milk in heavy saucepan. Cook sugar mixture to soft-ball stage, or until candy thermometer registers 235°. Pour over peanut butter mixture. Stir until mixed. Spread in buttered 8″ or 9″ square pan. Cool; cut into 64 1″ squares.

Lucille Dillon
Daviess County

GRANDMOTHER'S PEANUT BUTTER FUDGE

2 lb. brown sugar	butter size of an
2 lb. granulated	egg
sugar	1 lb. (about 1 c.)
1 c. light corn	peanut butter
syrup	3 c. milk

Combine all ingredients together except butter and peanut butter. Cook over low heat until sugars are dissolved and mixture comes to a boil. Stir constantly so it will not stick. Cook to soft-ball stage (235° on candy thermometer). Remove from heat and add butter and peanut butter. Beat until creamy and pour into buttered pan. Cool and cut into squares. Makes about 5 pounds.

Miss Christine Kaye Mohr
Marion County

WHITE FUDGE

2¼ c. sugar	2 T. butter
½ c. sour cream	1 T. white corn
¼ c. milk	syrup

¼ t. salt
2 T. vanilla
1 c. walnuts, chopped
⅓ c. candied cherries, quartered

Combine sugar, sour cream, milk, butter, corn syrup, and salt in heavy 2-qt. pan. Stir over moderate heat until sugar is dissolved and mixture reaches a boil. Boil 9–10 min. to 238° (soft-ball stage). Remove from heat and let stand until lukewarm (110°). Add vanilla and beat until mixture loses gloss. Quickly stir in walnuts and cherries; turn into greased pan. Let stand until firm. Cut into squares.

Lela Stevens
Martin County

CREAM MINTS

3-oz. pkg. cream cheese
2½ c. powdered sugar
food coloring
flavoring— almond, vanilla, or peppermint— as desired

Shape into tiny balls and flatten. Refrigerate overnight. Makes 50–60.

Peggy Hadar
Sullivan County

GO-TO-BED MINTS

2 egg whites at room temperature
pinch of salt
½ t. cream of tartar
few drops green food coloring
¾ c. sugar
1 6-oz. pkg. mint chocolate chips

Preheat oven to 375°. Beat egg whites, salt, cream of tartar, and food coloring until mixture holds its shape. Gradually add sugar, and beat until stiff but not dry. Add mint chocolate chips. Drop on ungreased cookie sheet. *Turn off oven.* Put candy in oven and leave for 7–8 hr.

Winnie Demass
Porter County

NUT GOODIE CANDY BARS

1 12-oz. pkg. chocolate chips
1 12-oz. pkg. butterscotch chips
1 c. peanut butter
1 lb. miniature marshmallows
1 pkg. Spanish peanuts

Melt chips over low heat; add peanut butter. Stir in marshmallows and peanuts. Put into buttered 12×15″ pan. Cool. Cut into 40 1×1½″ bars. Keep refrigerated.

Mrs. Wandalee Bonnewell
Owen County

PEANUT BRITTLE

2 c. unroasted Virginia peanuts
2 c. sugar
1 c. water
1 c. light corn syrup
¼ t. salt
1 t. butter
¼ t. soda

Blanch unroasted Virginia peanuts (raw Spanish peanuts do not need blanching). To blanch, cover peanuts with boiling water for 3 min. Run cold water over peanuts. Remove coating. Combine sugar, corn syrup, and water in heavy skillet. Cook slowly; stir until sugar dissolves. Cook to the soft-ball stage (238°). Remove the candy from heat while testing. Add nuts and salt to mixture. Cook to hard-crack stage (290°). Stir constantly. Remove from heat. Add butter and soda; stir to blend. Mixture will bubble. Pour onto greased platter; cool partially by lifting around edges with spatula. Keep spatula moving under mixture so it will not stick. When firm but still warm, turn over. Break in pieces when cold.

Sharon Haworth
Jay County

PEANUT BUTTER BALLS

1 lb. powdered sugar	3 c. Rice Krispies
2 c. chunky pea-nut butter	1 6-oz. pkg. chocolate chips
1 stick mar-garine, melted	1 large Hershey bar
	½ bar paraffin

Mix sugar, peanut butter, margarine, and Rice Krispies and form small balls. Freeze overnight. Melt chocolate chips, Hershey bar, and paraffin over hot water. Stick toothpick in frozen balls and swirl in melted chocolate. Dry on waxed paper.

Mrs. Hilbert Fischer
Dubois County

PECAN ROLLS (1)

2 c. sugar	1 c. light cream
1 c. brown sugar	½ c. pecans, chopped
¼ c. corn syrup	

Cook sugars, syrup, and cream to soft-ball stage. Cool to lukewarm and beat until creamy. Turn onto a board and knead. Shape into 3–4 rolls and roll in the nuts. Chill and cut in slices.

Beulah Nolting
Greene County

PECAN ROLLS (2)

1 12-oz. pkg. penuche fudge mix	½ lb. (about 28) caramels
¼ c. milk	1½ c. chopped pecans

Prepare fudge mix according to package directions. Cool slightly. Roll into 4 rolls about 1″ in diameter. Melt caramels with milk. Roll fudge mixture in the slightly cooled caramel mixture. On a sheet of waxed paper, roll fudge and caramel mixture in chopped pecans. Chill and cut into 32 ½″ slices.

Mrs. Terry Finney
Boone County

QUICK POPCORN BALLS

¼ c. cooking oil	½ c. popcorn
½ c. dark syrup	½ c. sugar
½ t. salt	

Heat cooking oil in 4-qt. kettle over medium heat for 3 min. Add popcorn. Cover, leaving a small air space at the edge of cover. Shake frequently until the popping stops. Meanwhile, mix together corn syrup, sugar, and salt. Add to popped corn in kettle and stir constantly over medium heat for 3–5 min., or until corn is evenly and completely covered with mixture. Remove from heat. Form into balls (use butter on hands, if desired). Makes 6 popcorn balls about 2½″ in diameter.

Ida Joe Temple
Dubois County

CARAMEL CORN

2 c. sugar	2 T. vinegar
1 c. molasses or sorghum	½ t. soda
1 T. butter	popcorn, popped, approx. 5 qts.

Boil first 4 ingredients until mixture snaps in cold water. Take from stove and add soda and stir. Pour over popcorn.

This recipe was my great-grandmother's and is more than 150 years old.

Mrs. Guye Call
Wells County

OVEN CARAMEL CORN

2 c. brown sugar	½ t. soda
1 c. butter	5–6 qts. popped
½ c. syrup, light	popcorn
or dark	1 c. salted nuts
1 t. salt	

Mix first 4 ingredients and boil 5 min. Add soda and pour over popped corn and salted peanuts in large roasting pan. Bake in 250° oven for 1 hr., stirring every 15 min. Spread out on cookie sheet to cool. Store in airtight container.

Pat Foster
Whitley County

POTATO CANDY

Add powdered sugar to ¼ c. leftover mashed potatoes until easy to roll out. Roll out to ¼″ thickness on powdered-sugared board. Spread with peanut butter. Roll up, refrigerate, and slice.

Margaret Alvey
Vigo County

SEA FOAM

3 c. brown sugar	1 t. vanilla
1 c. boiling water	salt
2 egg whites,	1 c. nuts,
beaten	chopped

Boil sugar and water to soft-ball stage. Pour slowly over beaten egg whites, beating constantly until stiff. Add nuts and vanilla. Drop from a spoon onto a buttered plate.

Carol Whaley
Pike County

SPONGE CANDY

1 c. sugar	1 T. vinegar
1 c. dark corn	1 T. baking soda
syrup	

Combine sugar, corn syrup, and vinegar in heavy saucepan. Cook over medium heat, stirring, until sugar dissolves. Continue cooking, without stirring, to 300° on candy thermometer, or until a little of mixture dropped in cold water becomes very brittle. Remove candy from heat. Quickly stir in soda; mix well. Pour into lightly buttered 9×9×2″ pan. Do not spread as candy will spread itself. Cool. Break into pieces. Makes about 1 pound.

Children love the way it falls to crumbs in the mouth; it is so porous they can almost whistle through the honeycomb structure.

Mrs. Wilfred A. Kocher
Knox County

CANDY STRAWBERRIES

2 3-oz. pkg.	¾ c. condensed
Strawberry	milk
Jello	red decorator
1 c. pecans, finely	sugar
ground	almonds, sliced,
1 c. flaked	blanched
coconut	(optional)
½ tsp. vanilla	

Combine Jello, pecans, and coconut. Stir in milk and vanilla. Mix well. Chill 1 hr. Shape into strawberry shapes and roll in red decorator sugar. Yields 1 pound, 3 ounces.

If you wish, tint sliced almonds with green food coloring to make leaves.

Mrs. Clarence Spuller
Marshall County

TAFFY

1½ c. sugar	⅓ c. light corn
¼ t. cream of	syrup
tartar	2 t. butter
¼ c. water	1 t. vanilla

Combine sugar, cream of tartar, syrup, water, and butter in saucepan. Blend well. Cook, stirring occasionally. Bring to boil or to 265°. Remove from heat and stir in vanilla. Pour mixture onto a well-buttered pan. Turn in edges when cool. After it is cooled, with buttered hands, roll in ball, then pull until white. Roll in long, thin rolls and cut off in 1″ pieces.

Mrs. Daniel Wessel
Dubois County

ENGLISH WALNUT TOFFEE

1 c. sugar	1½ c. English
½ t. salt	walnuts,
¼ c. water	chopped
½ c. butter	2 6-oz. pkg. semi-
	sweet chocolate

Combine sugar, salt, water, and butter. Cook to light-crack stage (285°). Add ½ c. chopped walnuts. Pour into well-greased 13×9″ pan. Cool. Melt chocolate. Spread ½ on top of cooled candy; sprinkle with ½ c. walnuts. Cool. Turn; repeat with remaining chocolate and nuts. When chocolate has cooled, break toffee into pieces. Makes about 2 dozen pieces.

Jane Rodman
Monroe County

TURTLES

144 pecan halves	36 light caramels
½ c. semisweet	2 T. light corn
chocolate	syrup (more or
pieces, melted	less)

Grease a cookie sheet and arrange pecans flat side down in groups of 4 on it. Place 1 caramel on each cluster of pecans. Heat in slow oven (325°) until caramels soften (about 4–8 min.). Remove from oven. With buttered spatula flatten caramels over pecans and cool. Remove from pan to waxed paper. Add enough syrup to melted chocolate, so that chocolate can be swirled on pecans and caramel. Makes 36 turtles.

Anna Lou Arnett
Randolph County

Food Preservation

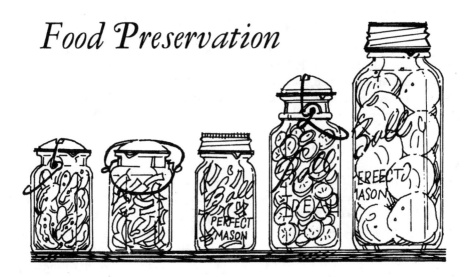

In the years before commercially canned foods were readily available, women spent many hot July and August days over the wood stove filling fruit jars or "puttin' up." A good housewife often "put up" 500 jars in a season. Today "homemade" is still a magic word when used to describe jams and jellies, and even though we know that pickles and relishes probably have little food value, we treasure them for their psychological food value.

Heat processing in a boiling water bath is recommended for all pickle products. For fermented cucumbers and fresh-pack dills, start to count processing time as soon as the filled jars are placed in actively boiling water. This prevents development of a cooked flavor and a loss of crispness.

Process butters, conserves, jams, and preserves 10 to 20 minutes at simmering in a water-bath canner. Read recipes carefully for processing times. It is not necessary to heat process jellies.

FROM 1 LB. BUTTER TO 2 LBS.

Soften ¼ c. (4 T. or 4 envelopes) plain gelatin in 2 c. milk, heat in top of double boiler over hot water to dissolve. Cut 1 lb. butter or margarine in pieces and place the bowl over hot water. Gradually whip gelatin mixture into the butter. Season with salt to taste. If milk appears, keep beating until it disappears. Pour into a mold or small bowls. If desired, chill before serving. Can be put in freezer until needed.

Barbara Snyder
Pike County

HOW TO PRESERVE EGGS

From *Conklin's Handy Manual,* 1891 edition:

To each pailful of water, add two pints

of fresh slacked [slaked] lime and one pint of common salt; mix well. Fill your barrel half full with this fluid, put your eggs down in it any time after June, and they will keep two years, if desired.

Kanda Walden
Gibson County

FRAGRANT SUGAR
Bury a small, very fragrant rose in a glass jar of powdered sugar. Screw top on tight. Place in sun for several days. Delicious on fruit or in tea.

Edith Wiseman
Crawford County

APPLE BUTTER

APPLE BUTTER

16 c. applesauce	¼ t. nutmeg
10 c. sugar	½ t. cinnamon
4 T. cider	1 c. red hots
vinegar	(candies)

Mix all ingredients. Cook on top of stove 20 min. or put in granite pan and bake in oven 30 min. at 350°. Makes about 10–12 pints. Process 10 min. in simmering water bath.

Mrs. Stella Burge
Jennings County

GRANDMOTHER'S APPLE BUTTER

5 gal. cider	1 bushel (about
5 lb. sugar	50 lb.) apples

In a copper kettle bring cider to a boil and allow to boil until there is a white froth on top. Carefully skim froth away and add peeled and quartered apples. Add sugar after apples have begun to darken in color. Cook about 4 hr., stirring continually with a big-handled wooden paddle

to keep apples from scorching. To spice or not to spice is a matter of personal preference. Pour into hot jars and process 10 min. in simmering water bath.

Gertrude Glasgow
Wells County

OLD-FASHIONED APPLE BUTTER
Wash and core apples. Add just enough water to keep from sticking. Cover kettles and cook until mushy. Run through colander (an old-fashioned potato masher works well). You will need 20 gallons of pulp after running through colander. Put apple pulp in copper kettle over open fire outside. Add 130 pounds sugar, 6 sticks cinnamon bark. Stir with long-handled wooden stirrer. Cook, cook, cook, stirring constantly. When "cooked down" to a little more than ½ of original amount, test a few tablespoonfuls. When it thickens as it cools slightly, pour into containers (may be put in canning jars and sealed or small stone jars and covered with clean cloth over top, keep cloth securely in place). The flavor cannot be duplicated by any other method of preparation. Yields approximately 10 gallons.

Note: To clean copper kettle, use salt and vinegar, rubbing with a cloth and rinsing well. This should be done just prior to using the kettle.

Betty Mae Sullivan
Greene County

JAMS AND JELLIES

BLUSHING PEACH JAM

2 c. crushed	2 c. red rasp-
peaches (1½	berries
lb.)	¼ c. lemon juice

7 c. sugar
1 bottle liquid
  fruit pectin

few drops almond
  extract

To peeled, pitted, and crushed peaches, add 2 T. lemon juice. Let stand while preparing raspberries. Crush berries and add remaining lemon juice. Combine peaches and raspberries with sugar in heavy kettle. Mix well and bring to full boil. Boil 1 min. Remove from heat and add pectin. Stir and skim for several minutes. Add extract. Pour boiling hot into hot containers and process in simmering water bath for 10–15 min. Makes 4½ pints.

Mrs. Charles McIntyre
Fayette County

ROSE PETAL JAM

2 c. red rose
  petals
2 c. hot water

2⅔ c. sugar
2 T. honey
1 T. lemon juice

To measure washed rose petals, pack tightly without bruising. Cut with scissors in ¼″ strips, discarding tough base. Add water, cover, and boil for 10 min. Drain and reserve rose petals. Combine liquid with sugar and honey. Simmer uncovered for 5 min. Add petals; simmer covered over low heat for 40 min. Stir occasionally. Add lemon juice; simmer covered for 30 min. Stir occasionally. Cool 5 min. Pour into hot jelly glasses and process in simmering water bath for 10 min. Makes about three 6-oz. glasses.

Edith Wiseman
Crawford County

PINEAPPLE-RHUBARB
REFRIGERATOR JAM

1 small can
  crushed pine-
  apple, drained

1 3-oz. pkg.
  Strawberry
  Jello

3 c. rhubarb   3 c. sugar

Cut the rhubarb into small pieces. Combine the sugar and rhubarb and cook until tender. Dissolve the Jello in hot mixture. Add the crushed pineapple and put into hot, sterilized jars. This recipe is also good as an ice cream topping.

Vera Lee Tweedi
Pulaski County

BEET JELLY

6 large uncooked
  beets
1 box Sure Jel

½ c. lemon juice
6 c. sugar

Peel and slice raw beets. Cover with water and cook until tender. Drain and save liquid. Mix 4 c. beet juice with lemon juice and Sure Jel. Bring to a boil and add sugar. Bring to a full rolling boil and boil 3 min. Seal in hot, sterilized jars. Makes 4 pints.

Mrs. Thomas Fisher
Randolph County

CORN COB JELLY

12 clean dry red
  corn cobs
3 qt. water
1 pkg. pectin

3 c. sugar
few drops red
  food coloring
  (optional)

Cut corn cobs into 4″ pieces. Place in a covered pan with water. Boil 30 min. Remove cobs and strain liquid. Take 3 c. liquid juice and pectin and let come to a boil. Add sugar and boil hard for 5 min. If a brighter color is desired, add a few drops of red food coloring. Pour into hot, sterilized jelly glasses.

Mrs. Kenneth Claudy
Steuben County

GOLDEN DANDELION JELLY

1 qt. fresh dandelion blossoms	5½ c. sugar
	3 drops yellow food coloring
2 qt. water	2 t. orange extract
1 pkg. Sure Jel	

Put dandelion blossoms in water. Bring to a boil. Boil for 3 min. Strain and press out all the juice. To 3 c. of juice add package of Sure Jel. Bring to a boil. And add all the sugar at once. Stir and boil 2½ min. During the last few seconds add food coloring and orange extract. Pour into hot, sterilized containers and seal. Fills about 10 small jars.

Linda Blocher
Putnam County

PEPPER JELLY

3 red bell peppers	3 hot peppers
3 green bell peppers	6½ c. sugar
	1½ c. vinegar
	1 bottle Certo

Remove seeds and grind peppers in food chopper. Combine sugar, vinegar, and peppers and cook for 7 min. Cool 2 min. and add Certo. Pour into hot, sterilized jars and seal.

Marie Tidler
Daviess County

APRICOT CONSERVE

1 lb. dried apricots, coarsely ground	1 c. water
	3 T. lemon juice
	4 T. orange juice
1 No. 2½ can crushed pineapple	4 c. granulated sugar

Soak all of above, except sugar, overnight. Add sugar. Cook in heavy pan over low heat until of desired consistency. Stir often. Pour into hot containers and process 10 min. in simmering water bath. Makes 4 pints.

Mrs. George Conrad, Sr.
Miami County

PEAR HONEY

1 gal. pears, peeled and ground	2 small cans crushed pineapple
sugar in amount equal to pears	

Cook peeled and ground pears and sugar until thick (about 15 min.). Add pineapple and cook until hot through. Pour hot into hot containers (pints and quarts) and process in simmering water bath for 10 min.

Olive Johnson
Sullivan County

QUINCE HONEY

4 quinces	2 qt. sugar
4 apples	1 qt. water

Dissolve sugar in water. Grind quinces and apples, then add syrup. Boil 20 min. Pour into hot, sterilized jars and seal.

Arphelia Ann Sheetz
(for Arzona Noyes)
Fulton County

RHUBARB PRESERVES

6 c. raw rhubarb, diced	1 small pkg. Strawberry Jello
6 c. sugar	

Stir rhubarb and sugar well and let stand overnight. Boil mixture for 10 min. Take off stove and add Strawberry Jello. Mix well and put in hot, sterilized jars. Keep in refrigerator or put in freezer. Makes about 3 pints.

Mrs. John Kuhn
Fulton County

MINCEMEAT

MINCEMEAT (1)

approximately 1 gal. meat, salted	1 qt. cider vinegar
4 oranges	2 lb. raisins
2 lemons	cloves to taste
4 lb. sugar	cinnamon to taste
5 lb. apples	allspice to taste

Cook meat thoroughly. Seed oranges and lemons; cut sections into thirds. Dice apples finely. Place all ingredients in large canner. Cook until apples are mushy. Immediately place in hot pint jars. Process 20 min. at 10 lb. pressure. Makes approximately 16 pints.

Ms. Jo Anne Ramey
Jennings County

MINCEMEAT (2)

2 pecks Stayman Winesap apples	1 c. white sugar
1 gal. cider	2 T. cinnamon
2 T. vinegar	1½ T. salt
2 lb. brown sugar	1 t. cloves
2 lb. dark raisins	1½ t. nutmeg
2 lb. currants	1 t. allspice
1 c. honey	4 lb. lean ground beef

Cook peeled apples in cider; boil down to 2 qt. Frizzle ground beef until red disappears. Mix all ingredients and heat to boiling. Pack in hot qt. jars and process at 10 lb. pressure for 20 min. Makes 10–12 quarts.

Mrs. George Conrad, Sr.
Miami County

HOMEMADE MINCEMEAT

Four pounds of lean boiled beef, chopped fine, twice as much of chopped green tart apples, one pound of chopped suet, three pounds of raisins, seeded, two pounds of currants picked over, washed and dried, half a pound of citron, cut up fine, one pound of brown sugar, one quart of cooking molasses, two quarts of sweet cider, one pint of boiled cider, one tablespoonful of salt, one tablespoonful of pepper, one tablespoonful of mace, one tablespoonful of allspice, and four tablespoonfuls of cinnamon, two grated nutmegs, one tablespoonful of cloves: mix thoroughly and warm it on the range, until heated through. Remove from the fire and when nearly cool, stir in a pint of good brandy and one pint of Madeira wine. Put into a crock, cover it tightly, and set it in a cold place where it will not freeze, but keep perfectly cold. Will keep good all winter.

In modern kitchens mincemeat may be put into closely sealed jars and stored in the refrigerator.

Genevieve Breeden
Monroe County

MEATLESS APPLE MINCEMEAT

4 lb. apples	½ t. ginger
1½ lb. seedless raisins	grated peel and juice of 2
½ c. brown sugar	lemons
1 t. nutmeg	rum or brandy
2 c. cider	flavoring to
1 T. cinnamon	taste
½ t. cloves	

Combine peeled, cored, and chopped apples, raisins, sugar, spices, and cider. Bring to a boil and simmer for 1 hr., or until thick. Add lemon juice and peel. Add flavoring. Pack in hot jars and process in boiling water bath for 25 min.

This recipe makes 4 standard pies. When making pies, add 2 T. butter and a small amount of citron.

Mrs. Gertrude Glasgow
Wells County

PICKLES

PICKLED BEETS

½ bushel small whole red beets	2 T. pickling spices, omitting some red peppers
2 c. vinegar	
4 c. water	
4 c. sugar	

Cook beets until tender; drain. Cold dip and slip skins. Combine vinegar, water, and sugar; add spices tied in muslin bag. Let mixture come to boil. Add cooked beets. Leave in pickling syrup while filling one jar at a time. Pour boiling hot syrup over beets. Process 30 min. in simmering water bath. Yield: 4 quarts.

Mrs. Richard Dunn
Scott County

CARROT PICKLES

4 c. carrots, sliced	½ t. cinnamon
2 medium onions, sliced	¼ t. ginger
	¼ t. cloves
1 c. water	¼ t. celery seed
¾ c. sugar	1 T. salad oil
¾ t. salt	2 c. vinegar

Cook carrot and onion slices in water over low heat for 10 min. Drain, add all remaining ingredients, and simmer gently for 15 min. Ladle into sterilized pint jars. Process 30 min. in boiling water bath.

Mrs. Elmo Taylor
Jay County

SLICED BREAD AND BUTTER PICKLES

5 qt. cucumbers, sliced	5 c. sugar
	3 c. white vinegar
8 small onions, cut fine	1 c. water
	1½ t. turmeric
2 mangoes, cut fine	1 t. celery seed
	2 T. whole
½ c. salt	mustard seed

Do not peel cucumbers; use slicer to make very thin slices. Mix cucumbers, onions, mangoes, and salt together. Mix through and cover with ice cubes from 3–4 trays. Cover and let stand for 3 hr. Drain thoroughly. Place in large kettle. Combine sugar, vinegar, water, turmeric, celery and mustard seed and pour over cucumbers. Bring to a boil and cook for 30–45 min. until pickles are clear. Process 15 min. Yield: 6 pints.

Mrs. George Conrad, Sr.
Miami County

15 MINUTE PICKLES

4 qt. small dill cucumbers, sliced or chunked	3 c. water
	1 t. cloves
	1 t. allspice
	3 t. salt
5 c. vinegar	1 onion, cut fine
5 c. sugar	

Mix vinegar, sugar, and salt. Put spices in a cloth bag, or just put in loose, and add. Bring to a boil. Add cucumbers and onion; boil hard for 5 min. Pour in hot cans and process in boiling water bath for 15 min.

Cecile Nicoll
Carroll County

KOSHER DILL PICKLES

4 c. vinegar	½ c. pickling salt
4 c. water	

¾ c. sugar
small red peppers
3 doz. 3–4"
  cucumbers

grape leaves
  (optional)
sprigs of dill
garlic cloves

Combine vinegar, water, sugar, and salt. Simmer 15 min. Place a grape leaf in bottom of each quart jar. Pack pickles, adding 1 garlic clove, 1 red pepper, and 1 sprig of dill to each jar. Pour boiling liquid over pickles. Seal. Process 10–12 min. in boiling water. Makes 3 quarts.

Mrs. Wilma Hall
Dubois County

SWEET PICKLE SLICES
  (Without Lime)

4 qt. unpeeled
  cucumber slices,
  ⅛" thick
7⅓ c. white
  vinegar
3 T. salt

1 T. mustard seed
6 c. sugar
2¼ t. celery seed
1 T. whole
  allspice

In covered kettle simmer cucumber slices in 4 c. vinegar with salt, mustard seed, and ¼ c. sugar for about 15 min., or until slices turn slightly yellow. Do not overcook. Drain; discard cooking liquid. Spoon slices into hot, sterilized jars. Bring to a boil 3⅓ c. vinegar, 5¾ c. sugar, celery seed, and allspice. Pour over pickles and process in boiling water bath for 10 min. Yield: 5 pints.

Mrs. James Bryan
Montgomery County

CRISP SWEET PICKLES
  (With Lime)

1 gal. or 7 lb.
  cucumbers,
  unpeeled and
  sliced

2 gal. cold water
1 c. lime (pur-
  chased at
  drugstore)

3 T. salt
2 qt. vinegar
8 c. sugar
1 t. celery seed

1 t. cloves
1 t. salt
1 T. mixed spices

Mix cucumbers, water, salt, and lime. Let stand 24 hr., stirring very often. Rinse in cold water 3 times. Let stand in cold water for 3 hr. Drain well. Combine vinegar, sugar, celery seed, cloves, salt, and mixed spices. Pour over pickles. Let stand overnight. Next morning, bring to boil and boil for 35 min. Put in hot jars and process for 10 min. in boiling water bath. Makes 4 quarts.

Barbara Brown
Parke County

WATERMELON PICKLES

2 lb. watermelon
  rind
4 c. sugar
2 c. white vinegar
1 T. whole cloves

1 lemon, thinly
  sliced
2 T. cinnamon
  bark

Trim green and pink parts off rind. Cut in 1" cubes. Soak overnight in salt water (¼ c. salt to 1 qt. water). Drain, rinse, and cover with cold water. Cook until tender; drain. Combine sugar, vinegar, lemon, and spices tied in a bag. Simmer for 10 min. Remove spices. Add watermelon; simmer until clear. Fill hot jars and process in boiling water bath for 10 min. Makes 3 pints.

Mrs. Hurley Fletcher
Lawrence County

ZUCCHINI PICKLES

2 lb. zucchini,
  cut in thin slices
2 small onions,
  sliced
¼ c. salt

2 c. sugar
2 c. white vinegar
1 t. celery seed
1 t. turmeric
2 t. mustard seed

Cover zucchini, onions, and salt with water and let stand for 2 hr., then drain. In saucepan mix vinegar, sugar, celery seed, turmeric, and mustard seed. Bring to a boil. Pour mixture over drained zucchini and let stand for 2 hr. Bring to a boil and let boil for 5 min. Pour into hot jars and process in boiling water bath for 15 min. Makes 3 pints.

Elma Viel
Dearborn County

RELISHES

CARROT-CUCUMBER RELISH

3½ c. unpeeled cucumbers, coarsely ground	1 c. onions, coarsely ground
1½ c. carrots, coarsely ground	2½ c. sugar
	1½ c. vinegar
	1½ t. celery seed
	1½ t. mustard
2 T. salt	seed

Combine vegetables and salt; stir and let stand for 3 hr. Drain. Combine remaining ingredients and bring to boil. Add vegetables and simmer uncovered for 8–10 min. Pour hot into hot jars and process 30 min. in boiling water bath. Makes about 2½ pints.

Martha J. Cox
Parke County

CORN RELISH

3 c. tender sweet corn kernels	4 green peppers, finely chopped
3 large onions, finely chopped	4 c. cabbage, finely chopped
1 red pepper, finely chopped	3 c. vinegar
	3 c. sugar

½ c. flour	2 t. salt (more or less to taste)
¼ c. dry mustard	
1 t. turmeric powder	2 t. celery seed

Add corn kernels to other vegetables. Set aside. Mix together vinegar, sugar, flour, dry mustard, turmeric, and salt and put in a canning kettle over medium heat. Add vegetables and cook ½ hr. Add the celery seed and pack into the size jars desired and seal according to the jar manufacturer's directions. Process 15 min. in boiling water bath. This relish will also keep in the refrigerator several days (tightly covered) without sealing.

Mrs. Ralph E. Partridge
Spencer County

CRANBERRY-ORANGE RELISH

½ large or 1 small unpeeled orange	2 c. raw or thawed frozen cranberries
1 c. sugar	

Put orange and cranberries through food chopper. Mix in sugar and let stand for several hours. Store in a covered jar and refrigerate. Ready to serve. Makes 1½ cups.

Kathleen Ingle
Crawford County

CUCUMBER RELISH

7 c. cucumbers, peeled, seeded, and ground	5 mangoes, ground
3 c. carrots, ground	⅓ c. salt
	3 c. vinegar
4 large onions, ground or chopped	4 c. sugar
	1 T. mustard seed
	1 T. celery seed
	1½ t. turmeric

Large yellow cucumbers may be used. Mix cucumbers, carrots, onions, and mangoes together. Makes about 1 gal. altogether. Sprinkle salt on cucumber mixture. Mix and cover with ice cubes. Soak for 3 hr. and then drain. Mix vinegar, sugar, mustard seed, celery seed, and turmeric and bring to boil. Pour over drained pickle mixture. Simmer 15–20 min. and put into hot, sterilized pint jars. Process 5 min. Makes 8 pints or more.

Olive Weaver
Switzerland County

HOT DOG RELISH

1 medium to large head of cabbage	green and red mangoes (optional)
1 jar dill pickles, drained	celery (optional)
1 large onion	red hot pepper (optional)
1 bottle catsup, small or medium size	2 T. sugar
	2 T. vinegar
salt to taste	1 T. water

Grind together cabbage, dill pickles, onion, and any or all of optional ingredients. Add catsup and salt. Add sweet vinegar mixture of sugar, vinegar, and water. Keeps well in covered container in refrigerator.

Susan Goldman
Spencer County

MRS. PARK'S SWEET RELISH

One quart each of	vinegar
onions	green tomatoes
celery	apples
cauliflower	green peppers
sweet pickles	red peppers
sugar	yellow peppers

Cut all ingredients into small chunks. Place in large container and add 1 T. celery seed and salt to taste. Cook until apples are tender. Put in jars and process at 10 lb. pressure for 10 min. Makes 12 pints.

Mrs. Oliver F. Russell
Lawrence County

SUMMER RELISH

5 c. onions	5 c. green tomatoes
5 c. green beans	
5 c. butter beans	4 stalks celery
7 c. carrots	2 heads cauliflower
5 c. red and yellow sweet peppers	2 large cucumbers
5 c. green sweet peppers	11 c. vinegar
	11 c. sugar

Cook green beans, butter beans, and carrots until partially soft. Add a handful of salt to all other ingredients, after cutting into pieces, and let stand several hours. Drain. Mix all ingredients together and let boil for approximately 10 min. Pour into hot, sterilized jars and process for 10 min.

Note: Celery seed, mustard seed, and a little alum may be added to each jar, if desired.

Mrs. Robert Loeffler
Vanderburgh County

TOMATO RELISH

3 qt. ripe tomatoes, peeled and chopped	1 c. green peppers, chopped
	2 c. sugar
3 c. celery, chopped	¼ c. brown sugar
	1½ t. pepper
2 c. onions, chopped	1½ t. mixed pickling spices
¼ c. salt	1 c. white vinegar

Combine tomatoes, celery, onions, green peppers, and salt. Let stand overnight. Drain in colander, but do not press vegetables. Place vegetable mixture in a large kettle and add sugar, brown sugar, pepper, mixed spices tied in cheesecloth, and vinegar. Bring to a boil, reduce heat, and simmer uncovered for 15 min. Ladle into hot jars and process in boiling water bath for 10 min. Makes 5½ pints.

Mrs. Lee Joe Welp
Dubois County

CHOPPED VEGETABLE RELISH

12 onions, ground (2 c.)	½ c. salt
	2 T. mustard seed
10 green tomatoes (4 c.)	1 T. celery seed
	1½ t. turmeric
1 medium cabbage (4 c.)	4 c. cider vinegar
10 green peppers (2½ c.)	2 c. water
	6 c. sugar

Mix onions and chopped vegetables together. Sprinkle with salt and let stand overnight. Rinse and drain. Mix last 6 ingredients. Pour over vegetables. Heat and boil for about 5 min. Pour into hot, sterilized jars and process for 10 min.

Eleanor Hankins
Vigo County

SAUCES

CHILI SAUCE

25 lb. ripe tomatoes	8 T. whole cloves
	6 T. mustard seed
25 medium onions	4 T. celery seed
	8 T. salt
12 green peppers	8 sticks whole cinnamon
2 qt. sugar	
3 qt. vinegar	

Remove skins from tomatoes and cut in quarters. Dice onions and peppers. Add to tomatoes and combine with vinegar and sugar. Tie spices in cheesecloth. Add to tomato mixture and cook slowly for 2 hr., or until thick. Pour into hot jars and process in boiling water bath for 15 min. Makes 12 pints.

Beulah Mull
Parke County

MOTHER'S CHILI SAUCE

30 large ripe tomatoes, peeled and diced	4 c. white vinegar
	4 c. sugar (add more according to taste)
6 large sweet peppers (mangoes), diced	4 t. salt

Put all ingredients in a large pan to cook. Let cook 1½ hr. or longer until thick and no water shows. Stir often. Put into hot jars and process in boiling water bath for 15 min. Makes about 13 pints.

Mrs. Andrew J. Mohr, Jr.
Marion County

HOMEMADE PIZZA SAUCE

1 gal. tomato juice, unseasoned	2 t. rosemary
	1 t. pepper
2 t. oregano	1 clove garlic
2 t. salt	2 bay leaves

Cook until thick enough to round up on a spoon. Pour into hot jars. Process 15 minutes in boiling water bath. Makes 4–6 pints.

Mrs. Thomas Zumbrun
Noble County

TOMATOES AND CATSUP

TOMATO JUICE

4 qt. juice	¾ t. celery seed
2 T. and 1 t. salt	¼ c. sugar

Wash tomatoes; cut out stems and blemishes. Cook and run through food mill. Combine juice and other ingredients and bring to boil. Pack into hot qt. jars and process 15 min. in boiling water bath. Makes 4 quarts.

Sandra Heckley
Allen County

CANNED GREEN TOMATOES

Select tomatoes about 2½" in diameter. Slice ¼" thick and pack in washed jars. Fill with cold water, and add 1 t. salt to each qt. Place in pressure cooker. Let pressure come to 10 lb. and cook for 15 min. Turn off cooker; cool and remove. When ready to fry, roll in flour. These taste as if they are fresh from the garden.

Mrs. Roy Lester
Greene County

OLD-FASHIONED CATSUP

2 gal. tomato juice	20 drops oil of cinnamon
8 T. salt	20 drops oil of cloves
6 T. cornstarch	
8 c. sugar	2 onions, shredded
3 c. vinegar	

Add salt to tomato juice and onions and boil down about one third. Mix together sugar and cornstarch. Add vinegar and oils to tomato juice and cook for ½ hr.

Then add sugar and cornstarch mixture, stirring constantly. Bring to a rolling boil. Pour into hot jars and process in boiling water bath 10 min.

Dorothy Esche
Posey County

COLD CATSUP

1 gal. uncooked tomatoes, peeled and chopped	¼ c. salt
	1 lb. brown sugar
	1 oz. mustard seed
2 c. celery, diced	4 c. vinegar
2 c. onion, diced	1½ c. (8 oz.)
2 c. green pepper, diced	grated horseradish

Prepare tomatoes, celery, onion, and green pepper. Combine with salt. Place in a colander and drain 6–8 hr. or overnight. Mix brown sugar, mustard seed, vinegar, and horseradish. Pour over tomato mixture. Let set for 2 days before using, and keep in refrigerator.

Mrs. Allan Simon
Noble County

GOOSEBERRY KETCHUP

2 qt. gooseberries	1 T. cinnamon
	1 T. cloves
2 c. vinegar	1 T. allspice
3 lb. brown sugar	

Cook slowly for 2 hr., being careful not to burn. Put into wide-mouthed jars and process in boiling water bath for 15 min. Makes 40 servings.

Ardella Reust
Whitley County

Cooking for a Crowd

Cooking for a crowd need not be overwhelming. Organization is no doubt the key word. Detailed advance planning will save many a headache. Plan also to use reliable recipes that are not too complicated since hands that are willing may not necessarily be experienced.

Be especially aware of what causes food poisoning when your "family" is a crowd. Keep your hot foods hot–place pans of cooked foods in roasters with hot water if necessary to hold foods hot until serving time. Cold foods need to be really cold. Store all perishable foods—meat, fish, chicken, cream puffs, layer cakes, etc.—in refrigerators. Check to make certain the temperature of refrigerators is below 40° F.

ELEPHANT STEW (Just for Fun)

1 elephant	2 rabbits
salt and pepper to taste	(optional)

Cut elephant into small bite-size pieces. This should take about 2 months. Add enough brown gravy to cover. Cook over kerosene fire at 465° for 4 weeks. This will serve 3800 people. If more are expected, 2 rabbits may be added, but do this *only* if necessary. Most people do not like to find hare in their stew.

Juan Knarr
Pulaski County

CHILI

12 lb. hamburger	7 T. flour, approximately
18 c. tomato juice	24 c. kidney beans
6 onions (3 c., chopped	

salt, pepper, and 18 c. water
chili powder
to taste

Brown hamburger and onions. Place in large kettle. Add all other ingredients and simmer for approximately 1 hr., or until flavors are blended. Serves 40.

Roselyn McKittrick
Ripley County

GOLDEN FRUIT SALAD

8 3-oz. pkg. ½ No. 10 can
Orange Jello grapefruit sec-
2 qt. hot peach tions, drained
syrup 1 pt. maraschino
2 qt. orange juice cherries,
1 No. 10 can chopped
peach slices, 2 lb. creamed
drained cottage cheese

Dissolve gelatin in peach syrup. Stir in orange juice. Chill until slightly thickened. Fold in remaining ingredients. Pour into shallow pans. Chill until firm. Cut into squares and serve on crisp salad greens. Serves 50.

Mrs. George Conrad, Sr.
Miami County

POTATO SALAD

12 lb. potatoes, 12 eggs, hard
diced and boiled and
cooked chopped
1 pt. mayonnaise 1 T. mustard
1 T. vinegar 1 pt. sweet
8 stalks celery, pickles,
diced chopped

Combine all ingredients and mix well. Serves 50.

Edythe Price
Clay County

SAVORY GREEN BEANS

2½ No. 10 cans ¾ c. cider
green beans or 8 vinegar
No. 3 cans, 13 large
drained pimientos
1½ lb. margarine salt and pepper

Boil down bean broth (liquid). Add other ingredients. Simmer to blend flavors. Serves 50.

Mrs. George Conrad, Sr.
Miami County

PANCAKE SUPPER CAKES

8 c. flour 8 eggs, separated
10 T. baking 2 quarts milk
powder 1 c. melted butter
4⅔ t. sugar or margarine
1 T. salt

Mix and sift flour, baking powder, sugar, and salt. Beat egg yolks; add to milk. Pour slowly on flour mixture. Beat thoroughly. Beat egg whites until stiff and fold into batter. Add melted butter. Drop by spoonfuls onto hot griddle. Cook on one side over medium heat, until bubbles appear on top of cakes. Turn and bake on the other side. Serve with butter and maple or other syrup. Makes 1 gallon of batter or 20 servings, three 5″ cakes to each serving.

Donna Handley
Union County

PIE CRUSTS THAT KEEP

10 lb. flour 1 c. sugar
4 lb. lard ½ c. salt
3 lb. Crisco 4 eggs
1 qt. water 1 pt. milk
½ qt. milk ½ t. vinegar

Step I: Mix well flour, lard, and Crisco. Put aside. Step II: Combine water and ½ qt. milk in pan. Put sugar, salt, eggs, 1 pt.

milk, and vinegar in blender. Blend well. Add blended mixture to milk mixture in pan. Mix together. Add Step II mixture to Step I *quickly*. Divide dough into amounts for 1 pie crust and place each in a plastic box. Freeze. To use: Take out of freezer 3 hr. before using. Makes eighteen 10″ single pie crusts.

Marjorie M. Frye
Greene County

BAKED CUSTARD

2½ c. sugar	20 eggs
½ t. salt	2 T. vanilla
5 qt. milk, scalded	2 T. nutmeg

Beat sugar, salt, and eggs until well mixed. Add scalded milk and vanilla. Pour into baking pans and sprinkle with nutmeg. Place pans in larger pans of hot water and bake 45 min. at 300°. Makes 50 servings.

Rice Custard: Use ½ of recipe and add 4 eggs to 6 c. cooked rice.

Mrs. Chester Smith
Perry County

SANDWICHES

BARBECUE

5 lb. boneless shoulder or chuck roast	3 onions, diced
5 lb. pork roast	4 15-oz. cans tomato sauce
½ c. water	2 cans water
4 medium carrots, diced	28 oz. tomato catsup
3 green peppers, diced	½–¾ c. brown sugar, according to taste
3 stalks celery, diced	2 T. chili powder
¼ c. vegetable oil	dash of Worcestershire sauce

Place both roasts in pan with ½ c. water; roast in 350° oven for 2½–3 hr., or until meat falls from bones. Cool. Meanwhile, sauté onions, carrots, peppers, and celery in oil until they are transparent. Add tomato sauce, water, catsup, sugar, chili powder, and Worcestershire sauce. Combine in deep, heavy kettle and simmer slowly, covered, for 1 hr. Slice meat into medium-sized pieces; add to simmered sauce. Simmer another hour, uncovered, stirring occasionally. Yield: 24 servings.

Mrs. Joseph O'Bryan
Floyd County

BAR-B-QUE FOR A CROWD

20 lb. ground beef	1 c. vinegar
margarine as needed	2 c. brown sugar
2 c. flour	few drops of Worcestershire sauce
4 c. ketchup	few drops of Tabasco sauce
5 c. water	
1 c. table mustard	

Brown ground beef and drain. Save drippings and add enough margarine to make 1 c. Place drippings in large kettle; add rest of ingredients. Cook until thick and pour over browned hamburger. This may be placed in an electric roaster and simmered until tender. Makes at least 100 sandwiches.

Mrs. Noble C. Fry
Putnam County

SLOPPY JOES FOR A CROWD

15 lb. hamburger	½ c. Worcestershire sauce
3 c. onions, diced	1 No. 10 can tomato catsup
3 c. flour	
enough water to mix with flour	

Fry onions and hamburger. Mix flour and

water. Add with rest of ingredients to hamburger mixture. Cook for 1½ hr.; stir with wooden paddle. Or put in oven and bake.

Fern Duguid
Steuben County

MAIN DISHES

CHICKEN LOAF

1 5-lb. hen, cooked until done, or 3–4 c. cooked chicken	1 can cream of mushroom soup
	2 c. celery, diced and cooked
¾–1 lb. crackers, broken into pieces	6 hard-boiled eggs, diced
1 qt. chicken broth	salt and pepper to taste

Remove chicken from bones; dice. Combine with other ingredients. Put in greased 10×14″ pan. Bake about 1 hr. in medium oven. Loaf may be served with sauce made from remaining broth. Serves 20.

Castleton Homemakers Club
Marion County

LAYERED CHICKEN LOAF

5 lb. bread, broken in pieces	12 whole chickens
24 eggs, beaten	30 eggs, boiled and chopped fine
2 qt. chicken broth	
salt and pepper to taste	15 cans cream of mushroom soup (do not thin)
sage and parsley to taste	corn flakes, crushed
5 lb. noodles	

Cook chickens and pick from bones. Reserve broth. Mix together the first 5 ingredients; put in dish for first layer. Cook noodles in broth; add to dish for second layer. Add chicken for third layer. Add hard-boiled eggs for fourth layer. Add mushroom soup for fifth layer. Top with corn flakes. Bake 30 min. at 350°. Serves 100.

Turkey or pork may be used in place of chicken.

Cora Krueher
St. Joseph County

CHICKEN AND NOODLE CASSEROLE

1 5–6 lb. hen	6 heaping T. flour
10 c. dry noodles	salt and pepper to taste
1 stick margarine	
1 can Milnot or half & half	4–5 hard-cooked eggs
2 cans cream of mushroom soup	buttered bread crumbs

Stew chicken and remove from bones. Divide and reserve broth. Cook noodles in weakened broth until tender. Melt margarine in large skillet, add flour. To this add 6 c. chicken broth, Milnot, mushroom soup, and salt and pepper and make gravy. Grease a large deep pan and alternately add cooked noodles, cut-up chicken, and hard-cooked eggs, then more noodles and the gravy. Top with buttered bread crumbs and bake 35–40 min. at 350°. Serves 20–25.

Zella L. Fouse
Randolph County

CHICKEN TETRAZZINI (1)

1 6-lb. hen	1 clove garlic, minced
1 lb. Italian-style thin spaghetti	¼ lb. butter
2 cans sliced mushrooms	¼ c. cooking sherry
¼ c. Parmesan cheese	1 c. almonds, finely chopped

5 T. flour	¼ t. garlic salt
2 t. salt	6 c. American
¼ t. pepper	cheese, grated
2 cans cream of	2 small jars
mushroom soup	pimiento,
1 t. Worcester-	chopped
shire sauce	2 c. milk
2 medium green	1 can whole
peppers,	mushrooms
chopped	

Stew chicken until done. Remove from bones in small chunks. Cook spaghetti in broth from chicken. Drain and rinse spaghetti. Melt butter in skillet over low heat. Add peppers and cook until tender. Add flour, mushroom soup, milk, pimientos, garlic, garlic salt, salt, pepper, Worcestershire sauce, sherry, mushroom slices, chicken, 4 c. American cheese, and Parmesan cheese. Cook slowly for 10 min. Alternately add spaghetti and sauce to large Pryex dish until almost filled. Sprinkle almonds and remaining cheese on top. Then place whole mushrooms on top. Bake 10 min. at 350°. Serves 16–20.

Mrs. William Rambo
Wayne County

CHICKEN TETRAZZINI (2)

1 onion, minced	1½ lb. shredded
1 clove garlic,	cheddar cheese
minced	1 4-oz. can
1 T. butter	pimiento,
pepper and	chopped
paprika	2½ qt. cooked
4 c. milk	chicken, diced
2 t. steak sauce	⅓ c. parsley,
4 cans cream of	chopped
mushroom soup	1½ c. spaghetti
4 cans cream of	(coiled spring
chicken soup	type is best)

Cook onion and garlic in butter for 5 min.; add steak sauce, milk, soups, and ½ the cheese. Cook until smooth. Add chicken, parsley, and pimiento and mix well. Cook and drain spaghetti. Rinse in hot water and put in large shallow baking pan. Pour chicken mixture over spaghetti. Sprinkle with remaining cheese and paprika. Bake at 375° for 30 min. Serves 25.

Lou Seely
Allen County

HAM LOAF

12 lb. smoked	Sauce:
ham, ground	1 c. tomato
4 c. bread crumbs	catsup
1 qt. milk	¼ c. vinegar
1 qt. tomato juice	¼ c. mustard
12 eggs	1 c. brown sugar
salt and pepper	
to taste	

Combine ingredients and shape into long loaves. Bake at 325° for 2 hr. Half an hour before loaves are done, add sauce made from last 4 ingredients. Serves 50.

Mrs. George Conrad, Sr.
Miami County

HAM LOAF WITH RAISIN SAUCE

3½ lb. smoked	Raisin Sauce:
ham, ground	2 T. ham
6½ lb. fresh	drippings
ham, ground	2 T. flour
10 eggs, beaten	½ t. dried
5 c. bread	mustard
crumbs, grated	1 c. pineapple
5 c. milk	juice
1½ t. pepper	½ c. seedless
salt to taste	raisins

Mix gently as for any meat loaf. Bake at 350° for 1 hr. Serve with raisin sauce.

Combine ingredients for sauce and cook until thickened. Increase as needed.

Betty Alcorn
Monroe County

BEEF STROGANOFF

9 lb. round steak, cut in cubes	6½ qt. fresh mushrooms, sliced
3 T. shortening	⅔ c. flour
3¾ qt. water	1⅛ c. cold water
⅜ c. tomato juice	2⅔ t. salt
⅜ c. vinegar	meat coloring (optional)
1⅔ c. shortening	6 c. uncooked rice
5 c. onions, ground	2¼ gal. water
1½ qt. sour cream	2¼ t. salt

Brown cubed meat thoroughly in 3 T. shortening in heavy-bottomed kettle. Add 3¾ qt. water to tomato juice and vinegar. Add liquid to meat, cover and let simmer about 2 hr., or until meat commences to become tender. Sauté onions in 1⅔ c. shortening until golden brown. Add sliced mushrooms and cook 5 min. more. Add onions and mushrooms to meat mixture together with sour cream. Cover and cook until tender. Remove meat and thicken stock and cream with flour mixed to a paste with cold water. Return meat to gravy, being careful not to break up meat. Cook rice in boiling salted water and when tender, drain and pour cold water over it. Reheat the rice. Serve approximately ⅔ c. of meat mixture with a No. 10 scoop of rice. Serves 50.

Mrs. Louis C. Notter, Sr.
Whitley County

PAWNHOAS (Old German Recipe)

6 qt. broth	5 c. cooked beef and pork
4 t. salt	

1 t. pepper	1 lb. (5 c.)
1 t. sage	rolled oats

To make broth, boil the beef and pork together. Remove the meat from bones and grind. Chill broth and remove fat. Bring broth to a boil, stir in ground meat, boil; then stir in rolled oats and seasonings. Cook slowly for 1 hr. Pour the mixture into two 9×13″ loaf pans and cool. Cover and store in refrigerator. When ready to serve, slice and fry until crisp and brown. This is a good recipe for breakfast. It substitutes for bacon or sausage. Serves 25.

Mrs. Waldo Feldmeyer
Marion County

CAMPFIRE STEW

5 lb. hamburger	5 large cans vegetarian vegetable soup
2 large onions, diced	

Brown hamburger and onion together in hot, dry, deep pot. Drain excess fat off before adding soup. This can serve 20 and be stretched by adding more soup. Be sure soup is vegetarian vegetable.

Canned biscuits may be added for dumplings if pot is covered with a lid.

Mrs. Jo Anne Ramey
Jennings County

FARMER JONES

1½ qt. uncooked rice	1 pt. onion, chopped
2½ T. salt	1½ qt. tomato purée
1 pt. celery, chopped	1½ qt. grated cheese
6 lb. ground beef	

Cook rice in salted water until done. Combine celery and onion with ground beef; cook. Drain excess fat. Add tomato purée. Spread cooked rice in four 9×12×4″ pans and cover with hamburger mixture. Sprinkle with cheese. Bake at 350° until cheese is melted. Serves 50.

Afra Mauder
Martin County

HAMBURGER-NOODLE BAKE

4 lb. ground beef	3 c. water
3 c. onion, chopped	¾ c. green pepper, chopped
16 oz. medium noodles, cooked and drained	½ c. chili sauce
	¼ c. canned pimiento, chopped
16 oz. (4 c.) sharp American cheese, shredded	3 c. soft bread crumbs
	6 T. butter, melted
3 10¾-oz. cans tomato soup	1½ t. salt
	dash of pepper

Divide beef and onion between 2 large skillets. Brown meat; drain off fat. Combine meat and onion with noodles, cheese, soup, water, green pepper, chili sauce, pimiento, salt, and pepper. Mix. Turn into 2 greased 13×9×2″ baking dishes. Combine crumbs and butter. Sprinkle on top of casseroles. Bake uncovered at 350° for 45 min. Serves 25–30.

Dorothy Rauh
Noble County

GOURMET CASSEROLE

3 lb. hamburger	2 cans chow mein noodles
4 onions, chopped	3 c. water
2 c. celery, chopped	1 c. uncooked Minute Rice
2 cans cream of chicken soup	2 cans cream of mushroom soup
8 T. soy sauce	

Cook hamburger until brown. Drain and put in large bowl. Add other ingredients except noodles. Bake in large casserole 1½ hr. at 350°. Remove from oven and cover top with noodles. Bake 30 min. longer. Serves 20.

Jane Barto
Allen County

MEAT PIES (*Kraut Barouk*)

1½ c. warm water (110°–115°)	Filling:
2 pkg. dry yeast	4 T. shortening
3 eggs, room temperature	3 c. (2 large) onion, finely chopped
about 6 c. flour	6–8 c. (1 large) cabbage, shredded
½ c. sugar	1½ lb. hamburger
½ c. soft shortening	2 t. salt
1 t. salt	

To make filling: Sauté onion in 2 T. shortening until tender. Add shredded cabbage. Mix and cook until cabbage is tender. Remove from pan to bowl. Cook hamburger in 2 T. shortening until pink color is gone. Add to cabbage-onion mixture. Add salt. Blend. To make dough: Dissolve yeast in warm water. Let stand 3–5 min. Add eggs, ½ the flour, sugar, shortening, and salt; beat until smooth. Stir in more flour, a little at a time, until dough cleans sides of bowl. Turn out on lightly floured board; knead until little bubbles can be seen beneath surface. Let rise in warm place until doubled (about 1 hr.). Punch down. Let rise 15 more min. Shape ½ of dough at a time as follows: Roll to 16″ square. Cut into sixteen 4″ squares. Put ¼ c. filling in center of each square. Fold sides over filling and pinch all seams to form little "cushions." Turn seamside down on greased baking sheet. Butter tops of dough and prick with fork. Shape second ½. Let rise in warm place 30–40 min., or until doubled. Bake about 30 min. until golden brown in quick moderate oven (375°). Serve either warm or cold. Makes 32 pies.

Alice Black
Tippecanoe County

5 CHEESE SPAGHETTI

1 lb. spaghetti	1 small roll
2 t. butter	smoky cheese,
1 T. salt	cut fine
4 qt. water	1 t. onion salt
1 c. sharp cheddar	1 t. garlic salt
cheese,	2 t. salt
shredded	pepper to taste
1 c. Swiss cheese,	1 T. Worcester-
shredded	shire sauce
1 c. Provolone	1 t. dry mustard
cheese,	3 T. butter
shredded	1 qt. milk (or ½
1 c. grated Par-	Milnot and ½
mesan cheese	water)

Add 2 t. butter and 1 T. salt to water and cook spaghetti until just not quite tender (about 10 min.). *Drain.* Toss together cheeses. Butter 4-qt. casserole and place in it layer of spaghetti and layer of cheese and dot with butter. Repeat 3 times. Mix Worcestershire sauce, mustard, and milk and pour over spaghetti. Insert a slotted spoon into spaghetti and let milk ooze throughout. Cover casserole and place in 350° oven. Bake until hot through (bubbling). Remove from oven; remove lid and with slotted spoon lift spaghetti from bottom to top. Again cover and return to oven. Thirty min. later, repeat the lifting and turning. Bake another 15 min., then lift and turn again. When ready to serve, the casserole should be creamy and not browned on top. Serves 20.

Lois Evelyn Bowman
Hamilton County

SPAGHETTI SAUCE WITH MEAT

1 medium stalk	60 oz. tomato
celery	paste
3 green peppers	32 oz. tomato
1 large onion	sauce
1 bunch parsley	32 oz. mushrooms
6 small carrots	with liquid
1 whole garlic	2 c. grated Ro-
bulb	mano cheese
2 c. olive oil	2 4- or 5-lb. pork
2 bay leaves	roasts
1 T. basil	water to make
1 t. cumin	4 gal.
1½ t. pepper	cornstarch, if
3 T. salt	needed
1 t. oregano	

Grind onion, celery, peppers, parsley, garlic, and carrots, using fine blade of food chopper. Heat oil in kettle large enough to hold 4 gal. Add ground vegetables to oil and cook about 10 min. Add spices and stir well. Add tomato paste and sauce, rinsing each can with a can of hot water and adding that. Cook over medium heat for 1 hr. Put mushrooms and their liquid in enough water to cover in separate pan and simmer ½ hr. Add to sauce and stir in cheese. Meanwhile, cook meat in oven until tender. Slice and add to sauce at this time. Add boiling water to make 4 gal. Simmer for at least 6 hr. Sauce will reduce by almost ½ and will thicken. If not thick enough, add a little cornstarch mixed with cold water and cook a little longer. Serves 20–25.

Mrs. Joseph O'Bryan
Floyd County

Old-Time "Receipts"

It was the hunter's skill that carried pioneer families through the first year or two. An early Brownstown settler remembered that in parts of southern Indiana in 1815 flocks of 500 wild turkeys were not uncommon, in the winter herds of 10 to 20 deer could be seen, and there were shoals of fish in the Driftwood River that covered half an acre. A week's supply of game could be killed in half a day. A Bloomington pioneer reported that at times pigeons darkened the sky flying in two-layered flocks 200 yards wide, and according to some witnesses 30 miles long.

In the woods there were hickory nuts, black walnuts, chestnuts, beechnuts, hazelnuts, pecans, and plenty of wild fruit—grapes, plums, strawberries, raspberries, and gooseberries. Since there was no flour with which to make pie crust, the pioneers used the fruit for sauce only. Blackberries were originally thought of as a nuisance. Early cookbooks mention blackberries as ingredients in medicinal remedies, such as blackberry syrup as a cure for cholera and summer complaint.

A much sought after treasure was the honey of wild bees found in bee trees. Sugar maple trees provided early settlers with syrup and sugar for sweetened foods. Forty gallons of maple sap and lots of evaporation resulted in one gallon of syrup. Another staple was sorghum made from juice extracted from sorghum cane. It is lighter in color than commercial molasses and has a more delicate flavor. The usual yield is about five gallons of sorghum from fifteen gallons of juice.

Salt was needed not only for seasoning but for preserving meats. Almost all of it had to be imported. The arrival of a new shipment at a store was a cause for celebration. Salt remained expensive until the coming of the railroads.

In the spring children were dosed with sulphur and molasses to ward off spring fever. After a winter diet of salted meats and root vegetables, milkweed shoots, dandelion greens, or the first stalks of wild asparagus furnished the badly needed Vitamin C.

Kitchenware needed for fireplace cooking included an iron pot or two, a skillet with legs called a spider, a griddle, and a Dutch oven. At first there were wooden bowls and spoons for tableware. Later came pewter plates, tin cups, iron spoons, two-tined forks, and knives. A great iron kettle swung over the fireplace could be used for many household needs— making lye soap or hominy, dying homespun linen, doing the laundry, or scalding the hogs that were butchered for the winter meat supply. Knowing how to season kitchenware was important, for example: The way to season a new black skillet is to heat it real hot with un-salted oil or fat in it, and then allow it to cool gradually. This treatment should be given a couple of times. Any sticking of foods will stop after the pan has been used for a while.

One of America's best-known pioneers is Johnny Appleseed Chapman. When the early settlers came to Indiana, some orchards, which he had planted, were already at hand. Johnny was a religious man who wore few clothes, traveled barefoot, and always carried a Bible and a supply of apple seeds with him. He repaid the kindnesses offered him in the cabins he visited by planting the apple seeds. He died in Fort Wayne in 1845.

TANNING SKINS WITH THE FUR ON

To tan a skin of any kind with the fur on, first take the skin and flesh it, which is done by laying the skin on the round side of a slab, with the flesh side out, and scraping it with the back of a drawing knife, until all the flesh is removed; then wash it thoroughly in soap suds until all the grease is removed, and rinse it in soft water. Then place it in a liquor made of one ounce of sulphuric acid and four quarts of soft water. Let it remain in this liquor half an hour, or until the skin looks tanned. Then take it out and work it dry. It will be soft and pliable.

Mrs. Allan Rogers
Dearborn County

KITCHEN "RECEIPTS"

YELLOW CHEESE

Take 3 gal. milk made into cottage cheese; squeeze out by hand. Curd must be quite dry. Rub it between hands so it crumbles and becomes quite fine. Add ½ c. butter in which 1 t. soda has been dissolved, ½ c. sweet cream, ½ c. sour cream, 4 t. salt, and ½ t. butter or yellow coloring (you may need more). Cook mixture in enamelware pan over boiling water, stirring constantly. It may get stringy but keep on stirring. Cook well until completely smooth and melted. Pour into an oiled pan to set and ripen. Cover when cold with paraffin.

Mrs. George Conrad, Sr.
Miami County

TO BOIL A TONGUE, CALF'S HEAD, AND PLUCK

If a tongue is fresh and tender, put it in your pot overnight, fix the fire so as to keep the tongue gently simmering. Two hours or so before dinner, brisk up the stove and boil well until dinner.

After cleaning the head nicely, soak in water until it is white. Then put on to boil, letting the tongue and heart boil an hour and a half, the head an hour and a quarter, and the liver an hour. Tie the brains in a bag and boil them an hour. Arrange the time so that all will be taken up together. Serve the brains with pounded crackers and butter; vinegar, pepper, and salt may also be served with them.

Mrs. Allan Rogers
Dearborn County

PREPARING PORK FOR SUMMER USE (From *The Dairy Farmer*, February 15, 1924)

After the meat is thoroughly cold, saw hams and shoulders into pieces four to six inches square and place closely, skin side down, in a large dripping pan or roaster. Season with salt and pepper and roast until the bones can be removed without meat adhering to them. Then remove bones and skin and add salt and pepper where these were removed. Roast until meat is thoroughly done, then pack in stone jars and completely cover with hot fryings or lard. When it has become thoroughly cold, tie heavy paper over the jar and set in a cool place. When any is taken out to use, be sure that lard covers what remains in the jar. Heat the meat slowly until hot clear through, and it will taste just as it did the day it was roasted. Meat cared for this way will keep all summer.

Mrs. Loys Rees
Rush County

TO SMOKE HAMS AT HOME

Take an old hogshead and fix a place to put a cross stick near the bottom to hang the hams and bacon sides on. Next, in the side, cut a hole near the top, in order to introduce an iron pan filled with hickory wood sawdust and small pieces of green wood. Having turned the articles to be smoked upon the cross stick, then introduce the iron pan in the opening and place a piece of red hot iron in the pan; cover it with sawdust and all will be complete. Let remain two days, all the while keeping up a good smoke. Wrap in white clothes and hang high from a beam to cure.

"Blue River Pioneer Cookin' "
Shelby County Historical Society

HOUSEHOLD "RECEIPTS"

SWEET BAGS FOR LINENS

Dry and blend leaves of lavender, lemon verbena, rose geranium, rosemary, and southernwood. Proportions may be to your taste, letting one scent predominate; or use one alone. Lightly fill small silk or muslin bags. Sew up or tie with ribbons and laces. Use these to scent linens and clothes.

POMANDER BALLS (A Christmas Fragrance)

For each pomander ball, you will need one orange, a box of whole cloves, powdered orris root, and ground cinnamon. Stick whole cloves firmly into skin of the orange, covering the entire surface. You may leave some space between cloves, as the ball shrinks. Combine orris root and cinnamon and roll orange in mixture, putting in as much as it will hold. Wrap ball in several thicknesses of tissue paper. Store in a cool dry place several weeks to dry and develop fragrance.

REMEDY FOR BEDBUGS

Salt is a sure thing on bedbugs. Wash the articles and places infested with the bugs with salt and water, and fill cracks and crevices where the vermin hide; they will give no more trouble. They cannot abide where salt is. Another way is to take a feather and apply a little coal oil to the places where the bugs hide. This is a sure remedy.

Mrs. Allan Rogers
Dearborn County

FLEAS (From an old *Indiana Farmers Guide Cookbook*)

When fleas get into the house, a very simple method of getting rid of them is to put on rubber boots and wrap them with flypaper. Then walk through the house and you will get them all. Fleas jump at any moving object and, since they cannot leap higher than 6 inches, they will be caught on the flypaper.

Ruby Luhrsen
Dearborn County

LYE SOAP (1)

To pioneer women soapmaking was a common household chore. They leached wood ashes by putting them in a hopper and pouring water over them to make an alkali solution. Scrap grease of any kind was used. Today soapmaking is a hobby. Commercial lye is used for the alkali, and vegetable fats make a lighter colored soap. Perfumes may be added; oil of sassafras is a good one to use. This soap is gentle to the hands and may be used on fine fabrics. To use it in automatic washers: Chip soap and let it stand in a crock with some water until it dissolves to jelly-like consistency.

Caution must be taken to prevent the lye solution from touching the skin. If it does, the skin should be washed with cider vinegar. This stops the action immediately.

Mix 1 can of lye with 2¾ pt. of cold

water in an enamel or iron kettle over open fire. It will get very hot. Stir with a wooden paddle. Let stand about 1 hr. Add 5½ lb. of warm grease—any kind. Stir until it resembles honey. Add 1 c. of ammonia and ¼–⅓ c. of borax. Add perfume, if desired. Pour into shallow pans or cardboard boxes. Cover so it does not cool too quickly. When set, but not hard, cut into squares or bars and remove from pans or boxes. Wrap in oiled paper. Will store indefinitely. Makes 6 pounds.

Miss Bessie Taylor
Jennings County

LYE SOAP (2)

Soap should be made out of doors because of the fumes. In a large iron kettle place 2 qt. of water and 2 cans of lye. Stir until dissolved. Add 1 gal. of lard or cooking oil. This can be any fat that has been used and saved, although if it is browned, it will not produce as white a product as fresh white lard will do. After adding fat, stir until creamy and mixture begins to thicken. Add about ¾ c. of borax dissolved in just enough water to fill the cup. Stir in 2 c. of ammonia and continue stirring until thick. Dip out into molds, if available. Empty ½-pt. milk cartons also make good molds. You may line cardboard boxes with waxed paper and pour a layer of soap into them. When cooled and firm, cut into desired size. My mother has used this recipe for years—and still does. It is a very mild soap.

Janet Ping
Monroe County

PAINT AND VARNISH REMOVER

Dissolve 4 heaping T. of cornstarch in 2 qt. of water in a wooden pail or stone crock and in another container dissolve 1 can of lye in 1 qt. of water. Pour the lye solution into the cornstarch very slowly, being careful to stir well all the time. This will make a thick paste without lumps.

Paint this on the surface from which the paint is to be removed with an old brush or swab, putting it on in an even thick coat. If on the body of an auto, it is best first to remove the fenders and running boards or to cover them with a thick coat of grease. A small section should be covered with the paste at a time and should be left on until it shows signs of drying. It then can be scraped off with a putty knife, wire brush, or steel wool. If running water is available, turn the water on parts treated and paint will let loose and run off like ink. When using this method, allow the paste to become almost dry. On parts where paint or varnish does not come off with the first application, a second application should be given.

Do not use this remover on aluminum parts or on cars with aluminum bodies. It is especially good for removing varnish or paint from furniture and is also very economical.

May Mullilin
Randolph County

RUG CLEANER

1 large bar Ivory soap (heated and melted in some of the water)	1 gal. water
	2 t. ammonia
	2 T. turpentine

Mix together and apply with brush. Sop up all moisture possible with sponge wrung out in clear water.

Mrs. Harry Kyle
Dearborn County

WALLPAPER PASTE

1½ pt. flour	4 qt. boiling water
1 qt. cold water	
1 T. alum	1 T. sugar

Mix flour and cold water to a smooth paste; add alum and sugar. Add boiling water to flour mixture, stirring to prevent lumps. Stir and simmer over low heat for 10 min. Cool before using.

Mrs. Robert E. Templin
Wabash County

DEPRESSION PLANT

1 c. warm water	1 T. bluing
½ c. salt	piece of coal

Take an odd-shaped piece of coal and put in dish. Make a solution of warm water, salt, and bluing and pour over coal. After 3–4 days drop different food colorings on coal. As the plant "grows," add a little warm water each day.

Donola Hysong
Fountain County

CHRISTMAS TREE SPRAY

1 16-oz. box borax	powdered boric acid
1 8-oz. box	4 qt. warm water

Dissolve first 2 ingredients in warm water and spray on the tree.

Mrs. Robert Morgan
Rush County

PLAY-DOUGH

1 c. flour	1 T. salad oil
2 t. cream of tartar	1 c. water
½ c. salt	food coloring

Mix flour, cream of tartar, and salt. Add salad oil, water, and food coloring. Put mixture in electric skillet. Stir. Cook at medium heat until mixture sticks together. Place on a sheet of waxed paper. Cool. Then knead to playable consistency. Keep in airtight containers.

Joanie Smith
Rush County

SALT BEADS

½ c. salt	½ c. flour
½ t. cream of tartar	1 t. powdered alum

Slowly add just enough water to make a paste. Color to suit preference. Place all in a double boiler and cook until thick. Work and mold into desired shapes. When hard, pierce.

Anna Belle Buskirk
Monroe County

MEDICINAL "RECEIPTS"

BLOOD PURIFIER

1 T. (rounding) cream of tartar	3 T. (rounding) epsom salts
2 T. (rounding) sulphur	

Pour boiling water to dissolve. Makes a quart can. Take 1 T. (rounding) each morning. Costs 5 cents.

Mrs. Harry Raudenbush
Adams County

CASTOR OIL COOKIES
(75-Year-Old Recipe)

1 c. sugar	1 t. soda
1 c. molasses	2 t. ginger
1 c. milk	flour to make dough
½ c. castor oil	
½ t. salt	

Mix ingredients well and use enough flour to make a dough that can be rolled. Roll out, cut, and bake in a fast oven (375°).

Two cookies are equal to a dose of castor oil.

Ruby Bedwell
Sullivan County

AID FOR REGULARITY

1 lb. figs	1 lb. raisins
1 lb. dates	5¢ senna powder

Put the fruit through the meat grinder and mix the senna powder through it. Put in glass jars with lids. Dose: a lump the size of a walnut.

Mrs. Harold Coffman
Union County

REMEDY FOR COLDS

Take 3 medium-sized lemons, boil for 6–8 min., then slice them thin with a sharp knife. Put them and their juice into a brown earthen pan, and put over them 1 lb. of clean brown sugar—the browner the better—and set the pan on top of the stove so that the sugar may melt gradually. When it is melted, move the pan to a hotter part of the stove, and let the mixture stew for about 3 hr. Then take it off, let it stand for ½ hr., and then stir into it a small tablespoonful of the oil of sweet almonds. When cold, it is ready for use. Two makings of this will drive the worst cold from the breast and throat, though one is generally sufficient for the purpose. A dose is a teaspoonful whenever you choose, provided you do not eat it up too rapidly.

Mrs. Allan Rogers
Dearborn County

COUGH SYRUP

Cook 1 lemon for 10 min., then strain the juice into a glass. Add 2 T. (1 oz.) glycerin. Stir, then fill the glass with honey.

Stir the mixture before each dose of 1 teaspoon. Take as needed day and night.

Mrs. Diane Hunteman
Ripley County

OLD-FASHIONED REMEDY FOR
A BAD COUGH

Take a brown paper large enough to cover the chest. Grease with lard or meat fryings, then pepper real well. Heat this and place on the chest, covering with a piece of flannel. It brings relief.

Mrs. Lewis Ringel
Wabash County

CURE FOR CROUP

Just before going to bed, grease the breast thoroughly with goose grease and lay on it a double thickness of flannel. If the strangling comes on suddenly, mix Scotch snuff and lard together, spread on a piece of brown paper, and apply instantly to the breast, meanwhile rubbing the throat with hot goose grease, lard, or oil. Or you can do this: Dip a flannel in water, as hot as it can be borne, lay it on the breast, then take salt butter, spread on a piece of brown paper, and apply to the breast and throat.

Mrs. Allan Rogers
Dearborn County

CURE FOR HOARSENESS OR
LOSS OF VOICE

⅓ c. fresh,   1 c. honey
  strained lemon   1 c. rum
  juice

Shake ingredients in jar and store in a cool place until needed. Use ½ c. of mixture to ½ c. of hot water; sip slowly. Makes 5–6 doses.

Joann Dant
Daviess County

GARGLE SOLUTION

1 glass hot water   ½ t. soda
1 t. salt   5 drops iodine

Donna Handley
Union County

CURE FOR HEADACHE

If the headache be accompanied with sick stomach, take an emetic of one teaspoonful of table salt in a little water. After vomiting, take ten drops of hartshorn in a tablespoonful of cold water, and lie down for half an hour or so. If you have only headache, bathe the wrists and arms in cold water and the feet in strong, hot mustard water, and take the hartshorn only. Lie down, and your headache will soon leave you.

Mrs. Allan Rogers
Dearborn County

GRANDMA'S LINIMENT

2 oz. ammonia   2 oz. turpentine
  (ask druggist   2 oz. apple
  for ammonia   vinegar
  that is used for 2 oz. whole egg
  medicinal pur-   (slightly beat,
  poses and not   enough to mix
  household   yolk and
  ammonia.   white)
Hartshorn is the
name.)

Mix well. Always use equal parts. Store in glass bottle; never use plastic. This liniment is an old recipe handed down from my grandmother. It is good for strained muscles, bruises, or sore places. Never put in an open cut or wound. Caution: Never wrap tight or it will blister. The original recipe said to blow out the contents of 1 egg and use the eggshell to measure the other 3 ingredients.

Frances Barden
Greene County

THRASHERS LINIMENT
("Receipt" over 100 Years Old)

6 oz. witch hazel	1 oz. sassafras
1 oz. ammonia aqua	1 qt. cider vinegar

Get first 3 ingredients at the drugstore. Add to vinegar. Shake well before using. Good for aches or sprains. Will not blister.

Mrs. L. L. Richeson
Tippecanoe County

FOR PERSPIRING FEET
(World War I)

Army regulations abroad require the soldiers to bathe their feet in cold, not hot, water, to have the inside of the stockings ironed, and to dust the feet freely every morning with a powder containing salicylic acid. Most of the powders consist in part of salicylic acid and in most cases a certain amount of talcum powder is used. Several combinations have been proposed:

Recipe 1

½ oz. salicylic acid	4 oz. boric acid
8 oz. violet powder	1 dr. eucalyptus oil

Recipe 2

1 dr. boric acid	5 min. (drops)
3 oz. French chalk	oil of Bergamot

Mix.

Recipe 3

16 oz. Puly. Amyli	16 oz. Puly. Acidi Borici
1 dr. Thymolis	1 dr. Camphorae

Triturate the camphor and thymol in a mortar until liquid, add the starch little by little, then the acid, and sift twice.

Mrs. Harry Raudenbush
Adams County

PEACH-TREE TEA

Steep a small handful of washed peach-tree leaves or bark of new limb in a pint of hot water. To be used freely as a drink. Best to make fresh daily. It is an excellent tonic, soothing to stomach. Use cold for colds and hot for fever. Also used for inflammation of bladder or kidneys.

Mrs. Pearl M. Hansen
Starke County

PERSONAL "RECEIPTS"

AUNT RUTH'S CLEANSING CREAM

1 t. borax	1½ oz. spermaceti
1 T. hot water	
4 oz. rosewater	1½ oz. white wax
1 pt. mineral oil	

Thoroughly dissolve borax in hot water. Add lukewarm rosewater and mineral oil to above mixture, stirring well. Melt spermaceti and white wax together. When lukewarm, add to above mixture. Pour into jars. Leave lids off until cool. Makes 1½ pounds.

Margaret R. Orman
Ripley County

TO REMOVE FRECKLES WITH BUTTERMILK (From *Grandmother's Household Hints*)

An excellent wash for freckles is made by scraping some horseradish very fine and letting it stand for some hours in buttermilk. Strain and use the wash night and morning.

Anne Reiff
Allen County

OIL TO MAKE THE HAIR CURL

Olive oil, one pound; oil of organum, one drachm; oil of rosemary, one and one-half drachms.

FOR WRINKLES IN THE SKIN

White wax, one ounce; strained honey, two ounces; juice of lily-bulbs, two ounces. The foregoing melted and stirred together will remove wrinkles.

These were taken from *The Everyday Cook Book* published in 1892.

Mrs. Willis Wiley
Monroe County

HUSKERS HAND LOTION

½ oz. gum of tragacanth	½ oz. bay rum
	perfume as
2 oz. glycerin	desired
2 oz. alcohol	1 qt. rainwater

Boil rainwater. Mix gum of tragacanth in a little hot water, then add to rest of water. Let stand overnight or until it thickens. Add rest of ingredients and bottle.

Donola Hysong
Fountain County

Index

PORK

Ham

CPSIA information can be obtained
at www.ICGtesting.com
Printed in the USA
LVHW101651011021
699240LV00014B/1244